Women's Studies (

An Educational Project at the Femini̲.̲.̲ ̲.̲.̲.̲.̲ ̲.̲.̲.̲.̲ ̲ ̲.̲.̲.̲ ̲.̲.̲.̲
Cooperation with Rochester Institute of Technology

Guest Editors for Current Issue
Frances Vavrus, Teachers College, Columbia University; Lisa Ann Richey, Roskilde University, Denmark, and Mailman School of Public Health, Columbia University

Editor
Diane Hope, Rochester Institute of Technology

Publisher
Jean Casella, the Feminist Press and the Graduate School and University Center, CUNY

Editorial Board
Lynne Derbyshire, University of Rhode Island
Jean Douthwright, Rochester Institute of Technology
Lisa Freeman, Kansas State University
Edvige Giunta, New Jersey City University
Dorothy O. Helly, *emerita,* Hunter College and the Graduate School, CUNY
Barbara Horn, Nassau Community College, SUNY
Alice Kessler-Harris, Columbia University
Wendy Kolmar, Drew University
Linda Layne, Rensselaer Polytechnic Institute
Tobe Levin, University of Maryland, European Division, and J.W. Goethe University, Frankfurt am Main, Germany
Kit Mayberry, Rochester Institute of Technology
Carol J. Pierman, University of Alabama
Nancy Porter, *Editor Emerita*, Portland State University
Lee Quinby, Hobart and William Smith Colleges
Carol Richardson, Rochester Institute of Technology
Deborah S. Rosenfelt, University of Maryland, College Park
Sue V. Rosser, Georgia Institute of Technology
Carole Anne Taylor, Bates College
Mari Boor Tonn, University of Maryland
Janet Zandy, *Editor Emerita*, Rochester Institute of Technology

Managing Editor
Jocelyn Burrell

Poetry Editor
Edvige Giunta

Copy Editors
Sara Cahill and Molly Vaux

Editorial Assistants
Abby Collier, Tyra Cooper-Davis, Jamie Stock

Administrative Assistant to the Editor
Cassandra Shellman

Contents

Reimagining Political Development: Identity, Power, and Possibilities

Creative Development: Prose and Poetry

Creative Development: Teaching and Learning

Book Reviews

Editorial

Women and Development: Rethinking Policy and Reconceptualizing Practice

Frances Vavrus and Lisa Ann Richey

It has been more than thirty years since the publication of Ester Boserup's groundbreaking book, *Women's Role in Economic Development* (1970). Since then, there has been tremendous growth in research on women's exclusion from development programs and in activism to increase women's participation in development activities in the "South." Boserup's book sparked demand for the inclusion of women as productive laborers in the development process, which eventually led to the formation of the women in development (WID) approach to addressing inequalities between women and men. Yet criticisms of WID's exclusive focus on equity have spawned alternative approaches toward understanding the nature of the development process and the relationships between men and women within it. In contrast to WID, the gender and development (GAD) approach emphasizes empowerment through the restructuring of gendered institutions and social relations (Kabeer 1997; Parpart 1995; Rathgeber 1990; Young 1997). By shifting the focus from "women" as a biological category to "gender" as a social construct, GAD advocates have expanded the parameters of the field of development to include analyses of identity and discourse. Indeed, we have now reached a point of considerable debate among feminist scholars, practitioners, and activists about the very concept of development and women's location within it.

This special issue of *Women's Studies Quarterly, Women and Development: Rethinking Policy and Reconceptualizing Practice,* provides a forum in which to discuss current perspectives on WID and GAD in light of contemporary geopolitical relations. It also creates a space in which to consider the growing literature on "post-development" and its articulation with feminist theory (Rosenau 1992; Saunders 2002). This issue reflects the outcome of an ambitious question posed by the coeditors to hundreds of potential contributors around the world: "What is development?" The selected articles, essays, teaching materials, poetry, and book reviews provide insightful responses to this central query. Moreover, they illuminate commonalities and differences in thinking about women and development in two important theoretical areas: (1) the problematization of development as an organizing concept in the social sciences and in the daily lives of women and men and (2) the analysis of discourses and practices in the contemporary Third World to understand what development actually "does" on the ground. The goal of this special issue is to reframe debates about development policy and practice using the tools provided by feminist theory in its many different forms.

Gender and Development: A Historical Overview

As academics and practitioners in the field of gender and development, we have long been concerned that feminist analysis of policy and practice has been slow to emerge from the "gender ghetto" of the WID office at the end of the hallway. We have also been troubled by the dichotomies that frequently divide "academic" from "practitioner" research, and separate men and women in this field. Many feminist scholars, such as economist Diane Elson, urge gender and development scholars to "stop talking only to ourselves" and to initiate an engagement with those "inside" the policy process. We believe that it is clearly in the best interest of academics that their scholarship become more relevant and timely and to the advantage of practitioners that their interventions become more theoretically informed and reflective. Similarly, the idea of mainstreaming gender into all aspects of development theory and practice has been embraced in theory, but this has been difficult to maintain in practice. There is still a strong association between gender and women both on the producing and the receiving sides of development. The fact that all of the contributors to this volume are women speaks to the limited progress toward integrating gender issues into mainstream development scholarship written primarily by men.

Historically, women have become a development constituency through their bodies and their dispositions. In colonial discourses, Third World women were viewed typically as the embodiments of the exotic, as sex objects, and as the most backward members of backward societies. Parpart notes that "during the colonial period, missionaries, colonial officials, and settlers put forward a blend of information, imagination, pragmatic self-interest, and prejudice to explain why Third World women were inferior beings, bound by tradition—either unable or unwilling to enter the modern world" (1995, 257). In the domains of education and health, in particular, colonial discourses often vacillated between heralding "traditional" attitudes and practices as the solutions to development problems in the colonies and criticizing the same beliefs and social relations for contributing to the "backward" state of affairs in the countries under their control (Colwell 2001; Vavrus 2002).

During the postwar decades of decolonialization, many development planners accepted these assumptions uncritically and virtually ignored them in their productive capacity. By the 1950s, economic and psychosocial theories of "development-as-modernization" focused on Third World men's potential contributions to their societies far more than they addressed women's roles (Peet 1999; So 1990; Vavrus 2003). However, women did receive attention in two development realms during this period: food aid and population (Kabeer 1997). It was assumed that once men became attuned to "modern," that is, Western, forms of political, economic, and social organization, women would naturally follow along. However, like the disabled and the sick, poor women in the Third World were understood to constitute a "vulnerable group" to whom relief would be offered. This "welfare approach," as described by Bulvinic (1983), is the oldest development strategy for women, assuming as it does that the "backward" ways of certain groups of women serve as an obstacle to progressive social change.

Questions of how to deal with women as productive economic subjects began to enter the discourse of development only in the 1970s with the work of Danish economist Ester Boserup . Boserup noted that development, identified as increasing levels of economic growth, could have negative consequences for women and children by increasing already existing inequalities between men and women. Her book provided insights into the relationship between colonialism and women's status, but it has also been criticized for accepting modernization theories of development and prevailing norms about the gendered labor of women and men.

Boserup's book sparked demands by liberal feminists for the inclusion of women as workers and producers in the process of development.[1] According to Kabeer (1997), the WID approach prompted the incorporation of "first-wave" feminism into international development organizations. After decades of limited concern about women in the Third World, the 1970s saw an upsurge of interest in their productive and reproductive lives. For instance, 1973 marked the passage of the Percy Amendment in the U.S. Congress, which stated that U.S. foreign assistance should be directed toward improving the status of women in developing countries by integrating them into the development process. The United Nations also declared 1975–1985 to be "The Women's Decade," and 1975 itself was designated the International Women's Year. Yet despite this heightened international recognition of women's role in development, the concept itself still described a process that was done "to women" or "for women" rather than "by women."

Following on the heels of the equity approach was the antipoverty approach. This strategy shifted the emphasis from reducing inequality between men and women to reducing income inequality and targeting poverty. The antipoverty approach was adopted by development agencies in response to two different problems with the equity strategy. First, donor agencies and developing country governments were, and continue to be, reluctant to become involved in the relations that are understood to be "cultural," including the "traditional attitudes" that Boserup and others believed were impeding modernization. Second, by the 1970s, a failure of modernization theory to tackle issues of income distribution or poverty had become apparent to donors (Moser 1989). Therefore, a new strategy aimed at poverty reduction was adopted by many development agencies (Finnemore 1997).

In response to the economic crises of the mid-1970s, "efficiency" became the next dominant approach. This approach "shifted the emphasis away from *women* and toward *development* on the assumption that increased economic participation for Third World women is automatically linked with increased equity" (Moser 1989, 813). Women came to be viewed not only as development "ends," but also as means of reaching project goals. The objective of the efficiency approach is to utilize the formerly untapped potential of 50 percent of the workforce by successfully incorporating women into national development efforts. However, critics of this process have shown that the efficiency approach often shifts the costs of development from the paid (and traditionally *male*) economy to the unpaid (*female*) economy. Here, women are considered only in their productive capacity, and questions of the unequally gendered nature of reproduction are seldom addressed. As the gender-arm of the structural adjustment programs that came into effect in the 1980s and 1990s, the efficiency approach is subject to many of the criticisms that have been leveled at adjustment policies and their impact on "vulnerable groups."[2] Nonetheless, efficiency has become the most common approach to women's issues in development assistance, and, notwithstanding changes in terminology, it still provides the underpinning of many contemporary approaches.

Despite its dominance, challenges to this particular construction of development have been raised from within the practitioner and academic communities. In the late 1970s a new approach originated from those groups that were viewed by policy makers as the beneficiaries of development aid. For example, Development Alternatives with Women for a New Era (DAWN), a network made up of researchers, activists, and policymakers from the Third World, published a challenge to "development feminists" in the late 1980s that marked a rethinking of many assumptions about gender relations held by First World scholars (The Association of African Women for Research and Development (AAWORD) also issued a sharp critique of Western feminisms' classificatory schemes and development strategies "for" women in the Third World (AAWORD 1982, cited in Kabeer, 1997). Therefore, in contrast to previous WID approaches, the new empowerment approach—gender and development (GAD)—situates gender domination within broader socioeconomic relations and seeks to restructure local, national, and international institutions in dramatic ways. It also places far more emphasis on the variability in gender relations across time and space than one finds in most WID analyses, which rarely discuss specific gender and class ideologies (Saunders 2002). In sum, these alterations in both the meaning of gender and of development have provided, for some, a different vision of the field of women and development.

Today, however, there is considerable debate about whether the key concepts of gender and development need further reconsideration. By shifting the focus from women to gender, GAD has undoubtedly provided greater opportunities for "talking to the boys" about gender issues, as Elson puts it (1998). Additionally, some pragmatic proponents of GAD argue that attention to gender has improved the ways that aid is currently disseminated, even if this has not led to a critical rethinking of the concept of development itself. Elson and Evers, for instance, begin with the premise that "reduction of gender inequality is not only a goal in its own right, but also is a contribution towards sustainable and equitable economic growth" (1997, 2). They contend that development aid can be provided in ways that reduce gender-based distortions in prices and patterns of resource allocation. Similarly, Standing (1997) proposes a framework for considering the gender implications of health sector reform by including specific "gender issues" within an existing framework. Both of these examples suggest sites for feminist interventions in the area of gender relations within the existent parameters of development organizations.

In addition, the recent attention that GAD has brought to the relationships between women and men has shown that supporting gender equality makes good economic sense.[3] However, as some scholars note, instrumentally promoting gender equality as a means for achieving other ends may be counterproductive. Jackson (1998), for example, shows how using gender to promote the poverty-reduction agenda does not tackle issues of gender injustice and often results in unintended consequences for policies intended to "empower" women. Indeed, as some scholars have shown, the shift from WID to GAD may actually imply advantages for men (see, for example, Kabeer 1997; Richey 2002). The articles in this volume, especially those by Boesten, Isserles, and Madhok, illustrate some of these unplanned outcomes of poverty alleviation policies. In addition, scholars Baden and Goetz (1997) contend that instrumental arguments run the risk of being discredited because they do not take into account the gendered nature of institutions themselves and how institutional organization affects the ways in which information is collected, analyzed, and prioritized. The importance of institutional analysis is highlighted in the articles in this special issue by Ghodsee on post-communist Central and Eastern Europe; by Hyndman and de Alwis on humanitarian responses to conflict in Sri Lanka; and by Salem, Ibrahim, and Brady on civil society institutions in Egypt.

A further critique of GAD comes from the emerging literature that incorporates aspects of poststructural discourse analysis to deconstruct the key terms and concepts that organize the field of women and development (Richey 2000). Many scholars utilizing this analytical framework are highly critical of conventional definitions of development as modernization, Westernization, and unbounded economic growth. As Escobar puts it, "development was—and continues to be for the most part—a top-down, ethnocentric, and technocratic approach, which treated people and cultures as abstract concepts, statistical figures to be moved up and down in the charts of 'progress'" (1995, 44). The articles in this issue on post-development thought in Bolivia (by Lind) and post-feminism in Colombia (by Murdock) are two examples of feminist scholars rethinking development from a poststructural perspective and carefully examining the construction of gendered social categories.

The importance of questioning the current consensus about gender equality in development programs is not to undermine the achievements of WID, GAD, and other approaches in the field of women and development. The goal of this special issue is to ensure that debate over the practice of policy continues, because without continued critical inquiry we run the risk of limiting opportunities for dialogue about what development means for those whose lives are most affected by it.[4] Without critical analytical bridges between GAD interventions and women's lived experiences, mainstreaming gender into development processes is likely to suffer the same drawbacks that have plagued earlier attempts at incorporating women into development

(Richey 2000). As several of the articles in this volume demonstrate, fieldworkers' and local administrators' discretion plays a large role in implementing development policy, and their gender biases can work to constrain or undermine equality goals. The authors' case studies of GAD "on the ground" draw attention to the lingering gap between rhetorical support for gender equality and development practice in specific contexts. Through careful analysis, these problems can be explored to enable the development of alternative interventions that are specific, focused, sustainable, and cognizant of local and global gender realities.

Overview of the Special Issue

Section 1, "Rethinking Economic Development Policy: Microcredit, Ecotourism, Information Technology, and Housing," examines four types of popular development programs intended to improve the lives of women. Kristen Ghodsee and Robin Isserles provide a critical analysis of microcredit programs in two different contexts, Central and Eastern Europe and South Asia, respectively. Both authors identify gendered assumptions about entrepreneurship and capitalist economic relations in programs designed to empower women by assisting them in starting their own small businesses. Through their careful research, Ghodsee and Isserles demonstrate the need for more critique of the popular microenterprise model for women's development. In "Gender, Culture, and Ecotourism," Barbara Dilly, also raises questions about common-sense assumptions regarding the benefits of ecotourism for women living in rain forests. Drawing on fieldwork in a Makushi community in Guyana, Dilly provides a rich description of the "multi-edged sword" of tourism designed to promote both economic development and environmental sustainability. Kristin Phillips examines another widespread view in the women and development field, namely, that increasing women's access to information technology will necessarily lead to economic development. Phillips combines a review of the recent literature on gender relations and information technology with her observations in Internet cafés in northern Tanzania to make a compelling argument for greater attention to development policy as social practice. In the final piece in this section, "A Poor Women's Pedagogy," Salma Ismail provides an insider's perspective on a "people-centered" housing development association in South Africa. Ismail's case study of the Victoria Mxenge Housing Development Association in an informal black settlement in Cape Town describes the many sites for women's social learning in this association, from building houses to creating savings programs to engaging in participatory decision making. This study greatly expands conventional notions of economic development and of participatory pedagogy.

Section 2, "Reconceptualizing Social Development Practice: Women and (Re)Productive Labor," delves into debates about the roles assigned to women in development programs. Jelke Boesten examines ideological assumptions about poor Peruvian women's domestic roles that shape family planning and food distribution programs in the country. Intended to alleviate poverty and empower women, these programs do not adequately address the ethnic and class divisions in Peru that limit program efficacy and reproduce social inequality. Donna Murdock's article takes us to neighboring Colombia, where she looks at the multiple meanings of "gender and development" among government officials and nongovernmental actors in Medellín. Through her astute analysis, Murdock shows how officials defined GAD to fit their political purposes and "to directly underwrite a critique of feminism." Similarly, Sumi Madhok explores the way state power operates in India through programs that, at first glance, appear to be grassroots efforts to increase women's participation in local development. Madhok focuses on the problematic relationship between local feminist organizations and the state in her analysis of the role of *sathins*, women trained to work at the village level to implement development programs in the state of Rajasthan. Her research raises a number of important questions about "feminist emancipatory politics" within state-supported women and development programs.

Section 3, "Reimagining Political Development: Identity, Power, and Possibilities," brings together four articles on different aspects of women's political engagement with governmental and nongovernmental organizations. "Negotiating Leadership Roles," by Rania Salem, Barbara Ibrahim, and Martha Brady, explores the lives of young Egyptian women as they become involved with new civil society institutions. Drawing from the experiences of a group of development "promoters," the authors demonstrate the importance of considering the sociocultural context when developing leadership training programs. Mangala Subramaniam also looks at the promotion of women's engagement in civil society in her case study of a women's empowerment program in India. Her analysis of how the program encourages "capacity building" among members of the Scheduled Caste—generally the poorest people in India—demonstrates the importance of education and networking in efforts to increase women's political power. Jennifer Hyndman and Malathi de Alwis consider women's engagement in humanitarian assistance programs necessitated by the longstanding armed conflict in neighboring Sri Lanka. Noting at the outset that all humanitarian programs are gendered, the authors powerfully demonstrate how concepts like "beneficiary" and "motherhood" mask local power dynamics that perpetuate violence in this context. This section concludes with a thoughtful article by Amy Lind that utilizes a post-development framework to study women's movements in Bolivia and to suggest ways of teaching about such movements in women's studies classes in the United States. Drawing on interviews with a Bolivian activist and a variety of other source material, Lind leaves readers with some of the tools necessary to, in her words, "envision a world different from what exists today."

"Creative Development: Poetry and Prose" is the fourth section of this issue, and it contains essays and poetry reflecting the complexity of women's lives the world over. Rebecca Winthrop's essay on rebuilding the education system in Afghanistan illustrates vividly the complex negotiations over gender and power relations that inevitably occur between international development "experts" and local community leaders whose views of women's roles in development are often vastly different. Lara Knudsen presents an account of conflicting expectations for women—local and foreign—in her essay about maternal health care in Uganda. In contrast to these essays about "difference," Nancy Nye Knipe's reflections in "Women of the Tent" explores commonalities between herself and the women she meets in a tent village for displaced persons following the 1999 earthquake in central Turkey. While sharing tea with women living in these temporary shelters, Knipe learns of the challenges they face in rebuilding their lives as they leave the supportive environment of the tent community and return to their somewhat isolated family situations. The three poems selected for the special issue, by Fawzia Afzal-Khan, Paola Corso, and Kylie Thomas, also portray the complex lives of women and the multitude of forces that impinge upon their "development."

This section is followed by resources for teaching about women and development. "Creating Development: Teaching and Learning" provides educators with illustrative examples and ideas about how to design courses that incorporate historical and contemporary perspectives in the field of women and development. The essay and syllabi demonstrate ways that teachers can bring into the classroom different disciplinary approaches to the study of women, gender relations, and development. The final section of this issue contains reviews of recent books that will be of interest to teachers, researchers, practitioners, and activists who want to broaden the scope of their expertise and deepen their understanding of key issues in the women and development field. These issues include gender and nationalism, post-colonialism, child care and domestic equity, and reproductive health. The contributors to this special issue of *Women's Studies Quarterly*, along with the many authors whose submissions we could not include, demonstrate the continued importance of women and development as a field of study and as an arena for social change.

NOTES

1. For a comprehensive review of liberal feminism see Tong (1989). For a description of different feminisms linked with development see Staudt (1998).
2. For gender critiques of structural adjustment see Bourginon et al. (1991); Cagatay et al. (1995); and Commonwealth Secretariat (1989).
3. For example, a recent cross-national study by Swamy et al. (1999) argues that policies designed to increase the role of women in business and politics may have an efficiency payoff of lowering corruption.
4. The adoption of a "gender policy" by development organizations sets a baseline position that all members of the organization must accept; thus, it is necessarily all-encompassing, perhaps to the point of having little real impact. Wallace's study of development NGOs shows also that a slick policy façade can be used to conceal conflict and a lack of commitment to gender equality (1998).

REFERENCES

Afshar, H. (1991). *Women, Development and Survival in the Third World*. London: Longman.

Association of African Women for Research and Development (AAWORD). (1982). The Experience of the Association of African Women for Research and Development (AAWORD). *Development Dialogue* 1–2: 101–13.

Baden, S., and A. M. Goetz. (1997). Who Needs [Sex] When You Can Have [Gender]? Conflicting Discourses on Gender at Beijing. In K. Staudt (Ed.), *Women, International Development and Politics: The Bureaucratic Mire* (37–58). Philadelphia: Temple University Press.

Boserup, E. (1970). *Women's Role in Economic Development*. New York: St. Martin's.

Bourginon, F., J. de Melo, J., C. Morrison (1991). *Adjustment with Growth and Equity. World Development* 19(11) (1485–1508}.

Bulvinic, M. (1983). Women's Issues in Third World Poverty: A Policy Analysis. In M. Buvinic, M. Lycette, and W. McGreevey (Eds.), *Women and Poverty in the Third World* (14–34). Baltimore, Md.: Johns Hopkins University Press.

Cagatay, N., D. Elson, C. Grown. (1995). Gender, Adjustment and Macroeconomics. *World Development* 23(11): 1827–1836.

Chowdhry, G. (1995). Engendering Development? Women in Development (WID) in International Development Regimes. In M. H. Marchand and J. L. Parpart (Eds.), *Feminism/Postmodernism/Development* (26–41). London: Routledge.

Colwell, A. S. C. (2001). *Vision and Revision: Demography, Material and Child Health Development, and the Representation of Native Women in Colonial Tanzania.* Ph.D. diss., University of Illinois, Urbana-Champaign.

Commonwealth Secretariat. (1989). *Engendering Adjustment for the 1990s.* London: Commonwealth Secretariat.

Cornia, G., R. Jolly, F. Stewart(1987). *Adjustment with a Human Face.* Oxford: Clarendon.

de Groot, J. (1991). Conceptions and Misconceptions: The Historical and Cultural Context of Discussion on Women and Development. In H. Afshar (Ed.), *Women, Development and Survival in the Third World* 107–138. London: Longman.

Elson, D. (1998). Talking to the Boys: Gender and Economic Growth Models. In C. Jackson and R. Pearson (Eds.), *Feminist Visions of Development: Gender Analysis and Policy* (155–70). London: Routledge.

Elson, D., and B. Evers. (1997). Gender Aware Country Economic Reports: Working Paper no. 2 Uganda. Manchester: University of Manchester Graduate School of Social Sciences GENECON Unit.

Escobar, A. (1995). *Encountering Development: The Making and Unmaking of the Third World.* Princeton: Princeton University Press.

Finnemore, M. (1997). Redefining Development at the World Bank. In F. Cooper and R. Packard (Eds.), *International Development and the Social Sciences: Essays on the History and Politics of Knowledge* (203–27). Berkeley: University of California Press.

Gilman, S. L. (1985). *Difference and Pathology: Stereotypes of Sexuality, Race, and Madness.* Ithaca, N.Y.: Cornell University Press.

Jackson, C. (1998). Rescuing Gender from the Poverty Trap. In C. Jackson and R. Pearson (Eds.), *Feminist Visions of Development: Gender, Analysis and Policy* (39–64). London: Routledge.

Kabeer, N. (1997). *Reversed Realities: Gender Hierarchies in Development Thought.* London: Verso.

Mohanty, C. T. (1991). Introduction: Cartographies of Struggle: Third World Women and the Politics of Feminism. In C. T. Mohanty, A. Russo, and L. Torres (Eds.), *Third World Women and The Politics of Feminism* (1–47). Bloomington: Indiana University Press.

Moser, C. O. (1989). Gender Planning in the Third World: Meeting Practical and Strategic Gender Needs. *World Development* 17(11): 1799–1825.

Parpart, J. L. (1995). Post-Modernism, Gender and Development. In J. Crush (Ed.), *Power of Development* (253–65). London: Routledge.

Parpart, J. L., and M. H. Marchand. (1995). Exploding the Canon: An Introduction/Conclusion. In J. L. Parpart and M. H. Marchand (Eds.), *Feminism/Postmodernism/Development* (1–22). London: Routledge.

Peet, R., with E. Hartwick. (1999). *Theories of Development.* New York: Guilford.

Rahnema, M. (1997). Towards Post-Development: Searching for Signposts, a New Language and New Paradigms. In M. Rahnema and V. Bawtree (Eds.), *The Post-Development Reader* (377–403). London: Zed.

Rathgeber, E. M. (1990). WID, WAD, GAD: Trends in Research and Practice.

The Journal of Developing Areas 24: 489–502.

ENBbuRichey, L. A. (2000). Gender Equality and Foreign Aid. In S. Robinson and F. Tarp (Eds.), *Foreign Aid and Development: Lessons Learnt and Directions for the Future* (390–429). London: Routledge.

———. (2002). Demographic, "Development" and Feminist Agenda: Depoliticizing Gender in a Tanzanian Family Planning Project. In J. Parpart, S. Rai, and K. Staudt (Eds.), *Rethinking Empowerment in a Global/Local World: Gendered Perspectives* (199–217). London: Routledge.

Rosenau, P. M. (1992). *Post-Modernism and the Social Sciences: Insights, Inroads and Intrusions.* Princeton: Princeton University Press.

Sachs, W. (Ed.). (1992). *The Development Dictionary: A Guide to Knowledge and Power.* London: Zed.

Saunders, K. (Ed.). (2002). *Feminist Post-Development Thought: Rethinking Modernity, Post-Colonialism, and Representation.* London: Zed Books.

Scott, C. V. (1995). *Gender and Development: Rethinking Modernization and Dependency Theory.* Boulder: Lynne Rienner.

Sen, G., and C. Grown (1987). *Development Crises and Alternative Visions: Third World Women's Perspectives.* New York: Monthly Review Press.

Shiva, V. (2002). *Water Wars: Privatization, Pollution, and Profit.* Cambridge, Mass.: South End.

Skjonsberg, E. (1992). Women in Development Towards the Year 2000. Discussion paper. Copenhagen: Danida.

So, A. Y. (1990). *Social Change and Development: Modernization, Dependency, and World-System Theories.* Newbury Park, Calif.: Sage.

Standing, H. (1997). Gender and Equity in Health Sector Reform Programmes: A Review. *Health Policy and Planning* 12(1): 1–18.

Staudt, K. (1998). *Policy, Politics and Gender: Women Gaining Ground.* West Hartford, Conn.: Kumarian.

Swamy, A., S. Knack, Y. Lee, O. Azfar (1999). *Gender and Corruption.* College Park, Md.: Insitutional Reform and the Informal Sector (IRIS).

Tong, R. (1989). *Feminist Thought: A Comprehensive Introduction.* Boulder, Colo.: Westview.

Vavrus, F. (forthcoming). *Desire and Decline: Schooling amid Crisis in Tanzania.* New York: Peter Lang.

———. (2002). Uncoupling the Articulation Between Girls' Education and Tradition in Tanzania. *Gender and Education* 14(4): 367–89.

Wallace, T. (1998). Institutionalising Gender in UK NGOs. *Development in Practice* 8(2): 159–71.

Young, K. (1997). Gender and Development. In N. Visvanathan, L. Duggan, L. Nisonoff, and N. Wiegersma (Eds.), *The Women, Gender and Development Reader* (51–54). London: Zed Books.

Frances Vavrus *is assistant professor of education at Teachers College, Columbia University, where she teaches courses on international education,* *gender and development, and education and demographic change. She was the recipient of an Andrew W. Mellon Postdoctoral Fellowship in Anthropological Demography at Harvard University, which allowed her to conduct a two-year research project on education, health, and the environment on Mount Kilimanjaro. Her current research interests focus on the impact of structural adjustment policies on women's education and reproductive health in Tanzania. She has written articles on educational inequality, HIV/AIDS, and postcolonialism in Sub-Saharan Africa, and she has recently completed a book on these matters entitled* Desire and Decline: Schooling amid Crisis in Tanzania *(Peter Lang).*

Lisa Ann Richey *is assistant professor of international development studies at Roskilde University in Denmark and a Soros Reproductive Rights Fellow at the Heilbrunn Department of Population and Family Health at the Mailman School of Public Health, Columbia University. She was a researcher at the Danish Institute for International Studies while editing this collection. She has published on issues of gender and development, family planning, HIV/AIDS, and population policy. Her current research is entitled "Gender, Wealth, and Modernity: Weaving International, National, and Local Interpretations of Population Policies in Uganda and Tanzania."*

And If the Shoe Doesn't Fit? (Wear It Anyway)

Economic Transformation and Western Paradigms of Women in Development Programs in Post-Communist Central and Eastern Europe

Kristen Ghodsee

Introduction[1]

From its inception in 1973, the Women in Development (WID) paradigm of incorporating gender into projects for economic growth has dominated the development establishment. Although this model has been critiqued and modified over time, WID scholars, advocates, and practitioners continue to dominate the field and to set the agenda in most multilateral and bilateral aid agencies, as well as in international nongovernmental organizations (NGOs) working in the developing world.[2] Since 1989, with the fall of the Berlin Wall, aid organizations have attempted to implement WID theory and practice within the former communist countries of Central and Eastern Europe. Despite the millions of dollars of aid dedicated to gender programs and the hundreds of projects throughout the region, these efforts have met with limited success.

This article will briefly examine just one of the possible reasons why WID projects have failed to reach women in Central and Eastern Europe: the long-suppressed history of WID–funded projects, which beyond liberal notions of development, have also served as covert tools to stem the spread of Marxist ideology in the developing world. Traditional accounts of the integration of women into American foreign assistance programs have ignored the Cold War context and the U.S. government's fears that communist insurgents were successfully mobilizing Third World women for revolutionary causes. In some part, the roots of the WID model are intricately linked with the fight against global communism.

Exploring these roots will provide important clues as to why WID and its heir, Gender and Development (GAD), have been largely unsuccessful in the former Eastern bloc countries. Central and Eastern European socialism and its legacies have not yet been totally erased from the collective social and cultural memory of the region's women, many of whom may prefer political rather than "self-help" solutions to their economic plight. This important, yet forgotten history must be reclaimed and integrated into the way scholars and development professionals study and theorize the WID model.

WID Aid to Eastern Europe

The fall of the Berlin Wall exponentially expanded opportunities for gender-related development work in Eurasia. The sudden implosion of communism was unexpected by scholars, politicians, and activists in both the East and the West. Feminists around the world were equally surprised by the momentous events that came to mark the end of the greatest social experiment of the twentieth century. Soon after, armies of democracy consultants and privatization advisers invaded the former Eastern bloc, riding a tidal wave of Western aid (Wedel 2001). Gender experts and Women in Development advocates and practitioners were not far behind

In the early years of the transition, Western feminist scholars (both liberal and Marxist) began researching and publishing about the negative effects that economic transition was having on women in the former communist countries (Corrin 1992; Einhorn 1993; Moghadam 1993; Funk and Mueller 1993; Rueschemeyer 1994; Alsanbeigui et al. 1994). Some scholars also felt it was necessary to "bring the Third World in" so that parallels between the transitioning and developing countries could be drawn (Moghadam 1993; Jaquette and Wolchik 1998; Kotzeva 1999; Verdery 1996). This research sparked the active interest of the WID departments of multilateral and bilateral aid agencies. These agencies, in turn, began offering grants targeted to local women's groups as part of "civil society" building initiatives throughout the region.

After the 1995 United Nations Fourth World Conference on Women in Beijing, cooperation among international women's agencies reached a zenith, and WID experts in the nonprofit sector began to "discover" Eastern Europe. International women's nongovernmental organizations based in the West recognized the plethora of opportunities available for gender-related work in the Central and Eastern European region and began applying for grants to do projects and carry out studies. "Feminist" networks, women's alliances, gender studies programs, and local women's NGOs have multiplied throughout the former communist world, and many millions of dollars have been spent on consciousness-raising activities, conferences, and gender assessments (Greenberg 2001).

For the most part, however, these activities have been unsuccessful in creating a broad-based women's movement in any of the former communist countries, even as women's status has continued to decline (Einhorn 1993; Holmgren 1995; Gal and Kligman 2000a, 2000b). In the few areas where Eastern European women have seen their status improve in the wake of the privatization of their economies, this has had less to do with Western aid efforts and more to do with the historical legacies of women's position under the previous regimes (Fodor 1997; Szalai 2000; Ghodsee 2003). Furthermore, women's NGOs and feminism in general have been met with great skepticism not only by the Eastern European societies as a whole, but specifically by the women in these societies (Kay 2000; Sperling 1999; Gal and Kligman 2000a; Grunberg 2000; Richter 2002; Jalusic and Antic 2000). Citizens in these countries were also wary because they felt that local NGOs were controlled by foreign donors and therefore had little legitimacy (Snavely and Desai 1994; Ottoway and Carothers 2000; Mendelson and Glenn 2000, 2002). Many Eastern European women feel that feminism is an alien ideology that does not address the real needs of women in post-communist countries.

These same frustrations and misunderstandings between East and West have been cited by many other feminist scholars and activists throughout the region (Funk 1993; Drakulic 1993). This essay, however, will focus on trying to untangle why WID and GAD paradigms designed to incorporate women into capitalist development have had such a hard time taking root in Central and Eastern Europe. Many misunderstandings might stem from incomplete accounts of the history of WID and GAD in the United States and the developing world. Without a nuanced exploration of how the threat of communism in the "Third World" propelled the incorporation of WID into the development efforts of the United States Agency for International Development (USAID), an understanding of the underlying tensions that hamper successful cooperation between women born and raised on either side of the capitalist-socialist ideological divide will be obscured.

History of WID

Work for the Revolution is more important than my marriage. Will the family disappear as a result? Fidel says, "Only love will hold the family of the future together."   (House of Representatives 1971)

Many scholars of WID mark the beginning of the field with the publication in 1970 of Ester Boserup's landmark book, *Women's Role in Economic Development* (Tinker 1983, 1984, 1990; Mosse 1993; Parpart 1995). They also cite the general influence of the United States women's movement on the United Nations and the international development community. Then there was the growing recognition of the failure of traditional development models in the Third World, which created industrial "growth" at the expense of social harmony and increased poverty. Taken together, these factors led to the inclusion of Section 113 in the 1973 amendment to the 1961 Foreign Assistance Act; this Percy amendment officially incorporated women into U.S. aid programs for the first time.

Other scholars (Kabeer 1994) recognized that the general atmosphere of social unrest and protest, both domestically and internationally, that marked the late 1960s and early 1970s may have shaped the ideas and opinions of the development community. Radical critiques, such as dependency theory coming out of Latin America, forced development practitioners to rethink their goals and priorities, and ultimately to consider the plight of those left out of more traditional development models that were focused exclusively on economic growth.

Yet in addition to the factors mentioned above, it is important to remember that the field of WID, like the project of Third World development itself, was created partially in response to fears of the spread of world communism.[3] In the context of the Cold War, the United States' recognition of women as an important constituency in development may have had less to do with genuine concern about the unequal hardships that modernization produced, than with the perceived threat posed by communists who were successfully mobilizing disenfranchised women (and rural peasants) for revolutionary causes throughout the developing world. This is not to say that the WID scholars and activists themselves were promoting WID as a way to fight Marxist ideologies, but that the U.S. government's fear of communism may have been one important reason why the Percy Amendment was accepted by the overwhelmingly male congress in 1973. Moreover, funds to support WID programming should be seen as part of a larger shift from direct military aid to more socially oriented types of aid that the 1973 amendment to the 1961 Foreign Assistance Act accomplished.

The history of how and why women became integrated into the international development establishment in the context of the Cold War has been largely lost. Reclaiming it will, in some small way, assist both scholars and practitioners in understanding why so many problems arise when WID projects are transplanted from the Third World to Eastern European soil. After all, if WID as a development paradigm was produced in response to the perceived successes of socialist and communist countries in granting women greater political and economic rights, it might prove difficult to apply the same model to the very women who were beneficiaries of the socialist system that the WID model was trying to displace.

The Birth of Development and "Basic Needs"

The goals of foreign aid to the Third World were bound up intimately with the Cold War and the need to suppress communist uprisings in the newly independent states emerging from colonialism across the globe (Leebaert 2002). Indeed, the rapid industrialization of the Soviet Union and other Eastern bloc countries that employed the communist model served as a powerful example to new nations hoping to modernize and catch up with both the First and Second Worlds. One of the foundational texts of development economics was Walter W. Rostow's *Stages of Economic Growth: A Non-Communist Manifesto* (1960). This book outlined a progressive, linear path to economic development that relied upon and celebrated individualism, entrepreneurship, and private property in contrast to the communal, centrally planned, state-owned economies of socialist and communist models.

The allure of communist ideologies in the developing world became especially relevant during the Vietnam War and the United States' failure to "save" the South Vietnamese from socialism. No one understood the consequences of communism in the developing world better than one of Rostow's colleagues in the Kennedy and Johnson administrations, Robert S. McNamara. Fresh from his tenure as secretary of defense after having fallen out with President Johnson over American involvement in Vietnam (McNamara 1995), McNamara assumed the presidency of the World Bank in 1968. He had spoken and published widely on the idea that poverty bred communism, and that the only way to fight socialism around the world was to raise the living standards of the poor and to soften the worst inequalities created and perpetuated by capitalism (McNamara 1968). He writes,

> Given the certain connection between economic stagnation and the incidence of violence, the years that lie ahead for the nations of the southern half of the globe look ominous. This would be true if no threat of Communist subversion existed, as it clearly does. Both Moscow and Peking, however harsh their internal differences, regard the modernization process as an ideal environment for the

growth of Communism. . . . It is clearly understood that certain Communist nations are capable of subverting, manipulating and finally directing for their own ends the wholly legitimate grievances of a developing society. (1968, 147–148)

McNamara's thirteen-year presidency of the World Bank ushered in an era of lending for projects based on a new paradigm—one called "redistribution with growth" by the World Bank and "basic needs" by the United Nations. This new paradigm focused on improving the living standards of the poor. World Bank lending would increase from $883 million per year in 1968 to $12 billion per year in 1981 when McNamara left the bank (Leebaert 2002). This new focus on human development saturated the development establishment and fundamentally altered development theory and practice.[4] Instead of focusing efforts on building roads, dams, factories, and airports, the World Bank and USAID began funding such things as water wells, primary schools, and hospitals.

Special attention was given to those who had been previously left out of development's modernization efforts: poor, rural populations and women. These two groups were particularly important because of their vulnerability to communist co-optation. On February 16, 1962, a classified telegram from the American embassy in Thailand warned that the communist National Front for the Liberation of South Vietnam had begun to infiltrate the south through the formation of "various affilists [*sic*] bodies," including the Liberation Farmer's Front and the Liberation Women's Front (Department of State 1962). While a September 1966 intelligence memorandum, "The Organization, Activities, and Objectives of the Communist Front in South Vietnam," included a list of the leaders of Hoi Phu Nu Giai Phong, the liberation women's organization, with detailed biographies (Central Intelligence Agency [CIA] 1966). This list demonstrates that the CIA recognized women as important leaders of the communist movement and marked them as potential enemies.[5] Another CIA report spoke of the "usual array of mass organizations (women's, youth, peasant and labor groups)" (1972, 47) that the Vietnamese communists mobilized for their own ends. The dedication and mobilization of Vietnamese women as soldiers for the communist cause (Turley 1972) must have also concerned the U.S. government.

Between 1970 and 1974, the Committee of Internal Security of the House of Representatives of the United States Congress held a series of hearings, the Theory and Practice of Communism. These hearings were held because the U.S. government felt that there exists a world-wide Communist movement whose purpose it is by espionage, sabotage, and other means to establish a totalitarian dictatorship in countries throughout the world . . . and that the Communist organization in the United States, together with other circumstances of the international Communist movement, presents a clear and present danger to the security of the United States and the existence of American institutions. (House of Representatives [HR] 1970, 4631)

The U.S. government had to acknowledge that women were an integral part of this clear and present danger. Testimony presented at the hearings supports the idea that women's organizations such as the Third World Women's Alliance and the Women's International Democratic Federation were considered "communist fronts," "founded and supported at all times by the international communist movement" (HR 1974, 2693). Moreover, the devotion of women in Cuba to Fidel's communism (Smith and Padula 1996) was yet another example of how leftist parties were successfully able to integrate women into revolutionary causes. A pamphlet prepared by two American women active in the U.S. women's movement and included in exhibits for the hearings demonstrates that communist governments had already included women in development—well before the capitalist world:

In every Cuban neighborhood women get together to discuss topics ranging from Jose Marti to day care, and from the struggles in Vietnam to problems of picking citrus fruits. Larger units of the Federation [of Cuban Women] organize women's work brigades to combat on one front or another Cuba's number one problem: underdevelopment. (HR 1971, 5569)

As the 1970s progressed, there were growing references to the role of women in the developing world. In later testimonies given in support of further incorporating women into USAID's projects and for soliciting funds from Congress to support the Voluntary Fund for the United Nations Decade for Women, advocates argued that women were essential for carrying out a basic needs paradigm of development (HR 1978).

In fact, the Percy amendment was part of a foreign policy trend away from direct military intervention toward indirect economic interventions in developing countries. This new strategy coincided neatly with McNamara's call for poverty alleviation as a way to fight communism. Thus, if women were essential to basic needs, and meeting basic needs was essential to fighting communism, then women were essential to fighting communism.[6]

> The imperative to integrate women into the development process turns out to be not a product of American feminism, as some have implied, but grows organically out of the situation of poor women and the needs of development. The everyday activities of the world's poor women intersect with a basic human needs approach. (Elsa Chaney, testimony, cited in HR 1978, 9)

A good illustration of the possibilities of a new women's focus on development (and one rarely mentioned with reference to the birth of the WID paradigm) was the very important role played by Chilean women in opposing Salvador Allende's socialist government in Chile between 1970 and 1973. After the Popular Unity's rise to power and its wholesale nationalization of the economy, Allende's three-year stint in power was punctuated by parades of women banging spoons on pots and pans to protest severe food shortages. This ultimately lent support to the U.S.–backed coup that brought Ugarte Pinochet to power (de los Angeles Crummett 1977; Townsend 1993). In the March 7, 1974, testimony of Hermogenes Perez de Acre before the Committee on Internal Security, the Chilean professor is asked directly about women in Chile, "You mentioned that the women had a demonstration with regard to pots and pans. Did the women play an important role with regard to the downfall of Allende's government?" Perez de Acre then explained in detail how women's "resistance to Marxism was much more than the one from men" (HR 1974, 2556). In an exhibit attached to this testimony, there is a newspaper article entitled "Women and Their Fight for Chile," which states:

> Undoubtedly the role played by Chilean women was one of the most decisive factors in the fight against Marxist oppression. . . . There can be no doubt that the women of Chile, of all ages and conditions, were the first to realize the crisis which afflicted our country. (HR 1974, 2639)

The political actions of El Poder Feminino in Chile proved definitively that women, if incorporated into a capitalist development paradigm, could be very valuable allies in the fight against socialism. Therefore, although the women's movement in the United States and Boserup's book were certainly influential voices, these brief examples demonstrate that the Cold War context must be considered when unraveling the creation myths surrounding WID. I will, however, reiterate here that the women who were advocating for WID had no visible interest in using women as a tool against communism. The focus needs to be shifted to the U.S. government. Was the government's receptivity to WID inspired by altruistic concerns regarding the moral imperatives for granting women equal rights and resources, or was it motivated by the perceived threat of communist infiltration? WID's underlying alliance to capitalism and its incorporation into mainstream development would eventually open it up to sometimes harsh criticism.

Women and Development, Gender and Development

Two other models of incorporating women into economic development, both of which censured WID for its liberal feminist and First World biases, subsequently critiqued the WID paradigm. The first critique was a neo-Marxist perspective that attacked WID based on its ideological adherence to capitalism. The Women and Development (WAD) school believed that only with radical, systemic reform could women benefit from development.[7] WAD theorists (Rubin 1975; Maguire 1984) would frequently point to the advances of women in communist countries where the state had abolished private property. In terms of the traditional development establishment, however, WAD was far too radical of a critique to be taken seriously in development practice. It fundamentally attacked the capitalist superstructure of developing societies, the very capitalisms that development was trying to preserve.

Proponents of the GAD paradigm leveled a second line of criticism. Much as women of color mounted an attack against the white, middle class feminists of the "Second Wave"[8] in the United States, so Third World women claimed that the WID paradigm exported First World feminist values that were not applicable to their lives and experiences.[9] Third World women in conversation with First World women created the GAD paradigm in order to modify and make WID more relevant to their lives (Mosse 1993; Visvanathan et al. 1997). GAD projects are supposed to be more participatory and sustainable than WID projects, often working to mobilize women at the proverbial grass roots. Furthermore, GAD recognizes that women in different countries, even in different regions within countries, may have very different goals. GAD strategies for development, therefore, are more varied and flexible. Despite these modifications, GAD theory and practice is compatible with WID in that it neither fundamentally challenges the capitalist model nor seriously considers a class-based analysis of women's oppression.

Today, gender has been "mainstreamed" into development projects at most multilateral and bilateral aid agencies, and grant-funding for gender-related projects has increased exponentially.[10] What is relevant to our discussion is that although WID has been critiqued and modified over time, one of its central goals has essentially remained unchanged: the incorporation of women into capitalist models of development. Indeed, the WID model may have been accepted precisely to contain the spread of communist ideologies. Because of this, the design of WID projects in former socialist countries cannot understand, in fundamental ways, the needs and concerns of women there. They fail to provide useful strategies for women's "development" because they are unable to identify underlying social and political tensions.

WID/GAD Projects in Central and Eastern Europe

Although there are many examples of less-than-successful aid projects in Central and Eastern Europe (Wedel 2001), in the interest of brevity and space, I will only focus on two specific types of WID programs. One example involves the ubiquitous WID/GAD promotion of microcredit schemes for women and/or their support of women's entrepreneurship. Microcredit banks extend small amounts of capital to groups of poor women. These women either use the money to meet immediate basic needs or to invest in some small, income-generating project that will allow them, after having made a profit, to repay the money. Profits are then used to pay for basic needs or saved and then put to use productively in some further income-generating scheme. A typical example of a WID-type microcredit scheme is the Social Entrepreneurship Center in Plovdiv, Bulgaria, funded by the European Union's PHARE Access Program: "The goal of the project is providing opportunity to unemployed women to integrate in new economic conditions through training on starting their own business as an active strategy for living standard increase [*sic*]" (NGO Resource Center 2002).

Support for women's entrepreneurship picks up where microcredit schemes leave off. Once women have enough capital to move beyond meeting basic needs, they need to be given the training and encouragement to start their own businesses. The hope is that these businesses will be sustainable and will realize a continuous stream of profits, which—in turn—will allow these women to meet their basic needs, reinvest in their businesses, and eventually be able to consume nonessential goods and luxury items. In other words, these kinds of projects help women become good entrepreneurs (i.e., capitalists), so that they can support themselves, and ultimately "get ahead" (i.e., become consumers).

A study for the Microcredit Summit Campaign (Cheston and Kuhn 2002) found that women in Eastern Europe "lag far behind" women in other parts of the world in microcredit participation. Recent USAID Gender Assessments have also found that women are far less likely than men are to take advantage of microcredit in Bulgaria (Nails and Arnold 2001) and Romania (Rosenberg and Arnold 2002). In Romania, the authors found that although women owned or managed approximately 44 percent of all businesses, women accounted for only 2.7 percent of the total amount of money loaned (loan value) in 1999. The study suggests that low levels of lending to women might indicate "a reluctance of women to borrow money," and recommends further research on the issue. In Bulgaria, there are at least twelve different sources for microlending and here too, women consistently borrow less than men.[11] Even when programs are specifically targeted to women, many women are reluctant to participate, even if loan amounts are relatively small. Although there has been an increase in women-owned-and-managed businesses in recent years, there is little evidence to demonstrate that this activity has been a result of microcredit schemes. Overall, microcredit in the region has met with very limited success.

The first part of the problem is the very definition of basic needs. In the prototypical developing country (the first Microcredit Bank was in Bangladesh), the women needed the money to meet the most basic needs of food, water, and shelter. These were things that the state had never provided, and the shift toward a more market-driven economy had further reduced in supply (Boserup 1970; Goulet and Hudson 1971; Mende 1972). These women never had jobs in the formal economy, few of them had educations, and many were illiterate. Despite this, development practitioners found that women were very resourceful with small loans, and that they most often used the profits they realized to increase the welfare of their families. As access to money increased, women used the profits to access the fruits of modernization: medicines, fertilizers, seed varieties, electricity, education, and more. These were "needs" newly created by development through the importation of Western technologies and Western ideas about universal education and "modern" living. Microentrepreneurship allowed women to have access to the benefits of a modernizing economy. In these circumstances, microcredit was a revolutionary strategy for empowering women and incorporating them into the formal, developing economy.

The problem with this model in Central and Eastern Europe is multifaceted. Whereas in the Third World, "needs" were imported by "successful" development projects and microcredit and entrepreneurship helped women to meet those needs, in the socialist context these "needs" already existed (at least rhetorically) as the basic *rights and entitlements* of the citizen. In other words, the introduction of "modern" technologies and institutions in most communist countries (i.e., universal education, Western medicine and health care, modernized agriculture, heating, electricity, etc.) was intimately bound up with the idea that it was the state's responsibility to provide them without cost to society. The communist or socialist state legitimated its existence through the provision of these goods and services to all citizens (Verdery 1993). Indeed, one of the greatest achievements of the communist countries was the high level of human development that they achieved. This was one of the core Marxist criticisms leveled at capitalism: that although communist and socialist citizens may not have been "free," they were certainly not hungry, uneducated, or unhealthy.

In the post-socialist period, these rights and entitlements have all but disappeared. The collapse of the communist states has relegated these "rights" to the status of "needs" for the first time in the history of many of these countries. This, for example, means that countries that were electrified under communism never had electricity that was not provided by the state as a public good. In other words, electricity did not exist in many places before it was introduced by the communists as proof of successful modernization by the "dictatorship of the proletariat."[12] In the First or Third World context, where for the most part these things were always constructed as needs (although even capitalist states have granted many social entitlements at different historical periods), programs and projects to support women's "self-help" in regards to meeting these needs are more likely to be successful. In the Central and Eastern European context, however, microcredit and women's entrepreneurship projects will be less easily implemented. Many women have not fundamentally accepted that it is their responsibility to meet these needs in the first place. Women in Central and Eastern Europe might have incentives to work for consumer items or to save money to travel abroad, but many might resist the idea of taking loans to start businesses to earn money to pay for the very same things they once had without cost, especially if they are expected to pay interest on the money they borrow (which can be as high as 26 percent). Studies have confirmed that women are less likely to start their own business (United Nations Development Report 2000), and the fact that women in Central and Eastern Europe are still more likely to vote for left-leaning or outright communist parties demonstrates an intransigent resistance to capitalism (Jalusic and Antic 2000). WID/GAD projects aimed at alleviating women's poverty based on microcredit or entrepreneurship programs fail to realize that Central and Eastern European women may prefer to put their energies into finding political solutions to their rapidly declining standards of living rather than participate in a system with which they fundamentally disagree.

Furthermore, WID/GAD projects often fail to recognize that Central and Eastern European women are highly educated, with many years of participation in the formal economy. Indeed, the former communist countries could once boast of the highest labor-force participation rates for women in the world. A further assumption or misconception is that Central and Eastern European women are not concerned with politics. On the contrary, Central and Eastern European women are politically savvy and incredibly discerning about the political process. Many projects based on increasing women's activities in politics, therefore, are also meet with resistance or simply go unnoticed.

For instance, throughout the region, there are several grants for local NGOs to organize high-profile media campaigns to increase women's political participation.[13] These grants, usually originating in the United States and Western Europe, are given to local NGOs (whose directors disturbingly often do have the "right" political affiliations) to advocate for "democracy promotion." However legitimate the need to encourage women to take part in the political process, many Central and Eastern European women believe that advocacy campaigns to "get women to the polls" are partisan efforts and that foreign governments use local NGOs to promote political parties favorable to the funders' interests. Furthermore, Central and Eastern European women may view *not* engaging in politics as a political act. A more useful project might explore why women are not involving themselves in the polity, rather than simply assuming that getting women to vote and stand for election (in a political system that they do not yet believe in) is somehow intrinsically in their own interests.

In the two brief examples given above, it should be clear that some WID/GAD projects effectively promote women's integration into the capitalist system, and actively discourage the creation of a more socialistic, welfare state closer to the Scandinavian model. Neither of the paradigms is sensitive to the political sophistication or ideological history of Central and Eastern European women, many of whom are still trying to negotiate their roles in society after 1989. A more appropriate paradigm for women in Central and Eastern Europe would be one which does not assume, a priori, that free-market capitalism is the only possible model for successful economic growth—not necessarily because this is not true, but because Central and Eastern European women may have yet to believe it. Furthermore, WID scholars, practitioners, and advocates (Tinker 1990) need to recognize that essentially free education, health care, child care, electricity, central heat, water, public transportation, etc., were and may remain basic *rights* in the popular imagination. Many Central and Eastern European women feel that these entitlements were taken away from them without adequate compensation—"freedom" has yet to pay the bills. Projects to address the needs of women may need to include politically "dangerous" strategies to help women decide for which "needs" they will work and for which "rights" they will fight. Only then will international efforts to raise the living standards of women in Central and Eastern Europe be both sensitive to the social and political history of the region and relevant to the daily struggles of women living through a most tumultuous (and often uninvited) period of economic transformation.

NOTES

1. The author would like to thank Irene Tinker for her comments and encouragement and Ed Leijewski at the WID department of USAID for taking the time to consider and comment upon my ideas.
2. The terminology used to refer to different regions of the "developed" and "developing" worlds has changed over time and displays particular affiliations with specific development paradigms. In this paper, while recognizing the political implications of different terminologies, I will use the terms First, Second and Third Worlds, core and periphery, less-developed countries (LDCs), and the global south interchangeably.
3. Arturo Escobar (1995) has done an excellent job of discussing the Cold War context of development as a whole.
4. McNamara 1973; Chenery et al. 1974; World Bank 1975; and International Labor Organization 1976 were all influential publications which legitimized the idea that poverty alleviation was an essential goal of development.
5. Similar lists of women in left-leaning women's organizations affiliated with the *Partai Komunis Indonesia* (PKI) were including in the lists that the CIA handed over to General Suharto of Indonesia in 1964. Suharto used these very lists to carry out one of the most brutal massacres of the Cold War – murdering an estimated 250,000 men, women and children in order to purge his country of communism (Leebaert 2002).
6. It should also be recognized that the development establishment would begin to recognize the importance of women in the Third World exactly as calls for women's liberation at home also began to point to the successes of the socialist model abroad (House of Representative 1971; Jenness 1972).

7. Informed as it was by dependency theory, WAD thinkers argued that the First World had underdeveloped the Third World in its own quest for development. The linearity of Rostowian stages of economic growth was challenged, with global capitalism seen as the system that would always and inevitably perpetuate inequality and exploitation. Just as proletarian classes were exploited by bourgeois classes within nations, so countries in the "periphery" were exploited by those in the "core." For the large part the ideological divide between the WID and WAD models fell along the same lines that traditionally divided liberal and socialist feminists for over a century; whereas the former believed that women were oppressed by patriarchy the latter laid the blame at the feet of private property. WAD theorists believed that poor men shared the same structural disadvantages as poor women and that men and women needed to work together for development.

8. Second wave refers to the U.S. women's movement in the 1970s when women advocated for legal and economic equality as well as reproductive rights.

9. Both women of color in the United States (for example hooks 1981; Lorde 1985; Anzaldua and Moraga (1983) and "Third World" women (for example Mohanty et al.1991; Narayan 1997 and Bulbeck 1998) have criticized the white, middle class bias of cultural feminism in the U.S. women's movement and the WID paradigm.

10. For instance, the World Bank now requires "Gender impact assessments" for all of its development projects.

11. For instance, The NACHALA Cooperative, The Resource Center Foundation, Caresback-Bulgaria, The Phare Program, Catholic Relief Services, The Bulgarian-American Enterprise Fund, National Network for Micro-Funding, etc.

12. Of course, the provision of these services in practice by the communist government was less than perfect. Power and water outages were endemic in both rural and urban areas, and the quality of these services was rarely consistent.

13. Two good examples are Project Parity, funded by USAID and implemented by the Women's Alliance for Development in Bulgaria, and a USAID project in neighboring Macedonia by two American gender consultants (Greenberg and McDonald 2000) aimed at increasing Macedonian women's political participation.

REFERENCES

Alsanbeigui, Nahid, Steve Pressman, and Gail Summerfield. 1994. *Women in the Age of Economic Transformation: Gender Impacts of Reforms in Post-Socialist and Developing Countries.* New York: Routledge.

Anzaldúa, Gloria, and Cherríe Moraga. 1983. *This Bridge Called My Back: Writings by Radical Women of Color.* New York: Kitchen Table, Women of Color Press.

Boserup, Ester. 1970. *Women's Role in Economic Development.* New York: St. Martin's Press.

Buckley, Mary. 1997. *Post-Soviet Women: From the Baltic to Central Asia.* Cambridge and New York: Cambridge University Press.

Bulbeck, Chilla. 1998. *Re-orienting Western Feminisms: Women's Diversity in a Postcolonial World.* Cambridge and New York: Cambridge University Press.

Central Intelligence Agency [CIA]. 1966. Intelligence memorandum. "The Organizations, Activities and Objectives of the Communist Front in South Vietnam." 26 September. Document no. 1603/66.

————. 1972. *National Intelligence Survey: North Vietnam, General Survey.* January.

Chenery, Hollis Burnley, et al. 1974. *Redistribution with Growth: Policies to Improve Income Distribution in Developing Countries in the Context of Economic Growth.* Oxford: Oxford University Press.

Cheston, S. and Lisa Kuhn. 2002. *Empowering Women Through Microfinance.* Illinois, USA: International Opportunity.

Corrin, Chris. 1992. *Superwoman and the Double Burden: Women's Experience of Change in Central and Eastern Europe and the Former Soviet Union.* Toronto: Second Story Press.

Daskalova, Krassimira. 2000. "Women's Problems, Women's Discourses in Bulgaria." In Gal and Kligman 2000b.

de los Angeles Crummett, Maria. 1977. "El Poder Feminino: The Mobilization of Women Against Socialism in Chile (in Women in Revolution)." *Latin American Perspectives* 4, no. 4. (autumn): 103–113.

Department of State. 1962. Outgoing telegram issued from the American Embassy in Bangkok. 16 February.

Drakulic, Slavenka. 1993. *How We Survived Communism and Even Laughed.* New York: Norton.

Einhorn, Barbara. 1993. *Cinderella Goes to Market: Citizenship, Gender, and Women's Movements in East Central Europe.* London and New York: Verso.

Escobar, Arturo. 1995. *Encountering Development: The Making and Unmaking of the Third World.* Princeton, N.J.: Princeton University Press.

Fodor, Eva. 1997. "Gender in Transition: Unemployment in Hungary, Poland and Slovakia." *East European Politics and Societies* 11, no. 3 (fall): 470–500

Funk, Nanette. 1993. "Feminism East and West." In Funk and Mueller 1993.

Funk, Nanette, and Magda Mueller, eds. 1993. *Gender Politics and Post-Communism: Reflections from Eastern Europe and the Former Soviet Union.* New York and London: Routledge.

Gal, Susan, and Gail Kligman. 2000a. *The Politics of Gender After Socialism: A Comparative-Historical Essay.* Princeton, N.J.: Princeton University Press.

Gal, Susan, and Gail Kligman, eds. 2000b. *Reproducing Gender: Politics, Publics, and Everyday Life After Socialism.* Princeton, N.J.: Princeton University Press.

Ghodsee, Kristen. 2003. "State Support in the Market: Women and Tourism Employment in Post-Socialist Bulgaria." *International Journal of Politics, Cultural and Society* 16, no. 3 (spring): 465–82.

Goulet, Denis, and Michael Hudson. 1971. *The Myth of Aid: The Hidden Agenda of Development Reports.* New York: IODC N. America.

Greenberg, Marcia. 2001. "A Beijing +5 Success Story: Women from Eastern Europe Strengthen Their Democracy Skills." In WIDTECH Information

Bulletin [March]. Available from www.widtech.org.

Greenberg, Marcia, and Kara Mcdonald. 2000. *Women's Political Participation in the Republic of Macedonia: Opportunities to Support Women in Upcoming Elections—and Beyond.* Washington, D.C.: WIDTECH.

Grunberg, Laura. 2000. "Women's NGOs in Romania." In Gal and Kligman 2000b.

Holmgren, Beth. 1995. "Bug Inspectors and Beauty Queens: The Problem of Translating Feminism into Russian." In *Genders 22: Postcommunism and the Body Politic,* edited by Ellen Berry. New York: New York University Press.

hooks, bell. 1981. *Ain't I a Woman: Black Women and Feminism.* Boston: South End Press.

House of Representatives [HR], Committee on Internal Security. 1970. *The Theory and Practice of Communism in 1970,* 91st Cong., 2d sess., 23, 24 and 25 June. Washington, D.C.: U.S. Government Printing Office.

———. 1971. *The Theory and Practice of Communism in 1971 (Latin America) Part 3,* 92d Cong., 1st sess., 5–7, 14 October. Washington, D.C.: U.S. Government Printing Office.

———. 1974. *The Theory and Practice of Communism, Part 5 (Marxism Imposed on Chile—Allende Regime),* 93rd Cong., 1st sess., 15 November 1973, and 7 and 13 March 1974. Washington, D.C.: U.S. Government Printing Office.

House of Representatives, Subcommittee on International Organization and on International Development of the Committee on International Relations. 1978. *International Women's Issues,* 95th Cong., 2d sess., 8 and 22 March. Washington, D.C.: U.S. Government Printing Office.

International Labor Organization. 1976. *Employment, Growth and Basic Needs: A One-World Problem.* Geneva: ILO.

Jalusic, Vlasta, and Milica Antic. 2000. "Prospects for Gender Equality Policies in Central and Eastern Europe." Working paper, no. 70, SOCO Project, Vienna.

Jaquette, Jane, and Sharon Wolchik. 1998. *Women and Democracy: Latin America and Central and Eastern Europe.* Baltimore, Md.: Johns Hopkins University Press.

Jenness, Linda. 1972. *Feminism and Socialism.* New York: Pathfinder Press.

Kabeer, Naila. 1994. *Reversed Realities: Gender Hierarchies in Development Thought.* London: Verso.

Kay, Rebecca. 2000. *Russian Women and Their Organizations: Gender, Discrimination, and Grassroots Women's Organizations.* New York: St. Martin's Press.

Kotzeva, Tatyana. 1999. "Re-imagining Bulgarian Women: The Marxist Legacy and Women's Self-Identity." In *Gender and Identity in Central and Eastern Europe,* edited by Chris Corrin. London: Frank Cass Publishers.

Leebaert, Derek. 2002. *The Fifty-Year Wound: The True Price of America's Cold War Victory.* Boston, London, and New York: Little Brown and Company.

Lorde, Audre. 1985. *I Am Your Sister: Black Women Organizing Across Sexualities.* New York: Kitchen Table, Women of Color Press.

Maguire, P. 1984. *Women and Development: An Alternative Analysis.* Amherst, Mass.: Center for International Education.

McNamara, Robert S. 1968. *The Essence of Security: Reflections from Office.* New

York: Harper and Row.

———. 1973. *One Hundred Countries, Two Billion People: The Dimensions of Development.* London: Praeger Publishers.

———. 1995. *In Retrospect: The Tragedy and Lessons of Vietnam.* New York: Random House.

Mende, T. 1972. *From Aid to Recolonization.* New York: Pantheon, 1972.

Mendelson, Sarah, and John Glenn. 2000. "Democracy Assistance and NGO Strategies in Post-Communist Societies." Carnegie Endowment Working Papers, Democracy and Rule of Law Project, no. 8. Carnegie Endowment for International Peace, Washington, D.C., February.

———. 2002. *The Power and Limits of NGOs: A Critical Look at Building Democracy in Eastern Europe and Eurasia.* New York: Columbia University Press.

Moghadam, Valentine. 1993. *Democratic Reform and the Position of Women in Transitional Economies.* Oxford: Clarendon Press.

Mohanty, Chandra Talpade, Ann Russo, and Lourdes Torres. 1991. *Third World Women and the Politics of Feminism.* Bloomington: Indiana University Press.

Mosse, Julia. 1993. *Half the World, Half a Chance: An Introduction to Gender and Development.* London: Oxfam Publications.

Nails, Donna and Julianna Arnold. 2001. *Gender Assessment and Plan of Action USAID/Bulgaria.* Washington D.C.: WIDTECH.

Narayan, Uma. 1997. *Dislocating Cultures: Identities, Traditions, and Third-World Feminism.* New York: Routledge.

Nongovernmental Organization Resource Center. 2002. "Encouraging Entrepreneurship and Providing Loans to Unemployed Women," available online at http://www.ngorc.net/en/programs/pred/default.htm

Ottoway, Marina, and Thomas Carothers. 2000. *Funding Virtue: Civil Society Aid and Democracy Promotion.* Washington, D.C.: Carnegie Endowment for International Peace.

Parpart, Jane. 1995. "Post-modernism, Gender and Development." In *Power of Development,* edited by Jonathan Crush. New York: Routledge.

Richter, James. 2002. "Evaluating Western Assistance to Russian Women's Organizations." In Mendelson and Glenn 2002.

Rosenberg, Ruth, and Julianna Arnold. 2002. *Gender Assessment and Plan of Action USAID/ROMANIA.* Washington, D.C.: WIDTECH.

Rostow, Walter W. 1960. *The Stages of Economic Growth: A Non-Communist Manifesto.* Cambridge: Cambridge University Press.

Rubin, Gail. 1975. "The Traffic in Women: Notes on the 'Political Economy' of Sex." In *Towards an Anthropology of Women,* edited by Reyna. R. Reiter. New York: Monthly Review Press.

Rueschemeyer, Marylin. 1994. *Women and the Politics of Postcommunist Eastern Europe.* Armonk, N.Y.: M. E. Sharpe.

Smith, Lois, and Alfred Padula. 1996. *Sex and Revolution: Women in Socialist Cuba.* Oxford: Oxford University Press.

Snavely, Keith, and Uday Desai. 1994. "The Emergence and Development of Nonprofit Organizations in Bulgaria." Working paper, The Aspen Institute, Washington, D.C.

Sperling, Valerie. 1999. *Organizing Women in Contemporary Russia: Engendering Transition*. Cambridge and New York: Cambridge University Press.

Szalai, Julia. 2000. "From Informal Labor to Paid Occupations: Marketization from Below in Hungarian Women's Work." In Gal and Kligman 2000.

Tinker, Irene. 1983. *Women in Washington: Advocates for Public Policy*. Sage Yearbooks in Women's Policy Studies vol. 7. London: Sage Publications.

———. 1984. Testimony. United States Senate Committee on Foreign Relations. *Addendum to Women in Development: Looking to the Future*, 98th Cong., 2d sess., 7 June. Washington, D.C.: U.S. Government Printing Office.

———. 1990. *Persistent Inequalities: Woman and World Development*. Oxford: Oxford University Press.

Townsend, Camilla. 1993. "Refusing to Travel *La Via Chilena*: Working-Class Women in Allende's Chile." *Journal of Women's History* 4, no. 3 (winter): 43–62.

Turley, William S. 1972. "Women in the Communist Revolution of Vietnam" *Asian Survey* 12, no. 9 (September): 793–805.

United Nations Development Program. 1998. *Women in Poverty Report*. Sofia, Bulgaria: UNDP.

———. 2000. *1999 Human Development Report: Bulgaria*. Sofia, Bulgaria: UNDP.

Verdery, Katherine. 1996. *What Was Socialism and What Comes Next?* Princeton, N.J.: Princeton University Press.

Visvanathan, Nalini, et al. 1997. *The Women, Gender, and Development Reader*. Atlantic Highlands, N.J.: Zed Books.

Wedel, Janine. 2001. *Collision and Collusion: The Strange Case of Aid to Eastern Europe*. New York: Palgrave.

World Bank. 1975. *The Assault on World Poverty*. Baltimore: Johns Hopkins University Press.

Kristen Ghodsee *is assistant professor in the women studies program at Bowdoin College. Her publications include "State Support in the Market: Women and Tourism Employment in Post-Socialist Bulgaria" in the* International Journal of Politics, Cultural and Society, *Vol. 16, No. 3 (Spring 2003), 465-82, and "Feminism-by-Design: Emerging Capitalisms, Cultural Feminism, and Women's Nongovernmental Organizations in Post-Socialist Eastern Europe" forthcoming in* Signs, *Spring 2004, vol. 29, no. 3. She is currently revising her book manuscript,* Sun, Sand and Socialism: Gender, Class, and Tourism in Postsocialist Bulgaria. *Kristen Ghodsee has received both Fulbright and IREX fellowships, and was a research fellow with the Eastern European Studies Program at the Woodrow Wilson International Center for Scholars in 2002.*

Microcredit

The Rhetoric of Empowerment, the Reality of "Development As Usual"

Robin G. Isserles

Introduction

From the beginning of the United Nations Decade for Women in 1976, feminist scholars and activists from across the globe have struggled to alter development thinking and practice. In doing so, they sought both to recognize women as important actors and to identify the many ways in which women's lives have been disrupted by the development process. The challenges they posed have had an impact on the policy-making of the major development institutions, particularly the World Bank, UN agencies, and nongovernmental organizations (NGOs): concerns for women have been increasingly incorporated into mainstream development policies and programs. Most major development institutions now have specialized gender departments that assist in the design, implementation, and evaluation of development programs, concentrating on the impact of such programs on women.

Many of the program initiatives that concern women are heavily focused on bringing them into the development process. Scant attention has been given to altering the overall development process, and even less to changing the oppressive gendered relations that the process often creates or maintains. The popular rhetoric employed by development specialists and institutions—specifically those that emphasize women's participation and empowerment—seems disconnected from actual practice. This seems especially true in the case of microcredit, which has often been presented as a cure-all, occupying a central place in new development protocol.

This essay provides a critical analysis of some of the ideological assumptions underlying microcredit and considers the implications it has on the lives of women it is supposed to empower. Such an analysis explores the disjuncture between rhetoric and reality, as it reveals the ideological commitments reinforced by neoliberal notions of development. The data presented come from a variety of sources: a critical analysis of some of the current writing on microcredit; interviews conducted between 1998-1999 with development workers who have been engaged in microcredit programs in developing countries;

and fieldwork I conducted at the Microcredit Summit in New York City in 1998.

Defining Microcredit

Microcredit is a poverty-relief program that grants very small loans to the poor for small business enterprises (Fairley 1998, 339). The average microloan in Bangladesh, for example, falls within the range of seventy-five to one hundred U.S. dollars (Hashemi, Schuler, and Riley 1996, 636). These microloans are used for small-scale enterprises: to encourage recipients to become petty traders, small shopkeepers, seamstresses, or street vendors. Normally, these loans are given to a small group of people, usually women, on a short-term basis, from six months to a year. Although there are some programs that give to individuals, without financial collateral, small groups are believed to perform better, and thus are more desirable clients. Most programs require weekly or biweekly payments as well as attendance at group meetings, at which time the payments are made. Since most loan recipients have few assets, the peer group serves as what is often referred to as "social collateral." The group provides the necessary pressure to ensure repayment. If one person defaults, the entire group is held responsible.

The originator of microcredit, as it is largely implemented, is Muhammad Yunus, a Bangladeshi economist. His Grameen Bank (*grameen* means "village") was established in 1983, and now serves as the model for most microcredit programs. Grameen is presently the largest microlending institution in Bangladesh, with 1,046 rural branches, covering 34,913 villages. Its cumulative investment is more than one billion U.S. dollars disbursed among 2.02 million members, 94 percent of whom are women (Rahman 1999, 67).

In the Grameen model, groups are usually composed of six nonrelated people with similar socioeconomic positions in terms of assets, housing arrangements, and property. At first, only two members are granted a loan, then after a month of good loan performance, the next two members receive loans. Good loan performance means that the borrowers have attended weekly meetings and have made their payments on time. At the end of the loan cycle, if the group members have consistently made their payments, the borrowers can then seek larger loans to expand their enterprises.

With a fairly extensive list of success stories (see, among others, Wahid 1994; Rahman et al. 1997; Counts 1997), microcredit has been depicted as the newest solution to the problem of poverty in both the global north and south. Moreover, with the changing rhetoric about the importance of including women, microcredit strategies address concerns that women benefit from the development process. Proponents present images of women who have been empowered, economically and socially, by the microloan. Consider this article from the *New York Times*:

> The pride of place belonged to a steaming stew of chicken and potatoes. A dozen guests sat cross-legged on the floor eating, and the woman in the new green dress at the head of the table could not contain her joy. Her eyes sparkled and she broke into a wide grin, four front teeth of gold shining brightly. A year ago, Minavar Salijanova and her family were close to starving. . . . Mrs. Salijanova could not even dream of owning a new green dress, let alone putting on a feast like the one she now spread for neighbors and the visiting United Nations officials who helped her toward previously unimagined prosperity. (Frantz 2000, A6)

The writer's excitement is almost infectious, and also highly consistent with the general "buzz" about microcredit among development practitioners and agencies. Though its successes may be exaggerated rhetorically, there is little doubt that some improvements have been made in the lives of the poor it has served. For women living in especially repressive environments, microcredit has allowed them to congregate with other women, and has given them access to skills and training, basic literacy, and health and nutritional education. Studies show that the use of contraception (Schuler, Hashemi, and Riley 1997) and child immunization (Amin and Li 1997) have increased not only among women participants of programs but also among nonborrowing women in communities where programs exist. In some programs, women participate in activities for the first time, from demonstrating group and family leadership to handling and saving money (Bernasek and Stanfield 1997). Programs have been shown to help families buy land and build new homes, freeing them from the bondage of exploitative moneylenders. There are also examples of small-scale businesses growing into larger enterprises.

In light of this evidence, it is not surprising that microcredit has been hailed as the way to combat global poverty. According to data compiled by the Microcredit Summit, a consortium of microcredit practitioners, advocates, educational institutions, donor agencies, international financial institutions, NGOs and governmental organization, there are 1,065 participating institutions, reaching 13.8 million people, 10.3 million (or 75 percent) of whom are women. From 1997 when the first

Microcredit Summit was held to 2001, there has been a dramatic increase in new participants: 82 percent (more than 6 million) new borrowers overall. This includes a 16 percent increase (1.4 million) in new women participants.[1] Clearly, this program is gaining worldwide attention, and is even being replicated in several impoverished rural and urban areas in the United States (Servon 1999).

The popularity of microcredit and the lack of critical reflection on its ideological bases lie at the heart of the critique presented in this essay. Such reflection is needed to enable us to see the gap between the rhetoric of microcredit and the everyday implications for the beneficiaries. As one of my interviewees said,

> Ah. Everybody believes that is going to solve everything. The focus on microcredit ignores a lot of things. It ignores that very often the credit may not even be for the women, only for their husbands, who may or may not meet the needs of the women. Many times it keeps them just as poor as they ever were. (KN: 11/22/98)

The Political-Economic Context: Globalization and the Aftermath of Structural Adjustment Programs

The reasons for the popularity of microcredit are wide and varied, and largely represent two opposing interpretations of recent global political and economic transformations. Those aligned with mainstream development thinking explain this shift by citing the increased necessity for efficiency, privatization, and self-initiative, combined with a growing skepticism about the benefits derived from large-scale development programs (Adams and Von Pischke 1992). Microcredit addresses these concerns: it is a market model, encouraging the entrepreneurial spirit of advanced capitalism, but is implemented on a micro-scale.

Another set of explanations, more critical but not as visible, suggests that the shift toward microcredit is a result of the economic and political consequences of globalization, trade liberalization, and more specifically the impact of structural adjustment programs (SAPs) (Scully 1997). SAPs, implemented as conditions for loans received by many Third World countries from the World Bank and the International Monetary Fund, contain requirements that call for privatizing nationalized industries, opening markets to foreign investments, and devaluing currencies. According to Scully (1997), this has effectively enlarged the informal economy by destroying small enterprises, farms, and formal-sector jobs, thereby limiting the potential for income opportunities within the formal economy. Thus microcredit is a way to adjust to what these policies and programs have helped to create: fewer employment opportunities within the formal sector, greater disparity between wealth and poverty, and an even greater marginalization of the poor. The structural changes occurring in the developing countries due to globalization and SAPs have resulted in the expansion of informal economies and not those within the formal economic sphere (notwithstanding those jobs created through the global assembly line). Microcredit has emerged as the answer to address the problems of unemployment, underemployment, low-wage jobs, and the growing poverty brought about through the process of globalization (Johnson 1998, 9; Scully 1997).

One of my interviewees offered a more nuanced understanding of this. He perceived the growing shift toward microcredit, especially from those in the international development agencies like the World Bank, as an "implicit acknowledgment of the failures of structural adjustment programs" (NH: 9/14/98). For him, this admission is "shrouded in an overexaggerated rhetorical set of promises of the self-reliance needed to escape poverty through credit" (NH: 9/14/98). In other words, as part of the conditions of SAPs, there has been a tremendous decrease in public-sector employment opportunities. In many developing countries, the public sector had provided the majority of jobs in the formal economy. So, when these jobs were lost, and not replaced in equal numbers by the mostly foreign private sector, high unemployment rates ensued. The self-employment advanced by microcredit was thus viewed as an antidote, but, ironically, it is also the one that is least likely to bring about major structural changes. As Linda Mayoux writes,

> What is disturbing about much of the recent enthusiasm for micro-enterprise development for women is its promotion in the wider context of neo-liberal market reform, particularly "rolling back the state," the removal of welfare provisions and the dismantling of all forms of labour protection. It is also widely seen as a viable and less socially and politically disruptive alternative to more focused feminist organizational strategies. (1995)

That credit garners much more attention as a potential solution to poverty than the need to create stable, formal sector employment reveals a neoliberal ideological understanding of the causes and consequences of poverty. The rhetoric, however, is deceptive: microcredit solutions are "packaged" through co-opting the very language that has embodied the critiques of neoliberal ideology and practice.

The Appeal of Microcredit: Neoliberal Ideology and Populist Rhetoric

The success of microcredit in the developing world has been attributed not only to high repayment rates but also to a growing awareness of the failures of earlier poverty-alleviation programs. The measure of such success, however, is often driven more by donor interests than the needs of the borrowers. As expressed by one interviewee, "Funding is always an issue with these organizations. . . . Now they can say, 'In the last three years our loan program portfolio has upped 1000. Several committees are now making head scarves and they are repaying their loans regularly.' And the donors eat it up" (NH: 9/14/98). Microcredit can be easily measured in terms of efficiency standards and cost-benefit analyses, as this quote reveals. But first it needs to be acknowledged that microcredit seems to be popular with both sides of the political spectrum. While many policymakers would argue that such accord is profoundly important for the success of social policy, it represents an ideological convergence on the problems of and solutions to poverty that is entirely market driven. The market has become the "functional equivalent of democracy," what Thomas Frank has called "market populism" (Frank 2000, 57). Furthermore, microcredit is ideologically akin to the liberal/neoliberal orientation where equal opportunity is advanced as the rhetoric, but the focus is on individual attainment.

Without blaming the failures of current economic-development policies or poverty-alleviation programs, microcredit becomes a vehicle through which to stress the importance and need for self-reliance, efficiency, and economic independence. The logic is that poverty can be eradicated through the entrepreneurship and hard work undertaken by the disadvantaged individual. This is merely a policy version of bootstrap theory, or the economic individualism so prevalent in U.S. political ideology. That is, anyone can make it if they work hard enough in the marketplace. The liberal component to this is that given the right tools, or social capital—specifically training, education, or in this case access to credit—anybody can be economically successful.

We saw this raised most visibly in the U.S. congressional debates leading up to the 1996 welfare reform act, befittingly called The Personal Responsibility and Work Opportunity Reconciliation Act. As part of this bootstrap ideology, "work" is the way out of the insidious cycle of dependency that social welfare programs like Aid to Families with Dependent Children had purportedly created. "Welfare queens" were exposed in the media, which fostered myths about their laziness and high fertility rates. The answer was a "tough-love" policy of making the poor and dependent work for their benefits.[2] While I do not want to suggest that no self-esteem or economic independence could be derived from working either for a wage or through self-employment, the overemphasis on "self-reliance" and the promotion of "any job is better than no job," carries an ideological imprimatur that requires further critical examination.

In the drive to make microcredit attractive to donors, an examination of the language utilized is very revealing. The poor are described as "creditworthy," poor women are considered "good credit risks," and the borrowers are "clients." Such language is found throughout the microcredit literature. I observed several examples of this at the 1998 Microcredit Summit. At one panel I attended, a speaker affirmed that, through credit, "women are placed in the driver's seat of their life." Often the rhetoric of empowerment had a condescending or patronizing tone, accompanied by the self-help jargon of "confidence," "self-esteem," and "responsibility." Several times there were statements made describing microcredit as a switch from "charity to empowerment" or a "hand-up instead of a handout." At one point, a speaker from a for-profit financial institution said, "All human beings are entrepreneurs," which incidentally was followed by a room full of approving applause. One banker explained that microcredit gives people a sense of self-worth by bringing them into the financial system: "[T]hey can be like everybody else," he added. We may surmise that "everybody else" means people in the "developed" world.

In this conception of development and progress, the market is the answer, and self-reliance is the idealized objective. While aid has become identified with creating dependency, microcredit has come to be seen as a perfect way to actualize the self-reliance and independence that will eradicate poverty. Poverty is thus treated as temporary, remedied by simply improving cash flow. With a little credit harnessed by certain value changes, the poor will rise to the occasion and join the rest of the world as developed people.

Much of the thinking that underlies such notions lacks a textured understanding of how poor people live their lives. The claim that microcredit will restore initiative and responsibility to the poor ignores the fact that the poor are usually creative and responsible precisely because survival is so precarious. In fact, the characterization that the program has helped create entrepreneurs is overexaggerated. Many poor people who subsist in the informal economy are already necessarily entrepreneurial. As one of my interviewees said,

> I don't like a lot of the very individualistic rhetoric that attracts this, but I also don't think it has much relevance to what actually does go

on in the field. Like all of this creating of these entrepreneurs. There is no such thing as a peasant farmer who is not an entrepreneur, they have their own land, they have very low assets, but they manage them, and they buy and they sell and that's their life. (LH: 8/17/98)

In addition to reinforcing a narrow notion of poverty, microcredit makes individual behavior central to overcoming poverty, avoiding structural analyses or critiques. Such a construction of independence as always virtuous, with dependence as always objectionable, once again echoes the ideological discourse of economic individualism, and has been critiqued by many feminist economists (see Ferber and Nelson 1993).

Microcredit has appropriated a very potent and popular rhetoric to appeal to those frustrated with the persistent problems of poverty. Marketing microcredit as distinct from earlier development approaches, its supporters no longer claim that the poor are poor because they are lazy or culturally deficient, but because they lack access to certain resources, specifically credit, education, and training. While this presents a well-intended, liberal interpretation of poverty, it nonetheless places all emphasis on the individual, in this case the individual entrepreneur, ignoring the larger structural processes that inherently create and intensify disparities between the poor and the affluent.

What is even more alarming is that there has not been any systematic way of tracking the number of businesses, or perhaps even more importantly, measuring the income attained with the microloans. Most of the studies thus far are more interested in the repayment rates and measuring other indicators such as the number of borrowers, the total disbursement, school enrollment, fertility, and contraceptive use. There is scant attention given to the impact of income on a borrower's household. Even the Microcredit Summit Campaign, in their 2001 yearly report, included the following passage:

> The Campaign is committed to ensuring a positive measurable impact on the lives of the 100 million clients and their families. Yet, as with poverty yardsticks, there was no consensus in 1997 on the need for action in this area. Again, conventional wisdom argued against this theme by saying that: 1) the added expense of impact monitoring was not justified, 2) high loan repayment rates suggested positive impact, and 3) impact assessments done by practitioners would not be rigorous enough to be considered reliable. These arguments, if put into practice, meant that most practitioners would have to remain in the dark concerning the impact their programs were

having on the lives of clients and their families. (Druschel, Quigley, and Sanchez 2001, 6)

A Project for Women or a Gendered Project? Prospects for Empowerment

The Grameen Bank, as well as other "successful" microcredit programs, reportedly has over a 95 percent repayment rate, a fact shared by both proponents and critics (Yunus 1999; Rahman 1999). There is evidence, however, that some of these claims may be overexaggerated and underscrutinized. As stated earlier, the "success" of projects is often defined by the repayment rates; that is, how much of the loan is paid back within the loan cycle. While this criterion follows the goal of "efficiency," using loan repayment as the sole indicator obscures exploration of what actually happens with the money. What microbusinesses have been started? What impact have these enterprises had on the social well-being of the borrower and her family? Have these businesses contributed to the growth of the local economy and social infrastructure? The reliance on loan repayment as a measure of success neglects some important qualitative concerns.

Since repayment rates have been accorded such a high standard in determining a program's success, it is no surprise that programs largely targets women. In its early years, credit from the Grameen Bank was extended to both women and men. Until 1984, membership in the bank was balanced almost equally between men and women. In 1983, male borrowers made up 55 percent of total members, but by 1994, men accounted for only 6 percent. During this same time period, the percentage of women borrowers increased 700 times. In 1997, women constituted more than 95 percent of the 2.23 million borrowers (Rahman 1998, 94).

Microcredit has become a good way for development institutions to carry out their promises of including women, while at the same time remaining committed to capitalist ideologies and practices. The social positions of women, especially those in rural areas of developing countries, make them much more vulnerable to pressures to repay. One of my interviewees who had done an evaluation of the Grameen Bank as part of her role at a UN agency said,

> Well, Grameen is run on very militaristic lines. And one could observe the way the loan officers were telling the women what to reply to our questions. Extremely patronizing. And one could observe that they had no respect whatsoever for the women. They embodied a culture

that these women are children. And you can't possibly hope to
empower anybody that you think is an idiot. (TN: 3/25/99)

The gap between rhetoric and reality is particularly important to
clarify, for it highlights deeper problems, especially in terms of the
implications for empowering women. The publicly stated rationale as
to why women are targeted for these programs is that women are
believed to spend the money on the welfare of their children and family. Through discussions with bank workers, Aminur Rahman (1999)
found that the real reason women are targeted is twofold: men are
more difficult to extract payments from, and women are much more
manageable. According to one of Rahman's interviewees, "In the field
it is hard to work with male members. They do not come to meetings,
they are arrogant, they argue with bank workers, and sometimes they
even threaten and scare the bank workers" (cited in Rahman 1999,
69). So women make the success of the program, measured in repayment rates, much easier to realize. One of my interviewees disclosed
her feelings about how microcredit is treated by the United Nations
Development Program (UNDP). She said,

> The trouble is that our own microfinance unit is very uncritical of
> the microfinance world and its social impacts.[3] And, not terribly
> interested in exploring the ramifications of the gendered aspects of
> it. They're quite satisfied with the idea that "yes, we want to help
> women because they're good payers." (TN: 3/25/99)

This disclosure reveals two important concerns. First, it suggests that
despite the UNDP's rhetoric of the importance of gender equity, its
microcredit program does not appear interested in genuine empowerment. Second, it confirms that women are targeted because the perceived success of the program depends upon it.

The Cult of True Womanhood Revisited

While making women central to development policies is certainly
important, an examination of the reasons why women are targeted
requires a gendered lens. Practitioners often use the term "better
credit risks" when referring to women because women's repayment
rates are higher. When women are the borrowers, it is argued, the general well-being of the family is assumed to improve, specifically its
income, nutrition, health, education, and family planning, though
these improvements are not yet clear. Men as borrowers have been

found to spend money on themselves and leisure activities (Goetz and Gupta 1996; Rahman 1998, 1999). They are also less interested in attending meetings because they have freedom to be more mobile.[4]

Yunus, in explaining to the United States Congressional Forum why such a high percentage of his loans go to women said, "Women have plans for themselves, for their children, about their homes, the meals. They have a Vision. A man wants to enjoy himself."[5] Such explanations reveal a "boys will be boys" mentality: men's behavioral patterns, already known to be detrimental to the lives of their families, are excused and rationalized. Historically, such treatment of gender roles has justified the repression of women, as much of feminist theory has exposed. "This instrumental approach to women as conduits for credit for the family plays on, and reinforces, traditional cultural notions of womanhood, with women seen as moral guardians of the household and policers of recalcitrant men" (Goetz and Gupta 1996, 55).

Women are idealized as "mother" and burdened with a new set of responsibilities because they are assumed to be more reliable and more caring. This essentialism can be dangerous and ultimately regressive, reinforcing gendered stereotypes and role expectations. Consider this quote from a representative from a development NGO: "We believe that women are more caring of the weak and if we empower women then they will be able to take care of their children better."[6] It seems then, that women are believed to be more caring, while men are removed from such practices because it is presumed they are not capable of caregiving.

Thus, in traditional patriarchal fashion, women, idealized for their responsibility, are rewarded by being made responsible for more and more labor activities. Little is done or even discussed to transform the oppressive sexual division of labor, whereby women throughout much of the world are responsible for the bulk of the subsistence work and unpaid home labor. While it may be a progressive step to include women in income-generating activity, if their responsibilities at home and in the field are not shared more equally, the standard of living for these women may not actually improve. This "stalled revolution" has occurred in the global north, specifically in the United States, where middle-class women have entered the labor force but have suffered the consequences of second-shift responsibilities (see Hochschild 1989). Making women central to the development process, from family planning to nutrition and now poverty eradication, has apparently had the effect of making women more constrained by more labor, while allowing men to evade such responsibilities. So, in some ways microcredit is empowering, but in other important ways, it is not.

The Vulnerability of Women: Causes for Alarm

It may be objectively true that women have better repayment rates. This may, however, be because of their lower status in society. In many places where microcredit programs have been implemented, the gendered environment is such that women are more easily coerced and pressured by loan officers. The UN gender specialist quoted earlier in this essay supported this:

> I think that women do repay better than men, but it's also very clear that in Bangladesh, the high repayment rates are because the loan workers work very hard to get them, and they use very coercive methods. And I think that the repayment rate is as high as it is, not because women are intrinsically responsible but because they are more easily coerced. They can be intimidated more easily. They have fewer resources that they can call on to resist the loan officers. So, the high repayment rate is actually dependent on women's low level of power and status. (TN: 2/13/99)

In a follow-up interview, this same interviewee reiterated this, requiring us to question the "reality" of women's empowerment as an achieved goal.

> There is a pressure to repay. The husband feels comfortable in telling the loan officer to "get stuffed," "I'll pay you next week" kind of thing, but it's harder for her to do and at the same time she can't put pressure on her husband. So she feels a lot of distress. (TN: 3/25/99)

The issue of women's vulnerability has further consequences, as recent evidence of increasing rates of domestic violence and physical aggression toward women in borrower households surface. One of Rahman's (1998, 1999) findings was an increase in domestic violence among borrowers in several rural villages in Bangladesh. In fact, all the women in his sample said they experienced violence of some kind, revealing the predominance of domestic violence in rural Bangladesh. He found verbal aggression and physical assault against 120 borrowers. While 21 women (18 percent of his sample) claimed a decrease in aggression and assault because of their involvement with Grameen, 69 (57 percent) saw a rise in verbal aggression, and 16 (13 percent) saw a rise in both verbal and physical violence since they received their first loans. Six borrowers encountered male violence because they refused to hand over their loan to male family members or because they challenged men's proposals for using the loans.

Rahman writes, "the escalation of the violence against women borrowers in the loan centre and in the household can be seen as a repercussion of current practices of grassroots lending to the poor" (1998, 158).

In addition to these findings, Rahman describes in detail the relationship between the rigid bank rules and the violence women suffered at home as a consequence. For example, if a woman does not attend a weekly repayment meeting, the rest of the group must stay at the bank's center until the absentee woman's installment is paid. This practice is in conflict with village husbands' demands that their wives come home quickly, and as a consequence, several times during Rahman's fieldwork, a borrower was beaten by her husband for not returning home on time. According to Rahman, women may suffer violence if they do not return home right away or if they do not get another loan or one for a higher amount. Many of these issues are out of the borrower's control. "Lending to women within the patriarchal structure of the society often fails to provide any acceptable alternatives for women—social, economic or legal entitlements—that are supported by society, including active individual or organized protest against aggression and violence" (Rahman 1998, 163).[7] The peer group structure may work for the success of the program, and it may even foster consciousness among the women that could lead to building collective resources, if such was emphasized. But at this point, too much is being left out of the evaluations.

Getting the Loan, but Losing Control

A few important studies have shown that women borrowers often lose control of the money once they bring it home. In one such study, 63 percent of the women had only partial, very limited, or no control over the loans they received from institutions (Goetz and Gupta 1996). The loan is managed and controlled by male relatives, yet women bear the responsibilities for paying it back. This practice undermines the main rhetorical appeal of microcredit, which aims to empower participants through economic self-sufficiency and personal development. Though promoted as a project for the empowerment of women, if women must cede management and control of the loan to their male relatives their empowerment is doubtful. The women may act as vessels for men's economic activity (Goetz and Gupta 1996, 55). The UN gender specialist I interviewed supported this. She said,

> I don't think it [microcredit] is about empowerment. It's about introducing modern economic forms into the deepest rural areas, the

penetration of capital away from the capital cities into rural areas, and transforming the way rural societies are structured. Microfinance is a very good way of doing it because it's within the reach of poor people, but it's still governed by the forces of finance, which are decided millions of miles away. (TN: 2/13/99)

She continued her critique by saying, "the effect of microfinance is to introduce these people into these relationships in an extremely subordinate way."

Complicating this further, there is evidence that many women rely on moneylenders to help pay back loans, further worsening their economic position. Rahman's data show that 57 percent of the weekly installments were paid from sources other than investment profits, usually loans from relatives or moneylenders (Rahman 1998, 183). So, even the basic supposition that women are improving their livelihood may not be accurate.

Microcredit focuses on bringing women into the development process, not on transforming the process to eradicate gendered structures of oppression. The UN specialist quoted above continued,

We know that gender issues are at the heart of development and this is a very good example where development is going on, without any gender concern, and it may be making things worse for men and women in a sense. . . . The loan officers have no concept at all that the relationship between men and women is problematic. They think they're helping women. I don't think they have any perception or think it's important at all to look at why it is that women are getting the credit. (TN: 3/25/99)

The Peer Group: Enhancing Solidarity or Individualistic Competition?

The Grameen model and others like it require women to form peer groups, sometimes called "solidarity groups" for loan disbursement. Once again, rhetoric veils what appears to be the real motivation behind group formation. It is generally believed that since most of these women have no collateral, the peer group becomes a proxy for social collateral, a safeguard for repayment (Rahman 1999, 71). But the rhetorical emphasis has been on the promotion and enhancement of social solidarity among women, especially in areas where women are restricted to their homes because of patriarchal social customs. The women borrowers in a village are expected to establish a loan center as a place for women to congregate; to discuss issues that are meaningful to them, such as education, health, and their enterprises; and to pay back their installments. These weekly meetings do seem to have the potential to bring about the "empowerment" that such programs are supposedly designed to effect. Two interviewees shared their perspectives with me on this. One said,

> [W]omen come to meetings b*ecause that's where the empowerment of women really occurs* [italics mine]. . . . And the good discussions are ones that are determined by the women. . . . They can talk about things that appeal to them: What's the best age for the children to get married?... It can also be business related: What are people doing? How do they go about getting more customers? We don't give lessons, there's no curriculum. But people can talk with each other. (UT: 11/12/98)

The other, who evaluated projects in Latin America, echoed this sentiment:

> I visited and talked with people. The women were borrowing, and they were paying back, and everything was going well on the financial end. But then they also used the group meetings as an opportunity to talk about nutrition, like what kinds of things you ought to be eating when you are breast feeding and other kinds of life-training and health-training. (DN: 7/22/98)

These interview excerpts suggest that the elements of empowerment that result from microcredit seem to come more from the support networks that are created among women participants than from the borrowing of the microloan and the entrepreneurial activity that ensues. This is particularly interesting because, as Rahman has discovered in the case of Grameen, as programs become more focused on loan repayment, less time and attention tends to be given to enhancing solidarity among the women. The meetings become focused on loan repayment. Once again, economic development trumps social development.

  While microcredit uses a group framework, espousing solidarity and promising empowerment, it is individual achievement and participation that is actually sought. Most programs do not include group loans that would foster cooperative enterprises. Each woman, though part of a peer group, is expected to borrow for her own, individual enterprise. As one of my interviewees said,

> It's very individualistic. And it doesn't focus on group enterprises. It's
> for individuals to do their own thing. It's not like a group of six to eight
> women start up an organic farm. I think that microcredit could move
> to groups, but so far it has focused on individuals. (KN: 11/22/98)

These groups are formed to ensure loan repayment and not to create
collective income-generating activities, which would benefit women in
a different way. One of my interviewees compared the dynamics of the
peer groups, in practice, to "spying." Transforming individuals into
entrepreneurs, according to the precepts of free-market capitalism,
requires individuality, competition, and concerns for efficiency and
rationality. Such attitudes are encouraged through the co-optation of
values that represent a different and antithetical way of thinking and
operating—cooperation, solidarity, group interdependency. Microcredit is about using solidarity to foster individuality and competition,
advancing values and behavioral patterns which are perhaps insulting
and offensive to the borrowers.

Microcredit That Works: Collective Goals, Savings, and Empowerment

Though most microcredit programs suffer from the limitations
addressed earlier, in some programs the rhetoric of empowerment
seems more in line with reality. These are generally smaller programs,
run by local NGOs, which encourage collective enterprises. The structure and implementation of these programs are determined and
designed by the women participants, informed by their own experiences. Some programs are established by community-run organizations, and begin with a savings component, where the members put in
a small amount each week, perhaps equivalent to one day's pay. From
this, members borrow microloans for community enterprises.

One organization that seems to demonstrate this is Grassroots
Organizations Operating Together in Sisterhood (GROOTS). GROOTS
is a network of grassroots organizations that focus primarily on rural
development, housing, savings, and credit. The organization was
founded after the Third United Nations Conference on Women, held
in Nairobi, in response to the exclusion of grassroots women from policy and program discussions. One of GROOTS' member organizations
from Zimbabwe, Organization of Rural Associations for Progress
(ORAP), initiated a savings program before giving out loans to its members. With the savings, the women members reconstructed kitchens and
bought utensils to cook and sell food. To assure the participation of the

very poorest, the cooking is always prepared in and sold from the home of a very poor family. A percentage of what the family makes from the sales is then deposited into the savings for future activities.

Another member organization of GROOTS, Swayam Shikshan Prayog, in Maharashtra, India, emphasizes women's collectives and community-owned institutions. In addition to credit-related activities, these groups have become quite involved in local government issues, monitoring the delivery of public health and educational services.

Such small-scale, collective-oriented programs exist but are difficult to find in the shadow of Grameen and some larger programs. In collective-oriented groups, women learn how to manage money as a group, as they also learn to trust and work with one another. A representative structure for decision making is created through reliance on deeply held social relations. The women make decisions collectively to determine how money should be used. The methodologies used in such groups seem to be more consistent with the goal of empowerment advanced, but unrealized, by mainstream microcredit institutions. Such programs may have to maintain their small, local scale, for if they become larger and more bureaucratic, they risk compromising their more radical attributes.

Concluding Thoughts

Microcredit is girded by the current ideological disdain for dependency and an ongoing infatuation with "self-reliance." While there are some very real, albeit contested, political and economic transformations that have made microcredit programs more attractive and necessary, the driving force seems to be a strong ideological attachment to neoliberalism. The market is the panacea for economic and social development. Ideological commitments to economic individualism, especially as they inform understandings of and solutions to the problems of poverty and underdevelopment, support such a market-driven framework.

In addition to this particular economic ideology, there is also a powerful gendered ideology at work. In recent years, women have become the primary targets of programs. On the surface, this responds to feminist demands for making development policies and programs relevant to women. Beneath the rhetoric, however, lie some very troubling assumptions. The reasons cited for granting loans to women reproduce traditional and patriarchal notions of both women's and men's expected gender roles and responsibilities in society. Gendered stereotypes are reinforced through the ruse of empowerment.

Self-reliance, and programs that encourage self-initiative, should not be aborted. What I am suggesting, however, is that this peculiar attachment to self-reliance (and paralleling this, the current anti-dependency crusade) is part of a Western-driven, patriarchal bias of the hegemonic neoliberal economic paradigm, the framework currently operating, without much challenge, in the United States and in development practice generally.

More careful attention needs to be devoted to questions of who benefits, how, and in what ways. Looking beyond repayment rates, an evaluation of the qualitative issues raised in this essay is needed. What types of businesses are being created? Are the enterprises themselves sustainable, generating for these borrowers profit or just more debt? In what ways are borrowers able to contribute to the betterment of the community? Are the borrowers empowered in ways other than economically? Are unpaid hours considered? Are there corollary mechanisms set up to protect borrowers economically, socially, and psychologically, so they are not turned into overworked, overburdened entrepreneurs who internalize their own failure? Such considerations are important and they must be addressed before more policymakers and funders join the bandwagon.

A further question that should be addressed is what the popularity of a program like microcredit says about how "development" is defined. Turning people into indebted entrepreneurs and self-employed workers may only serve to intensify Western ideological assumptions that the developing world should mirror the First World. The consequence is an overly narrow conception of what it means to be a "developed" society and what constitutes "progress." Economically empowering women, if that is actually happening, means getting them involved in income-generating activities, privileging the productive sphere, but does little to change the cultural practices of the gendered division of labor. How then, could this be truly empowering or emancipating? When empowerment is linked only to income generation, one's value and worth becomes reduced to income-earning labor. Microcredit is symbolic of the strong ideological attachment of development to the primacy of unfettered capitalism, where humans are reduced merely to productive workers, in this case entrepreneurs. But is this development? Does this allow humans to flourish?

NOTES

This essay draws on a chapter of my Ph.D. dissertation in sociology, "Ideology, Rhetoric and the Politics of Bureaucracy: Exploring Women and

Development" (The Graduate Center at the City University of New York, February 2002).

1. See www.microcreditsummit.org/campaigns/report00.html.
2. For a wonderful account of the real-life effects of the welfare reform act, see Ehrenreich 2002.
3. Many in the UN use the word *microfinance* instead of *microcredit.*
4. For many women, the group meetings are the only forum for them to talk with other women, interact with bank and NGO officials, etc. (Schuler, Hashemi, and Riley 1997).
5. Excerpted from www.gdrc.org/icm/wind/wind.html.
6. From *The Earth Times,* 16–30 September 1998, People section.
7. Unfortunately, this issue does not seem to be garnering much attention among development practitioners, despite the rhetorical emphasis placed on eradicating violence against women. Further investigation into this connection is warranted, but beyond the scope of this essay.

REFERENCES

Adams, Dale, and J. D. Von Pischke. 1992. "Microenterprise Credit Programs: Déjà vu." *World Development* 20(10): 1463–1470.

Amin, Ruhul, and Yiping Li. 1997. "NGO-Promoted Women's Credit Program, Immunization Coverage and Child Mortality in Rural Bangladesh." *Women and Health* 25(1): 71-87.

Bernasek, Alexandra, and James Ronald Stanfield. 1997. "The Grameen Bank as Progressive Institutional Adjustment." *Journal of Economic Issues* 31, no. 2 (June): 359–366.

Counts, Alex. 1997. *Voices from the Field: Interviews with Practitioners for the Poor.* Malaysia: Cashpor Publication.

Druschel, Kate, Jennifer Quigley, and Cristina Sanchez. 2001. "State of the Microcredit Summit Campaign 2001 Report". Microcredit Summit: 1–22. Available online at www.microcreditsummit.org

Ehrenreich, Barbara. 2001. *Nickel and Dimed: On (Not) Getting By in America.* New York: Metropolitan Books.

Fairley, Joanne. 1998. "New Strategies for Microenterprise Development: Innovation, Integration and the Trickle Up Approach." *Journal of International Affairs* 52(1):339–350.

Ferber, Marianne A., and Julie A. Nelson. 1993. *Beyond Economic Man: Feminist Theory and Economics.* Chicago: University of Chicago Press.

Frank, Thomas. 2000. *One Market Under God: Extreme Capitalism, Market Populism and the End of Economic Democracy.* New York: Doubleday Press.

Frantz, Douglas. 2000. "A Chicken in Every Kyrgyzstan Pot: Take a $10 Microcredit Loan. Multiply. Get a Taste of Freedom." *The New York Times,* 3 December, A6.

Goetz, Anne Marie, and Rina Sen Gupta. 1996. "Who Takes the Credit? Gender, Power and Control over Loan Use in Rural Credit Programs in Bangladesh." *World Development* 24(1):45–63.

Hashemi, Syed, Sidney Ruth Schuler, and Ann P. Riley. 1996. "Rural Credit

Programs and Women's Empowerment in Bangladesh." *World Development* 24(4):635–651.

Hochschild, Arlie. 1989. *The Second Shift.* New York: Avon Books.

Johnson, Margaret A. 1998. "An Overview of Basic Issues Facing Microenterprise Practices in the United States." *Journal of Developmental Entrepreneurship* 3(1):5–23.

Mayoux, Linda. 1995. "From Vicious to Virtuous Circles? Gender and Micro-Enterprise Development", Occasional Paper No. 3, UNRISD, UN Fourth World Conference on Women, May. Available online.

Rahman, Aminur. 1998. "Rhetoric and Realities of Micro-Credit for Women in Rural Bangladesh: A Village Study of Grameen Bank Lending." Ph.D. diss., University of Manitoba.

———. 1999. "Micro-Credit Initiatives for Equitable and Sustainable Development: Who Pays?" *World Development* 27(1):67–82.

Rahman, Sayeeda, et al. 1997. "Microfinance: Helping the Poor to Help Themselves." *UNESCO Courier* 50 (January): 10–39.

Schuler, Sidney Ruth, Syed Hashemi, and Ann P. Riley. 1997. "The Influence of Women's Changing Roles and Status in Bangladesh's Fertility Transition: Evidence from a Study of Credit Programs and Contraceptive Use." *World Development* 25(4):563–575.

Scully, Nan Dawkins. 1997. "No Panacea for Poor Women." Available online at www/igc.org/dgap.

Servon, Lisa J. 1999. *Bootstrap Capital: Microenterprise and the American Poor.* Washington, D.C.: Brookings Institute.

Wahid, Abu N. M. 1994. "The Grameen Bank and Poverty Alleviation in Bangladesh: Theory, Evidence and Limitations." *The American Journal of Economics and Sociology* 53, no. 1 (January): 1–15.

Yunus, Muhammad, with Alan Jolis. 1999. *Banker to the Poor: Micro-Lending and the Battle Against World Poverty.* New York: Public Affairs.

Robin G. Isserles, *Ph.D., is assistant professor of sociology at the Borough of Manhattan Community College, City University of New York. Her current research project draws on feminist theories of care to revisit existing theories of international development. She dedicate this article to the memory of Robert R. Alford, an exceptional mentor and friend.*

Gender, Culture, and Ecotourism

Development Policies and Practices in the Guyanese Rain Forest

Barbara J. Dilly

Ecotourism and the Meeting of Gender, Local Culture, and Development

The gendered effects of neoliberal development policies and practices upon indigenous tropical rain forest communities are evident in the expanding ecotourism industry. Ecotourism is an economic development strategy that, in developing countries, often replaces intensification of horticulture and offers an alternative to manufacturing or extractive industries (Boo 1990, 2). Ecotourism, like many other forms of tourism, is a form of economic, social, and cultural exchange between "host" cultures, often depicted as "exotic" and "primitive," and "guests," typically affluent consumers from "sterile," developed cultural environments who are seeking "authentic" cultural experiences in "pristine" environments.

This essay addresses the dynamics among gender, economics, and politics that emerged from the creation and implementation of an ecotourism development program among the indigenous Makushi people of the Guyanese rain forest. Drawing on ethnographic data and my own fieldwork, I identify three anthropological concerns regarding women and the development of ecotourism. First, rain forest ecotourism provides economic opportunities for women to develop a nonextractive, nonindustrial, and nonagrarian industry—often without the need for capital, the labor resources of men, a large consumer base, or proximity to markets. The cultural viability and sustainability of economic development projects that directly benefit women but do not also integrate men, however, are questionable. Second, in concert with many of the anthropologists who evaluate neoliberal global development policies and programs, I argue that the empowerment of indigenous communities should be central to development processes (O'Rouke 2002, 14). Further, I assert, the effectiveness of specific local ecotourism programs must be evaluated in terms of local gender relations, as well as potential for economic gain, and should further the rights of both men and women. Third, development agencies must acknowledge that the adaptation of culture to development programs is a gendered process. Men and women experience opportunities differently.

In this essay, I discuss how development policies and programs directed toward women will be more economically successful, more individually empowering, and more culturally authentic when the process of cultural adaptation to development programs considers both male and female roles and supports positive gender relations. And while cultural change is certain to occur with new forms of economic development focused on the needs of women, I argue that some forms of cultural continuity, in terms of gender relations, are necessary for stable development. Local gender relations—even though they will be transformed through processes of cultural adaptation to development programs, and perhaps often should be—are significant dimensions of local cultures, which should not themselves be the primary targets of change. This is particularly true when local gender relations have been egalitarian for generations, and have only recently been transformed by externalities that marginalized women. The development problems that affect women, then, should not be seen in terms of problems inherent in the local culture or in the recent shifts in gender relations that have marginalized women, but in terms of the externalities that marginalize both men and women.

My work explores these dynamics within a specific, local context: it traces the experience of the Makushi people of the Surama community, just outside and to the south of the Guyanese international rain forest preserve Iwokrama.[1] Drawing on ethnographic field data, I assess the roles and relationships of men and women as they negotiate among several development opportunities. I also explore the practical implications of ecotourism as a means for sustaining Makushi cultural autonomy and identities, as well as the egalitarian gender roles they value but have not recently fully enjoyed.

The Transformation of Makushi Egalitarian Gender Relations

The Makushi are a Carib-language-speaking people of the north Rupununi District savannas of interior Guyana and of the frontier state of Roraima in Brazil. Approximately six thousand Makushi live in small, dispersed villages near the foothills of the Pacariama Mountains in the Guyanese interior. Most reside within one hundred miles of the Brazilian border, which they regularly cross, both legally and illegally, to work, trade, and visit relatives. The population in any village at any given time is highly variable, owing to temporary out-migration of adult male labor to Brazil and to the Guyanese coast.

The youth population of Makushi villages fluctuates with the periodic absence of children who attend regional boarding schools.

The traditional egalitarian gender roles of the Makushi were first transformed by the cultural influences of the British colonial government, and then, since the 1960s, by the cultural influences of Brazilian and Guyanese national development policies which have increasingly drawn the Makushi into education, wage labor, surplus production, and urban consumerism. The Makushi are not, therefore, strangers to global economic structures of development, nor are they naïve about the exploitative effects of such structures. They quickly perceive those opportunities that result from their interaction with national development policies. They readily send their children away to school, and most learn to speak English and Portuguese in addition to their native language and Wapishana, the language of their neighbors and many of their relatives.

Such cultural shifts, of course, impact the local community. Because children's labor was an integral part of subsistence horticulture, Guyanese anthropologist Janette Forte, who serves on the Amerindian Research Unit, University of Guyana, argues that children's time spent away at school contributed greatly to the decisions by men to seek economic opportunities beyond local cassava production (Forte 1996, 73). Then, on another level, the cross-cultural contact between Makushi children and others at Christian mission and government schools further influenced changes in the local culture through the sharing of new languages and cultural ideas. It also promoted intermarriage among Amerindian groups. The nationalist agenda, which advanced integration by bringing together children from diverse cultures, further broke down the distinctiveness of local cultures as it promoted the development of a Guyanese national identity among Amerindian children.

It was the acculturation demands of the former English colonial government that most significantly affected the gendered structure of social interaction: male labor was reorganized to focus on extractive industries. Beginning in the early twentieth century and until the 1970s, balata bleeding and peanut farming altered the subsistence economy through payment and bartering for exported goods, including wheat flour, rice, sugar, and matches (Forte and Melville 1989, 11). Cash payments from peanut farming introduced Makushi men to Western technology and such market goods as shotguns, which men then used to intensify their hunting of wild game (Forte and Melville 1989). This form of economic development gave male "heads of household" provider-status, from the perspective of Western cultural norms, but it did not remove men from the family and community as economic contributors. Nor did it destroy the horticultural cooperative household labor system for the production of traditional foods like cassava. Peanut farming required the labor of men, women, and children, thereby sustaining the traditional household production system and preserving the local culture

Since the 1970s, wage labor in mining and logging industries, in both Guyana and Brazil, offered greater cash incentives for men than peanut farming. The loss of children's ability to contribute to the household economy while they attended school, combined with a lower commodity price, reduced the profitability of peanut farming. Hence, Makushi men, fully acculturated by cash incentives, were increasingly drawn away from their families and communities into individual wage-labor employment opportunities. The current development decisions by local men and women are derived, then, from gender roles that have been modified by external realities over the last century. But these cultural changes also reveal persistent cultural patterns of gender equality and cooperation.

Local Decision Making

Makushi men and women currently choose among various gendered development alternatives, all consequences of global and national development agendas. The options vary for each sex. Makushi men may temporarily, or permanently, migrate for wage labor in mining and logging. They may also choose to remain in the community, if they leave for a time, to become teachers. They may also participate in the expansion of a community-based United Nations agricultural development program. Some Makushi men may even elect to compete for limited opportunities to participate in ecotourism development. Makushi women, particularly those with children, are encouraged to participate in the community-based agricultural development program designed to produce surplus cassava. Younger Makushi women may participate in an ethnobotany program, developed by Oxford University, to collect local pharmaceuticals. And all Makushi women may also compete for still limited ecotourism opportunities.

It is significant to note that the Oxford ethnobotany project and the UN program to produce surplus cassava by transforming slash-and-burn horticultural practices into a semi-intensive agricultural system, were designed primarily for women. These projects were intended to compensate for the loss of male labor from an egalitarian, but gendered, food production system. Within such a system, men's work is complemented by the cooperative work of women, who maintain garden plots, gather wild fruits, and process and prepare foods. Male labor has always played a vital role in sustaining the Makushi traditional horticultural system, which produces the staple cassava and other garden vegetables. Men hunt wild game and fish, clear land for farming, and also assist with the gathering of wild fruits; all of which significantly contributes to the nutritional balance of the local subsistence food production system.

The loss of male labor directly affects local food supply: It reduces the amount of land cleared for rotated plots within a slash-and-burn horticultural production system, threatening the household production system. It also decreases the supply of food made available from hunting and fishing, thereby diminishing protein sources. The loss of such labor is further exacerbated by a shortage of locally grown vegetables, which has led to an increase in malnutrition and greater dependence on food imports. Increasingly, in response to a government program addressing nutritional deficiencies, Makushi women are advised to raise chickens in sedentary locations to meet dietary needs. This program requires cultural adaptation to animal husbandry and has yet to become successful.[2]

Clearly there is a need for economic development to meet Makushi women's needs. Nutritional problems are evident in the health of children and women. Few women can now depend on men to help sustain their daily food needs (by working within the traditional Makushi production system) or to regularly supply them with the cash necessary for imports. The out-migration of Makushi male labor threatens the social and economic viability of Makushi communities. The absence of male laborers and matriculating young adults leaves women and very small children vulnerable to starvation and violence. It also impoverishes communities of developmental potential. But women and children have no options outside the community. In this context, community-based development programs for women are seemingly the best policy.

Ecotourism Development Options for Women Without Men

The question that I address here is whether development options for women without men are directed towards women's best interests. Despite the dramatic global efforts directed toward alleviating women's suffering and promoting their empowerment, development policies have focused more on nation-building agendas than on feminist issues (Scott 1995).[3] Recent development projects designed to aid Makushi women focus on developing their potential contributions to national economies. While development agencies like the World Bank and the United States Agency for International Development took a welfare approach to women's development up through the 1970s, defining women as passive and needy (Moser 1993, 231), the United Nations Decade for Women (1975–85) promoted women as active participants in economic and political systems (Ward 2003, 239). This shift has been positive, but development agents must work to recognize the specific gendered experiences of women within particular developing systems.

Empowering local women to define, shape, and participate in their own development projects has challenged both masculine ideologies and Western feminism. Modernization and dependency theories of development display the patriarchal ethnocentrism of Western development models (Scott 1995). Women in the Third World have learned that such models are not always effective: they may reinforce the domination and subordination of women within their own cultures, or they may liberate them. But, even more, these women have learned that preserving relationships within their own cultures must be evaluated in relation to outsiders and their agendas. Women in developing nations are suspicious of Western feminist agendas that focus on the oppression of women by men but do not address racism and class barriers within national governments, international development agendas, and private organizations (Ward 2003, 239).

The economic potential of ecotourism and its direct consequences for women must be evaluated from local models of development and empowerment. Ecotourists, as agents of Western models of development, may disrupt local cultural processes by furthering inequality, creating internal conflicts, and straining local resource distribution. As a result, hosts of ecotourism risk the marginalization of their cultural identities and the erosion of authenticity, as well as of their self-reliance, as they are "colonized" by the hegemonic cultures of their consumer guests (Nyoni 1987, 53).

Theoretical and empirical analyses of ecotourism highlight positive and negative consequences for local economic, social, and cultural institutions (Boo 1990; Cohen 1979; DeKadt 1979; Graburn 1995; MacCannell 1992; McKean 1976; Smith and Eadington 1992). Tourism-generated activities have varied effects on local cultures and environments, ranging from exploitation to conservation. Problems are likely to result when local environments are overdeveloped and cultures are commodified by market-driven global development agencies, especially those that impose their own agendas over those of the local people. This need not be the case, however. A growing body of evidence suggests that development policies and programs focused on tourism can promote and provide benefits for host cultures (Boo 1990; DeKadt 1979).

Due largely to the work of anthropologists from the Amerindian Research Unit, University of Guyana (Forte 1996), local peoples in peripheral regions as remote as the Guyanese rain forest are aware of the drawbacks of exploitative national development policies and international programs directed from core economic and political global institutions.[4] Anthropologists and human rights workers have worked to inform indigenous communities of their rights to cultural autonomy and the preservation of their intellectual, territorial, and environmental domains.[5]

The Makushi approach change cautiously, but confidently, seeking to play active and collaborative roles in defining development policies and programs that meet local, national, and international needs. While it is certainly too early to declare the Makushi development program a huge success, my field observations and activities from the mid-1990s and subsequent monitoring of ecotourism developments in the Guyanese rain forest appear to illustrate the hypothetical goal of Smith and Eadington (1992, 3) that both hosts and guests can experience a positive exchange. To foster such successful exchange, program goals must be ambitious, extending beyond mere economic success. It is hoped that ecotourism in the Guyanese rain forest may help reduce the rate of social disintegration that has already occurred due to the out-migration of male laborers into extractive industries.[6]

Ecotourism As Development: Toward Local Cultural Survival, Nation Building, or the Globalization of Environmental Protection?

The economic and social problems of the Guyanese interior have drawn increasing attention from national and international development policies and programs. Since Guyanese independence from Britain in 1966, the interior populations have been drawn more closely into the nexus of a developing Guyanese political economy. In 1989, the Makushi were invited by the Guyanese government to participate in the development of Iwokrama, a 900,000-square-mile international rain forest reserve and research program.[7] The intersection among international tourism development, protection of the rain forest, and local community development is a consequence of increasing globalization. The rain forest reserve has become the locus of these development agendas. The development of ecotourism is also an outgrowth of the Guyanese government's interest in supporting indigenous economic opportunities and cultural identities, cooperating with global environmental organizations, and profiting from external agency development agendas that meet local, national, and international goals.

A model of global ecotourism that coordinates and sustains Makushi horticulture, hunting, fishing, and food gathering with national development and international rain forest protection programs and policies is emerging in the Guyanese interior. This model acknowledges the specificity of gendered roles and encourages cooperation in the development of local opportunities.

The emerging rain forest ecotourism program developed out of the Iwokrama research camp and its growing international clientele. Located deep in the interior of Guyana, the Iwokrama preserve can accommodate the basic food needs of twenty guests per day through its local subsistence food production system. Food for guests is also imported, but at great transportation cost. The camp director seeks to expand the number of guests the camp can accommodate without straining the local environment. Rather than intensify food production at the camp and risk environmental degradation, the director of the Iwokrama program has begun to coordinate accommodations for additional visitors in nearby villages. This ecotourism program is intended to provide local economic development for the Makushi in an isolated region where few other development programs can be defined. The program promises also to meet the specific needs of Amerindian women and children in several surrounding communities, as well as for the Makushi.

The Makushi of Surama are eager for such development opportunities, and according to Forte, who evaluated their potential, quite capable of engaging in cultural contact and developing their own program. In 1995, as a faculty representative for a small, Midwest liberal arts college, I evaluated the site for potential as an ecotourism/service-learning program for students. I was encouraged by the confidence and hospitality of the local Makushi and returned the following year with thirty students. Aware that local food supplies were limited, we transported most of our food from Georgetown on the coast, a nine-hour, four-wheel truck drive away, for a two-week stay. Because certain supplies were nonexistent in the interior, we brought our own hammocks, cots, towels, and personal supplies. Half of the students stayed at the research camp, half in the village. The students rotated at the end of the first week. In line with our previous arrangement to pay U.S.\$20.00 per day per person, we paid the community council cash for lodging in their community center and the use of their fresh-water well and outhouses. We also paid cash to individuals designated by the community for their services as guides, cooks, and lecturers (who taught a short but highly effective course on rain forest ecology). The cash was used to develop the tourism infrastructure.

Two years later, screened barracks for eight to twelve people, with toilets and showers and a kitchen with a vented stove, awaited the 1998 student delegation. The lodging fees collected from each group of guests goes toward the development of more barracks for more guests, up to a limit of twenty guests at a time in any location. The program plan is to develop the surrounding communities so that each can host up to twenty guests at any given time.[8] The development of eleven communities surrounding Iwokrama enables the program director to attract researchers and tourists to the area, without straining the local ecology of the research camp or any particular village. Ongoing reports reveal slow but steady developments and success.

My field observations and interviews with local residents suggest that program success depends somewhat on whether or not the Makushi and their neighbors can guarantee a food supply for guests who may not wish to transport all of their supplies. Despite our truckload of grocery items, we soon depleted our supply of fresh fruits and vegetables, which, we learned, were out of season at the time of our stay. We also ran out of some staples like flour, which the locals sold to us for cash, thereby making sacrifices from their own larders. This was done only after careful consultation among Makushi community members. They decided that it was worth it, aiming to cultivate a positive relationship with our group.

The cash payment to the Makushi village council for the use of the community center, fresh water, and the pit latrine would, as distributed by community leaders, benefit nonproductive members of the community as well as for productive individuals. Consideration was also given to establishing a remuneration system that would benefit a wide range of individuals. Makushi men were paid to guide tours into hunting and fishing areas. Men also demonstrated their weaving skills and lectured about Makushi culture and life. Makushi women were paid to lecture on cassava production, processing, and cooking, as well as their experiences with child- and health care. Women were also paid to cook for us. We did our own laundry, but under the supervision of the Makushi women who showed the students how to use a washboard and a bucket.

The cash remuneration rate for these activities followed the Iwokrama Preserve's established scales, which ranged from $7.00 to $10.00 per day. This wage is competitive with money earned in logging and mining camps. Ecotourism positions, however, are more desirable for both men and women because they normalize local social relations, particularly at the household and community level. These positions also offer better working conditions and higher status than logging and mining work.

Through ecotourism employment, women are rewarded for their traditional food production activities, while men are rewarded for hunting and fishing activities. Both are making economic contributions to their families without leaving the community. Beyond cash-earning opportunities for a few individuals, the money paid to the community council for lodging benefits the entire community. After investing a portion of the money in the barracks and cooking center, the community leaders distribute the remaining money to meet the basic needs of local residents, particularly older women, and mothers and small children whose male family members are absent.[9]

There are problems that still must be addressed by the community. An increasing number of visitors to the region may exacerbate regional food shortages. Flooding can destroy local cassava crops. Competitive cash sale of surplus foods to then visitors can deplete otherwise sustainable levels of production and erode the cooperative local market exchange system.

Local food production intended for guest consumers should be based on sustainable agro-ecological models that ensure that local communities gain and secure favorable economic returns, without exacerbating environmental degradation and social inequality. Such a model would preserve egalitarian social structures and the informal local economy of the Makushi and their Amerindian neighbors. It would retain gender balance in the production of food and in the development of the ecotourism infrastructure. Such a model is highly desirable: it coordinates food production by women *and* men, enabling men who had been reliant on migrant work to reintegrate themselves within the community. While the entire Makushi community was aware that the female leaders and few male leaders who remained in the village were highly effective in coordinating activities and presenting the lectures for guests, it was also clear to the Makushi women that they could not guarantee surplus food for such guests without first adjusting their plantings, which required planning six months to a year in advance. The increased workload would require the return of their men.

Even if large numbers of men could return to clear land and cultivate crops, the women were aware that this was no guarantee of a high yield—the weather could always interfere. A supply of fresh fruit and vegetables, so often sought by guests from developed countries, was the most difficult to ensure. My study shows that tourists' demand for food interferes with local food distribution practices, heightening the potential for negative social effects of Western development. I would argue, however, that a moderate increase in such nonlocal demand for food can help alleviate the undesirable effects on local cultural systems that have already been affected by the global development of mining and logging industries. The feasibility of revitalizing and transforming subsistence horticultural practices to supply the food needs of local people and guests *must* provide additional competitive economic incentives for men. Without such incentives, men are not likely to remain in the community, where they are needed to increase food production and sustain ecotourism programs.

In the meantime, Makushi women participate in a surplus cassava production project developed by the Guyanese government and a United Nations development program. Rather than undertake the somewhat dangerous and physically demanding work of clearing family plots in the highlands,[10] the women are encouraged to work in a community co-op to intensify cassava production on lower lands near the Surama village center. These lands are typically dryer, but subject to flooding during the wet season.

The community co-op produces cassava for the families of elderly widows and of mothers with small children whose male partners, in the course of seeking wage labor, have either abandoned them or are away for long periods of time. This program promotes the development of surplus cassava through which local women meet basic food needs and are drawn into the production of commodities for cash exchange. The production of surplus cassava for local and potentially national markets is intended to meet the development needs of women who also desire material goods.

The program developers contend that the machinery they brought in to mechanize the local processing of cassava will yield not only products for local needs but also derived products such as cassareep, tapioca, and farine for commercial export.[11] The program trained local women in quality control, labeling, and processing techniques.[12] The Guyanese government provides free local transportation of products. It is hoped that the growing potential the plant offers for stable, wage employment might encourage men to return to the village. This has not yet occurred, although the men who remain in the village actively support the project.

If the surplus production of cassava is to be sustained for any length of time, and certainly if the project generates increasing amounts of surplus, the local market structure will be transformed. The local farmer's markets, where in-season crops are sold at prices agreed upon through the local political structure (protecting locals from middlemen), will likely collapse under external market forces. Such a shift will further threaten the guarantee of local food supply and the primarily reciprocal economy of the region.

Although regional development prospects that further access to, and incorporation within, a global market may be desirable at some levels, the current cassava program is likely to lead to debt and dependency on imported goods, particularly food. Further, a development strategy of this sort, which is intended to offset the economic instability of women in particular, may in fact, make them more vulnerable to the vagaries of the global market and local weather conditions, a tragic reality for agriculturalists throughout the globe.

Another global development strategy that impacts gender relationships among the Makushi is the plan for a road that would begin in Roraima, Brazil, and extend through the Guyanese Rupununi region to Georgetown. The road would provide market opportunities for Makushi surplus production and certainly improve access to the region for potential ecotourists, who must now endure a nine-hour truck drive over the frequently flooded, often impassable logging roads to the interior. There is an airport within one hour of Surama and two hours of the Iwokrama Rain Forest Preserve, but the roads to these sites also require four-wheel drive. These vehicles are currently in short supply and can carry only four to six passengers and limited supplies. Each truck needs to reserve room for shovels and chain saw needed for frequent road clearing.

A more developed road that would accommodate trucks transporting raw materials and finished goods would primarily benefit Brazilian economic development. Such activity would facilitate contact with the nearby, more-developed Brazilian economy, heightening its cultural influence. The Guyanese government fears that more Makushi men would be lured into Brazilian wage labor and that, in turn, the Makushi people would become more dependent on Brazilian consumer goods, while not contributing equally to the economic development of Guyana.

To date, it is unclear whether international or national programs to promote environmentally and socially sound ecotourism can resist or reverse the deterioration of egalitarian gender relations in the globalization of subsistence economies. Trends include the wage-labor exploitation of males in extractive industries, which contributes to the decline in local food production and community nutrition, the spread of sexually transmitted diseases, alcoholism among males, and domestic abuse. These trends are in stark contrast to cooperative subsistence practices that promote equality in gender relationships and provide balanced diets for local families, as well as an informal market for sharing local surplus. Able to make a viable living in their local community, workers need not be subjected to the alcohol, drugs, and prostitution that so often plague migrant labor camps.

Questions remain regarding so-called enlightened development programs that promote gender-based division of labor, especially when such segregation dramatically alters local gender traditions that are more egalitarian. Extended male absence from family and community creates a variety of social and economic problems. It is reasonable to assume, however, that if the women's community cooperative cassava project was successful without men returning to the village, women would gain greater control over resource allocation, business decisions, and distribution of economic rewards. Without male contributions to their economic livelihoods and social lives, women would presumably also gain more personal independence. Can they adapt to this social and economic shift, the absence of so many men, and also secure and stabilize family and community life? Can they preserve their cultural identities? A development policy that promotes surplus production of a monocrop is likely to reduce women's ability and incentive to produce the variety of basic foods necessary for balanced nutrition. My preliminary social-impact study suggest that the local ecology is best preserved through the ecotourism project, which sustains gender cooperative horticulture, than through intensified cassava production, which focuses on the needs of women alone.

It was already apparent, from my field observations in 1996, that for those few men who remained in the community, strategies to revitalize Makushi culture through development of women's social and economic roles often diminish males's social status. For example, tensions exist between male and female leaders, primarily over the direction of outside development assistance. The cassava production center draws its resources from the United Nations. Ecotourism draws resources from the Guyanese government. The ethnobotany project, sponsored by Oxford University, which also installed a satellite-transmitted Internet service, perhaps brings the greatest potential for further external resources.

Conflicts between male and female community leaders over opportunities to attract and distribute resources are evident at each level of development, and may jeopardize the cooperative coordination needed to secure these essential, but still inadequate, resources. As men and women perceive opportunities for individual remuneration over community compensation, competition for cash incentives becomes more common. These gendered conflicts are also complicated by kinship conflicts. Some families have more members actively involved in individually compensated positions with Iwokrama, and others have more men who regularly contribute wages, from external labor, to household needs.

The current local leadership seeks to balance and coordinate development opportunities within the community so that all households can participate, but competition for individual economic opportunity is evident. This is another reason why the community-based ecotourism project promises long-term sustainability. The profits from the rental of barracks and the use of water and latrines go to the community, rather than to individuals, to be distributed among those with the greatest needs.

Conclusion

Development policies and programs that influence the transformation of gender roles, especially those with roots in traditionally egalitarian societies, pose significant challenges to external and internal decision makers. I argue that the coordination and development of the opportunities for and talents of both men and women in cooperative endeavors will provide the most hope for long-term success. Within the framework of Western capitalism, however, it is difficult to advance the need for the development of nonexploitative infrastructures—ones that also promote just and sustainable opportunities for men and women. We need to work toward this. In doing so, we cannot limit ourselves to a static model of success. Anthropologists argue for periodic social and economic impact studies, which are intended to reveal external biases and identify local processes.

Significant among the development factors affecting Makushi men and women is that the current national-political structure of Guyana accommodates local cultures as it seeks international support. The Guyanese government, a latecomer to global development, has had time to learn from other developing nations. The Guyanese government recognizes the importance of garnering international support through validating the human rights of indigenous peoples and actively participating in rain forest preserve management. It acknowledges the contributions of indigenous people in protecting national sovereignty along unpatrolled borders. It also recognizes that without careful regional management, the competition among the local rain forest communities for specialized development projects is likely to be divisive and counterproductive.

In the final analysis, the success of diverse development strategies for Makushi men and women will depend upon the development of local leadership through key individuals. These leaders must work to identify and sustain national and international opportunities and structures of support. To be effective over the long term, men and women must develop their skills and creativity in coordinating external and local cultural resources, without commodifying their culture or destroying their cooperative community through competition. This requires the participation of both men and women who can develop their own local agendas, fostering mutual respect and equality between men and women. In doing so, they will have to resist the behaviors and attitudes of tourists and other outsiders who may or may not respect their egalitarian ethos.

During the time that my students and I visited Surama, the Makushi village, it was clear to the Makushi women that North American males did not show them the same respect that Makushi men showed them. My male students related to the Makushi women who cooked for them as they would relate to their mothers. They related to male and female lecturers as they would relate to male and female faculty, which generally defers greater status to males. My male students did not generally respond as enthusiastically to the directions of Makushi female leaders as they did to Makushi male leaders.

In contrast, when several Makushi men sought to enlist the aid of my students (a providential, if temporary, easing of the labor shortage) in rebuilding a bridge that had been washed out by a flood, they were met with overwhelming support. My male students were surprised, however, to discover that women were also invited to participate in the construction project. Makushi women and their female student peers were assigned tasks as strenuous as those assigned to the men.

The bridge-building project helped my students better understand the Makushi cultural attitudes and behaviors associated with gender equality and respect. My males students were given long poles to use as levers to remove fallen timbers from the collapsed bridge site. This was not because they were men, but because they were quite tall, considerably more so than Makushi men and women, who do not exhibit the same degree of sexual dimorphism evident in most North American populations. Because there was no mechanized equipment, both men and women were needed to hoist the huge logs back into place, with only the aid of ropes and carefully coordinated heaves. Perhaps an even more telling indicator of gender equality among the

Makushi, was the sharing of bawdy sexual humor at the bridge site. My male students were shocked by the unabashed behavior of Makushi women, who took the same opportunities as Makushi men to comment on the sexual symbolism of laying huge logs into position. In their community life, Makushi men and women enjoy many opportunities to bridge differences between each other, and there is much North Americans can learn from them. Along similar lines, development strategies that advance gender equity as a core principle enable broader forms of development at the levels of individual, family, community, and culture.

NOTES

1. A map of Guyana and the location of the Iwokrama Forest can be found on Guyana's ecotourism Web site at http://www.jetsettersmagazine.com/archive/jetezine/globe02/samerica/guyana/ecotourism.html.

2. Makushi women are unfamiliar with strategies to protect chickens from the carnage of hawks. The government was unable to deliver wire netting for protection of the chickens, and the women were uninterested in my suggestions to build coops from local materials. Their response to the problem was, "If the government wants us to raise chickens, then they can send us chicken wire."

3. See the World Bank report on Guyana and its indigenous peoples, available at http://Inweb18.worldbank.org/External/lac/lac.nsf/Countries/Guyana

4a. For a feminist critique of modernization and dependency theories see, Scott, Catherine V. 1995. *Gender Development: Rethinking Modernization and Dependency Theory." Boulder: Lynne Rienner Publishers,* El-Bushra. Judy. 2000. "Rethinking Gender and Development Practice for the Twenty-First Century." In *Gender in the Twenty-First Century,* edited by Caroline Sweetman, 55–62, Stivins, Maila. 1996. *Matriliny and Modernity: Sexual Politics and Social Change in Rural Malaysia.* Austrailia: Allen and Unwin, and Sweetman, Caroline, ed. 2001. *Gender Development and Money.* Oxfor: Oxfam.

4. See the World Resources Institute report, "Challenges to and Opportunities for Profit Without Plunder: Conflicts over Amerindian Lands and Rights," available on their Web site at http://www.wri.org/wri/biodiv/guyana/103e-pwp.html.

5. United Nations Development Programme, "National Report on Indigenous Peoples and Development" (UNDP, country office: Guyana). Available at http://www.hartford-hwp.com/archives/41/318.html.

6. The loss of male laborers in horticultural societies, however, is less disruptive than is the case in agricultural societies. This is not due wholly to their labor contributions, but to the nature of women's social positions in horticultural societies. Kinship organization within horticultural societies guarantees that women and children are not dependent upon

male-dominated patterns of descent and residence for resource distribution, status, and decision-making opportunities.

7. The Iwokrama Web site describes the project's mission and shows photos of its infrastructure; available at http://www.iwokrama.org

8. This only pertains, however, to the dry season. All of the roads in the region are flooded during the rainy season, between June and August.

9. Household units depart from Western-based conceptions of the nuclear family. Makushi households are often comprised of extended families in which men and women rear children, with the assistance of in-laws, until they become financially independent and can establish their own households.

10. The danger is due to the need to sometimes stay overnight in isolated locations, five to six miles from the village. Wild animals, particularly jaguars, are a threat to temporary campsites. The slashing and burning of trees is both difficult and dangerous, requiring the containment of fires. Traditionally, entire families engaged in this work, but men provided the major share of the physical labor, as well as the hunting skills needed to protect the family from predatory animals.

11. Cassareep is a boiled juice extracted from bitter cassava. It is a seasoning similar to soy sauce, used on rice and fish. Farine is a dried cereal staple consumed like rice or dried beans. It can be stored indefinitely.

12. Photos of this process are available upon request.

REFERENCES

Boo, Elizabeth. 1990. *Ecotourism: The Potentials and Pitfalls.* Country Case Studies, vol. 2. Washington, D.C.: World Wildlife Fund.

Cohen, E. 1979. "The Impact of Tourism on the Hill-Tribes of Northern Thailand." *Internationales Asienforum* 10(5):5–38.

DeKadt, Elizabeth, ed. 1979. *Tourism: Passport to Development?* Oxford: Oxford University Press.

Forte, Jannette. 1996. *About Guyanese Amerindians.* Georgetown, Guyana: Jannette Forte.

Forte, Jannette, and Ian Melville. 1989. *Amerindian Testimonies.* Georgetown, Guyana: Jannette Forte.

Graburn, Nelson H. 1995. "Tourism, Modernity, and Nostalgia." In *The Future Of Anthropology: Its Relevance to the Contemporary World,* eds. Akbar S. Ahmed and Cris N. Shore, 158–178. London: Athlone Press.

MacCannell, Dean. 1992. *Empty Meeting Grounds.* New York: Routledge.

McKean, P. 1976. "Tourism, Culture Change, and Culture Conversion." In *Ethnic Identities in Modern Southeast Asia,* ed. D. Banks. The Hague: Mouton.

Moser, Caroline. 1993. *Gender Planning and Development: Theory, Practice, and Training.* New York: Routledge.

Nash, Dennison. 1995. "Prospects for Tourism Study in Anthropology." In *The Future of Anthropology: Its Relevance to the Contemporary World,* eds. Akbar S. Ahmed and Cris N. Shore, 179–202. London: Athlone Press.

Nyoni S. 1987. "Indigenous NGOs: Liberation, Self-Reliance, and Development."

In *Development Alternatives*, ed. Anne Gordon Drabek, 51–66. Oxford: Pergamon Press.

O'Rouke, Diane O. 2002. "Women's Worlds 2002—Making Connections in Kampala." *Anthropology News*, November, 14.

Scott, Catherine V. 1995. *Gender and Development: Rethinking Modernization and Dependency Theory*. Boulder: Lynne Rienner Publishers.

Smith, Valene L., and William R. Eadington, eds. 1992. *Tourism Alternatives: Potentials and Problems in the Development of Tourism*. Philadelphia: University of Pennsylvania Press.

Ward, Martha C. 2003. *A World Full of Women*. 3d. ed. Boston: Allyn and Bacon.

Barbara J. Dilly *is assistant professor of anthropology at Creighton University in Omaha, Nebraska. Her applied research interests focus on rural social and economic development in Latin America and the American Midwest. Her current projects include comparative and longitudinal studies of rural communities in Iowa undergoing social and economic transformations. Her essay "Volunteer Labor: Adding Value to Local Culture" in* Labor in Anthropology *(Society for Economic Anthroplogy Monograph, Volume 22), edited by E. Paul Durrenberger and Judith E. Marti, will be available in fall 2003.*

The Gender Regime of "Women's Work"

A View from Tanzanian Internet Cafés

Kristin Phillips

International organization policies pertaining to gender and information technology address gender in terms of the relations between men and women as defined by sociocultural norms. In doing so, they do not account for how technology is itself gendered, or how people use technology in ways that call up and reproduce gendered relations in society. Certain assumptions that underpin these policies—that argue that there exists an imminent danger of losing women because of a lack of technological skills—even serve to reproduce gender relations in the realm of information technology.

In this article, I deal with three questions. First, how are issues of gender and information technology conceptualized in the international educational policy literature? Second, what are some limitations of this policy conceptualization that surface in Internet café settings in northern Tanzania? The two issues I specifically investigate are the extent to which policy focuses on women's access to technology and the role that policy plays in the positioning of women as knowledge- and technology-poor. Third, how can we discuss these issues without either relying on an ethnocentric discourse and theory of gender relations that privileges white, Euro-American perspectives, or by reducing gender power relations to a faulty cultural logic in which sociocultural norms are blamed for imbalances of power?

In order to address these questions, I offer a conceptual language for thinking about gender and information technology through invoking the concept of "gendered social regimes." Crediting Foucault (1977, 1978), cultural anthropologists and gender theorists (Connell 2002; Escobar 1995; Ong, 1999) have used the concept of power and knowledge "regimes" to address ways that gendered structures of power and knowledge are normalized. A "regime" is a "structure of relations" that "defines possibilities and consequences" (Connell 2002, 55). I argue that there exists a gender regime of technology, which in concrete terms manifests itself in the sexual division of labor in the realm of information technology. While I show that this regime is composed of gendered arrangements that draw on both global and local relationships and discourses, I also highlight how these arrangements are shaped in part through policy discourse that reproduces ideas about Third World women as knowledge- and technology-poor.

Method

This article concerns itself most directly with the language and direction of international education policy dealing with issues of gender and information technology. I ground it in an extensive conceptual and discursive analysis of two information technology policy documents (UNCSTD Gender Working Group 1995; Hafkin and Taggart 2001) that I have selected as representative of the themes and language of a broader sample. I locate these policy documents in the research and policy debates, which they both reflect and shape, and then offer a critique informed by recent anthropological analyses of the conceptualization of technology and by interpretations of several gendered dynamics of Internet cafés that point to the problematic nature of policy objectives, strategies, and outcomes.

My understanding of Internet cafés as gendered spaces derives mainly from conversations with Internet café owners, managers, staff, customers, and other townspeople during a two-month period I spent in northern Tanzania conducting anthropological research on a separate project. Although this article draws on my daily experiences in at least seven cafés, I highlight one in particular, the Safari Internet Café (a pseudonym), located in a medium-sized city in northern Tanzania where as many as ten Internet cafés have opened in the last five years. I offer my thoughts on these gendered dynamics not as evidence derived from a systematic long-term study, but rather as vignettes in which I highlight issues and raise questions regarding the direction of international policy in information technology.

Literature Review

Gender, Information Technology, and Development

The question central to most discussions of gender and information technology in international development policy is "whether the Internet and other digital technologies will become agents of transformation or reproduce the inequalities of the status quo" (Robins 2002). Arguments for technology as the agent and opportunity for transformation (Keohane and Nye 2001) are grounded on the potential technology may offer for increased participation by women in democratic processes, access to information and a "global" culture, and the expansion of business, employment, social, and educational opportunities. Those who see technology as a new means for sustaining the status quo argue that technology and its applications are mediated by sociocultural norms that prevent women's access and that in general technology benefits those who already have resources (Allison 2002; Mercer, forthcoming). They also maintain that information technology is yet another tool of First World or capitalist domination that sustains dependency, since technology is enacted within existing political and economic structures (Mazrui and Ostergard 2002; Steele and Stein 2002; Stienstra 2002) and that basic needs such as health care and education must be met before technology can assist women in the developing world (Gates 2000). Other scholars have argued that while technology offers many opportunities for women in developing countries, these will be available only if they are supported by "deliberate policies to ensure participation, ownership, education, and ICT [information and communication technology] training for women."

A number of edited volumes on the subject (Mitter and Rowbotham 1995; Allison 2002; Harcourt 1999) document the impacts of information technology on the lives of women in developing countries; examine the Internet as the source of change, continuity, conflict, and cooperation; assess the possibilities and limitations for democracy in the world that the Internet offers; and analyze women's emerging Internet use and cyberculture. As this literature offers an ample supply of preliminary conclusions on the impacts of information technology on women's lives, this article pursues a different agenda, namely, to reflect upon the processes through which gender is brought to bear on information technology and to inform current conceptualizations of this process within policy.

International Education and Technology Policy

Two reports representative of recent policy orientations in gender and technology are: the Gender Working Group of the United Nations Commission for Science and Technology Development's (UNCSTD) report *Taking action: Conclusions and recommendations of the Gender Working Group* (UNCSTD Gender Working Group 1995) and the United States Agency for International Development's (USAID) study *Gender, information technology, and developing countries: An analytic study* (Hafkin and Taggart, 2001). In this section I review these policies with respect to their conceptualizations of the sexual division of labor in technology and the relationship of women to information and gender, and I relate these conceptualizations to those in the broader literature.

Women's Work in Technology

Policy reports express considerable concern for the division of labor in information technology work and the feminization of certain kinds of employment in the sector. The USAID study notes that women in developing countries "tend to be poorly represented as administrators and managers and concentrated in lower level, end user positions" (33). The UNCSTD Gender Working Group notes the need to increase the number of women involved in technology decision-making and policy and that while information technology has increased employment opportunities for women, it has also displaced women in many existing industries (such as manufacturing). Furthermore, the UNCSTD group notes, new jobs require a higher skill level and women are faced with limited training opportunities in comparison with men. Similar concerns have been reflected by other groups, such as the Gender and Information Working Group of the International Development Research Centre (IDRC) in Canada (IDRC Gender and Information Working Group 1995), which expresses a concern for the "devaluing of clerical work," in which "computer and technological skills tend to be gender-labeled," with women using computers only in low-paying positions, while "positions requiring highly skilled use of computers and other technology are most often held by men" (275).

The USAID study attributes the hiring and firing of women at particular levels of information technology jobs to "sociocultural norms" (20) that discourage women in their studies and feminize women's occupations, although the role of "traditional attitudes" as the root of social problems has recently been called into question (see Vavrus 1998). The USAID report charges that "the gender stereotyped division of labor in information technology that regards women as unsuited or unqualified for certain types of jobs frequently stems from employer attitudes" (34) and that "during economic downturns, women are the first ones to be laid off, and men are given preference for vacant positions, because of men's traditionally perceived role as family breadwinner in most societies" (34). This framing of culture as the source of blame for inequity in the sexual division of labor is problematic, in that it in no way accounts for larger social, political, and economic structures and relationships that are always at play in labor relations.

This phenomenon of gender-labeled work has been explained in other ways as well. Some theorists see the education system as merely reflecting the demands of the employment market. Connell (2002) notes that a division of labor necessarily leads to the division in the education system preparing people for work. And Escobar (1995)

reflects that "only men [have been] considered to be engaged in productive activities, and, consequently, programs intended to improve
agricultural production and productivity [have been] geared toward
men" (172). These theories, in contrast to the USAID study's explanations, suggest that the division of labor occurs before, or separately
from, the process in which women are weeded out of the system during their education. A significant body of research has indicated that
what actually qualifies as technology is in fact shaped in discourse with
gender. In its analysis, the USAID study includes mention of a "feminization of certain IT occupations" in which the entrance of many
women into a given occupation results in a drop in wages, status, and
working conditions. The study cites Reardon's warning (1998) that

> as computer-based skills become more commonplace, and as the
> need for more workers to use them in a greater variety of ways grows,
> more women will again be recruited. But this will be at a lower wage
> because these will no longer be considered specialist skills, merely
> something that women can do. (14)

As Reardon suggests, the notion of technology itself has been widely
contested in such debates. A broader definition of technology, which
considers not only hardware but also "skills, expertise, organization,
techniques, and knowledge, all of which are connected to production
processes" (IWTC 1990, 289), has allowed feminist researchers to rein-
terpret women's historical role in science and technology (Harding
1995; Mitter and Rowbotham 1995). Rowbotham (1995) charges that
"who is remembered and revered is not a matter of chance but bound
up with how science is defined and what mode of the relationship
between science and technology is adopted; it indeed depends on how
knowledge is constituted" (55). The IDRC Gender and Information
Working Group (1995) suggests the need to examine whether important technologies "are being overlooked because they are associated
with women's work, and because women's knowledge is not generally
considered scientific and valuable" (286). With the introduction of
ethnographic evidence in a later section, I attempt to build upon these
other theories of the engendering of labor in order to move beyond
sociocultural deterministic explanations.

Information

Another concern addressed in information technology and gender
policy is women's relationship to the information communicated in

information technology practices. The USAID study warns that "women are few and far between as *producers* of Internet content, programmers, designers, inventors, and fixers of computers" (Hafkin and Taggart 2001, 19–20) and that they are only passively engaged in information technology processes: as users of communication and consumers of information.

While the USAID study challenges this role for women, the language and logic that it uses throughout the report reproduce women's relationship to "information." Much current development policy echoes the USAID language when it expresses concern for "those left on the other side of the digital divide—the division between the information 'haves and have nots' . . . women within developing countries are in the deepest part of the divide—further removed from the information age than the men whose poverty they share" (2001, 1). The representations of this divide range from pathological interpretations in which women are conveyed as unable to meet their basic needs, to geographical interpretations that focus on the isolation of women as a factor preventing their access to information technologies. As Hafkin and Taggart have noted (2001), "The geographic location of public Internet centers also affects women's access to information technology in developing countries. Women's mobility is considerably more limited than men's in most societies" (25).

The UNCSTD report distinguishes between the "development, diffusion, and use of modern science-based technologies and the local knowledge and traditional technologies that have evolved within communities over many years of trial and error" (1995, 1). "Local knowledge" is historically and contextually situated, to be traded only with other local actors, while "modern science-based technologies" are universally applicable, if sufficiently translated to be "the information of most value to poor people . . . 'locally-contextualized,' 'relevant' information" (Heeks, in Hafkin and Taggart 2001, 83). In both cases, the role of local actors, presumably women, is one of prepackaged consumption, not critical reflection or translation. In this model, women are creatures of the local, the rural, the periphery, while the men's world is enacted in urban centers that are closer to the global center in the web of international relations. I take issue with this representation of women, which floats freely in Internet discourse and practice.

Gender and Gender Regimes

In the UNCSTD Gender Working Group report *gender* "refers to the distinct roles that men and women are assigned in any society" (3).

The knowledge and experiences that are acquired in the specific tasks of these roles "lead women and men to have different needs and aspirations" (3). This working definition of gender in the UNCSTD report views gender categories as stable and culturally bound. The USAID study implies a similar understanding of gender when it maintains that "girls and women's ability to access IT [information technology] is also shaped largely by sociocultural norms that determine female behavior and interests" (26).

There are two problems with this conceptualization. First, it overlooks the view that gender categories are "inherently unstable" and produced in discourse and in practice, not "determined" by any given social structure (Butler 1990; Connell 2002). Second, it places a monolithic "developing country culture" in the center of discussions about obstacles to technology and development, ignoring geographic, political, and historical diversity and implying that modernization must follow a Western cultural model, a common flaw in development discourse (Escobar 1995; Rahnema and Bawtree 1997).

Taking the view that power operates within knowledge and gender regimes (Escobar 1995, 156; Ong, 1999, 113), I argue that a gender regime of technology—composed of gendered arrangements that are naturalized in relation to other institutions (Connell 2002, 55)—is enacted and sustained, in part, through a policy discourse on Third World women and technology that reproduces conceptions of the Third World as knowledge- and technology-poor. In the following analysis, two gendered arrangements patterned by and sustaining the gender regime of technology are described and illustrated in context: technology work and information. These depictions of the gender regime challenge notions of gender and information technology as represented in policy discourse, and also offer a new language for information technology and international education policy formulation.

Internet Cafés in Northern Tanzania

Storefronts in the larger cities of northern Tanzania are increasingly marked by signs announcing Internet services. Internet cafés offer a new space for communication and interaction for those of the urban population in Tanzania who can afford the price. These cafés generally make five or six computers available for customer use, and prices are consistent across cafés and cities. One hour of Internet use in July 2002 cost 1,000 Tanzanian shillings, or approximately one dollar. With a 1999 per capita GDP of 270 dollars (United Republic of Tanzania, 2001a), this price equals more than a day's wages for the majority of

Tanzania's population of 31 million. In fact, statistics from 2000 indicate that in Tanzania only 0.8 percent of the population used the Internet (International Telecommunication Union, 2000). It is therefore important to keep the problems identified in this article in perspective with the broader social and material context. In light of these statistics, the relevance of exploring a setting that seems irrelevant to as much as 99 percent of the Tanzanian population may seem questionable. My purpose here is not to make generalizable statements about Tanzanians and technology, but rather, in light of the international policy emphasis on access, to examine what is happening in gender relations at sites where women already have access to information technology.

In at least one of these cafés, North American and European tourists, researchers, medical volunteers, and missionaries made up the majority of the clientele. In other cafés, however, customers overwhelmingly represented one of two Tanzanian demographic groups, both of whom came to socialize as well as to make use of the Internet: middle-aged men dressed in business attire who came to conduct both business and personal communications using word processing applications and the Internet, and young women and men, most of whom were secondary-school graduates, who came to engage in personal communications as well as to investigate personal, professional, and educational opportunities through research and contacts on the Internet. In addition to these two groups there were also several middle-aged professional women who would often use the Internet and leave quickly. As Form Four graduates, who are at a level similar to vocational high school graduates in the United States, nearly all of these individuals represent a middle-class elite of the population, particularly in terms of access to education and technology. According to 2000 statistics, only 2.8 percent (25,456 of 894,894 students) of those enrolled in the first year of school, Standard One, continue on to Form Four (United Republic of Tanzania 2001b).

The cafés I frequented were all privately owned, for-profit businesses, as opposed to telecenters opened by internationally funded information and communication infrastructure programs elsewhere on the African continent (Economic Commission for Africa 2002). Most cafés were attended by one young woman or man who assigned customers to computers. Drinks (cold, bottled sodas) could be purchased from a Coca-Cola mini-refrigerator in a corner. Internet connection speed varied from fast to frustratingly slow, depending on the cafe, but electricity outages were universal and service was often cut off for several hours at a time. Except in the café serving mainly foreigners, which emptied quickly, the periods of power outage were among the most social and interactive in the cafés, as customers and employees passed the time chatting and joking. At least three other cafés had modeled themselves into business centers that, besides offering the amenities already mentioned, marketed photocopy and fax services, and customer service provided by three or four employees. One of these Internet cafés, and its environment, services, and personnel is described in greater detail below.

The Gendered Arrangement of Technology Work: When Less Education Gets You Further

A small brown building tucked away on a dusty side street houses the Safari Internet Café. Young people, often employees and their friends, gather on its porch, which is decked with stools and a narrow bar table that runs along the café's perimeter. A sign outside proclaims, "Good service is our motto." Inside, in a tiny room of perhaps ten by fifteen feet, six computers are crammed into a set of carrels. The owner has tucked a printer against the carrels and a photocopier against one of the walls, and an air conditioner blasts cold air into the room through the only window. In a smaller room, off to the side, benches are pressed up against two adjacent walls, and a coffee table lined with newspapers is wedged between them. A single office behind plate glass windows is tucked into the back of that room.

At any given time three young women and one young man, all sharply dressed in business attire, perform their respective duties as employees of the café. Juma, in his late twenties, who has been trained by the owner of Safari, manages the network and personnel and attends to technical problems. Two young women in their mid-to-late-twenties, Pili and Zakiya, work as full-time secretaries who do "whatever is needed," while Rosa interns as a secretary in order to complete her certification at a local technical institute. The three women show customers how to use the computer and how to email and type business and personal work for customers at their request. Juma works long hours, allowing Zakiya and Rosa to go to the mosque to pray several times a day, and giving Pili her day of rest on Sundays so that she can attend church. Several times a week both Pili and Juma teach computer classes in the café to young people wanting to increase their skills. Pili has also trained both Zakiya and Rosa in their new roles as secretaries.

At first glance, these observations point to the promise of policy objectives. Both the manager and the secretaries are offering more than just service at their Internet café; they are offering opportunities for young people to engage in informal continuing education and are also taking advantage of such opportunities themselves. But a closer look at the training and qualifications of the employees presents a problem: the young women are concentrated in lower-level positions than that of the young man, a trend that is reflected in data from the policy literature. Not only did both Pili and Zakiya—the two secretaries—have the same six-month computer training course as Juma, they also had an additional six months of training, in the form of a secretarial course, and Pili worked at the café for five months before Juma started. Juma, having not attended the secretarial course, has less training than Pili and Zakiya and no professional experience, but he was hired above them. Apparently the secretarial course was not of value in the matter of Pili's position. This scenario begs an answer to the question, What role did the secretarial course play in Pili's hiring and in her lack of promotion?

As seen in the literature discussed above, ideas about what actually qualifies as technology are shaped in concert with gender. Since the structural and social gender patterns of employment delimit job possibilities for young women, and as young women increasingly move into emerging fields, the structural and social patterns are reinscribed. When high numbers of women enter a profession, salaries, status, and working conditions often drop, thus turning the profession into a "feminized" occupation (Hafkin and Taggart 2001, 35). As skills become translated into pre-existing gender divisions (such as secretarial/ managerial work) they become engendered. What may have previously been unacceptable for women is now open to them as a possibility, and this access is described as a victorious moment in USAID policy:

> the positive aspect of women's new entry into the labor force in jobs related to information technology, albeit largely in end user entry level secretarial positions or manufacturing jobs, brings many women disposable income for the first time, raises their status in their own eyes and in those of their family, and frequently leads to their desire for more training and upgrading of skills. (Hafkin and Taggart 2001, 35)

Yet as the market floods with women who find new doors open to them, the supply of labor inflates, resulting in a drop of wages and loss in status. This feminization of certain technical jobs increases possibilities for participation and access for women, yet it later marks them as they seek additional training and promotion. Pili's preparation in a secretarial course, in addition to the six-month technical course that she and Juma have both completed, most likely won her the secretarial position. Yet as these occupations become retracked along gender lines, this very qualification marks her as ineligible for further on-the-job training. And without opportunity for further training, her career is stilted, or as Mitter warns:

> it is not enough to give women workers one-time access to computer training. In this rapidly changing field, skills must be upgraded continually. Women's entry into new occupations has so far been mainly as clerks and typists. These are precisely the jobs that are likely to be automated in the next phase of technology development. (1995a, 229)

Connell (2002) offers a historical perspective on this phenomenon. He notes that being a clerk was "originally a man's job" but with the invention of the typewriter and growing amount of office work, "clerical work increasingly involved women; in fact it became archetypical 'women's work.'. . . But with the advent of the computer and word processing, 'the secretary' is disappearing as an occupational category. Clerical work is again, increasingly, being done by men" (60–61). As this scenario shows, this gendered arrangement has shifted once again, as more positions have appeared and women gain access to training and skills.

This dynamic set of ever-shifting gendered arrangements is squarely situated in local (though not closed) contexts. Yet these arrangements consistently reproduce the overarching gender regime of technology, which transcends culture and nation. Van Zoonen (1992) writes that "in the cultured construction of genderedness, women are largely absent from the realm of what counts as technology" (in UNCSTD Gender Working Group 1995, 272–73). I argue differently: that women, through these gendered arrangements of labor, come to embody technology; or, rather, that the internalization of formerly inaccessible skills represents the ultimate demystification of the skilled labor that is associated with technology. As new technologies are produced, they are mystified by those people who have access to them, in order to defend their market value. This mystification occurs in both employment and education. As those technologies become demystified through their demand-based circulation, and as they reach those least positioned to learn them—women in developing countries—their manipulation becomes naturalized into labor. This arrangement comes to be seen as commonsensical, as part of what the body can do. I mentioned at the beginning that I wanted to challenge the emphasis on access in gender and technology policy. I would like to demonstrate in this scenario that access, far from being the ultimate solution for women, is actually itself implicated in the process of sustaining gendered power relations through the sexual division of labor.

The Gendered Arrangement of Information

A second gender arrangement that became clear to me at the Safari Internet Café was that the role women play in technology practices is inscribed within a particular sphere, which excludes the actual production of information and, in certain cases, its critical assessment. On the one hand, there was clear evidence that young women were seizing the opportunities that information had made available to them; they were expanding their social and professional networks, improving their language skills, developing their understanding of other countries, and accessing information on sensitive topics like HIV infection. Zakiya frequently showed me advertisements for various agencies and organizations purporting to help students to study medicine in the Ukraine or facilitate relationships with French hotels that, in exchange for more internationally experienced staff, will provide lessons in French. Aisha, a frequent customer at Safari, uses the sponsorship section of a popular U.S. Internet search engine to look for financial support for higher education in the United States. Until she finds it, she will attend Makerere University in Uganda, which she found out about on the Internet. And nearly all the young women I spoke with at a number of Internet cafés used a particular Internet chat room to make acquaintances and build friendships and support networks all over the world. Rosa indicated that it was with these friends throughout Tanzania, and in the United States, Nigeria, and Canada, that she could be open and honest and be advised on her relationships, friendships, family, and even concerns about AIDS.

Yet I often found myself concerned about the lack of filtering of information that my own experience had taught me about, particularly with regard to the young women's perpetual search for sponsorship to work or study overseas. Nearly all the young men and women I spoke with both inside and outside Internet cafés had heard "that story" (of which there were several versions) about the young man or woman who had "made it" to America or Europe and had thereafter become quite wealthy based on one Internet contact. This myth often supported a faith in technology and its content of which my own e-mail box, overloaded with junk mail and promises of "undergraduate diplomas," and my privilege of nine previous years of Internet use (and mistakes) had made me skeptical.

Beyond concerns about Internet scams, I came to be aware also that information was not necessarily something that would be produced by young women in the Safari Internet Café. During one afternoon, I showed Rosa, Zakiya, and a third young woman how to design their own Web sites using a free Web page editor. In very little time, Rosa had designed her own Web page. But there was one problem: she said she had "nothing to say." Although Rosa was an incessant e-mailer with friends from all over the world she had met in chatrooms and on other Internet sites, the act of posting a written document stopped her in her tracks. She didn't know any information.

Now it is only in the context of my broader interpretation of the Internet café as a social space that this comment and observation really come to signal the positionality of the young female employees with regard to their role in information technology. While the maleness of a young customer at the Internet café was enough to qualify him as an ad hoc consultant to the manager when the server or other hardware broke down, the secretaries' relationship to both information and technology was one of consumption, communication, education, and embodiment (as I described earlier), but not one of production.

One of the consequences of the separation of women's work from the production of Internet content is that content sources are mystified and therefore can appear more objective or scientific than perhaps is warranted. Women's passive role in relationship to the information and technology of information technology contributes to a "self-peripheralization" (Liechty 1995) of young women as they internalize the notion that they are information-poor without technology. This notion is threaded throughout the analysis in the USAID study: "[Information technology] is uniquely beneficial to women's empowerment in developing countries by helping to end their information isolation, a phenomenon from which women suffer most" (Hafkin and Taggart 2001, 62). Without information, women, as represented in policy, are unable to meet their basic needs in today's complex society and left vulnerable to exploitation:

> When information is not accessible to all, those who don't have it can be exploited. One of the hallmarks of women's situation in developing countries, particularly among poor women and most markedly among poor women in rural areas, is their information poverty, which reflects the general disparity between men and women in terms of access to all development resources. If information is power, lack of information is disenfranchisement. (Hafkin and Taggart 2001, 61)

Hafkin and Taggart attribute women's vulnerability to a lack of access to technology. I would like to acknowledge, at least, that the exploitation to which women are vulnerable may be more appropriately attributed to an international policy discourse that constructs them as lacking knowledge and skills of value more than to a lack of information technology at their fingertips.

Information used this way designates knowledge that has been extrapolated from its context, scientifically and centrally processed, and mass-distributed, through technological means. Information technology plays a central role in legitimating and redistributing knowledge. As Foucault notes, "what is considered valid information in a particular society is often produced and transmitted under the control, dominant if not exclusive, of a few great political and economic apparatuses" (in IDRC Gender and Information Working Group 1995). The gender regime of technology is one of these apparatuses. This regime is sustained by a gendered arrangement where gender, understood to be linked with relative location and a certain degree of generalizability is selectively decontextualized and celebrated as either formal and modern or as indigenous and local. While there exist knowledge and data that can assist women in rural areas to go about their lives, and while such policy language undoubtedly attracts development aid, this language is debilitating in its perpetuation of what Fatma Alloo (1995), founder of the Tanzanian Women's Media Association (TAMWA) calls the "'poor and powerless' myth" (303), which "[makes] us believe there is something wrong with our continent" (309).

Knowledge categories such as "global," "local," "information," and "traditional" are enacted in part by their positioning in the information technology mechanism and the gendered nature which that implies. In its present mode, international education policy reproduces these distinctions and the gendered roles implicit in them. In any case, a new analytical framework for gender and information technology policy, that of the gender regime, can reframe women's relationship to technology and information.

Conclusion

Technology is a tool that women use toward their own ends, collective and individual, as well as a tool that can sustain or reinscribe gender hierarchies, which, as many scholars have predicted, will usually be to the detriment of women. Yet information technology also represents an arena, which is by no means new, in which gender is enacted and defined. In this article, I have argued that a gender regime of technology, composed of gendered arrangements, is mediated in part through a policy discourse on women and information technology that reproduces women in developing countries as knowledge- and technology-poor. I have offered descriptions of one information technology context that illuminates these arrangements and how they serve to support a gender regime.

There are two reasons why I find the idea of the gender regime so particularly compelling. The first is in response to a critique of both feminist theory and of Women in Development/Gender and Development (WID/GAD) policy, which contests the pursuit of a universalizing and ethnocentric discourse and theory of gender relations, an agenda that has often been set by white feminists from Europe and North America (Mohanty 1991). The countervailing challenge, however, is to take into account context and social relations and dynamics, without reducing gender power relations to faulty cultural logic or attributing social problems to traditional attitudes that others have already called into question. In appropriating the concept of gender regime for this article, I draw on its capacity to provide a conceptual language in which the enactment of gender relations is neither culturally bounded nor universal.

In the space provided I have been able to sketch only briefly the way in which international education policy comes to bear on gender relations in information technology settings. In closing, I would like to point to the need to examine further this tension between the need for policy language to prioritize strategy (in order to effectively attract and allocate funds) over representation. My hope is that this article's attempt to grapple with the question of representation may inform the future development and investigation of policy's strategic nature.

ACKNOWLEDGMENTS

I wish to thank Amy Stambach, Sarah Robert, Adriane Williams, Mike Abelson, and the reviewers at *Women's Studies Quarterly* for their comments on earlier drafts of this essay.

REFERENCES

Allison, J. E. (2002). Information and international politics: An overview. In J. E. Allison (Ed.), *Technology, development, and democracy: International conflict and cooperation in the information age.* Albany: State University of New York Press.

Alloo, F. (1995). Using information technology as a mobilizing force: The case of the Tanzania Media Women's Association (TAMWA). In S. Mitter and S. Rowbotham (Eds.), *Women encounter technology: Changing patterns of employment in the Third World.* New York: United Nations University Press.

Butler, J. (1990). *Gender trouble: Feminism and the subversion of identity.* New York: Routledge.

Connell, R. W. (2002). *Gender.* Cambridge, England: Polity Press.

Dogar, R., and C. Power (2000). Mapping a Virtual Planet. *Newsweek,* December 1999–February 2000, 78–82.

Economic Commission for Africa (2002). *Development of national information and communication infrastructure plans.* Retrieved 23 November 2002, from http://www.uneca.org/aisi/nici.htm.

Escobar, A. (1995). *Encountering development: The making and unmaking of the third world.* Princeton, N.J.: Princeton University Press.

Foucault, M. (1977). *Discipline and punish: The birth of the prison.* New York: Pantheon.

————. (1978). *History of sexuality* (Vol. 1). New York: Pantheon.

Gates, B. (2000, October). Paper presented at the World Resources Institute's Digital Dividends Conference, Seattle.

Hafkin, N., and N. Taggart (2001). *Gender, information technology, and developing countries: An analytic study.* Office of Women in Development Bureau for Global Programs, Field Support and Research, USAID. Retrieved November 15, 2002, from http://www.dec.org/pdf_docs/PNACM294.pdf

Harcourt, W. (1999). *Women@Internet: Creating new cultures in cyberspace.* London: Zed Books.

Harding, S. (1995). Just add women and stir? In UNCSTD Gender Working Group (Ed.), *Missing links: Gender equity in science and technology for development.* New York: UNIFEM.

Heeks, R. (1999). *Information and communication technologies, poverty and development.* Retrieved October 10, 2002, from http://www.man.ac.uk/idpm/diwpf5.htm.

IDRC Gender and Information Working Group (1995). Information as a transformative tool: The gender dimension. In UNCSTD Gender Working Group (Ed.), *Missing links: Gender equity in science and technology for development.* New York: UNIFEM.

International Labour Organization (2001). *The information technology revolution: Widening or bridging gender gaps.* Retrieved October 6, 2002, from http://www.ilo.org/puclic/english/bureau/inf/pkits/wer2001/wer01ch4.htm.

International Telecommunication Union (2000). *Internet indicators, 2000.* Geneva, Switzerland.

IWTC (International Women's Tribune Center) (1990). *Filling the information gap: How do women get information and technologies appropriate to their needs? Proceedings of a communications workshop, June 1990, New York.* New York: IWTC and UN Development Fund for Women.

Keohane, R. O., and J. S. Nye (2001). *Power and interdependence* (3rd ed.). New York: Addison Wesley Longman.

Liechty, M. (1995). Media, markets and modernization: Youth identities and the experience of modernity in Kathmandu, Nepal. In V. Amit-Talai and H. Wulff (Eds.), *Youth cultures: Across-cultural perspective.* New York: Routledge.

Mazrui, A. A., and R. L. J. Ostergard (2002). Technology transfer in the computer age: The African experience. In J. E. Allison (Ed.), *Technology, development, and democracy: International conflict and cooperation in the information age*. Albany: State University of New York Press.

Mercer, C. (Forthcoming). Engineering civil society: Information and communication technologies and NGOs in Tanzania. *Review of African Political Economy, 98, (December)*.

Mitter, S. (1995a). Who benefits? In UNCSTD Gender Working Group (Ed.), *Missing links: Gender equity in science and technology for development*. New York: UNIFEM.

Mitter, S., and S. Rowbotham (Eds.) (1995). *Women encounter technology: Changing patterns of employment in the Third World*. New York: United Nations University Press.

Mohanty, C. (1991). Under Western eyes: Feminist scholarship and colonial discourses. In C. Mohanty, A. Russo, and L. Torres (Eds.), *Third World women and the politics of feminism*. Bloomington: Indiana University Press.

Moser, C. O. N. (1993). *Gender planning and development: Theory, practice and training*. London: Routledge.

Ong, A. (1999). *Flexible citizenship: The cultural logics of transnationality*. Durham: Duke University Press.

Rahnema, M., and V. Bawtree (Eds.) (1997). *The post-development reader*. London: Zed Books.

Reardon, G., in collaboration with S. Mitter and C. C. S. Ng (1998). *Globalisation, technological change and women workers in Asia* (Vol. 2002). Maastricht, Netherlands: UNU/INTECH.

Robins, M. (2002). Are African women online just ICT consumers? *Gazette: International Journal for Communication Studies,* 64(3): 235–50.

Rowbotham, S. (1995). Feminist approaches to technology: Women's values or a gender lens? In S. Mitter and S. Rowbotham (Eds.), *Women encounter technology: Changing patterns of employment in the Third World*. New York: United Nations University Press.

Stambach, A. (2000). *Lessons from Mount Kilimanjaro: Schooling, community and gender in East Africa*. New York: Routledge.

Steele, C., and A. Stein, A. (2002). Communications revolutions and international relations. In J. E. Allison (Ed.), *Technology, development, and democracy: International conflict and cooperation in the Information Age*. Albany: State University of New York Press.

Stienstra, D. (2002). Gender, women's organizing, and the Internet. In J. E. Allison (Ed.), *Technology, development, and democracy: International conflict and cooperation in the information age* . Albany: State University of New York Press.

UNCSTD Gender Working Group (1995). Taking action: Conclusions and recommendations of the Gender Working Group. In UNCSTD Gender Working Group (Ed.), *Missing links: Gender equity in science and technology for development*. New York: UNIFEM.

United Republic of Tanzania (2001a). *Country presentation by the United Republic of Tanzania*. Paper presented at the Third United Nations Conference on the Least Developed Countries, Brussels, Belgium.

———. (2001b). *Basic statistics in education: 1996-2000: National data*. Dar as

Salaam, Tanzania: Ministry of Education and Culture.

Van Zoonen, L. (1992). Feminist Theory and Information Technology. *Media, Culture, and Society, 14,* 9-29.

Vavrus, F. (1998). "Schooling, fertility, and the discourse of development: A study of the Kilimanjaro Region of Tanzania." Ph.D. diss., University of Wisconsin-Madison.

Kristin Phillips *is a graduate student in the departments of anthropology and educational policy studies at the University of Wisconsin, Madison. Her dissertation research will examine the implementation of a national primary school reform in Tanzania and trace the relationships between schools, communities, and international educational policy.*

A Poor Women's Pedagogy

"When Ideas Move in People's Hands and Hearts, They Change, Adapt, and Create New Solutions"

Salma Ismail

> *Women are singing;*
> *Ululating, dancing,*
> *Marching*
> *Carrying placards of their different housing associations,*
> *Wearing T-shirts which read—*
> *People's Dialogue for Housing and Shelter*
> *We Want!*
> *Power! Money! Knowledge!*

> *The songs they sing tell of the hardships they endure in the shacks, The threat from fire, rain and the wind and from eviction even under a new government.*

> *Now they have started to build houses by saving R2 a day*

> *These women are marching to the mass meeting in Hout Bay settlement Imizamo Yethu. The atmosphere is electric, there is lots of energy, excitement and anxiety as the different housing savings groups take the courage to say enough is enough, we are tired of this kind of life, and don't want to die in fires any longer and they say, "We work with all our hearts to do the good work and do not want to be pitied and we will rebuild our lives as we build our homes."*

> *They shout: "We will make it work!"* —documenting the spirit of the launch of the Imizamo Yethu savings group and model house display, 26 August 2000 (video recording by John Valentine and Salma Ismail)

Introduction

This article is concerned with processes of learning within a community housing project called the Victoria Mxenge Housing Development Association. The research sets out to describe and analyse how women learn to save for and build their own homes in a community context. It also seeks to show how these processes of learning have contributed to the social construction of knowledge and to the achievements of Victoria Mxenge Housing Development Association (VM). The article describes one social learning event in this process—a mass meeting organised by VM in an informal black settlement known as Imizamo Yethu (Our Striving) that has mushroomed in Hout Bay, Cape Town. This is the paradise land of rich white South Africans situated on lush mountain slopes between harbour and farmland.

Qualitative research methods such as observations, individual and group interviews, and a video recording of the mass meeting were used for gathering data. The analysis seeks to identify the critical educational strategies used by VM and to discuss how VM's philosophical and political perspectives translate into different forms and traditions of learning, advocacy, and social action. In this project the approach to gender and development is populist and people-centered, as the leadership claims that the model has developed from ordinary people's actual experience of development projects. The focus is on the empowerment of poor people; it emphasizes the values and interests of marginalized people and is in favour of decentralised, self-managed modes of organization. The leadership draws on populist views of development from the South (Wignaraja 1993) and argue that they do not subscribe to one grand and glorious development meta-theory and that they avoid being dogmatic. They further argue that development must result in relevant development praxis, which is concerned with an overall improvement in poor people's quality of life as well as with control of resources and sustainable forms of living that conserve land, energy, and progressive cultural systems that do not undermine and oppress either women or men. The pedagogical approach of the South African Homeless People's Federation, VM's supporting organization, combines popular and feminist pedagogy, as the core orientation to learning is that learning is participatory and valorises local knowledge. This form of learning affirms adult education principles in that it starts from where the people are situated and works to develop a broader understanding of structures and how these can be transformed. The education is positioned to support the struggles of women in oppressed communities (Walters and Manicom 1996).

South Africa faces a huge problem in redressing the backlog of housing needs, which is the legacy of the apartheid policies and is exacerbated by the problems in delivery on the part of the new government.[1] This problem is compounded by rapid urbanisation evidenced in the growth of 1,088 informal settlements throughout the country (Tabane and Sefara 2003). Housing and land are inextricably linked, and the redress of one affects the other. The local authorities have made very little inner-city land available for housing the poor. Since the democratic election in 1994 only 2 percent of the land has been redistributed (Tabane and Sefara 2003). The visible implications of this are overcrowding in the townships and rapid growth of informal settlements on the outskirts, which in turn lead to conflict, land invasions, rampant child abuse, and crime.

In this project's populist model of development, the constituency owns the development process and they are party to decision making and to setting goals. Members act using the democratic process and act on the basis that the state has an obligation towards poor people. There is a strong emphasis in the project on citizenship, participation, and redistributive justice.

Description of the VM project

VM is being held up as a model social development project of the South African Homeless People's Federation and has taken a leadership position in Cape Town in advocating for its model of housing delivery. The organization is based in Philippi, Cape Town, and it has a membership of 251 women and 5 men.[2]

Many women in the project have some schooling; this varies from two or three to eight or more years of schooling. They have migrated from poor rural areas, and have lived under African customary laws, in particular the principle that the male is the head of the household and that women have no right to own land. They live on the outskirts of the city in often hostile environments. Their main sources of income are domestic work, selling fruit and vegetables, and providing child care. Under the apartheid government, the communities where these women live were regarded as illegal and therefore the state provided no housing or basic services to the communities. The VM women have a long history of struggle for basic services. They have suffered constant forced removals by the apartheid state and vigilante groups, and now criminal elements threaten their new homes.

Through another South African nongovernmental organization (NGO) called People's Dialogue,[3] VM formed linkages with similar NGOs in India, Brazil, and Philippines. The members have successfully pooled their resources and have realised their dreams of financing, building, and owning their own homes. The women have built houses in their community and more than 800 houses for other Federation savings groups and a community centre, which includes a crèche, a shop, and the offices of VM.

The standard model of housing delivery for the poor is to build with a state housing subsidy. The normal procedure is to access the subsidy through a developer. This usually means that most of the subsidy is paid to the developer, and the homeowners have to borrow more money to build their homes. Houses built by private developers tend to be small and identical, and there is very little involvement of the homeowner in the building process. The Federation provides an alternate model for housing delivery which seeks not only to address a housing need but also to redress poverty and create sustainable, cost-effective systems of development, which are people-controlled, not just people-centered. The VM organization poses significant challenges to the contractor-driven model for housing. In the VM model, the homeowners become the developers and are involved in all the decision-making processes, from financing, to design, to building their own homes. Their participation continues beyond housing delivery and is characterised by participation in other activities, which will sustain the community.

VM's model of saving schemes, participatory decision-making, and control from the bottom up has resulted in more than just building houses. It has provided a foundation on which a learning community has been built. VM's slogan emphasises the importance of this foundation: "We are not only building houses but people and communities." Previous research (Ismail 1999) suggests that VM projects have lessons to offer the state and community housing initiatives in South Africa. These include how to secure subsidies given the tedious bureaucratic process; how to build within the state subsidy and construct a bigger and better-quality product than most private developers can; and how to ensure that during this process each person has acquired skills, such as bricklaying, financial managing, and negotiation and has the potential to enter the formal or informal economy. The objective is not only to build houses but also to empower the poor and to build learning communities.

Saving for Change

The Federation model is publicized mainly through the formation of housing savings schemes. Small groups of about twenty women form a savings scheme. The women in the group save any amount on a daily basis; each member of the group has a responsibility to save. Within the group someone will be nominated to keep a record of the savings of each member. The women come together on a weekly basis to check the records, to see who is contributing regularly, to learn who attends and participates in the meetings, and also to scrutinize the record keeping. The women's savings are then deposited with Federation bookkeepers. In this way women learn to save, to keep records of their savings, and to trust the group effort. Saving is one of the most important of all the practices in this social movement. These savings groups form the lifeblood of the Federation, as it is in this way that the organization grows and sustains itself.

Some members describe their understanding of the practice of saving in the following ways: Veliswa, who in 1996 was the technical advisor says, "Savings schemes collect people, and they collect resources, so when we negotiate with the government we come with resources in our hands." Xoliswa, who was the savings co-coordinator in 1996 says that the saving scheme is a "breath of life, the pulse, the glue that keeps people together; it's a strong idea and links with savings practices within African communities. People have been saving for funerals, weddings since they were unable to access credit from banks due to apartheid laws and today, by being poor". Rose Maso, who was the building supervisor in 1996, says, "Bank managers don't know us, the people in the savings scheme do know us. They come from our community and they are our people; they know where I live and when my daughter is sick." Xoliswa says, "The daily collectors are like social workers. They see the situation of every house and then we hear who is sick and who is in need of work. It is in the groups where all the problems are heard and can be potentially solved."[4]

Members devote a lot of energy to promoting, reviving, and refining the scheme. There are three kinds of savings operating that allow members access to low interest credit: the crisis savings, from which money can be borrowed for funerals; the income-generating savings, from which money can be borrowed to set up stalls to sell produce; the housing savings scheme (group savings plus money from foreign donors), from which loans for housing are made.

Finding New Solutions: A Case Study

One of the strategies the Federation uses is to train the women in the savings group to build a model house to put on display and to host a mass meeting with all the relevant stakeholders. The stakeholders in this case are the local councilor, the mayor, the chairperson from the all-white residents' association, the local and provincial administrative authorities from the housing board and land committees, national and regional Federation members, and local and national savings group members. "The mass meeting and the model house display are used as a way of celebrating, to mark a milestone and say that this savings group is ready to build its own homes [and that they] need land and resources from the State" (Asian Coalition for Housing Rights 2000, 6).

The Federation nominated VM to support and strengthen the savings group in the informal settlement of Imizamo Yethu (IY) in Hout Bay. The IY savings group forms a small part of this settlement and has a membership of women. Most of the people living in this settlement have no rights to the land because they have migrated here from rural areas and have no money to purchase this land.

Preparation Before the Meeting

Preparation for the mass meeting stirs up a lot of excitement amongst the members of the savings groups. The women's confidence and energy increase as a number of arrangements and details have to be finalized. First, they have to secure a plot of land from the local authority to build the model house to show to the community and public officials, in particular, the state representatives. During this week, the building of the model house is used as an opportunity to train the savings group on surveying the housing needs of the savings group and designing their dream houses. The women also learn the most important steps in design and house building. The training and building of the model houses bring together a critical mass of learners, and demonstrate a collective commitment, challenging the belief that poor women have no skills. Moreover this process shows that women can acquire knowledge that was exclusive to professionals and experts. It emphasizes that what poor women don't have is space and monetary resources to use to support and refine their skills.

VM and local savings scheme members erect a huge tent because there is no building to hold the meeting. They also hire chairs, tables, and a sound system, prepare food for the visitors, and inform the national television station of the event to secure news coverage. They furnish the model house and collect data to present at the meeting, such as the cost of building the house and sketches of the house plans.

During this week of preparations they host the national representatives of the South African Homeless People's Federation members who travel down from the different provinces, including providing for Federation members' accommodation and food. VM involve Federation members in the ongoing activities of the organization, such as finalizing the program and confirming the invitations for speakers at the meeting. These exchanges allow community leaders to meet, talk, and see what other poor people are doing. The exchanges begin an education that allows the leaders to explore the lives and situations of other people and to pick up ideas that may be useful back home. This process builds trust and partnerships where teaching and learning from each other become quite natural. It is a key strategy for education and mobilization of the poor by the poor (Asian Coalition for Housing Rights 2000).

The Mass Meeting and Model House Display

The mass meeting brings together a number of different stakeholders, to ensure that different groups are represented. The purpose of the meeting is to show concretely what poor women can achieve and to advocate for more land and finances for the poor.

A number of educational tactics are used in this mass meeting, such as a march through the settlement in which women carry banners and sing and shout slogans. The singing continues throughout the meeting. The women sing various hymns and traditional songs, which they often combine with protest songs from the liberation movement and new protest songs from the Federation. They sing about the hardships of living in shacks, especially how they are prone to fires, rain, and evictions. The women clearly want proper houses, land, and an increase in the state housing subsidy. Their slogan is "We want power, knowledge and money." There is also dancing. The membership and visitors are attired in traditional or smart clothes, which signify the importance of the meeting and the audience. Iris, the host of ceremonies, brings humor to the meeting by acting as a provocateur, interpreter, and facilitator and she keeps the audience interested and attentive. An example of this is when she asks the government officials to add their voices to the meeting when the women sing their songs, or when she lambastes them for not doing enough to house poor women.

The technical and publicity documentation that VM has collected are displayed in the model house. This house has separate rooms, such as a kitchen, bedroom, and so forth—important features, because houses built by developers usually have only one central room. This display is a powerful demonstration of women's planning and mobilizing tools, and it makes effective evidence for bargaining in negotiations to secure land tenure and for approval of development plans. The climax of the meeting is when the parliamentary official cuts the ribbon to the model houses. This act symbolizes the state's approval of the model of delivery and the product.[5]

In a climate of rising costs, growing unemployment, and declining real social and welfare expenditures, there is an inevitable growth of informal settlements. However, the sustainability of houses built by community-based projects is under threat. The women of VM continuously develop new strategies for survival and new relationships with NGOs and the state for support in this uncertain climate.

Their optimism and vision of building houses and communities are directly linked to their successful integration of education and development. Through their activities everyone is learning continuously, and the knowledge of the basic principles is widespread and has helped to create local leaders. Personal confidence has grown amongst the leadership and this has encouraged them to continue and not to be discouraged by the slowness of the process. The VM women are strongly driven by the need to offer their children decent places to grow up and thrive.

Analysis: Learning in a Framework of Gender and Development

The central question in understanding development in this context is, How does the social action of VM relate and contribute to different theories of adult education, feminist pedagogy, and development? There are many and varied definitions of development, gender, and feminism. These include the idea that feminism is a method of analysis whose central concern is the social distinction between men and women (Mitchell and Oakley 1976, cited in Roberts 1984, 185). In African gender politics, "feminism is the popular struggle of African women for their liberation from various forms of oppression they endure" (Mama 1995, 38). Socialist feminists argue that feminist methods conceptualise gender divisions as a set of social relations. Gender relations, it is argued by some, are distinct from those of class but are, however, embedded in the social relations of production and reproduction in that the subordination of women serves the interests of capitalism as well as those of patriarchy (Roberts 1984, 175). Feminism is "the awareness of the oppression, exploitation and or conscious subordination of women within society and the conscious action to change and transform this situation" (Reddock 1986, 53).

These definitions represent different approaches to the inequality of women in society and are pertinent in a society such as that of South Africa, wherein patriarchy and capitalist relations oppress women. The strength of these definitions in the South African context is that they stress multiple systems of oppression including not only class and gender but also race and ethnicity. The postmodernist definitions have criticised other feminisms for failing to emphasise the plurality of women's experiences, identities, and constructions of realities. These critiques are important in any consideration of social action, as they highlight the fact that men and women are not homogenous groups who will naturally act in the interests of the group. Third World feminism as expounded by Maria Mies (1986 in Youngman 2000) has also pointed out the negative impact of structural adjustment programmes on women's economic and social situation and provides an important influence on populist models of development. In Mies's proposals of alternative models of self-sufficient development, she considers small-scale models of development rooted in indigenous practices and survival struggles of grassroots movements (Youngman 2000, 144–47).

The VM women do not necessarily see themselves as feminists but rather as protectors of the family and community. In their songs, they sing of women as mothers of the nation. This must be seen in the particular circumstances of apartheid and traditional South African culture rather than as a statement of domesticity that one might find elsewhere. The role of the mother was politicised during apartheid, as men were largely absent from the home working as migrant labour, or were absent due to state repression.

African women's activism can be compared to Pnina Werbner's (1999, 221–40) descriptions of motherhood movements that valorise maternal qualities. In these movements, women capture the moral high ground because their members' mixed agenda and embeddedness in local traditions enable them to mobilise ordinary women on a vast scale and attain a measure of autonomy. The VM women do not see their organization as threatening to men, yet their activism has been of concern to their husbands and partners and sometimes threatens the delicate power balance of relationships. These men are aware that their wives are skilled and knowledgeable, as they have built the houses. This creates a tacit understanding that relationships, expectations, and the demands made of each other have changed. For instance, VM women say that they can now talk about contraception and family planning with their husbands and partners.

The definition of development used in this organization incorporates broader constructs. "It calls for people to look for alternatives from below so as to ensure that societies answer the needs of people" (Clarke 1991, 19). The ingredients of this alternative view include development of infrastructure, economic growth, poverty alleviation, equity, natural resource protection, democracy, and social justice. The people-centered/populist approach described by Clarke is oriented to meeting basic needs, and it concerns linkages between local and national people, bureaucrats, and intermediaries in project choice, planning, and implementation. It is also committed to valuing local knowledge and solutions to problems, using local resources, fostering self-reliance, and addressing not only projects but also overall development policies (Sen and Grown 1987). This approach to development is also common in many social movements and resonates with most feminist approaches to women in development.

In this model, development is seen as a continuous process. It begins with a critique of power and stresses participation of the community in planning, choosing, criticizing, and having control over the development process. There is a process of empowerment, which aims to help communities enhance their own contribution to addressing their basic needs. The people-centered approach lays its emphasis on the richness of people rather than their poverty, and their potential for action rather than their role as recipients of development aid. It gives back agency to individuals, groups, and communities whose actions can take a diverse range of forms that can impact at the local, national, and international levels. This approach also gives human action and consciousness a central role in development.

The development literature (Sen and Grown 1987; Rowbotham and Mitter 1994) that locates gender in the present era of globalisation and postmodernism argues that if the goals of development include improved living standards and the removal of poverty, then it is quite natural to start with the poor and therefore with women. Women, it is argued, are the majority of the poor and suffer more because of additional burdens placed on them through gender-biased hierarchies and subordination by men. Women in many poor communities are solely responsible for child care, food production, and sanitation, and their labour is dominant in paying for household needs. Therefore, a woman's viewpoint is critical to any understanding of development strategies.

Other feminist scholars of development, such as Pearson and Jackson (1998,) take a different view, arguing that the above perspective on development buys into conventional ideas and mainstreams gender into development policies. For example, Pearson and Jackson assert that conflating the concerns of women with poverty alleviation falls short of an understanding of how men's and women's experiences differ according to the different constraints and responsibilities they face. Pearson and Jackson argue that "poverty refers to more than the level of household income and includes the context in which household survival takes place—the public space, access to services and opportunities for change—and that gender concerns are both mediated by poverty and transcend the poverty debate" (11).

Both viewpoints have relevance for African women, and rather than seeing them as antagonistic, it is important to be critical of the process that mainstreams gender into poverty alleviation. The key issue according to Rowbotham and Mitter (1994) is the extent to which poor women are able to gain greater control over social and economic conditions and more democratic power over state policies. Generally the South African state's development polices are gender blind, but government officials, the project leaders, and donors of the Federation have women as their primary target group. Historically in South Africa, as is still true today,[6] race, class, and gender inequalities intersect. Thus Black and African can be translated into the poor, and the most vulnerable of the poor are usually women and children. Overcoming these positions of weakness has never been easy but being organized makes women less vulnerable to oppressive forces (Rowbotham and Mitter 1994).

In the VM project, learning happens within a framework of popular education and strongly echoes feminist pedagogy. As said earlier, the pedagogy works towards consciousness raising, and it values working with women's experiences, local knowledge, collective decision-making, and participation at all levels of the program. The development practitioner comes in as an advisor and learns from the community to provide technical expertise in a nonauthoritarian way. There is usually a strong emphasis on making the curriculum relevant to the learners' context, on democratic decision-making, and on using participatory styles of learning. The concepts of learning and empowerment are central to improving the quality of the learners' lives. It is in different ways of learning that women in this case are creating new forms of social action and devising new strategies to demand basic needs like housing.

Learning in the VM project is used comprehensively to include technical, social, cultural, and political education. It can be formal, informal, deliberate, incidental, experiential, unplanned, and tacit, and it can be powerful (Foley 2001). Within this framework, indicators for empowerment are women's development of confidence, a sense of achievement, and self-reliance. This new consciousness allows women then to reflect on their situation and act to change oppressive gender and other social relations. In this process women learn that the political will for those in power to promote change depends in part on women to organise and demand change.

The women within the housing collective educated themselves to work in teams and learned to save, keep financial records, survey a community's needs, design their dream houses, measure and cost a house, and make bricks and build their own homes. Throughout the learning process the more experienced members led the groups. Between 1992, when Patricia Matolongwe started the housing collective and 1994, membership grew from 8 to 286 members, of whom 85 percent were women. The initial lessons of surveying, planning, and so forth, were learned from networks in India. Some of the first members, like Mama Msiza, learned to make bricks from local brick-making companies, and a builder in the community passed on his construction skills to the first group of women. The first building team helped to demystify the tasks ahead, and their efforts illustrated that poorly schooled women can build houses.

The VM women do not romanticize their learning or the arduous process of obtaining subsidies and building houses. They echo these words when they talk about their experiences, "Women learn as they struggle, they live their experience and these are complex and contested; their struggles and solutions involve ethical judgements and choices around which there is often conflict" (Foley 1999, 7). Women are the majority in leadership positions in the collective and many of the mediators encourage women to join the organization. This, together with the fact that the women have not constructed themselves as dependents of men, has disrupted traditional interpretations of gendered need and has attracted hostility from the target community. Patricia Matolengwe became the target of angry husbands who objected to her political involvement and the fact that she was an unmarried mother. She organised house meetings with the men and encouraged them to take an active interest in the savings scheme by pointing to the fact that in rural areas it is the women who build homes. This approach won their confidence and respect (Ismail 1998). The group approach has given women mutual support and a sense of solidarity to challenge discriminatory customary laws, and to gain the right of women to own land and to register their homes in their names.

Strong connections can be made between VM's learning through a development paradigm (Rogers 1992; Snyder and Tadesse 1995; Wignaraja 1993) based on a people's driven process and theories of experiential learning; informal learning; popular, social action learning; and feminist pedagogy (Freire 1972, 1983; Foley 1999; Rowbotham and Mitter 1994; Walters and Manicom 1996; Barr 1999). In these paradigms theorists argue that people learn from their own experience, and from dialogue and critical reflection, which lead to social action and solving problems. In VM learning is in action, in the activity of forming savings groups, learning to save, learning to dream about houses that women design and construct, learning from national and international exchanges. All of this learning is individual and collective. There is a shared experience of meaning in this action. There are direct links between this practice of learning and Wilder-meersch and Jansen's (1997) characterisation of social learning. The central concepts of social learning are problem solving involving processes of action, reflection, communication and cooperation, in which the different actors in the learning process intervene; issues of power, creativity and responsibility prevail throughout the process, as this project is action- and experience-directed. In solving problems, critical reflection is involved, and it is dialogical as well as multi-actor oriented.

Social action learning theorists draw heavily on Freire in their explanations of how learning occurs in social movements. Generally, women in social movements belong to a community and learn in struggle for the collective good and for the future of their children. In the action learning approach the participants learn mainly informally; they develop an understanding that guides practice. In this pedagogy the experiences of the learner occupies central place in all considerations of teaching and learning. Connections can also be made to Lave and Wenger's (1996, 150) theory that takes "learning to be participation in socially situated practices." VM's experience demonstrates that their pedagogy is about changing participation in "changing communities of practice." VM's pedagogy can be called feminist, although the members would not call themselves feminists, because the members see themselves as mothers and protectors of the family. The pedagogy is participatory, democratic, and nonhierarchical; it encourages creative thinking that breaks through embedded formats of learning. It strives to foster both personal and social empowerment (Walters and Manicom 1996).

The Federation calls this form of learning horizontal learning. They believe it is more equitable to learn in a collective in which the measurement is in the act of doing and of solving a problem. Each person and organization uses what works for them. The Federation believes very strongly that learning needs to be supported: therefore, all exchange visits and training are done in a collective. Learning is a collective and social process, and knowledge is a collective asset (Asian Coalition for Housing Rights 2000).

For the women in the project there is a qualitative difference between learning from peers and formal training. As one member of the collective says, "When you see ideas being put into practice by people as poor as you, it's powerful, you see possibilities that did not come from a textbook or an expert" (Asian Coalition for Housing Rights 2000, 6). In this way poor women become committed to learning how to build houses even if it takes a long time. Each participant feels responsible for her own learning, as it is through this process that she will secure finance, land, and housing. Learning is based on poor people's own learning systems, based on critical consciousness and learning what is relevant and useful in improving a situation and solving problems (Asian Coalition for Housing Rights, 2000).

The learning that occurs outside of institutions consists of a broad ensemble of activities, as witnessed in the mass meeting. In VM's campaigns they use common symbols and ritual, such as prayers, songs, and dress to create a shared meaning. This helps to "shift learning to its transformative power by pointing to possibilities that point to social action" (Wildermeersch and Jansen 1997, 468). These communities have shared histories of learning and they share their competence with new generations. For them learning is not about memory but about creating identities, and it is in a continuous process of negotiation with other poor communities. It is about creating rhythms and being human (Wenger 1998).

The women's experiences in the mass meetings produce stories, which enable people to critique and challenge the status quo. In these meetings and in the training and building of their homes, they unlearn dominant paradigms about their self-worth, gain a critical view of authority, and recognize their own ability to influence decision making. There are direct links between Freire's theories of reflection and action and the development of a critical consciousness and empowerment in these groups. "Critical consciousness is brought about, not through an intellectual effort alone but through praxis—through the authentic union of action-reflection" (Freire 1983, 87).

The organizational structure and the shared philosophy that poor women need each other support democratic participation. These systems regard everyone as a leader and part of the decision-making process. This is seen as the central concept of a people-centered development and is demonstrated in VM's pedagogy, in which women insist on using dialogue to solve problems and to find solutions. There is a sense that empowerment occurs through discussion and involvement of members in all the activities of the organization. The strategy of continuous training prevents the consolidation of resources in the hands of a few. In their struggle to gain resources the women constantly have to reflect and critique strategies, and in this way, too, they are empowered. This is illustrated in VM's acknowledgement of the women's ownership of their homes, which has shifted the gender balance in their homes. It has given them greater freedom of speech and movement, and the ability to participate in the organization's activities without their husband's permission (Ismail 1999). The culture in the organi-zation is sufficiently secure to allows "women to be confident and effec-tive . . . men do not feel threatened and work with women in authority" (Yasmin 1997, 204).

As a result of their experiences with builders, developers, and tech-nical support from local and provincial government, this community is cautious of academics and experts. In their interaction with typically male-dominated organizations, the VM women usually negotiate their plans in a group. In these negotiations they stress the necessity of work-ing from their own knowledge, seeing this as the discourse of the poor that presents a challenge to the mainstream. This strategy echoes that of Freire (1983). Wendy Luttrell (in Barr 1999, 108) distinguishes between common sense knowledge and school-wise intelligence, that is, between knowledge produced through experience and knowledge available from textbooks written by experts. In her study of working-class women, she notes that the women shared similar ideas about their common sense abilities to care for others and regarded common sense as a way of judging truth. Luttrell suggests that the claim to have com-mon sense knowledge—for example, relying on friends who know the ropes, seeking advice from people who can be trusted, not because they are professional experts but because they share the same problems—recognises and validates working-class solutions to problems despite the power of scientific knowledge. Barr (1999) argues that this knowl-edge—which developed in the collective and is born out of practice—is often more trusted than expert knowledge. The VM women help and empower others by listening and understanding or by teaching others what they know from their own common sense and from building their own homes, and this experience gives them more confidence.

In this populist model, learning is connected to helping women "toward community, power, and integrity. Such an education facilitates the development of women's minds and spirits" (Belenky et al. 1986, 228). Patricia Collins reflects on the way that black women claim their knowledge as "motherwit" or wisdom. This knowledge, she says, comes from the ability to work hard and get material things they need with-out a man's support (Barr 1999, 108–111).

The women experience some systematic education and transfer of cognitive skills and knowledge in learning to build a house. The teaching is based on sound adult education principles that start from the knowledge of the participant. The trainer starts off with the per-son's knowledge and slowly includes new strategies for teaching more complex measurement and procedures. The trainer uses visual and physical measurements within the new homeowners' understanding and costs it according to these understandable measurements (People's Dialogue 1994, 6). This lengthy process must be accurate. Thus, knowledge in this project is created in a collective process and in this process new kinds of knowledge, ideas, and relationships develop. VM's pedagogy and their emphasis on knowledge production, as is evidenced in their slogan "We want Power, Knowledge and Money," reflect Eyerman and Jamison's (1991) account of cognitive praxis in a social movement—that knowledge is central, its creation is a collective process, that activists learn by doing, and that learning cannot be measured by what is in people's heads. This way of learning, Eyerman and Jamieson inform us, is the core of a social movement's cognitive practice and identity.

How do VM women determine what is learned, how it is learned, and how to assess the role of learning in reaching development goals? There are no easy answers to these questions, as the women's learning is difficult to measure, and a range of issues affects the learning process both positively and negatively. Lessons produced by this study were that learning and consciousness raising were not straightforwardly incremental and that these were difficult, ambiguous, and contested concepts. Moreover, we saw that learning and development is not linear and that cumulative skills often develop in unanticipated ways. Assessment occurs through both qualitative and quantitative measurements, in terms of the quality and number of houses built, the amount of land secured, the savings collected, the stability and security of the community, the impact of the group on the state's housing policy, the women's control over resources, and the personal development of their membership (Ismail 1999). VM women evaluate and monitor themselves by their slogan "We build houses, people and communities."

Generally in the literature on adult education, women in development, and social movements, women belong to a community and learn in struggle for the collective good and for the future of their children. In the development literature there is a strong emphasis on women's empowerment to challenge gender relations, women's access to resources, and women as the central agent in development, as the women are the caregivers, toil the soil, and generally keep the family intact. There is a strong emphasis on the ownership of the process, learning in a collective, keeping the learning people-driven, and ownership of the knowledge by the participants. The experiences of VM illustrate these emphases and demonstrate that it is possible in the changed political situation of South Africa to create a social movement that speaks with the language of hope and possibility.

NOTES

I would like to thank the women of VM for their time and patience and the National Research Foundation of South Africa who provided financial assisstance for the research.

1. The latest estimation of the numbers of homeless in South Africa is 7 million. In Cape Town alone there is a backlog of 220,000 houses. A recent study has shown that each year 10,000 new individuals pour into the city from the Eastern Cape and move into existing settlements (Ashley Smith, *Cape Times* July 27, 2002).

2. The South African Homeless People's Federation (SAHPF) was established in 1994 and has a membership of 30,000. It grew out of a network of savings schemes with a focus on making credit available for development and involves mainly women.

3. People's Dialogue on Land and Shelter is a nongovernmental organization that explores ways in which support can be given to homeless urban dwellers internationally so that they can address their own housing needs. VM has formed linkages with the slum dwellers association in India (Mahila Milan,) with homeless organizations in Brazil (Cearah Periferia), and with an urban homeless people's organization in the Philippines (The Lupang Pangako Urban Poor Association). The People's Dialogue facilitates exchanges between the different homeless savings groups nationally and internationally.

4. From interviews with Xoliswa Tiso, Rose Maso, and Veliswa Mbeki in July 1996.

5. Because of the success of the Federation's and other NGOs' models of housing provision the state has shifted its own policies to include more enabling finance legislation, identify more land for urban use, and pledge its support for a people's housing process.

6. South Africa has an economically active population of 13.8 million, of whom 4.7 million are unemployed (34 percent); unemployment is particularly acute amongst Africans, particularly African women (South African Survey 1999).

REFERENCES

Asian Coalition for Housing Rights. 2000. *Face to Face: Notes from the Network on Community Exchange.* January. Bangkok: Asian Coalition for Housing Rights.

Barr, J. 1999. *Liberating Knowledge, Research, Feminism and Adult Education.* London: National Organization for Adult Learning.

Belenky, M. F, et al. 1986. *Women's Ways of Knowing, the Development of Self, Voice and Mind.* New York: Basic Books.

Clarke, J. 1991. *Democratizing Development.* Bristol: Guernsey Press.

Eyerman, R., and A. Jamieson. 1991. *Social Movements: A Cognitive Approach.* London: Bristol.

Foley, G. 1999. *Learning in Social Action: A Contribution to Understanding Informal Education.* London, Zed Books.

————. 2001. *Strategic Learning: Understanding and Facilitating Organizational Change.* Sydney: Centre for Popular Education.

Freire, P. 1972. *Cultural Action for Freedom.* Hammondsworth: Penguin.

————. 1983. *Pedagogy of the Oppressed.* New York: Continuum.

Ismail, S. 1998. "When Women Take Control: Exploring the Social Activism of the Victoria Mxenge Housing Development Association in Meeting the Need for Shelter." *Agenda* (38):51-62.

————. 1999. An Evaluation of the Victoria Mxenge Housing Development Association from a Gender Perspective." In *Breaking Through,* ed. C. Mendel-Anonuevo. Hamburg: UNESCO.

Mama, A. 1995. "Feminism or Femocracy? State Feminism and Democratisation." *Nigeria in African Development* 20(91): 37–58.

Pearson, R., and C. Jackson. 1998. "Interrogating Development, Feminism, Gender and Policy." In *Feminist Visions of Development,* eds. C. Jackson and R. Pearson. London: Routledge.

People's Dialogue. 1994. "Regaining Knowledge, An appeal to Abandon Illusions: Innovative Community-Based Shelter Training Programmes." September, Cape Town, People's Dialogue.

Reddock, R. 1986. "Feminism and Feminist Thought: An Historical Overview." In *Feminism and Nationalism in the Third World,* ed. N. Jayawardna. London: Zed Books.

Roberts, P. 1984. "Feminism in Africa: Feminism and Africa." *Review of African Political Economy,* 175–184.

Rogers, A. 1992. *Adults Learning for Development.* London: Cassel.

Rowbotham, S., and S. Mitter. 1994. *Dignity and Daily Bread.* London: Routledge.

Sen, G., and C. Grown. 1987. *Development Alternatives with Women for a New Era.* London: Earthscan.

Smith, A. 2002. *Cape Times* [daily independent newspaper, Cape Town], 27 July.

Snyder, M. C., and M. Tadesse. 1995. *African Women and Development—A History.* London: Zed Books.

South African Survey. 1999. *Millennium Edition on Land, Housing and Unemployment.* Braamfontein: Institute of Race Relations, 147-155

Tabane, R., and M. Sefara. 2003. "Comment on the HSRC Report." *Cape Times,* 23 April.

Walters, S., and L. Manicom. 1996. *Gender in Popular Education.* London: Zed Books.

Wenger, E. 1998. *Communities of Practice, Learning, Meaning, and Identity.* Cambridge, U.K.: Cambridge University Press.

Werbner, P. 1999. "Political Motherhood and the Feminisation of Citizenship: Women's Activisms and the Transformation of the Public Sphere." In *Women and Citizenship and Difference,* eds. N. Yural-Davis and P. Werbner. London: Zed Books.

Wignaraja, P., ed. 1993. *New Social Movements in the South—Empowering People.* London: Zed Books.

Wildermeersch, D., and T. Jansen. 1997. "Strengths and Limitations of Social Learning as a Key Concept for Adult and Continuing Education in

Reflexive Modernity." In *Proceedings of the 27th Annual Scrutrea Conference, Birbeck College, London,* eds. P. Armstrong, N. Miller, and M. Zukas. London: Birbeck College Press.

Yasmin, T. 1997. *"What Is Different About Women's Organizations?"* In *Getting Institutions Right for Women in Development,* ed. A. M. Goetz. London: Zed Books.

Youngman, F. 2000. *The Political Economy of Adult Education and Development.* London: Zed Books.

Salma Ismail *is a lecturer at the Center for Higher Education and Development at the University of Cape Town, South Africa. She convenes and teaches for the Programme for the Advanced Certificate for Adult Education, and she assists faculty with staff development and equity research. She is currently doing research for a doctoral degree in the processes of teaching and learning among women in a low-cost, community-based housing project.*

Poor Women in Peru

Reproducers of Poverty and Poverty Relievers

Jelke Boesten

Between 1990 and 2000 in Peru, the Fujimori government justified governmental social programs directed at poor women with discourses regarding both the development and emancipation of women. In presenting these social programs, the government combined internationally promoted discourses of integration and equity in development practices with traditional notions of womanhood. On the one hand, the government saw women as being responsible for the biological reproduction of a social reality; they were mothers of the poor. On the other hand, the government represented women as guardians of the survival of the family and the community alike.[1] The state used these popular images of what a woman is to treat poor, mainly indigenous or mestiza women both as reproducers of poverty in population programs and as poverty relievers in food distribution programs. By examining a minute book of a grassroots women's organization in Ayacucho, a region in the southern Andes and one of the poorest in Peru, I will show in this article how poverty relief programs were implemented and how women used their roles as mothers to expand their agency in a society in which social relations are over-proportionally built on divisions of gender, ethnicity, and class.

When examining the relation between developmental and emancipatory discourses in the promotion of social programs directed at women during the Fujimori administration, we will see that a modern rhetoric of equity was used for developmental purposes. The scholar Naila Kabeer argues that women's empowerment to achieve gender equality as an end in itself has politically weak winners and powerful losers. As such, developmentalist arguments for gender equality "would offer policy makers the possibility of achieving familiar and approved goals albeit by unfamiliar means."[2] In Kabeer's argument, gender equality and development are equally important and equally pursued within the policy arena, although under a developmentalist discourse. However, as I will argue in the first part of this article, the Peruvian state has pursued developmental goals under the disguise of women's emancipation, instead of the other way around, as Kabeer proposes.

In the second part of this article, I will show what the role of targeted women was in the construction of womanhood in government policies and how women and the state used these constructions in practice. Women were not just "victims" of the government's developmental interests, but negotiated with local authorities over resources and the power to control those resources. Possibilities for agency did often depend on the agency of others—such as governmental institutions or the municipality—and their deployment of power. Women's agency is analyzed within its context, on the assumption that agency does not exist outside of existing social realities and hierarchies, but is shaped by them.[3]

As a number of scholars have pointed out, neoliberal governments, supported by World Bank and International Monetary Fund policies, devolved many social responsibilities to nongovernmental organizations (NGOs).[4] In the case of many so-called Third World countries, this did not solve social problems, as NGOs do not have the capacity to reform or structurally carry out state responsibilities such as health care, education, or justice. Nor can they enforce the law.[5] Still, neoliberalism contributed to the "NGOization" of civil movements, such as feminist organizations, and also of grassroots women's movements that took over social responsibilities of the state.[6] In a sense, the alliance between NGOs and grassroots women's movements reproduced old hierarchies and inequalities between groups of people, as differences in class, education, and ethnicity were at the heart of those alliances. However, as I will show, the NGOs were and are also an alternative source for information, training, resources, and even justice.[7]

To highlight the character of the policies of the Fujimori administration, I will first examine how and why the government targeted women. Second, I will show how social programs functioned in practice through a case study on food distribution programs. The experiences of women are analyzed through a minute book of a large women's organization based in the Andean city of Ayacucho for the years 1995–99. These findings are complemented with discussion of personal conversations with women conducted in 2000–2002 in Lima and in Ayacucho.

Women and Social Policies in Peru

Social hierarchies steeped in discrimination based on ethnicity, class, and gender have made Peru an unequal society in which some groups are more vulnerable than others. Full citizenship is not available for all Peruvians; large parts of the population are excluded from social services, such as proper education, health care, and even water and electricity; from free political participation, as clientalism and electoral manipulation are widespread; and from justice, as many police officers and judges are prejudiced and corrupt.

To cover basic necessities that were not provided by the state, beginning in the late 1960s, poor women in urban migrant communities and rural areas alike organized themselves in *comedores populares* (soup kitchens) and *clubes de madres* (mothers' clubs) to alleviate the consequences of economic crises by cooking and taking care of small children and sick family members communally. Migrant women from the provinces who settled in urban slums not only organized their household tasks together but also fought to obtain social services and neighborhood infrastructure.

These well-structured women's organizations became a target for charity and state programs. Just as church-based charities had an interest in the souls of people, political parties had an interest in the votes of people. First ladies of the nation would distribute foodstuff and kitchen utensils to women's organizations in poor neighborhoods during election time. These sporadic and paternalist campaigns were not devoid of attempts to do good by "civilizing" the poor. For example, Violeta Correa de Belaúnde, first lady of Peru between 1963 and 1968, personally visited the settlement of San Martín de Porres, Lima, and organized a contest among women's organizations. Those women who could show the cleanest houses, even the cleanest children, would receive sewing machines, cooking utilities, or food.[8]

Since the 1970s, governments have sought to bind women's organizations to the ruling party. For example, under the military government of General Juan Velasco Alvarado (1968–75), a state institution was appointed to supervise all donations and social projects, limiting the freedom of people to seek funding and support without interference of the state. During the government of Alan García (1985–90), only organizations that were members of his party were recognized and received donations from the state. In the same period, a municipal program was set up that guaranteed a daily glass of milk to all children under the age of six. The fact that the *vaso de leche* (glass of milk) program was not under the auspices of the state offered more continuity to the beneficiaries. However, special mothers' committees were set up to distribute the milk, an arrangement that generated confusion and competition among the women's organizations. As we will see, the program's independence from the state has not prevented manipulation of the women's *vaso de leche* committees either. Thus, from the beginning, women's organizations have had to negotiate levels of autonomy.

When Fujimori came to power in 1990, the country was socially, economically, and politically bankrupt as a result of huge inflation and the devastating war initiated by Shining Path in 1980. Shining Path, originally a Maoist political party, emerged as an extremely violent opponent of any existent social structure holding the country in terror, especially its poor urban and rural sectors in Ayacucho and since the late 1980s also in Lima. To deal with these problems, Fujimori created an authoritarian-populist rule with a flavor of democracy. The new president promised to "give back" democracy to the people; no white elite, no patriarch would govern the people of Peru, but he, as a personal hero, would liberate the people.[9] From the start, Fujimori used a rhetoric of social integration and emancipation. Despite his promises, the new president started his governmental period with severe economic measures, which stabilized the economy but also impoverished the population. However, several economic and social achievements—not to mention the dismantling of Shining Path by the capture of its leader, Abimael Guzman, in 1992—gave Fujimori large support from society. Fujimori also used his mandate to create a system of unprecedented control over society. After a "self"-coup in 1992, the judiciary system, the military, the police, and large parts of the media were controlled by the president and his secret service.[10]

The economic shock of 1990 worsened the situation of the poor. The government needed to secure popular support by alleviating the situation of the majority of the people. To achieve this, Fujimori institutionalized the "sporadic and paternalistic" support given to grassroots women's organizations by setting up a permanent institution for food distribution, the National Program of Foodstuff Support, PRONAA. In doing so, the government converted temporary poverty relief into a structural practice that depended entirely on the voluntary work of women. By 1995, at least 76,300 grassroots women's organizations provided food to 25 percent of the population, contributing almost 5 million U.S. dollars to the economy.[11]

Following the World Conference on Women held in Beijing in 1995—where the only male head of state present was the Peruvian president—Fujimori created the Ministry for the Promotion of Women and Human Development, PROMUDEH. Under the rhetoric of gender equality and the "promotion of women" on the one hand and the importance of mothers in development on the other, PROMUDEH was given the responsibility for most social programs.[12] Although the emphasis on women's emancipation had various positive effects on the position of women in legislation and political representation, poverty-relief–related programs under the auspices of

PROMUDEH failed to stimulate equality between the sexes or between classes and ethnicities.[13]

At the same time the government created the National Population Program under the auspices of the Ministry of Health. This program was to reduce population growth by reducing the high fertility rates among poor and mainly rural families. At Beijing, just before the Peruvian population program was vigorously implemented, Fujimori stressed the importance of women's right to make decisions regarding their own bodies and the necessity of providing access to reproductive health-care services for women of all classes. The discourse with which Fujimori justified these policies fitted neatly within national and international discourses of development and women's emancipation. However, by 1998 the family planning program had to be stopped after accusations of sterilizations forced upon poor and mainly indigenous women.[14]

In its promotion material, PROMUDEH is described as follows: "A ministry for the woman. To appreciate her, to support her, and to promote her development and that of her family; to give her the primordial place in our society and in the political and economic development of the country that she deserves." The leaflet stresses the important role that women play in the development of the nation. PROMUDEH was created, the leaflet says, "as gratitude to her invaluable support." The promotion leaflet also states that the ministry will work for "a world of equity." However, this world of equity is based on a maternalist discourse of development and on the role that women played, are playing, and should play as "natural" mothers and caretakers of the family and the community. In effect, the pictures in the leaflet resemble the images that international development agencies use to encourage the Western world to donate money; the front page shows a poor but enchanting indigenous girl with a dirty face and hanging mucus. The whole leaflet radiates the government's commitment to reduce poverty with the support of Peruvian mothers, not its commitment to the promotion of women as autonomous beings.[15]

Food Distribution

The aim of the food distribution program, PRONAA, was to improve the level of nourishment of the most critical groups in society. The target groups of the program were children under the age of six, pregnant and breastfeeding mothers, old people, and victims of "temporal situations of emergency."[16] Law 25307, issued in 1991, legalized PRONAA's activities. This law stated that women's organizations would receive the bulk of the foodstuff to be handed out to the other target groups, as community-based women's organizations had the infrastructure to do the distribution. Additionally, the women's organizations would receive kitchen utensils, support in the "integral development of woman," technical assistance, literacy campaigns in rural areas, and financial support for the *comedores populares* of Lima and Callao.[17] To avoid political manipulation, the women's organizations would be approached as independent *organizaciones sociales de base,* (grassroots social organizations), which would ensure the political autonomy of the women involved. As we will see, autonomy was not guaranteed, nor was technical or educational assistance given, and the "integral development of woman" proved hard to find.

As several scholars have shown, PRONAA, like other governmental social programs, was used for political purposes. The increases of state spending on social programs prior to elections were notorious.[18] Foodstuff came with aprons and cooking hats in orange, the color of Fujimori's movement, and with the PRONAA logo, and there was the obligation to paint the kitchen with state-issued orange paint and put PRONAA on the kitchen's façade. A large picture of the hero of the nation, Alberto Fujimori, had to be hung on the façade of the building as well. Of course, loyalty to the government was enforced by the threat—made real when necessary—of the withdrawal of alimentary support.[19]

Women and Poverty Relief: Ayacucho

The district of Ayacucho has a history of severe political violence, as it was the center of the war between Shining Path and the army from 1980 to 1994. The department of Ayacucho is located in the high Andes, and many of its communities are difficult to reach. The majority of the population is Quechua-speaking and lives on family- or community-run agriculture. Geographic inaccessibility, poverty, and weak presence of the state made the department amenable to guerrilla warfare. Survival became increasingly difficult. The local economy was severely affected by the war, and many people left their rural communities to settle in urban areas, fleeing from violence and poverty.

Women in Ayacucho organized themselves during the war in *clubes de madres* to create safety nets around themselves and their families. They coordinated hiding places for family members at risk—adolescents and men—leaving the elderly in the communities and taking the youngest ones to travel around the region to keep kinship and refugee networks going. They organized searches for the disappeared, coordinated information on the dead and detained, and exchanged information on rights and legal mechanisms. According to Isabel Coral, who studied and worked with the women of Ayacucho for many years, the women's organizations created one of the strongest opposition networks against the violence in the region during the late 1980s.[20]

The women needed solid networks of information and support to coordinate their resistance to the war and to increase their safety. Hence, in 1988 the first provincial federation of *clubes de madres* was set up in the city of Ayacucho, a move that was soon followed by all provinces in the department of Ayacucho.[21] In 1991, these provincial federations united under a departmental federation, the Federación Departamental de Clubes de Madres de Ayacucho (FEDECMA). By 1995, this federation united eleven provincial federations, 1,400 *clubes de madres,* and approximately 80,000 women.[22]

The Minute Book

When I spoke with Vilma Ortega, president of the FEDECMA, in 2001, she explained that the women's organizations worked mainly in secrecy during the years of war. Vilma remembered that she and other women carried their minute book, hidden in their clothes, all over the province to be able to reach as many people as possible.[23] Unfortunately, the minute books of the years of war were not available to me as they have been lost or are perhaps still in "hiding." What I did get to study was the minute book of the years 1995–99.[24] This is the book of the Federación de Clubes de Madres de la Provincia de Huamanga (FECMA), which is one organizational level below the FEDECMA. The minute book is a record of meetings with the "bases", which include *comedores populares* and *vaso de leche* program committees, and *clubes de madres.*[25] The book also contains records of meetings with local officials and program executors, such as mayors and program administrators, and with benevolent lawyers and NGO workers.

In the minute book the Federation's members referred to themselves as needy mothers. Although the women's organizations emphasized their motherhood as their motivation for public activities, they also sought non–mothering-related activities that were directed at improving their position as women. However, the emphasis on motherhood when organizing activities was important for their survival. Gender relations at home were restrictive with regard to women's roles. Rules of what it is to be a good woman revolved around women's domestic qualities and their devotion to the family. Thus, within a gender hierarchy where women were assigned a limited role, women expanded their agency by drawing domestic responsibilities into the public sphere.[26] Another reason for emphasizing motherhood well into the 1990s had to do with the political situation. Motherhood provided a political "disguise," during the 1980s as armed parties tended to see mothers as politically innocent. Although motherhood has not prevented death threats directed at female community leaders and actual assassinations during the early 1990s, it did provide grassroots women's organizations with a relative political autonomy.[27] However, women's emphasis on motherhood and community care-taking not only provided women with an alibi, but also gave the government the free workforce it needed to implement poverty relief programs.

The targeted women's organizations acknowledged the problem of temporary poverty relief without structural reform. The minute book of Ayacucho shows that the lack of education and the consequential marginalization was a big problem in dealing with the food distributions. The signatures of representatives of participating *clubes de madres* show that many members were illiterate; many women signed with their fingerprint. The monolinguality and illiteracy of members of the Federation made women particularly vulnerable to manipulations by municipal officials, as they would do their transactions in Spanish and produce written documents that needed to be signed. To avoid deceit based on language, women would turn to the Federation, which could help them to coordinate and control distributions in their regions. The high level of organization that the *clubes de madres* of Ayacucho achieved was a form of protection against manipulation. However, as distances in the highlands are huge and transportation and money scarce, the coordinating function is time-consuming. It actually distracted the Federation from dealing with other issues, such as the lack of education that made this form of manipulation possible in the first place. Still, the demand for schooling, that is, bilingual education and literacy campaigns for women, was strong.[28] According to the minute book, in 1997 a feminist NGO from Lima started literacy courses especially for women.

Controlling and supervising the food programs in cooperation with the designated officials generated many conflicts. Various references are made in the minutes to authoritarian and manipulative bureaucrats who did not live up to their promises; for example, in the minutes of August 7, 1997: "We also ask that the *señor* administrator stop dividing the *clubes de madres* and that he does not participate in internal organizational problems."[29] The minutes confirm the widely held interpretation among scholars that the governmental social programs served political interests. Local authorities used their power to secure the loyalty of the women's organizations in their regions. The minute book refers to various cases of politics of divide and rule by spreading rumors, favoring one organization over the other, and interfering in organizational structures. The existence of the Federation of Clubes de Madres was important because it mediated in disputes and oversaw the manipulating politics of state institutions better than individual women's organizations could.

Occasionally, the Federation even blamed officials for internal fights that may occur in any organization, thus turning the disadvantage of manipulating officials into a function of the unity of the Federation and its members. For example, on September 9, 1997, a meeting was held with a *club de madres* in one of the migrant settlements surrounding the city of Ayacucho. The leaders of this club obliged every new member to pay a fee of three *soles* to become a member. When some new members refused to pay, other members joined in, claiming that "the old members (*socias*) always marginalized them." Internal fights over power such as these can hardly be attributed to outsiders. However, on the next page the secretary of the minute book wrote "that the *señor* administrator is to blame for this division." The shift from the relatively normal internal problem to the accusation that the problem was probably the administrator's fault sounds like an easy way of dealing with internal disputes and strengthening solidarity at the same time.

To defend their organizations against the unjust interferences of bureaucrats, the Federation fell back on the law. The minutes are peppered with recurrent phrases, such as, "the *clubes de madres* have at their disposal public records and there is even a law that qualifies us as grassroots social organizations."[30] Recognition by the law was important for the women, as it allowed them to defend themselves against manipulative practices and to demand a fair and adequate execution of programs. The women would stress the democratic character of their organization; they would demand to see municipal accounts and they would demand a voice in municipal committees for food distribution. The women's organizations were allowed to do so according to the law.[31] The women saw the food distributions as a right, rather than as a favor.

However, knowing the law and living up to it were not enough, as the women had hardly any power to force others to do so. While the minute book shows that the women knew their rights, it also shows that the Federation had little power to enforce those laws. On June 28, 1996, a lawyer, Mario Cavalcanti Gamboa, was present at a meeting of the Federation. The women explained their problems to him in general terms: "the policies are bad," "they maltreat us," "there is discord," "the federation doesn't have experience and does not know the laws,"—an assertion that proves to be mistaken when one reads the many references to the law in the minute book. However, Mario Cavalcanti Gamboa was prepared to become "advisor of the *clubes de madres* of Ayacucho."[32] Apparently, the Federation searched for long-term alliances with professionals who might be able to defend the Federation's rights when necessary.

The minutes confirm the idea that state foodstuff distributions generated many problems for the women involved. The most important features of the programs, the food and milk, did not always arrive; the foodstuffs were selectively distributed and often did not arrive at remote communities. The most inaccessible communities were the poorest, so the Federation did its best to oblige the distribution centers to reach as many communities as possible. The Federation itself was prepared to travel to the communities to inform local women of the procedures and to help them supervise the distribution. The Federation even demanded copies of the bank accounts of the local distribution centers to control the monthly budget and they subsequently donated food and milk, something they were allowed to do, according to the law.[33]

The distribution centers seemed to benefit from the legal distinction between the municipal *vaso de leche* program and the state-led food distributions by PRONAA. Officials accused the women of taking double advantage by combining the two programs under the same organizing committee, assuming that the women were taking double portions. The Federation argued that it was not they, as individual women or as an organization, who took advantage, but the final and legal beneficiaries within the general population. The Federation argued that the difference between the programs lay in the different beneficiaries, not in the ones who prepared the food and milk. Actually, it was the other way around; the government took double advantage of the voluntary work of women.

The state pretended to support women in their work but instead put them to work in, for example, reforestation projects in exchange for food, so-called "food-for-work" programs. Besides using a rhetoric of "encouraging local production," the state sought to persuade women with accusations that they were not willing to work. At least, as the minute book witnesses in the context of a food-for-work project, "one should change the working mentality,"[34] and "one should work and not wait for food."[35] These kinds of comments were in fact accusations of laziness, implying that the population was receiving food without doing anything. Instead of interpreting the voluntary efforts of organized women to take care of the community as an economic activity that ensured the livelihood of many, the state imposed a discourse of dependency, laziness, and favoritism. The use of offensive language as a means of persuasion was not uncommon and worked well, as the women themselves appropriated the idea that one should do "real" work for the donated food. If the women protested against food-for-work projects, the government stopped the food programs. Judging from the minute book, the women—and many times their families—did participate in this kind of food-for-work projects.[36]

Weakening resistance by using humiliating language was a proven tactic, used especially against the most vulnerable in society. The same tactic was used in the coercive population program. In 2000, women in the district of Pamplona Alta in Lima drew up an impressive list recording the humiliating treatment they received from health care personnel.[37] A report of a human rights organization that investigated the forced sterilizations records many humiliating remarks used by healthcare workers about women's sexual behavior, their stupidity, their marginal position, and their weak legal position.[38] Urban poor and rural women claimed to feel discriminated against, or rather abused ("*maltratado*") by health-care personnel and local authorities alike.

By 1997, not only was the state intervening in the women's organizations in the Ayacucho region, but national and international nongovernmental organizations increasingly were setting up support and educational campaigns as well. The minute book mentions literacy workshops held by one feminist NGO, workshops on domestic violence, family planning, and women's rights held by others. Workshops in textile production, handicrafts, management, and civil rights were also offered. International funding organizations entered the region, financing locally organized projects. The women's rights course made a particular and lasting impression on the Federation; after the first reference to the course in 1997, the discourse as expressed in the minute book becomes stronger, emphasizing "their rights"—not just referring to law 25307—as a defense against malpractices of every nature. A phrase that is used frequently after 1997 is "that they appreciate us as human beings," a phrase that proved useful in standing up to the authoritarian attitude of many——male—state officials. The minute book shows, and my interviewees confirmed, that these extra sources of information and support were welcome.

Conclusion

Under the Fujimori government, social programs for development were justified with emancipatory discourses for three main purposes: first, to steer the activities of large and well-coordinated women's organizations at the grassroots; second, to use the enormous capacities for voluntary work that women put into the development of their communities without having to mobilize a paid workforce; and third, to justify "developmental" goals such as the control of population growth under a "modern" discourse regarding the emancipation of women. Instead of helping women to gain equality with men, the government deployed women's reproductive capacity for economic reasons. These policies of poverty relief and reduction maintained and reinforced the disadvantaged position of poor women and their families, as no structural improvements were made. Hierarchies of gender, ethnicity, and class were efficiently deployed and enforced by these policies, as we saw, for example, in the issue of literacy and monolinguality.

The emphasis that grassroots women themselves put on motherhood for various reasons was used by the government to control and manipulate the women's work and their votes. Even the revaluation of women as mothers did not work; many women stated that they worked so hard in the various social programs that they hardly saw their children. As one of my interviewees said, "We are thieves of the time for our own children."[39] Organized women put their spare time into the governmental programs, while the object of organizing domestic tasks communally was to create time to do other things, such as generating an income or improving their capabilities through courses.

The state limited the agency of women by targeting them as poor mothers, not as full citizens of the Peruvian nation.[40] At the same time, the state appropriated the power of distribution of the organized women without implementing social reforms that would make the distribution of resources, knowledge, and power more equal. However, as we have seen, the high level of organization that the targeted women's organizations had reached at least enhanced their capacity to negotiate.

It is difficult to reconceptualize the policies and practices in development programs directed at women in Peru on the basis of these conclusions. We will have to go beyond the obvious in what the Peruvian government did wrong and should do better. Nevertheless, the experience of women in Peru demonstrates that a "gender" perspective can do harm when it is interpreted as focusing on women and their supposed roles in society. But even a more profound gender perspective, such as the one feminist NGOs tend to deploy, cannot resolve all problems in the emancipation and development of women. Ethnic, cultural, and class divisions in a society that denies full citizenship to large parts of its population and that strongly influence the actual execution of development projects should equally be taken into account.

NOTES

I would like to thank Nikki Craske, Maruja Barrig, Paulo Drinot, and the anonymous reviewers for commenting on previous versions of this article. The contents of the article are obviously my responsibility. Translations of quoted material originally in Spanish are my own.

1. For a discussion of women as "reproducers of the group," see: Yuval-Davis, N. (1997). *Gender and nation*. Thousand Oaks, Calif.: Sage Publications; Radcliffe, S. A., and Westwood, S. (1996). *Remaking the nation: Place, identity and politics in Latin America*. New York: Routledge.

2. Kabeer, N. (1999). Resources, agency, achievements: Reflections on the measurement of women's empowerment. *Development and Change* 30(3): 435–64, 436.

3. My interpretation of agency stems from theories of power and resistance as formulated in, for example, Scott, J. (1985). *Weapons of the weak: every day forms of peasant resistance*. New Haven, Conn.: Yale University Press, and feminist deconstructionist analyses of difference as formulated in, for example, Mani, L. (1992). Multiple mediations: Feminist scholarship in the age of multinational reception. In H. Crowley and S. Himmelweit (eds.) *Knowing women: Feminism and knowledge,* Cambridge: Polity, in assocation with the Open University; and Kabeer, N. (1994). *Reversed realities. Gender hierarchies in development thought*. London: Verso.

4. Craske, N. (2000). *Continuing the challenge: The contemporary Latin American women's movement(s)*. Research Paper 23. Liverpool, England: University of Liverpool; Schild, V. (1998). New subjects of rights. In S. E. Alvarez, E. Dagnino, and A. Escobar (eds.) *Cultures of politics, politics of cultures: Revisioning Latin American social movements*. Boulder, Colo.: Westview Press; Alvarez, S. (1994). The (trans)formation of feminism(s) and gender politics in democratizing Brazil. In J. Jaquette (ed.) *The women's movement in Latin America. Participation and democracy*. Boulder, Colo.: Westview Press. According to Morris-Suzuki, the World Bank evaluated the presence of NGOs in Third World countries as measurements of "good governance" during the 1990s. Morris-Suzuki, T. (2000). For and against NGOs. The politics of the lived world. *New Left Review* 2: 63–84.

5. As Molyneux argues, neoliberalism emphasizes individual rights. However, in countries with large social, economic, and political inequalities, the "social reality" catches up with the enforcement of individual rights, or in these case studies, even with the rights of large groups. Molyneux, M. (2000). *Women's movements in international perspective: Latin*

America and beyond. Basingstoke, England: Palgrave, 201.

6. Craske, (2000). *Continuing the challenge*.

7. Maruja Barrig has put forward similar arguments concerning negative and positive effects of NGOization. See: Barrig, M. (2000). *El mundo al reves*. Buenos Aires, Argentina: Consejo Latinoamericano de Ciencias Sociales(CLASCO).

8. Blondet, C. (1986). *Muchas vidas construyendo una identidad: Las mujeres pobladoras de un barrio Limeño*. Lima, Peru: Instituto de Estudios Peruanos, 45.

9. In 1992, an "independent" television station made a propagandistic miniseries that was broadcast by all national channels. In this program— starting a week before the elections for the Congreso Constituyente Democrático—Fujimori was presented as the saviour of Peru. The series pretended to cover the whole of republican history, with the "big change" starting in 1990. In Vega-Centeno, I. (1994). *Simbólica y política: Perú 1978–1993*. Lima, Peru: Fundación Friedrich Ebert.

10. Cotler, J. (1994). *Política y sociedad en el Perú: Cambios y continuidades*. Lima, Peru: Instituto de Estudios Peruanos, 165–222; Crabtree, J., and Thomas, J. (1998). *Fujimori's Peru: The political economy*. London: Institute of Latin American Studies. 11. Cueva Beteta, H., and Millán Falconi, A. (2000). *The women food organizations and their relationship with the government*. Report prepared for the comparative regional project Civil Society and Democratic Governability in the Andes and the South Region, Ford Foundation and Catholic University of Peru, Social Sciences Department. Facsimile.

11. Cotler, J. (1994). *Politica y sociedad en Perú. Cambios y continuidades*. Lima: IEP, 165–222; Crabtree, J. & Thomas, J. (1998). *Fujimori's Peru: The political economy*. London: ILAS.

12. These included the state programs for children (INABIF), displaced persons (PAR), food distribution (PRONAA), social participation (COOPOP), indigenous peoples (Asuntos Indígenas), literacy (PNA), child care (Wawa Wasi), adolescents (Promoción de la Niñez y la Adolescencia), and, as I argue, last and maybe least, for the promotion of women (Promoción de la Mujer). In Presidencia de la Republica and PROMUDEH. (n.d.). *Avanzamos hacia un futuro mejor.* Promotion leaflet. Lima, Peru: Ministerio de la Promoción de la Mujer y del Desarrollo Humano (PROMUDEH).

13. See also: Schmidt, G. D. (2003). *All the president's women: Fujimori and gender equity in Peruvian politics*. Paper presented at the Latin American Studies Association (LASA) Conference, Dallas, Texas, March 26–29.

14. Fertility control policies are dealt with in another paper: Boesten, J. (2003). *Free choice or poverty alleviation? Family planning under Fujimori*. Paper presented at the Latin American Studies Association (LASA) Conference, Dallas, Texas, March 26–29.

15. Presidencia de la Republica and PROMUDEH (n.d.). *Avanzamos hacia un futuro mejor.* Promotion leaflet. Lima, Peru: Ministerio de la

Promoción de la Mujer y del Desarrollo Humano (PROMUDEH).

16. Normas Legales, Decreto legislativo (October 20, 1996) *El Peruano.* Retrieved from Warmi, CENDOC-Mujer. CD-ROM.

17. Law 25307: Grupo Impulsor/CESIP (2000). *El PRONAA y los comedores populares: Yo te doy, pero si no me apoyas yo te quito.* Lima, Peru: Centro de Estudios Sociales y Publicaciones(CESIP).

18. A detailed economic analysis of social programs and electoral interests is: Schady, N. R. (1999). *Seeking votes: The political economy of expenditures by the Peruvian social fund (FONCODES) 1991–95.* Washington, D.C.: World Bank. http://wblnoo18.worldbank.org/research/workpapers.nsf/. Peruvian studies specifically directed at the practices of PRONAA are: Grupo Impulsor/CESIP (2000). *El PRONAA* and Portocarrero, F., et al. (2000). *Economia y politica de los programas gubermentales de apoyo alimentario en el Perú: el caso de PRONAA.* Lima, Peru: Centro de Investigación de la Universidad del Pacífico. www.idrc.ca/lacro/foro/seminario/portocarrero. A more general analysis of transitions in the relation between Peruvian politics and social programs is Roberts, K. (1995). Neoliberalism and the transformation of populism in Latin America: The Peruvian case. *Word Politics* 48 (Oct.) 82-116.

19. Grupo Impulsor (2000). *El PRONAA.*

20. Coral, I. (1998). Women in war: Impact and responses. In S. Stern (ed.) *Shining and other paths: War and society in Peru, 1980–1995.* Durham, N.C.: Duke University Press.

21. Administratively, Peru is divided into departments, which in turn are divided into provinces.

22. Coral. (1998). *Women in war,* 359.

23. Interview with Vilma Ortega, Ayacucho, August 2001.

24. *Constancia de apertura de libro de actas de la Federación de Clubes de Madres de la Provincia de Huamanga-FECMAPH 1995–1999.* Unpublished; onwards called *Libro de Actas.*

25. Contrary to the situation in Lima, in Ayacucho all these organizations formed part of the same federation.

26. See also: Corcoran-Nantes, Y. (2000). Female consciousness or feminist consciousness? Women's consciousness raising in community-based struggles in Brazil. In B. G. Smith (ed.) *Global feminisms since 1945.* London: Routledge.

27. The most well-known case was that of María Elena Moyano, who refused to stop her activities after death threats. In 1992 Shining Path murdered her on the public square of her neighbourhood. See, for example: Barrig, M. (1998). Female leadership, violence, and citizenship in Peru. In J. S. Jaquette and S. L. Wolchik (eds.) *Women and democracy: Latin America and Central and Eastern Europe.* Baltimore, Md.: Johns Hopkins University Press.

28. Asamblea extraordinaria, 20-1-1996, *Libro de Actas,* 51.

29. Asamblea general de clubes de madres de distrito de Huamanga, 2-8-1997, *Libro de Actas,* 289.

30. Reunión Extraordinaria, 15-7-1997, *Libro de Actas,* 287.
31. 02-12-91 Ley No.25307: www.congreso.gob.pe.
32. Reunión extraordinaria de la FECMA-Phga, 28-6-1996, *Libro de Actas,* 134.
33. Reunión extraordinaria, 15-7-1997, *Libro de Actas,* 283.
34. Asamblea Ordinaria de San Juan Bautista, (s.f)., *Libro de Actas,* 97.
35. Reunión Extraordinario de Tambillos, 19-4-1996, *Libro de Actas,* 114.
36. We have to consider that the indigenous communities of the Andes had a history of *mita:* voluntary work, or *corvee,* for the good of the larger community. Especially during the colonial period, but also during the republic, this tradition was often exploited by governors to obtain an unpaid workforce.
37. Meetings at the Casa de Bienestar, Pamplona Alta, supervised by local representatives of the feminist NGO Manuela Ramos, Lima, Peru.
38. Comité Latinoamericano para la Defensa de los Derechos de la Mujer (CLADEM) (1999). *Nada personal. Reporte de derechos humanos sobre la aplicación de la anticoncepción quirúrgica en el Perú, 1996–1998.* Lima, Peru: CLADEM.
39. Interview with Amalia. Lima, Peru. July 2001.
40. This point is also made by Craske, N. (1998). Remasculinization and the neoliberal state in Latin America. In V. Randall and G. Waylen (eds.), *Gender, politics and the state.* New York: Routledge, 106–107.

Jelke Boesten *is a Ph.D. candidate at the University of Amsterdam. Her thesis, under the provisional title "The 'New Woman': Discourses on development, emancipation, and women in Peru (1970–2000)" will be presented for defense in the autumn of 2003. Besides food distribution, she deals with family planning policies and domestic violence programs as areas of contested changes primarily directed at women.*

Neoliberalism, Gender, and Development

Institutionalizing "Post-Feminism" in Medellín, Colombia

Donna F. Murdock

> Those of us in this type of institution, I think we sometimes, in order to main-
> tain ourselves there, have to lower the tone of critique that subverts, or
> the permanent subversion of the daily-ness of the patriarchy . . . and in
> fact, you do not have to be feminist in order to work in a program for
> women in NGOs. What are the qualifications that they require? Women
> who have knowledge of the theory of gender![1]
> —Feminist NGO director, Medellín, Colombia

In what context does this woman's distinction between being a "feminist" and having "knowledge of the theory of gender" make sense? After
all, it is feminists who have created the theory of "gender" and who have
worked hard for its integration into mainstream development work.
How is it that a woman in Medellín, Colombia, has come to see knowledge of gender as not feminist, perhaps even "anti-feminist?"

Like all theoretical tools and discourses, the theory of gender is
always interpreted by persons within particular social contexts and
with particular orientations to the social world. In the context of an
increasing neoliberal hegemony, states are shrinking their development budgets, seeking new ways to economize, and gender policies
are of course implicated in these changes (Babb 2001; Rosen and
McFedyen 1995). At the same time, feminists have been so successful
at flagging the importance of considering women's participation in
development that governments are compelled to attend to gender
issues if they want to receive development monies (Young 1993;
Álvarez 1999). With the need to downsize and yet still attend to
women, states increasingly turn to feminist NGOs to provide services
and expert knowledge. What the quotation above refers to is the tendency for an increasing number of these NGOs to provide states with
knowledge of the theory of gender *minus* the feminist critique of gendered power relations (see also Álvarez 1999; Lebon 1996, 1998;
Thayer 2000, 2001; Lind 2000; García Castro 2001).

From 1998 to 2000, I conducted ethnographic fieldwork among

state and city development agencies as well as several feminist NGOs in Medellín, Colombia. Knowing that discourses rarely (if ever) translate directly, I asked, What does *gender perspective* mean in the context of Medellín? What is the impact of the substitution of *gender perspective* for earlier references to *feminist?* Is it a move "beyond" feminism, as some in Medellín claimed? Or is it more like the "anti-politics" machine that Ferguson (1994 [1990]) claimed for development discourses more generally and that Scott (1988) and others have cautioned against in relation to the term *gender* in particular?

In this article, I discuss how both state officials and local feminist organizations used the gender perspective discourse. While there were some positive associations with this discourse, there was also evidence that under neoliberal regimes, it could justify a hostile reception to subversive feminist politics. Specifically, when used by state actors, it seemed to delegitimate feminist critiques of essentialized linkages between femininity, women, and motherhood. As Babb (2001) observed in Nicaragua, I found the local government in a neoliberal economic context eager to reinscribe domesticity upon women, to reassociate them with their children and families as against feminist attempts to establish women's individual subjectivity.

Feminists working in NGOs appreciated the ability of the "gender perspective" to "move beyond" feminists' exclusive focus on women. However, they also feared the retrenchment it seemed to signal in some hands, especially as the reinscription of domesticity signaled a particularly hostile attitude toward the most controversial feminist issues, such as abortion and homosexuality. Far from a move "beyond" feminism, it seemed more like a move around feminism, toward a "post-feminism" that would arrive long before the subversive promises of feminism were realized.

Gender as a Development Discourse

The discourse of gender and development grows out of a complex set of feminist concerns and scholarship. Concerned that the uncritical use of the term *woman* tended to reinforce essentialist notions of the links between biology and behavior, as well as denying the real differences existing between women, feminist scholars began talking about *gender* instead (Scott 1988). According to Scott, many feminists wanted a term that would focus on the "social quality of distinctions based on sex" and that would accomplish two tasks: refute biological determinism *and* note that gender is constituted by social relations of power that involve both women and men (Scott 1988, 29). In addition to these usages, as Scott notes, *gender* is also sometimes substituted for the term *women* in an effort to gain academic legitimacy for feminist scholarship. Scott argues that *gender* may sound more "neutral and objective" than the term *women,* which carries connotations of "the (supposedly strident) politics of feminism" (1988, 31–32).

Similarly, in the development field, use of the term *gender* has signaled a desire to recognize the social construction of differences between women and men and the wide diversity in women's experiences. The gender and development (GAD) approach has been associated with Marxist-feminist critiques of the development-as-modernization paradigm, and focuses upon empowering women and men to transform gendered social relations (Marchand and Parpart 1995; Rathgeber 1990; Young 1993; Parpart 1995). To underscore the extent to which this perspective is supposed to move beyond integrationist approaches to women's experiences in development, Young calls GAD the "radical feminism of development" (1993, 143).

Like all discourses, GAD is grounded in political, economic, and cultural/historical contexts and may be used by actors for different purposes at different times (Foucault 1972; Bakhtin 1981). The uses to which GAD may be put, and the consequent meanings it may have, clearly shift as the user and the context itself shift. Elson (1992), for instance, distinguishes between feminist uses of GAD and its uses by men and women who enter the development field without a commitment to feminist critiques of gender inequality; the latter tend to view gender as simply another variable rather than a field of power relations. In such a case, gender and development can actually become a development discourse that functions like an "anti-politics machine" (Ferguson 1994 [1990]).

Perhaps because of the radical critique of development and gendered power relations that GAD calls for, it has been adopted by governments and development agencies only in a piecemeal fashion. In fact, many scholars have found its adoption only at the level of rhetoric, without the concomitant social changes that would imply a deep integration of the theory into mainstream development practice (Marchand and Parpart 1995; Parpart 1995; Young 1993). More disturbing than this piecemeal adoption is the charge by some that the GAD framework has actually allowed for the depoliticization of feminist development practice. This depoliticization has taken several forms. The most potent of these is the tendency for GAD to be used by state and other non-feminist actors to underwrite a twisted version of gender theory, such that women's difference from men is recognized, but its basis in unequal power relations is not (Baden and Goetz

1998, 19). Two especially negative outcomes potentially arise from this interpretation. First, there is the reinforcement of notions that women's difference from men lies in their maternal role. This may make the already controversial issues of abortion and homosexuality even more difficult for feminists to raise and defend (Baden and Goetz 1998, 28). Second, because there is no analysis of inequality, but rather a mandate to recognize both men's and women's conditions, the GAD framework may allow states to drop their exclusive focus on women, and even to switch focus entirely from women to men (Kabeer 1994).

To the extent that this discourse is used by governments or other development agencies to absolve themselves of dealing with gendered power relations, the discourse functions to turn gender into a technical problem, a variable to be accounted for. In the past, the discourse has expanded state power by calling for the creation of state agencies to deal with gendered development issues. However, in the increasingly neoliberal context of development practice today, it is not so much direct state bureaucratic expansion that is at stake, but rather the delegitimation of feminist critique.

In the context of neoliberal Medellín, I found GAD being used to justify a turn away from feminist concerns for women's experience. Instead of focusing exclusively upon women or considering how gendered power relations impinged upon women's ability to participate in development, government officials argued that according to the tenets of GAD, such concerns were discriminatory. Twisting the insight that gender is a social relation to their own uses, they argued that women must always be considered in relation to men, or their families, and never treated simply as individuals. They used gender and development discourses, such as the gender perspective discourse, to directly underwrite a critique of feminism.

It might be expected that state agencies would use GAD in this way. Perhaps more disturbing about the uses of GAD in Medellín was that feminist NGOs, formerly the site of contestation and opposition to state-sponsored gender regimes, were also required to use this discourse. Although these NGOs attempted to use it differently, the context into which they spoke made the feminist uses of GAD less intelligible and therefore less potent. The consequences are a state-sponsored reinscription of traditional associations between women and motherhood and a weakening of feminist institutions' ability to challenge these. The implications for a consideration of womens' rights to control their own sexualities, apart from the needs or desires of their families and apart from their traditional social role as mothers and wives, were quite worrisome.

Neoliberal Development, Feminist Success, and the Disciplining of Feminism

The disciplining of feminism in Medellín has occurred through an odd historical conjuncture. Feminist successes on the development field have collided with neoliberal development policies to produce a situation in which formerly radical feminist organizations have become increasingly close to the state, and at the same time, have been pushed to abandon their radical political claims.[2]

In Colombia, radical feminism surged out of the growing strength of the New Left in the 1970s. Eschewing institutional politics and critical of the Left's failure to live up to promises of participatory democracy, feminists began to form their own antihierarchical organizations in the late 1970s. Beyond its critique of institutional structures, this radical feminist line combined attention to sexuality and reproduction with a critique of social class structures. These feminists saw the artificial division of social life into "productive" and "reproductive" spheres (or the "public/private" split) as problematic. They argued that capitalist social organization played a role in this division, and they disagreed with the liberal feminist belief that women's greater participation in traditionally conceived economic and political practices would resolve gender inequality (Restrepo and Orrego 1994, 39–40, 153). However, they also rejected Marxist feminisms that placed "class above gender" in the analysis of women's problems, and disagreed with the argument that feminist politics were divisive and weakened the overall struggle for social justice in Latin America. Instead, they combined class and gender analyses, seeing reproduction and sexuality as central to sexist oppression, but also seeing how these oppressions were crosscut and informed by social class (Schmidt 1988). Not satisfied with consciousness-raising and forums for themselves, radical feminist groups began working with women from the popular sectors in the late 1970s, providing education on women's rights and sexual and reproductive health issues, among other topics (Villareal 1994, 176). Their organizational forms were diverse; some became "centers," others "groups" or "collectives," and they rejected affiliation with the state, the academy, or any other hierarchically-organized institutions (Villareal 1994, 184).

Quite soon, however, a number of national and international forces contributed to these groups' re-integration into the institutional frame. In 1975, the First World Conference on Women was held in Mexico, kicking off the United Nations' International Women's Year and the International Decade for Women (1975–1985). This event deepened the Colombian women's involvement in transnational feminist networks, and began the intensification of the Colombian state's consideration of women's participation in development as well. In 1981, Bogotá hosted the first Latin American and Caribbean Feminist Meetings (Navarro 1982). In the same year, the Colombian state ratified the Convention for the Elimination of All Forms of Discrimination Against Women (CEDAW). During the 1980s, Colombian feminism grew in strength and began participating in the society-wide calls for democratization.[3] With the creation of the new 1991 constitution and a deeper commitment on the part of the Colombian government to increase women's participation in development, feminists' roles began to change. More groups began to found NGOs, and began to serve as "experts" for a state that was expected to foster women's participation in development, but did not exactly know how (Villareal 1994, 184).

At the time of my fieldwork, most well-known feminist groups in Medellín were either NGOs themselves, or were coordinated through NGO offices. Although I was told that the majority of Medellín's feminists were not affiliated with any institutions, it was also true that the major feminist organizations—the Pacific Route[4] and the Colombian Women's Network for Sexual and Reproductive Rights ("the Network")—were coordinated and headed by principal women's NGO figures. For instance, the Pacific Route was headed by the director of one feminist NGO, and the Network was headed by a founding member of another. These positions rotated, of course, but these two NGOs in particular were regularly at the head of feminist initiatives organized outside the purview of the state. Whenever there were important commemorations, such as International Women's Day, or the International Day Against Violence Against Women, or the rare street protest, NGO women seemed to be in the forefront. With fax machines, copiers, computers, and wide networks at their disposal, they were well equipped to coordinate and bring off these large actions.

There were ongoing debates about the effect of an NGO strategy on the movement overall, with both gains and losses clearly visible to almost everyone involved. The extent to which NGO structure would permit feminists to retain a radical feminist line combining both sex and class critiques with a critique of institutionalized forms of power and inequality remained to be seen. Many believed that feminists' adoption of a structured, hierarchical organizational practice, and the abandonment of previously antagonistic relations with the state constituted a straitjacketing of feminist practice. More specifically, it was unclear what role feminism as a critique of gendered power relations was to play in the new relationship between feminist NGOs and states. The question became more pressing for many women with the intensification in the late 1990s of neoliberal economic reforms that highlighted the differences between a radical feminist line and the gender perspective espoused by a Colombian state that appeared little interested in feminism.

Gender Perspective and the State

In the 1990s, the Colombian government followed other Latin American states in adopting neoliberal policies.[5] This entailed blaming government bloat and inefficiency for much of the development failures of previous decades, and involved downsizing state bureaucracies and shifting the burden of social welfare programs and services to civil society (Álvarez 1999, 195). This process accelerated in Colombia in September 1998 when President Andres Pastrana declared an economic and social emergency and instituted a neoliberal economic program that included cuts in social spending and decreased budgets for state agencies (Morales 1999). State-run women's development programs were also affected, and in this context, feminist NGOs became increasingly important actors in gender and development practice.[6]

The kinds of services and advice governments expect to get from NGOs are quite specific. For instance, a Colombian official told Sonia Álvarez, "Now things have changed, it's no longer that radical feminism of the 1970s, now it's policies with a gender perspective." Álvarez has argued that this usage of *gender* seemed to signify the Colombian state's ability to do exactly as some feminists have feared, turning gender into yet another modern development technique and failing to recognize it as a "power-laden field of unequal relations between women and men" (Álvarez 1999, 192).

What is interesting is the extent to which this depoliticization of the gender discourse appears to vary with political contexts. The Women's Department of Antioquia, for instance, has variably embraced feminist critiques and rejected them, depending upon the political context of the moment. In 1992, Governor Juan Gómez Martínez made a pact with feminist organizations in Medellín. In exchange for their electoral support, he founded a women's department (La Consejería Para la Mujer) for the State of Antioquia. This governor envisioned the Women's Department as part of the overall modernization project of the state, involved in the larger context of democratization, economic opening, and a transformation in the model of social development. In particular, he believed that the state must find ways of "increasing the collective returns of social investment." One such way involved pushing for women's participation according to the "new conception and role which she should fulfill in society." The first department director was long-time feminist, Margarita María Peláez. Under her leadership, the state launched a series of wide-ranging projects that coordinated efforts between state agencies, NGOs, and other women's organizations. Using a gender and development approach, the Women's Department had a mandate to consider the obstacles that traditional gender relations placed in the way of women's wider political participation.

However, by the time I began fieldwork in 1998, changes in the interpretation of gender and development were afoot. President Andres Pastrana's fiscal conservatism was matched by social conservatism in the arena of gender equity as well. For instance, the president announced early in his term that no one would be allowed to enter the senate or congress in either blue jeans or mini-skirts. More seriously, in response to women's mass protests for stronger negotiations with the Revolutionary Armed Forces of Colombia (FARC) for the release of captive soldiers, the president suggested in his 1999 Mother's Day radio address that women could best contribute to the peace process from the home *["desde el hogar"]*.[7]

The new governor of Antioquia, Alberto Builes Ortega, facing budget restrictions, was also less sympathetic to women's issues, and the Women's Department found itself facing a number of changes. First, the department contended with a budget crisis. Although they had moved up several floors in the building (which supposedly signified higher status), their offices were less inviting than before. Employees were quartered in a tiny room where the backs of their chairs bumped. Staff members confided to me that while the budget had been prepared for the department's functioning that year, the funds had not been released. In addition, they had not received travel reimbursement for months, and were concerned that their salaries would be cut or even suspended. The once-influential Women's Department appeared to be limping along, hoping to hold out long enough to survive into the next administration.[8]

Second, the Women's Department was reorganized so that its once pioneering (because singular) focus on empowering women was expanded to include work on the elderly, youth, children, and the disabled. A government employee who had worked at the Women's Department since before the policy change reported that the new governor had justified the change with these remarks: "We cannot speak of women without also speaking of children." In fact, as in the situation reported in Nicaragua by Babb (2001), the Women's Department appeared to be shifting from an earlier emphasis on integrating women into development—and specifically, the market—toward an emphasis on women's domestic role.[9]

The beginnings of this shift can be traced to President Ernesto Samper's 1995 development plan, The Social Leap. This plan made a linkage between development and social equity, and argued that gender equity was essential to the nation's democratic development. It established the Policy for Women's Equity and Participation (EPAM), which sought to make visible and at the same time to empower women's contribution to society. Interestingly, EPAM called for the eradication of a "masculine universe which is exclusive, dominant, and violent," which could be accomplished with a "gender" approach to development. Despite its progressive language, EPAM interpreted the GAD approach as requiring a "cultural change" that would revalorize the feminine in society, revalorize the domestic sphere, and promote equitable relations between the sexes in all areas of social activity.[10] It sought to value "diversity" between women and men, and not to interfere with "the particularities of women's gender, this is their practice as mothers and wives." An attempt at equity was made by encouraging men to value women's domestic labor, and to participate fully in child care.[11]

By 1998, the ambivalence in government policy toward women was clear in that the most visible government program for women was the day-care system known as Community Welfare Homes (Hogares Comunitarios de Bienestar) run by "community mothers" *("madres comunitarias")*. Under the auspices of the Colombian Institute for Family Welfare, women in the poorest communities who were willing to run day-care centers out of their homes were supported by the state. In exchange, they received a small subsidy; some training in nutrition, child psychology, recreation, and healthcare; and could take out small government loans for home remodeling (Puyana 1991, 141–45). In Medellín, there were 8,000 community homes in which local women cared for and fed more than 120,000 children on weekdays from eight A.M. to five-thirty P.M. Women were paid 17mil pesos (about $10) a month and were provided with food, supplies, and so forth to cover children's needs. Aside from the service this provided to working mothers able to enlist their children in the program, the most positive effect of this program was its demonstrated ability to decrease the problem of malnutrition among the poorest children.

For the community mothers themselves, the picture was less clearly positive. As Puyana argues, the program both facilitated some women's work outside the home by providing reliable and affordable day care in their own communities and at the same time reinforced traditional gender ideologies that see women as the appropriate caretakers of children, and women's work as domestic (Puyana 1991, 129). Feminists in Medellín frequently worked with community mothers' organizations and saw their organizational and social critique skills increase (Villareal 1994, 184). In fact, they were especially supportive in 1999 when these women threatened a strike and march on Bogotá after their demands for a minimum-wage salary met with the decision to close the program down. Although feminists were interested in seeing government support for child care continue, they did not approve of the tendency to treat community mothers as housewives. They felt that the failure to pay these women adequately showed that women were visible to this government only in their role as mothers, that is, unpaid caregivers, and not as individuals with needs that could not be met by programs for children.

The Feminist Critique: Supporting Lesbians and Libertines

Unlike the majority of development interventions offered at that time to women, feminists had a desire to contest the dominant vision of women as "domestic subjects," as they put it. In particular, they were interested in contesting the region's predominant gendered traditions associating women with motherhood. They argued that hegemonic Latin American feminine identities were too frequently associated with the home ("*la casa*") and, especially, with motherhood. One woman disparagingly called this traditional feminine self the "woman/mother binomial" ("mujer/madre binomio").[12] In Antioquia particularly, traditional feminine ideals have suggested that women should bear as many children as possible and should also remain physically inside the home as much as possible, whatever their social class and need to work (Gutiérrez de Pineda 1996; Bohman 1984). As one local feminist scholar put it, "In Colombia, where femininity still equals maternity, we need to offer other images of what it means to be a woman."

In fact, feminists recognized that today, women of all social classes in Medellín work, go to school, and participate in community activities.[13] Women in Medellín are not exclusively occupied with mothering, nor are they physically confined to their homes as a literal reading of "the woman belongs to the home" ("la mujer es de la casa") ideal might suggest. However, feminists argue that the notion that women belong to the home, and the consequent reading of feminine subjectivity as being almost exclusively about motherhood, does impact women, making their participation in other activities difficult.[14] In particular, it makes women's ability to control their own sexuality and reproduction more difficult, especially to the extent that this is perceived as a rejection of the traditional wife-mother role. Crucial struggles on this front included the controversial issues of abortion and homosexuality.

Reproductive and sexual rights issues are widely recognized as among the most controversial issues in Latin America.[15] Further, they are clearly associated in common parlance with feminist political projects. For instance, women in Brazil's Rural Women Workers' Movement who privately identified as feminist were afraid to do so in public for fear of what would be thought about their "stance on controversial issues such as abortion" (Stephen 1997, 276). Similarly, as Escandón argues, abortion is a controversial issue in Mexico, both uniting women in the struggle for decriminalization and dividing them as well (1994, 207).

In the city of Medellín, these issues are equally controversial. In fact, although family planning projects have existed in Colombia since the 1960s, and sex education in high school appears to be quite common,[16] there is evidence that women's control of their own sexuality and reproduction—such as the use of birth control—is associated with "promiscuity." For instance, a feminist scholar who sits on the Young Women's Council of Medellín said that she had heard from young working-class women who had tried to use birth control pills and had found their families and boyfriends so opposed to the idea that they would hide the pills or even throw them away. The scholar believed that these girls' families associated a woman's desire to control her own reproduction with being promiscuous and appeared to prefer that young women become pregnant rather than risk their reputations. That risking a pregnancy should be more acceptable than attempting to disrupt the connection between sexuality and maternity suggests that the freedom to have premarital sex with a boyfriend is not the same as female control over sexuality and reproduction.

If the use of birth control is deemed unseemly, the issues of abortion and homosexuality are even more controversial. Despite, or perhaps because of, their controversial nature, whenever either issue was presented publicly as a viable option for women, the presenters invariably self-identified as feminists, often before saying anything else about the topic. For instance, a feminist sociologist who brought up female sexuality in a talk she gave at a public university in 1999 started out by saying that before the feminist movement began in Colombia, young girls like herself did not know the words *homosexual, lesbian,* and *pregnant.* She said, "The feminist movement has changed a lot of things, has questioned a series of myths about women, and shown that we do not all have to be mothers. Feminism has supported the achievement of a more relaxed sexuality, a sense of pleasure in sexuality."

However, the director of the Colombian Women's Network for Sexual and Reproductive Rights,(the Network) noted that even feminists were sometimes divided on these issues: "Those who enter [the Network] have to agree with our principles, such as the decriminalization of abortion, and not everyone is in agreement with this. . . . We also need to work on 'free choice' ['libre opción'] and this touches upon homosexuality and bisexuality."

Abortion

Colombia is one of three Latin American countries (along with El Salvador and Chile) that does not permit abortions, although there is legal provision for medical discretion under "special circumstances." Social class and the ability to pay for first-rate abortion services are of course crucial in getting access to that special treatment. In fact, botched illegal abortions are among the leading causes of maternal death, particularly for poor women.[17]

In 1999, the national headquarters for the Network was located in Medellín and I was able to speak with the director about their campaign to decriminalize abortion. Interestingly, she told me about the case of a young woman charged with killing her infant that had recently been adopted by the Network as a signal fight in this campaign.

Alba Lucía Rodriguez was a young, unmarried rural woman who had traveled to Medellín for work, became pregnant, and subsequently returned home to have her baby without benefit of medical care. Delivering the child herself, she claimed it was born with the cord wrapped around its throat. Delirious and frightened, she buried the child and tried to recover alone. When she finally went to the doctor, she was charged with the murder of her child. She was sentenced almost immediately to forty-two years in prison and had already served three years of that term by the time I heard about the story (Rivera 1999). The director of the Network explained that they had taken up the case

> because with the case of Alba Lucía we see the possibility of working on all kinds of rights, the quality of attention, the judicial misogyny.
> . . . they had to give her 42 years that they have never even given to

a drug trafficker! It seems that Alba Lucía is paying for what all of us have done—for the sole fact of being different, for having the possibility of enjoying sex and because they cannot define us. They charge us because we want . . . the possibility to decide. . . . So the Network decided to deal with this case whatever it costs.[18]

Homosexuality

The issue of homosexuality was more complicated than that of abortion. The gay rights movement had accomplished legal reforms in Colombia, at the same time that feminists and non-feminists alike continued to express ambivalence on the issue. On September 10, 1998, the Constitutional Court declared that teachers could not be dismissed simply for being homosexual, as this would be a violation of constitutional protection against discrimination for reasons of sex ("sexo"). According to the court, the United Nations Committee on Human Rights declared that *sex* included "sexual orientation" as this pertains to "personal privacy" (Duque 1998). Similarly, on July 14, 1999, the Constitutional Court declared that sanctioning homosexual soldiers is a violation of their human right to the free development of their personality.

However, this positive legal atmosphere was not reflected in the public sentiment I heard expressed. For instance, a female lawyer who attended workshops at one of the feminist NGOs I studied once complained to me about "those terrible posters [in the NGO] that had captions about homosexuality, actually condoning it!" She said, "This is horrible; you cannot do this kind of thing in a school of good quality!" In another workshop on sexuality and gay rights, a leader of a women's group said flatly, "It does not matter. Homosex-uality is a sin."

Feminist stances on homosexuality were complicated. An indication of just how complicated comes from the fact that while I routinely observed feminists defending homosexual and lesbian rights in general, I also understood that discussing women's own sexuality was a taboo subject. Observing the intense closeting that went on even within the close-knit circles of the feminist community, and knowing that "social cleansing" squads (at least in other cities) were responsible for the deaths of "known" homosexuals, I was reluctant to press the issue.[19] As women themselves never raised the issue with me either, I never learned their personal stakes in the matter or why the subject seemed so taboo.

However, there were moments in which feminists found themselves "on the line" in front of a somewhat hostile audience, and nevertheless defended the exploration of attitudes toward homosexuality. For instance, during a workshop at a feminist NGO, one feminist said, "I have homosexual tendencies like everyone, but this scares us and makes us uncomfortable. . . . But if we really want to change society, we have to study many 'dark points' *['puntos oscuros']*, including sexual options such as homosexuality."

Feminists received little social support on this issue from their larger circle of NGO friends, despite the fact that these usually were quite progressive and even radical in their overall political stance. At an NGO gathering in December 1999, women from a feminist NGO mounted a protest against the fact that the couple voted "worst" in the dance contest were two women, and that the three finalist couples were all "traditional" (i.e., male-female) couples. The protest was made lightheartedly with lots of joking, but nevertheless the speech they made was taken seriously enough that one male bystander said, "Oh *please,* we are on vacation here!" Later, while in line for food, the male contest judge joked, "They just accused me of something I'm willing to admit—being a heterosexual!" Although the women in line with me laughed, and he hugged one of the women right away, I thought the point was not quite settled for them, so I said, "No, it is not *heterosexual,* it is *heterosexist.*" He did not seem to have heard me, but the other women repeated it to him just before he walked away.

In the company of others, feminists seemed quite united in their commitment to defend homosexual rights, but amongst themselves, the association drawn between feminism and lesbianism caused friction. Some feminists complained to me that other feminists in Medellín were "homophobes" with whom they had had numerous arguments in favor of homosexual rights and in defense of lesbian-feminists' open presence at conferences in other parts of Latin America.[20] Some women objected to the stereotypes associating feminism with lesbianism, and this made for a complicated feminist response to the issue.

The Meanings of Feminism in a Neoliberal Age

Feminism was of course associated with a rejection of traditional gender norms, and stereotypes about lesbianism, "man-hating," and so forth, abounded. Most women were used to this, and being a feminist in Medellín required a willingness to accept a certain amount of negative stereotyping. What was especially troubling in the neoliberal context was the extent to which the state began to feel comfortable using the internationally sanctioned gender perspective discourse as a way of reinforcing these stereotypes. Further, the delegitimation of feminist critique that followed was also a justification for the states' cutbacks on programs for women.

It did not surprise Medellín's feminists that the Colombian state stepped back from its previously progressive stance on gender and development programs. They believed the political climate as a whole had shifted to the Right. However, it did irritate them that the gender perspective discourse was interpreted under new regimes as a justification for discontinuing some programs for women. The loss of the exclusive focus on women once provided by the Women's Department was especially galling to Medellín's feminists. One woman especially outraged by this change said, "We cannot allow institutions that don't have a profound analysis . . . to keep indiscriminately using gender perspective for economic gain. . . . The State and other institutions are cutting the projects they used to have specifically for women in the name of 'gender perspective' which means you have to have 'equality' for men and women." In fact, many women argued that under conservative state government, the gender perspective discourse was actually being used to claim that a feminist focus was discriminatory.

An employee from the Women's Department inadvertently confirmed this view for me. While we were talking about the changes from a singular focus on women to a more inclusive focus on women, children, the elderly, and the infirm, she complained to me that while these changes were in the planning stages, radical feminists working in some of the city's most prominent women's NGOs protested against Governor Builes's remarks concerning women and children. She characterized these women as "radical" feminists "who don't want anything to do with men or children." Later, she revealed to me that many people had opposed the existence of the Women's Department when it was focused solely upon women because they felt that "women are not the only people with problems, there are lots of people with problems." Focusing solely upon women was interpreted as being "against men" *("en contra de los hombres")*. She admitted that women working in the Women's Department during this later period had been afraid to call themselves feminists because of this assumption.

In fact, it is quite clear that despite the government's increasing reliance on feminist development expertise, social attitudes toward feminism and feminists remain basically negative. As Restrepo and Orrego report, feminists in general, and radical feminists in particular, were perceived as women "engaged in a direct and head-on fight with men" *("una mujer que está en una pelea frontal y directa con el hombre")* (1994: 183). Restrepo and Orrego continue, "In Medellín, it is customary to hear that feminists are 'ugly, old-maids, or lesbians.' The feminist movement is seen as produced by resentful women that do not have a man by their side" (1994, 184).

These stereotypes about feminism are part of the background against which women working in Medellín's NGOs choose to identify themselves as feminist or not. One woman noted that it was acceptable for *women* to participate in the creation of development policy, but *feminists* were not welcome. Whenever she mentioned women, or noted that gender inequalities were being left out of planning ideas, people said things like "of course, you have to be the feminists!" *("claro, tienen que ser las feministas!")*. She added that sometimes women working in these government agencies were more critical than were men, "and one of the things you find is that on the part of some women there is always the recrimination and sanction, more than some male colleagues, so they say 'again with the complaints, again the feminist!'"

Several women talked with me about some of the more negative meanings that *feminism* had in Medellín:

> You still get jokes, or men say, "And these crazy women, where did they come from?" Or [they say,] "Here come the witches."

> "Feminista" also can mean a "female 'machista,'" a woman who wants to arrive home late and drunk, stay in the street, wake up on the corner, smoke, etc.

> Very "radical" and "lesbiana" and "en contra de los hombres" [against men] . . . the stereotype that all feminists are "lesbians" or "marimachi."[21]

It is interesting to note that in 1975, Schmidt found Colombian women reporting that even though they believed in women's political empowerment, they were not feminist because they associated feminism with promiscuity or being a libertine ("libertinaje"). The fact that today's stereotypes are more likely to include "lesbian," "man-hater," or "witch" signals a neoliberal ratcheting up of feminist stigma. These negative stereotypes about feminists and feminism have made educating the public about gender roles, power imbalances, and women's rights difficult. Beyond that, it has provided the state with ample excuse not to confer with or include self-identified feminists in the production of state policy for women (Restrepo and Orrego 1994, 183; Red Nacional de Mujeres 1994). Under neoliberal conditions, when states become increasingly dependent upon feminist NGOs (and vice versa), the definition of feminism itself as discriminatory may force feminist NGOs to deradicalize their politics.

Gender Perspective and Feminist Politics

Feminists in Medellín had mixed feelings about the new gender perspective discourse. Many feminists appreciated the way that the term *gender* allowed them to broaden their analysis. They viewed the switch to *gender perspective* as an indication that feminists' previous exclusive concentration upon women has been superseded and amplified into an investigation of gender, viewed as a relational phenomenon whose transformation will require the work of women *and men*. One woman said, "Initially they talked about feminism as a political option for revision of these relationships, but then realized they couldn't stay there just with women . . . because women are in a context, in relationships with others, with men. So now they use gender perspective." Another added, "I don't want to say that gender perspective means you *have* to work with men and women, but I think that if we want to create social and cultural transformations it is fundamental to work with both men and women because it will not serve if women change, . . . if there is no change in men."

However, women also identified problems with the gender perspective discourse. One woman said she did not think gender perspective had done much good for women, despite the fact that NGOs receiving international funding have been forced to work with the concept. She noted that government agencies do not usually interpret the policy directive of gender perspective in ways that are satisfactory to feminists, and that in fact gender perspective

> has done more harm than good in terms of our more profound vindications for women, like in the case of abortion. . . . the more strategic things have gone, being lost and drowned in this gender perspective. . . . it could serve, but it could also allow us to lose, and maybe it is better to continue questioning ourselves about the causes of women's subordination.

Several argued that gender perspective had been adopted because it was easier than confronting feminist stigma. One said, "You cannot say 'feminista' because it makes their hair stand up on end *['pelo parado']*." Another stated explicitly that "gender perspective is a category of analysis that . . . entered into feminist organizations in order to diminish the political importance of feminism."

A long-time feminist activist and NGO director explained the "profound abyss" between work based on feminist principles and work based in a gender perspective. She argued that feminists attempt to get at the power relations that create obstacles to women's development while others simply try to devise "correctives" to get around these. She continued, "The discourse of 'gender' which is what most NGOs use, is not subverting anything! . . . it does not subvert the existing patriarchal order." This woman made a connection then between what women working in NGOs call themselves and the kind of approach they take to solving women's problems. Along with others, she asserted that the most radical or profound work is done by women who call themselves feminists. For these women, the biggest problem was that while feminist theory appeared to have moved beyond its exclusive focus on women, feminist NGOs were still working in a context where feminist goals had not yet been reached.

Conclusion

The current context of Medellín, Colombia, is one where women's right to control their own reproduction and sexuality is not guaranteed by the state. Abortion is one of the leading causes of maternal mortality, and despite recent legal reforms, homosexuality remains a highly controversial subject. In terms of gender and development programs, the Colombian state has shown itself to be ambivalent, tending toward the recognition and even reinforcement of gender differences, but not the recognition of gender inequalities. The state's most important program for women provides for children's day care, a useful support to working women. However, the inadequate remuneration paid to women who provide the day care underscores yet again the tendency to see women as wives and mothers before anything else.

The emergence of all of these issues is part of a larger shift toward fiscal and social conservatism that was intensified in 1998 with the Pastrana administration's neoliberal approach to governance. Within this larger context, the interpretation of gender and development discourse has taken a decided turn away from its radical promise of a transformation in gender roles and development models (Young 1993). Instead, the gender and development discourse has been used to underwrite a retrenchment from radical feminist politics, and indeed, even a delegitimation of the same.

Under these terms, gender and development discourse may indeed become a sort of anti-politics machine (Ferguson 1990). The insight into the relationality of gender may be used to reinforce notions of women as always, already wives and mothers. This may be heterosexist in its failure to recognize lesbian lives, and may also work against women's right to control and/or to refuse their reproductive capacities. The institutionalization at the state level of a post-feminism that presumes to go beyond feminism before the crucial struggles of feminism have yet been won is worrisome. The threat that even the critique that feminist NGOs have previously offered may be muzzled by the resurgence of anti-feminist rhetoric couched as the "latest" in development thinking is more worrisome by far. I suggest that the gender perspective discourse constitutes a threat to feminist politics precisely because of what is perceived to be its strength, that is, that it goes beyond feminism to focus explicitly upon both women and men, but has gone beyond before the work was finished. As Toril Moi aptly states, "If post-feminism is simply another name for a depoliticized approach to sexual difference, the gap between pre- and post- would seem to shrink to nothing. . . . true post-feminism is impossible without post-patriarchy"(1987, 12).

The term *gender* and the related phrase *gender perspective* clearly mean different things in different contexts. The *Gender and Development* framework is useful insofar as it attempts to account for differences between women, and for the socially constructed nature of gender identities. However, feminists cannot control the uses of our theories, nor can we assume that they travel in exactly the way we want them to. This means that we have to attend to how our theories are used in different contexts, and also that we must work hard to create contexts in which the meanings of our frameworks are not subverted. Now that feminist struggles and development projects are intertwined around the world, it is increasingly incumbent upon us all to monitor the conditions of development. Neoliberal development frameworks in particular appear to threaten turning feminist gains into potential losses.

NOTES

I would like to thank Bruce M. Knauft, Peggy Barlett, Carla Freeman, and Sonia Álvarez for their insightful comments on earlier incarnations of the material in this article. Thanks also go to the editors of this special issue of *Women's Studies Quarterly,* and to the anonymous reviewers who helped to make this paper stronger. Fieldwork funding was provided in 1998 by a Social Science Research Council International Dissertation Research Fellowship and in 1999 by a Fulbright fellowship. Dissertation write-up funding was provided by a National Science Foundation predoctoral grant and by an Emory University graduate fellowship. My deepest thanks go to the people in Medellín who graciously shared their lives and work with me.

1. All translations from the Spanish are my own, unless otherwise indicated.

2. See also Álvarez 1999; Lebon 1996, 1998; Thayer 2000, 2001; Barrig 1998; García Castro 2001; and Ewig 1999 for examples of this process in other Latin American countries.

3. Unlike other Latin American countries during the 1980s, Colombia was not suffering under a military regime. However, there was a call for electoral reform and negotiation with armed opposition groups during this period, as well as the creation of a new constitution expanding the political rights of Colombia's marginalized peoples (Bushnell 1993; Villareal 1994; Martz 1997).

4. The Pacific Route (La Ruta Pacífica) is a national women's peace organization that recently won an award from The United Nations Development Fund for Women (UNIFEM).

5. President Gaviria's development plan (1991–94) accelerated the economic opening ("apertura") begun tentatively in the 1950s; with a more neoliberal economic policy, foreign investment in Colombia doubled between 1990 and 1994 (Bergquist, Peñaranda, and Sánchez G. 2001, xvi), and international goods entered the country at an unprecedented rate. Reina argues that the *apertura* "devastated broad sectors of Colombian industry and agriculture thus exposed to the competitive pressures of the world market" (2001, 75).

6. Part of the impact of the neoliberal context is that first it appears to have enabled the "NGO boom," and at the same time, to have increased competition among NGOs for funding so that only the more "professional" ones are likely to survive. See Álvarez 1999; Gill 1997; Lebon 1998; Hulme and Edwards 1997.

7. Pastrana began peace negotiations with the Revolutionary Armed Forces of Colombia [Las Fuerzas Armadas Revolucionarias de Colombia (FARC)] in 1998. Mothers, sisters, wives, and daughters of soldiers held captive by the guerrilla group staged vocal national-level protests demanding that Pastrana agree to exchange them for FARC members held as political prisoners.

8. In fact, they never received the budget they needed to function at full speed, but were still in existence when I left the field in December 1999.

9. Babb (2001) suggests that this shift has to do with the government's need to cut spending and shrink state employment. Here economic policies coincide with gendered power relations with the result that women, even single mothers, are deemed expendable employees who can rely upon male economic support and are encouraged to "go home."

10. The preceding is all taken directly from the text of Law 188—EPAM—provided to me by Women's Department staff.

11. The preceding is taken from two documents supplied to me by Women's Department staff—"Democratic Leadership with a Gendered

Perspec-tive: Projection of EPAM" and "Toward Planning with a Gendered Perspective."

12. *Binomial* is defined in *Webster's Ninth New Collegiate Dictionary* (1998) as either "a mathematical expression consisting of two terms connected by a plus sign or minus sign" or "a biological species name consisting of two terms." I think it was the latter definition to which this woman alluded.

13. Puyana and Orduz (1998) argue that women's roles have changed considerably along with enormous social changes occurring during the past fifty years in Colombia. Processes of urbanization, along with expansion of the education system and changes in the structure of employment have been accompanied by changes in the family structure and women's status. The systematic use of contraception has resulted in lower fertility rates, there are more women in the labor force and education system, and there is more divorce and separation today than in the 1950s.

14. Stephen argues that "in Latin America, dominant cultural ideologies proposing that women's proper place is in the home are still powerful obstacles to women's political mobilization" (1997, 8).

15. The designation of women's control over their sexuality and reproduction as core feminist issues and the fact that abortion and lesbianism are the most controversial of these are widely accepted in the literature on Latin American women's movements (Chinchilla 1994; Stephen 1997).

16. See Puyana and Orduz (1998) for more information about the population control effort in Colombia and how it led to increased sexual education for women.

17. The National Women's Network (Red Nacional de Mujeres) argued in 1991 that botched abortion was the third leading cause of death among poor women in Colombia (1994, 47). Jean Franco notes that "74.5% of maternal deaths are the result of botched abortion" in Colombia (Franco 1998, 283, citing "Católicas por el Derecho a Decidir de Bogotá, 'Demandas a la Jerarquia Eclesiastica,'" *Conciencia Latinoamericana* (September–December 1994): 19.

18. Of course, the state is not always free to act as it pleases, either. In November 1998, the senate was considering reforming the legal code to decrease the penalty for abortion in the case of nonconsensual sex and life-threatening fetal deformities. The Catholic leadership argued that abortion was unacceptable under any circumstances (Suárez 1998). I heard a dramatic proof of the church's stance when Monsignor Giraldo, head of the Episcopalian Conference in Medellín, publicly equated abortion with the massacres committed by Colombia's armed groups.

19. I cannot discuss the details of my knowledge that "closeting" was going on without revealing more than I should about these persons' lives.

20. These issues are widespread. For instance, the Sixth Regional Latin American and Caribbean Feminist Meetings sparked a great deal of controversy in El Salvador; local newspapers carried stories entitled "Vienen las Lesbianas?" [Are the Lesbians Coming?] (Stephen 1997, 18–19).

21. *Marimacho* is defined in *Larousse Diccionario Usual,* 7th ed., as *"una mujer de aspecto o modales masculinos"* (a woman with masculine aspects or behavior). I have also heard that it can be similar in meaning to the English *tomboy.* In the context of the entire comment, I took it to have connotations of lesbianism, specifically "butchness."

REFERENCES

Álvarez, Sonia E. "Advocating Feminism: The Latin American Feminist NGO 'Boom.'" *International Feminist Journal of Politics* 1 (1999):181–209.

Babb, Florence E. *After Revolution: Mapping Gender and Cultural Politics in Neoliberal Nicaragua.* Austin: University of Texas Press, 2001.

Baden, Sally, and Ann Marie Goetz. "Who needs [Sex] when you can have [Gender]? Conflicting Discourses on Gender at Beijing." In *Feminist Visions of Development: Gender, Analysis and Policy.* Eds. C. Jackson and R. Pearson. New York: Routledge, 1998. 19–38.

Bakhtin, Mikhail M. "Discourse in the Novel." In *The Dialogic Imagination: Four Essays by M. M. Bakhtin.* Trans. Caryl Emerson and Michael Holquist. Austin: University of Texas Press, 1981.

Barrig, Maruja. "Los Malestares del Feminismo LatinoAmericano: Una Nueva Lectura." Paper delivered at the Latin American Studies Association Conference, Chicago, 1998.

Bergquist, Charles, et al, eds. *Violence in Colombia 1990–2000: Waging War and Negotiating Peace.* Wilmington, Del.: Scholarly Resources, 2001.

Bohman, Kristina. *Women of the Barrio: Class and Gender in a Colombian City.* Stockholm, Sweden: Stockholm Studies in Social Anthropology, 1984.

Bushnell, David. *The Making of Modern Colombia: A Nation in Spite of Itself.* Berkeley: University of California Press, 1993.

Chinchilla, Norma Stoltz. "Feminism, Revolution, and Democratic Transitions in Nicaragua." In *The Women's Movement in Latin America: Participation and Democracy.* Ed. J. S. Jaquette. Boulder, Colo.: Westview, 1994.

Duque, Andrea Dominguez. "Determinó la corte constitutional via libre a profesores homosexuales." *El Colombiano* (Medellín), September 10, 1998: 12(A).

Elson, Diane, ed. *Male Bias in the Development Process.* Manchester, England: Manchester University Press, 1992.

Escandón, Carmen Ramos. "Women's Movements, Feminism, and Mexican Politics." In *The Women's Movement in Latin America: Participation and Democracy.* Ed. J. S. Jaquette. Boulder, Colo.: Westview, 1994. 199–222.

Ewig, Christina. "The Strengths and Limits of the NGO Women's Movement Model: Shaping Nicaragua's Democratic Institutions." *Latin American Research Review* 34.3 (1999):75–102.

Ferguson, James. *The Anti-Politics Machine: "Development," Depoliticization, and Bureaucratic Power in Lesotho.* Minneapolis: University of Minnesota Press, 1994 [1990].

Foucault, Michel. "The Discourse on Language." In *The Archaeology of Knowledge and the Discourse on Language.* Trans. A.M. Sheridan Smith. New York: Pantheon, 1972.

Franco, Jean. "Defrocking the Vatican: Feminism's Secular Project." In *Cultures of Politics, Politics of Cultures.* Eds. S. Álvarez et al. Boulder, Colo.: Westview, 1998. 278–92.

Garcia Castro, Mary. "Engendering Powers in Neoliberal Times in Latin America: Reflections from the Left on Feminisms and Feminisms." *Latin American Perspectives* 28.6 (2001):17–37.

Gill, Lesley. "Power Lines: The Political Context of Nongovernmental Organization (NGO) Activity in El Alto, Bolivia." *Journal of Latin American Anthropology* 2.2 (1997):144–69.

Gutiérrez de Pineda, Virginia. *Cultura y Familia en Colombia.* Medellín, Colombia: Editorial Universidad de Antioquia, 1996.

Hulme, David, and Michael Edwards. *NGOs, States and Donors: Too Close for Comfort?* New York: St. Martins, 1997.

Kabeer, Naila. *Reversed Realities: Gender Hierarchies in Development Thought.* London: Verso, 1994.

Lebon, Nathalie. "The Professionalization of Women's Health Groups in São Paolo: The Troublesome Road towards Organizational Diversity." *Organization* 3.4 (1996): 588–609.

———. *The Labor of Love and Bread: Professionalized and Volunteer Activism in the São Paolo Women's Health Movement.* Ph.D. Dissertation, University of Florida, 1998.

Lind, Amy C. *Negotiating the Transnational: Constructions of Poverty and Identity Among Women's NGOs in Bolivia.* Paper presented at Latin American Studies Association Conference, Miami, Florida, March 16–18, 2000.

Marchand, Marianne H., and Jane L. Parpart. "Exploding the Canon: An Introduction/Conclusion." In *Feminism/Postmodernism/Development.* Eds. M. H. Marchand, J. L. Parpart. New York: Routledge, 1995. 1–22.

Martz, John D. *The Politics of Clientelism: Democracy and the State in Colombia.* New Brunswick, N.J.: Transaction, 1997.

Moi, Toril. Introduction to *French Feminist Thought: A Reader.* London: Basil Blackwell, 1987. 1–16.

Morales, German Jimenez. "Catarata de Alsas." *El Colombiano.* January 4, 1999, 1B.

Navarro, Marysa. "First Feminist Meeting of Latin America and the Caribbean." *Signs: Journal of Women in Culture and Society* 8 (1982): 154–57.

Parpart, Jane L. "Deconstructing the Development 'Expert.'" In *Feminism/Postmodernism/Development.* 221–43.

Puyana, Yolanda. "Mujer y Política Social: El Caso de los Hogares Infantiles." In *Mujer, Amor y Violencia.* Ed. Grupo Mujer y Sociedad. Bogotá, Colombia: U. Nacional Tercer Mundo Editores, 1991.

Puyana, Yolanda, and Cristina Orduz. 1998. "Que Mis Hijas No Sufren Lo Que Yo Sufri: Dinámica de la Socialización de un Grupo de Mujeres de Sectores Populares. Estudio de Caso Sobre la Región Cundiboyacense." *Mujeres, Hombres, y Cambio Social.* Bogotá, Colombia: Facultad de Ciencias Humanas, Universidad Nacional, 1998. 23–84.

Rathgeber, Eva M. "WID, WAD, GAD: Trends in Research and Practice." *The*

Journal of Developing Areas 24 (1990): 489–502.

Red Nacional de Mujeres. *Nuestro Pensamiento y Palabra También Cuentan: Una Mirada Crítica a la Política Integral Para las Mujeres.* Bogotá, Colombia: Antropos, 1994.

Reina, Mauricio. "Drug Trafficking and the National Economy." In *Violence in Colombia 1990–2000: Waging War and Negotiating Peace.* Eds. C. Bergquist, et al. Wilmington, Del.: Scholarly Resources, 2001. 75–94.

Restrepo, Claudia Patricia, and John Jairo Orrego. *Proceso Organizativo Del Movimiento Feminista en Medellín 1970–1994: O de Cómo Las Mujeres Construyen Su Autonomía.* Thesis. University of Antioquia, Medellín, 1994.

Rivera, Alejandro Higuita. "La exfanfarria con teatro documental: Al Alba, prisionera de la justicia." *El Colombiano* (Medellín), February 19, 1999: 1(D).

Rosen, Fred, and Deidre McFedyen, eds. *Free Trade and Economic Restructuring in Latin America.* New York: Monthly Review Press, 1995.

Schmidt, Steffan W. "Women in Colombia: Attitudes and Future Perspectives in the Political System." *Journal of Interamerican Studies and World Affairs* 17 (1975): 465–89.

———. The Origins of Gender Values: Notes on the Colombian Case. *Journal of Popular Culture* 22 (1988): 17–36.

Scott, Joan Wallach. "Gender, A Useful Category for Historical Analysis." In *Gender and the Politics of History.* Ed. J. W. Scott. New York: Columbia University Press, 1988.

Stephen, Lynn. *Women and Social Movements in Latin America: Power from Below.* Austin: University of Texas Press, 1997.

Suárez, Julian Giraldo. "Iglesia Católica se opone al proyecto de código penal." *El Colombiano* (Medellín), November 5, 1998, 12(A).

Thayer, Millie. "Traveling Feminisms: From Embodied Women to Gendered Citizenship." In *Global Ethnography: Forces, Connections, and Imaginations in a Postmodern World.* Eds. M. Burawoy, et al. Berkeley: University of California Press, 2000. 203–33.

———. "Transnational Feminism: Reading Joan Scott in the Brazilian Sertâo." *Ethnography,* 2.2 (2001):243–71.

Villareal, Norma. "Movimientos de Mujeres y Participación Política en Colombia: 1930–1991." In *Historia, Género y Política: Movimiento de Mujeres y Participación Política en Colombia 1930-1991.* Eds. L. G. Luna, N. Villareal. Barcelona: University of Barcelona, 1994. 59–194.

Young, Kate. *Planning Development with Women: Making a World of Difference.* London: Macmillan, 1993.

Donna F. Murdock *is assistant professor of anthropology at Sewanee University of the South. She coauthored a* Feminist Studies *article on Latin American/Caribbean feminist ethnography with Carla Freeman and wrote an article on NGOs forthcoming in* Ethnos. *Currently she is working on a manuscript based on eighteen months of field research with feminist NGOs in Medellín, Colombia.*

A Limited Women's Empowerment

Politics, the State, and Development in Northwest India

Sumi Madhok

Feminist development theorists and practitioners face a growing challenge from an increased appropriation of their conceptual language and categories by international and state-level organizations or what I shall term here "institutional feminism." This institutionalized feminism employs the language but not the feminist explanatory frameworks in identifying and providing solutions to women's subordination. Above all, institutional feminisms lead to the depoliticisation of the feminist development agenda and the consequent blurring of the distinction between a feminist emancipatory politics and the gender policy frameworks of many institutions. For instance, the World Bank, several United Nations agencies, nongovernmental organizations (NGOs), and policies of nation states share the "empowerment platform" with feminist theorists and activists. While empowerment has become a "motherhood term" (Parpart, Rai, and Staudt 2002, 3) and a common ideological meeting point for disparate actors, its widespread deployment by no means masks the different conceptual, procedural, and substantive concerns that underlie the commitment of different institutions to women's empowerment. For feminist development theorists and practitioners, empowerment not only signifies an "expansion of freedom of choice and action" (World Bank 2002, 11) through increasing the efficiency and responsiveness of institutions but also involves a radical restructuring of gendered social and political structures of power (Batliwala 1994; Agarwal 1994; Young 1993) through political engagements and activism (Batliwala 1994; Kabeer 1994; Staudt 2002) in order to "redistribute power and resources" (Stein 1997, 1). In light of this distinct deployment of the empowerment language, can there be any prospects for a collaborative politics between feminists and other institutional development actors? Is a feminist grassroots politics compatible with policies for women's development sponsored by states? In this article, I shall analyse the nature and limits of collaborative politics between feminists and state-led development agencies by focusing on the experience of the Women's Development Programme (WDP) sponsored by the state government of Rajasthan, in Northwestern India. This programme, I argue, serves well as a test case for analysing the interface between feminist ideas of development and those upheld by the institutions of the state.

The WDP is an effective test case for an analysis of the relationship between state initiatives and feminist politics for the following reasons. The programme drew on a variegated set of development ideas. It incorporated ideas espoused by the internationalist women's development frameworks, feminist conceptual frames, and the development goals set by the Indian state in its sixth five-year plan. The development programme conceived its principal role and activities in consultative exercises with women's development experts, activists, researchers, and NGOs, an exercise that resulted in the adoption of a development ethos markedly different from the top-down, skill-disbursement nature of common development programmes of the time. This departure from other development programmes was reflected in the WDP's focus. It shifted its emphasis away from the mechanisms delivering benefits to the recipients of development policies, to the subjects of development, that is, to women. The development mantra embodied in the WDP was one of women's "self-development" and "self-empowerment." Women were addressed as subjects of development policy rather than as incidental beneficiaries of development policies aimed at households and children. A novel alliance was forged between the state and nongovernment actors, which in turn led to the creation of new administrative structures within the WDP to accommodate and articulate the concerns of the feminist researchers, activists, and NGOs. This partnership fostered in its wake a new and direct relationship between development policies and women and established a linkage between rural and urban women, with the latter taking on responsibility of training the primary workers of the programme, the *sathins* (literally, female companions). Over the years, however, the programme has undergone changes in its orientation. In its early years, the programme enjoyed relative independence from the state development bureaucracy, which lent the programme considerable flexibility in its development activity. In the last decade, however, the programme has seen a radical shift in its operational strategy and ideological outlook. It has become closely tied to the development activities of the state and is now mostly used to strengthen the delivery mechanisms of the development state.

In this article, I first describe the objectives of the WDP and the institutional mechanisms that oversee its workings. I then shift my attention from an institutional discussion to one that is experiential in content and focus on the experience of women known as the *sathins,* who are the primary workers within this programme and in effect are responsible for bringing about "women's development" in the villages. Finally, I highlight the conflict between the state and its "agents of change" or the *sathins.* The *sathins,* largely illiterate or semiliterate and belonging mainly to the lowest castes, learned through their training in feminist pedagogical methods to incorporate the importance of personal self-transformation in their understanding of "development" and in time challenged the state-led initiatives on women's development.

The WDP: Genesis, Objectives, and Structure

In independent India, while economic and social development was distinguished in Indian intellectual debates from the 1950s, development remained a general, all-embracing objective that all sections of society were expected to share. The development of women was declared as a policy concern of the Indian state in the sixth five-year plan (1981), where it was discussed as a separate chapter in the plan document. It has since continued to be mentioned as an objective of development policy.[1] The WDP was set up in Rajasthan as a response to the failure of various other development programmes to involve or to benefit women though the development interventions of the state.[2] While there existed several development programmes with a female component, it was conceded by the state development bureaucracy that these had little or no effect on improving the inclusion and the participation of women within development.[3]

The WDP was announced formally in April 1984. It was launched in six districts of Rajasthan, with UNICEF providing funds for five districts and the sixth designated as a "tribal sub-plan area" and incorporated within the tribal development programme (WDP, DRDPR, 1984, 1).[4] The programme described itself as a "pioneering attempt to improve the status of women by raising their awareness levels and thereby increasing access to various developmental interventions." In a conceptual paper, the WDP stated that it recognised that most governmental schemes floated were inaccessible to poor rural women because of the latter's lack of "receiving mechanisms," and therefore it set itself the task of creating "such mechanisms through flexible and diversified structures backed by effective participation of women at the grass roots level" (WDP, DRDPR, 1984, 1).[5] The objective of the policy for women's development, it was stated, "should consist of a shift of attitude from one of compassion and welfare to that of treatment of women as equal partners with men in the family, in the social situation and economic activity, in education and culture" (WDP, DRDPR, 1984, 20). The document declared that women were not merely passive recipients of development schemes but possessed independent problems that needed to be recognised and prioritised.

The broad aim of the WDP was stated "to empower women through communication of information, education, and training and to enable them to recognise their social and economic status" (WDP, DRDPR, 1984, 1). Education and training were upheld as "the basis of development, as the critical facilitating factor in the participation of women as agents, animators and beneficiaries of development" (WDP, DRDPR, 1984, 20).[6] In order to achieve the empowerment of women, it was considered important to "encourage and create agencies, groups and individuals to articulate concern towards indignities and discrimination against women" (WDP, DRDPR 1984, 1). These concerns were translated into the following practical measures:

1. Support for the development of women's groups at the village level;
2. Allocation of space within the government institutional framework to women's activists, NGOs, and academics. They were entrusted with the responsibility of training the primary workers to meet the challenges of the programme.

No government programme before the WDP had declared its overriding goal to develop capabilities of women so that they would be able to benefit from the various development projects and schemes sponsored by the state. Consequently, a new administrative structure was set up in order to meet the structural needs of the WDP. The administration of the WDP set up linkages and administrative networks between a government department, local NGOs, and an academic institute. Local nongovernment bodies were involved in the development of training and information modules for the programme and the Institute of Development Studies (IDS) Jaipur was assigned the task of preparing evaluations for the programme. The external funding of the programme by UNICEF ensured the noninterference of government departments in the everyday functioning of the programme.

The new institutional setup that owed its origins to the WDP was the Information Development and Resource Agency (IDARA), which provided an institutional framework for technical support and training. The IDARA was set up both at the state as well as at the district level (see Table 1). The state-level IDARA was entrusted with the task of training the project directors and prachetas (a person of "learning and commitment") within the WDP and the district IDARAs were entrusted the responsibility of training the *sathins*. At the top of WDP's administrative hierarchy at the district level is the project director, who is the chief coordinator and is required to work in tandem with local government institutions, government departments and voluntary agencies. On the second rung of the district administrative hierarchy are the prachetas. They function as principal animators within the programme and are entrusted with the responsibility of selecting and supervising the *sathins*. At the lowest rung of the WDP ladder are the *sathins*. While they are not regarded as part of the formal administrative hierarchy, they in effect constitute the "recognizable face" of the programme at the village level.

Table 1
Organizational Structure of the WDP

Level	Organization/Worker	Function
State	Department of Women, Nutrition, and Children	Overall coordination and administration
	State Information and Development And Resource Agency (IDARA)	Information, training, staff selection, newsletter
	Institute of Development Studies, Jaipur (independent, nongovernmental body)	Monitoring, evaluation
District		
	District Women's Development Agency	Administration
	District Information and Development and Resource Agency	Information training, district newsletter
Field		
Pracheta	Supervisor of 10 *sathins*	Block-level worker
Sathin	Trainer, liaison person	Main field functionary, organizer/animator
	One in 10 villages	of groups

Source: Das 1992.

It is important to note that two competing ideas of development influenced the workings of the WDP. The first was a standard, Women in Development(WID)-influenced idea, but the second was a more radical perspective. This radical perspective, favoured by the non-government component of the programme, introduced the feminist empowerment framework of development into the programme. The permeation of this empowerment framework into the WDP can be attributed to the following three reasons:

• The structural partnership envisaged within the WDP allowed for different development perspectives to coexist within the programme. The state participated in the programme together with its nongovernment partners, namely the NGOs, women's activists, and academics. This exercise, with its distinct partners, resulted in the influence of distinct ideological frames informing the programme.

• The financial arrangements of the programme made it possible for these divergent perspectives on women's development to coexist. The programme was accorded a low priority by the state government. This meant that other groups involved in the programme could take advantage of the low-profile development status of the programme, tailoring it according to their intellectual and ideological leanings.[7] The reasons behind the low-priority status of the WDP were the following: the funding of the programme by UNICEF in the first six years of its existence meant that the programme was not accountable to the state financially and, since the monitoring and evaluation tasks were entrusted to IDS Jaipur, the state bureaucracy exercised no effective role in monitoring the progress of the programme. The difference in the understanding of the concept of women's empowerment in the state and its nongovernment partners can be see in at least two areas of the WDP: in the roles and activities of the *sathins* and in the design and content of the *sathin* training modules.

• The empowerment and WID perspectives are not watertight in character and do have overlapping concerns. The shared nature of these concerns, although understood differently by the proponents of both the approaches, are often upheld and supported by both as important policy goals. For instance, both the WID and Gender and Development(GAD) approaches stress the need for women to organise themselves into groups or collectives. However, the ends to which this mobilisation is aimed differ. The accent of the WID approach on women's collectives and groups is to ensure and increase their bargaining power in the market, whereas the emphasis of the GAD approaches is towards increasing women's political voice (Young 1997).

The difference between the development concerns of the state and those of its partners within the WDP, women's activists, NGOs, and academics is most acutely reflected in the training of programme workers who were meant to implement the development goals in the villages. The training of the WDP workers was not confined to dispensing skills that would lead to their employment or economic advancement. The resource persons responsible for the training component of the programme patterned their pedagogic exercises on feminist perspectives of empowerment and consciousness raising, which challenged popular notions of women's place within society and of their work and agency.[8]

Collaborative Politics, Social Change, and the Sathins

The *sathins* were the main actors within the WDP. They were entrusted with the responsibility of implementing WDP goals in the villages. Their tasks included motivating people to adopt family planning methods and to send girls to school; discouraging child marriages; and raising awareness against domestic violence, alcoholism, and the practice of dowry. The *sathins* involved women in credit and other development schemes and encouraged them to participate in political meetings of the *panchayats* (elected village councils)[9] and to exercise their votes. Above all, the *sathins* were instrumental in informing women of their rights and entitlements and for demystifying the abstract nature of the state institutions.

The radical nature of the *sathins*'s work in the villages was anything but a spontaneous outcome of their involvement within the WDP. It was the product of a deliberate project conceived and designed by the feminist academics-activists responsible for the training of the *sathins*. The first training of the *sathins* was held at the village of Bada Padampura and lasted for month. It had twenty-four participants (twenty-three *sathins* and one *pracheta*) who belonged to all castes and were between the ages of sixteen and fifty-five. Although not explicitly described as such, the training exercise developed by the resource persons designated as trainers within the programme bears a strong resemblance to the concept of empowerment education devised by Paulo Freire (1972). The trainers worked with the Freirian assumption of collective knowledge emerging from a group sharing experience in which the participants were looked upon as subjects who had their own contributions based upon their own understandings and reflections on the various issues brought to their notice by the trainers.

In addition to the activity of familiarising the *sathins* with the administrative organization of the WDP and the state bureaucracy through discussions and trips organised to the local government institutions, there was extensive training in the objectives of "team work, leadership skills, self reliance, self expression, decision making, concerted action, internalisation, consolidation of information, establishing rapport, creating solidarity, introducing and elaborating on issues" ("Report on the Training Programme" 1984, 15). Sessions were held during the training encouraging the women to express themselves and to relate their life experiences through the rewriting of popular folk songs and the staging of plays. Discussions and activities revolved around stereotypes of the "good" and the "bad" woman and the role of socialisation in corroborating these prototypes, and involved examining attitudes towards caste and religious differences and attitudes towards one's own body. The training modules introduced notions of marital rape and control over one's body; the necessity of control over one's earned income; and the relationship between property rights, inheritance laws, and women's status in society. Legal discussions examined fundamental rights and the constitution of India; the vagaries of the legal system, including aspects of local reality, such as the local *thana* (police station), the power of the *thaanedar* (police constable), the ultimate authority of the constitution and civil rights. According to a note of the state IDARA, "the nonhierarchical, free, adventurous mood of the training had its transforming effect on the *sathins*. They went back to their villages charged with a feeling of abandon and confidence, ready to begin something and everything at their own level without waiting for anyone to call a start. It was probably an overdoing" (Jain et al. 1986, 14).

Upon their return from the training, the *sathins* found a hostile reception to their ideas and plans. It must not be assumed that once the *sathins* joined the WDP their lives were somehow instantaneously or indeed remarkably transformed. It can be said, however, that the injustice of the practices central to their lives became more apparent to them once they had completed their training and returned to their villages. The efforts of the *sathins* in spreading this consciousness of subordination amongst other village women made them targets of social animosity and even aggression. Some of this mistrust was related to the visibility of the *sathin* in the village, her "newfound" confidence and boldness evident in her questioning of age-old social practices. The *sathins* began querying the basis of many entrenched beliefs and social practices and the administrative decisions within the village. For instance, they questioned the decisions and practices of the *sarpanch* (chairperson of the *panchayat*),[10] particularly in relation to the extension of state benefits and subsidies to landowning castes and powerful interests in the community. The suspicion of the *sathin* was compounded when she attempted to form women's collectives in the village and to organise regular meetings of women:

> In the beginning, the villagers were suspicious about us sathins conducting meeting with the village women. I was accused of ruining households and family life by my ideas. *'Yeh to maro ghar bigaregi'* (she will ruin my house) was what they used to say of me. In the beginning, very few women came out to attend the meetings. They said that meetings were held by men and attended by men. I had to work hard at making them understand that even women could get together and form a group.[11]

The social opposition to the *sathins* highlights the deep mistrust and cynicism in the event of any attempt to change the social attitudes towards women and in the comportment of women themselves. In time, however, the unwritten social rule laying down the invisibility of women in the village public spaces was challenged by the emerging women's presence through their collectives and other WDP activities. Women who were not allowed out of their homes except to carry out household chores or to work in the fields or graze animals were now meeting and deliberating on their own and some of them (the *sathins*) were beginning to travel to other villages and even cities for meetings and overnight stays. Many *sathins* found the travelling to be the hardest. Their absence from their homes over several days on WDP assignments fueled rumours and scandal about their personal lives. A common contributing factor to the general suspicion of the *sathins* was the popular perception of a "connection" between the state and the *sathin*. She was popularly held as a *"sarkari"* agent or "agent of the state" or belonging to its criminal investigation arm, the Criminal Investigating Department(CID). Even today, while most *sathins* who were interviewed view themselves as accepted and even highly regarded in their villages,[12] they do speak of the trailing suspicion that comes to the fore when any incident in the village draws attention to the "outsiders." This happens most notably in the event of a report of "child marriages" (marriages of children and infants):

> If a marriage of children is organised by a family or if the news of its
> imminent occurrence gets around, then our life becomes terrible.
> The villagers gather around us and think that we must have been the
> ones to inform the police or other officials. Especially on Akha Teej
> the villagers really trouble the *sathins*. However, there is already an
> official alert around these dates and often there is an enormous
> police presence. The villagers conduct weddings in secret as they fear
> that if they organised these openly, then we would inform the police.
> They often gather around my house and threaten me against inform-
> ing the police.[13]

The position of the *sathin* within the state administrative apparatus was at best ambivalent. According to the original terms of her
employment, she was not a government functionary. However, the
presence of the WDP state officials in the villages in their frequent
dealings with the *sathins* established the physical visibility of the state
in the village. The documentary practices of the state, in the form of
newsletters and other information addressed to the *sathins,* sealed
this popular perception. Organised meetings of women from other
villages and even districts, frequent village visits of WDP officials in
their vehicles, the official monthly document, *kagaj,* addressed to the
sathins, all contributed to the popular perception of the "official
access" enjoyed by the *sathin* and of her capacity to reach the nerve
centres of state decision-making apparatus. The *sathins* admitted that
the arrival of the *kagaj* (official letter informing them of the upcoming meetings and events and their official participants) every month
was seen by all the villagers; "even the postman used to be scared of
the *kagaj* that used to come for Kalyani."[14] Again, the perceived association with the state was double-edged. While this perceived proximity with the state lent the *sathins* a sense of physical security, it was
also a source of conflict.[15]

Finally, it is the equation between personal emancipation and development that marks the *sathins* as unique agents of development. The
sathins see themselves as role models introducing into their everyday
practice many of the "new" ideas that they discuss with the women in
their villages.[16] The idea of personal change in their own lived conditions was stressed not only at the time of their training,[17] but it also
came to be expected of them by by the state officials of the WDP.[18]
There are numerous incidents related by the *sathins* that bring to light
their struggles in making these changes in their own lives. The changes
are indicative of an attempt not only to engage with but also to inter-
nalise many of the general rights-based ideas they encountered at the

time of their training. With the increasing internalisation of many of these ideas by the *sathins,* as evidenced through the changes that they sought to introduce into their lives, there occurred a gradual discomfort with the development outlook of the state. An instance of the move away from the statist discourse was the criticism of the bureaucratic and impersonal treatment of women's issues by the officials responsible for the WDP. They no longer saw themselves only as agents of the government involved in propagating its agenda but also as being involved in spreading the idea of rights and fighting for social justice:

> In Loonawas village (Narwa Kalan Panchayat) in Nagaur district, there was a young girl of *Nai* caste who was burnt to death by her in-laws. We wanted to raise the issue and create awareness about the ill treatment of young married women but the WDP office was not ready to support us as the case had taken place outside Jaipur district. The *sathins* however believe that we must respond to women's circumstances in other districts too and we must do away with these district barriers in respect of women's development.[19]

Reclaiming Dominion, Redefining Development, and Limiting Empowerment

Today the WDP continues to exist, although it is no longer the only development programme aimed at rural women in Rajasthan.[20] The radical empowerment component of the programme has been effectively silenced and it exists only as a caricature of the original programme. This winding down of the programme began in the early 1990s, during which the WDP witnessed a systematic appropriation by the state of the spaces within the programme that had epitomised its nonhierarchical and participatory character and functioning. The change in the WDP is evidenced in the increased bureaucratisation marked by administrative procedures, reports, and inspections and the collection of statistics and setting of tangible development targets to calculate the usefulness of the work of the *sathins.* The *sathins* are now required to assume the new responsibilities and work profile of these programmes, and their work is dominated by the implementation of predetermined vertical government programmes. The WDP no longer recruits new *sathins,* although there continue to exist vacant *sathin* positions. Even the *prachetas* are now recruited on a contractual basis through "contractors" in order to avoid recruiting staff and paying benefits on a long-term basis.[21] Both the *prachetas* and the *sathins* have formed workers' unions and have initiated legal proceedings against their employer, the state of Rajasthan.

As mentioned earlier, the official profile of the WDP was unremarkable. In the initial years, the state remained a dormant partner, not being responsible for the training, funding, and monitoring and evaluation of the programme. Three events brought the program within the sharp focus of the state. The withdrawal of financial support for the programme by UNICEF in 1990 placed financial matters for the WDP under the management of the state, and consequently the WDP had to provide evidence of its achievements in quantifiable terms that could be statistically recorded. Public demonstrations organised by the *sathins* in protest against the *sati* of Roop Kanwar[22] and those in the aftermath of the rape of *sathin* Bhanwari Devi of village Bhateri[23] drew the attention of the state and national media and women's activists to the primary workers within the programme.[24] This display of collective solidarity by the *sathins* encouraged them in several instances to weave an identity independent of their association with the state and to participate in various citizen issues and activities organised by other women's groups and other NGOs in Rajasthan. A telling example of this newly emergent spirit of defiance was the participation of nine *sathins* at the National Conference of Women's Movements held at Kozhikode, Kerala, in December 1990. These *sathins* were a part of a group of forty women from Kekri Panchayat Samiti in Ajmer, who attended the conference and collectively identified themselves as members of the women's group Kekri. This identification of many of the *sathins* in that delegation as members of a women's group, rather than as employees of the WDP, led to the dismissal from the programme of the five *sathins* from Kekri Panchayat Samiti, along with their pracheta, Kiran Dubey, on February 15, 1991. The reason proffered was that the women were under the *sathin* programme of the government and could not attend the conference under the banner of women's group Kekri.[25]

The dismissal of the *sathins* of Kekri marked a significant turning point in the state-WDP-*sathins* relationship. It did so in three ways. It drew attention to the status of the *sathins* within the WDP; it signalled the state's increased involvement in and influence over the programme; and it marked the beginning of the end of the radical influence of the WDP itself. Following the dismissal of the Kekri *sathins* the position of the *sathins* as state employees within the WDP became the focus of debate. The dismissal of the *sathins* was defended on the grounds of their being state employees, a reason that was in marked contrast to the declared intent of the state, which had regarded the *sathins* as "voluntary workers." In dismissing the Kekri *sathins*, the state inadvertently bestowed upon the *sathins* the status of "state employee." Ironically, it was to assert their status and rights as state employees that the *sathins* initiated legal proceedings against the state. On May 9, 1991, the *sathins* filed a writ in the High Court of Rajasthan against their arbitrary dismissal.[26]

In 1992, the WDP was extended to nine districts of the state. However, there was to be one change. The *sathins* were no longer to be the defining face of the programme. In a note on the functioning of the WDP, the department of Directorate of Women and Child Development(WC&N), spelt out the following reasons prompting the shift in strategy within the programme.[27] According to the file note, the *sathins* had failed to mobilise and reach out to the women of the whole *Gram Panchayat*. They had been able to relate only to the women of their own villages and had been unable to fulfill the original expectations of the programme. Furthermore, it was felt that the *sathin* programme was based on a model of a "lone crusader," which in turn increased the vulnerability of the *sathin* to caste-based and other hostilities. These drawbacks, it was argued, would be overcome by adopting a "group model" of women's development, which would pay increased attention to credit schemes, income and skill-generating activities.

The adoption of the women's group model of women's development within the WDP placed it firmly along the lines of a WID pattern of development. Principal among the WID prescriptions is the unmistakable faith in income-generating activities, training, skill disbursement, and access to credit. It is for these purposes that the WID advocates lay stress on the organization of women into collectives (Young 1993). The promotion of the women's group model of women's development has led to an increase in the cash-credit schemes of the state to the detriment of its earlier vision of regarding this programme to be essentially a vehicle of disseminating new ideas and creating a new "way of thinking" among the women in the villages. This new wave within the WDP was realised fully with the floating of the concept of the "self-help groups," which was given the shape of a scheme in 1998. According to a District of Women's Development Agency (DWDA) file note titled "Self Help Groups," the scheme would "improve the access of rural women to the institutional credit network."[28]

Recent WDP documents released by the state continue to list the WDP as an important programme among the several existing development programmes for women. They acknowledge the achievements and successes of the WDP,[29] but fall short of extending credit to the village women who made possible the radical change demanded by the programme. They do not, for instance, endorse the work of the *sathins,* who in most cases embodied the radical message of the programme in its initial years and helped to unmask and explain within the village the exploitative nature of social practices that denied dignity to women. The *sathins* are instead regarded with suspicion and are considered as unreliable and disloyal workers of the state.

For their part, the *sathins* continue to voice concern about the women's-group model of development, which, according to them, replaces the empowerment component of the WDP with the more "conventional beneficiary model of women's development."[30] The sathins have won their battle in the Indian supreme court against their arbitrary dismissal. On February 28, 2001, a division bench of the Supreme Court of India in *Smt Geeta, Jhuma, Nausar, Nandu v. The Government of Rajasthan* ordered the Women's Development Programme to reinstate the four *sathins* within the WDP. While one of them, *sathin* Patasi has died, the ten-year legal struggle of these rural, poor, and largely illiterate women for their rights against arbitrary conduct of the state has been truly remarkable.

Conclusion

In this article I have addressed the question of the nature and limits of a feminist collaborative politics. I have outlined the case of the WDP as a representative model based on a partnership between the state and feminist groups. The WDP experience can be seen as an unsuccessful experiment in feminist collaborations with the state primarily because the radical quintessence of the WDP was short-lived, a tragic denouement of the increased state control, which led the WDP to slip into the form characteristic many of the other state-sponsored schemes. However, there were some lasting vestiges of this collaboration. Despite the erosion of the radical nature of the programme, the women trained to perform the role of "principal animators" within the programme continue to display many of the ideals of their empowerment training through their engagement with dominant patriarchal practices and corrupt and inefficient bureaucracy and through their espousal of women's equality before law and their rights to property, equal wages, education, and political office.

NOTES

This article is based on my doctoral fieldwork on the rights narratives of the *sathins.* The fieldwork was conducted in the districts of Jaipur and Ajmer in Rajasthan, northwestern India, over eight months, between September

1998 and April 1999. The fieldwork was made possible by a doctoral field-work grant from the Central Research Fund, University of London, and the Inlaks foundation.

1. The sixth five-year plan was the first to acknowledge the "backward" condition of women and the "drawbacks" that had led to their disadvantaged status. Repeated pregnancies, lack of education (formal and informal), social prejudices, and economic dependence were identified as the main causes of women's lack of development. The plan announced the economic emancipation of the family, with a special emphasis on women, as the focus of development policy for women. It observed the role of voluntary action and grassroots-level organizations in generating support for fighting social prejudice against women (*Sixth Five-Year Plan* 1981). The seventh five-year plan also included a chapter "Socioeconomic Programmes for Women"(*Seventh Five Year Plan 1985).* The current ninth five-year plan, now in place, includes a chapter titled "Empowerment of Women and Development of Children" (*Ninth Five-Year Plan* 2000).

2. See *Women's Development Project Rajasthan (DRDPR): Concept Paper* 1984. Henceforth, references to this document will be (WDP, DRDPR, 1984). See also *Prashasnik Prativedan avam Pragati Vivaran* [The annual reports of the department of women, child development and nutrition 1995–99].

3. In 1984 there did exist several programmes on women's development in the state. Programme areas included functional literacy for adult women under the Integrated Child Development Services (ICDS) programme, special nutrition, women's polytechnics, the industries departments programme of 1,000 household industries, and the various schemes of the department/board for social welfare (WDP, DRDPR, 1984, 18).

4. See *Development of Women and Children: A Brief on the Efforts Made in Rajasthan* 1999, 2.

5. At the outset, the districts of Jaipur and Ajmer were included in the six districts selected for the experimental running of the WDP. In 1995, the WDP was extended to fourteen districts in the state, and by 1996 it was extended to thirty-one districts.

6. Accordingly, the official stated objectives of the WDP were pronounced as the following: to identify programmes for women's development and to create mechanisms for their implementation. Women's development, it was felt, must especially concentrate on women who suffer from social disabilities resulting from societal oppression and gender discrimination. It was recognized that child bearing and caring were intimately linked to women's welfare and that therefore ante-natal, post-natal, and motherhood care must be a crucial part of any development initiative. Finally, in order to enhance the social and economic status of women, the official WDP documents noted the need to extend financial support to nonstate institutions involved in the development and concerns of women (WDP, DRDPR, 1984, 1).

7. Interview with Sharada Jain, Jaipur, Rajasthan, March 1999.

8. For a detailed account of the training modules, see "Report on the

Training Programme" 1984, 9. The *panchayat* represents the bottom rung of a three-tiered system of local government in India. Above the village panchayat (also known as the *Gram Panchayat*) is the *Panchayat Samiti*, which is a block-level institution, and on top rests the *Zila Parishad*, which is a district-level local government body.

10. Interview with Rampyari, Village Kharkhada, *Panchayat Samiti*, Jumwa Ramgarh Jaipur, Rajasthan, December 22, 1998. According to her, "In the beginning, (when I had just joined the WDP) I had taken five women to get sterilised. The *sarpanch* said that I should get them done on his name. During that time there used to be sterilization targets handed out to all officials and he wanted me to put those cases under his name so that he could make up his targets. He said that he would pay me money for it. I refused. In my first meetings with the village women, I was told that I had entered into a confrontational relationship with the villagers by refusing to do as the *sarpanch* asked."

11. Interview with Rampyari.

12. Interview with *sathin* Kalyani, Village Mokhumpura, *Gram Panchayat* Mokhumpura, *Panchayat Samiti,* Dudu, district Jaipur, Rajasthan, December 14, 1998. She said, "Earlier they used to oppose, even used to fight with us. Now whenever there is a *bada kaam* (important work), the *sarpanch* calls for me and says " *Kalyani ki durrie le aao*" (the *sarpanch* calls for a rug to be placed for Kalyani).

13. Interview with *sathin* Prem, Village Teetriya, district Jaipur, Rajasthan, December 20, 1998. *Akha Teej* is the festival celebrated on the third day of the fortnight of *Baisakh*—the month of May in the Hindu calendar. It is notoriously linked to the custom of marriages of infants or children in Rajasthan.

14. Interview with *sathin* Kalyani.

15. According to Unnithan and Srivastava (1997), the demand of the *sathins* to be included within the official state administrative structure was resisted by the IDARA and the IDS research team, although they supported the *sathins* in their bid for increased remuneration.

16. Interview with *sathin* Kalyani. According to her, "I have stopped the marriage of my infant daughter. . . . the marriage of the little girls of neighbours can only be discouraged once the infant marriages in one's home are stopped. My younger jeth's (brother-in law) daughter was only six months and mine was 3 years old when the family decided on their marriage. I was firm in my resolve not to let the marriage take place. . . . There was a great deal of familial opposition to my decision."

17. Interview with Savitri Sharma a retired *pracheta*, Jaipur, Rathasthan, February 27, 1999.

18. The insistence that the *sathins* embody many of the ideas they were involved in spearheading is at times questioned by the *sathins* themselves. According to many of them, the authorities did not realise the monumental nature of everyday struggles that were involved in bringing about social change.

19. Interview with Gulli Devi, Village Moondoti, Panchayat Sambhar, district Jaipur, Rajasthan, March 16, 1999.
20. The Rajasthan government has introduced the following programmes, which run in tandem with the WDP and in some cases are even implemented by the WDP. These include the Development of Women and Children in Rural Areas(DWCRA), which fosters development of women and children in rural areas; Ladli, which is aimed at adolescent girls; and the Mahila Rajgir Yojana, which introduces nontraditional income-generating activities for women. For a full description of these programmes see *Development of Women and Children, A brief on the efforts made in Rajasthan* 1999.
21. A monthly Hindi newspaper published from Jaipur raised the issue of the exploitation of the *prachetas* by the newly introduced private contract-based system of *pracheta* employment. According to the newspaper report, the prachetas are no longer hired by the state but by private contractors who pay them as little as 800 to 1,400 rupees per month, as opposed to those *prachetas* who were hired under the WDP recruitment drive in the initial phase of the programme, who were paid nearly 5,500 rupees per month. The newly recruited *prachetas,* the paper claims, are not given employment contract papers and do not receive employment benefits, such as paid sick leave, travel, and dearness allowances, also know as costt-of-living adjustments. See *Ujala Chadhi* (Jaipur), October 1998.
22. Roop Kanwar was an eighteen-year-old girl who was burnt alive on the pyre of her husband as a *sati* on September 4, 1987, at Deorala village in district Sikar, Rajasthan.
23. The gang rape of *sathin* Bhanwari Devi took place on September 22, 1992, as a "punishment" for trying to stop a child marriage from taking place amongst the Gujjar community in the village of Bhateri, in the *Panchayat Samiti* of Bassi. However, the rape itself constituted only the first in a long list of humiliations and betrayals suffered by Bhanwari Devi. The local police refused to register a First Information Report of the incident. After considerable pressure by the project director of the DWDA Jaipur, a report was filed, but Bhanwari was denied a medical examination for fifty-two hours after the assault. In a women's rally organised a month after the rape of Bhanwari, on October 22, 1992, thousands of women activists from other states and rural women from Rajasthan marched through the streets of Jaipur in protest at the failure of the state to apprehend the rapists. The investigation of the rape itself was protracted, with none of the accused charged in the first year. The first arrest was made seventeen months after the rape occurred. In November 1995 the judge (the sixth appointed on the case) at the district and sessions court acquitted all the five accused (Rajan and Mathur 1994).
24. Interview with Sharada Jain.
25. Interview with Deepa Martins, Ajmer Mahila Samooh (Ajmer Women's Group), Ajmer, Rajasthan, March 18, 1999.

26. Delivering a judgment on the *sathin*'s writ petition on March 10, 1992, the high court judge, Justice S. N. Bhargawa, declared the summary dismissal of the *sathins* as a breach of the natural principles of justice and ordered the immediate reinstatement. However, the government of Rajasthan was successful in obtaining a stay on the reinstatement of the *sathins*. A subsequent two-bench judgment of the high court quashed its earlier decision and defined the *sathins* as volunteers rather than workers of the WDP. The *sathins* proceeded to raise their case in the supreme court.

27. The file note is titled "Need for Reexamining the Structure at the Grassroot Level in WDP: The *sathin* model vis-à-vis women's group strategy," Department of Women, Children and Nutrition, Government of Rajasthan, File Records, Jaipur, no date.

28. The file note on the WDP is titled "Self Help Groups'," Department of Women, Children and Nutrition, Government of Rajasthan, File Records, Jaipur, no date).

29. In a brief prepared for the Parliamentary Committee on Women's Empowerment in 1997, the office of the DWDA, Jaipur, listed ten areas in which positive changes had been brought about in the thinking of rural women as a result of the work of the WDP. The achievements of the WDP are also elaborated upon in *Draft Policy for Women in Rajasthan* 1998.

30. Annual report of the Mahila Vikas Abhikaran *sathin* Karamchari Sangh (the third state-level meeting of the Sathins Workers Union), October 14–15, 1996.

REFERENCES

Agarwal, Bina (1994) *A Field of One's Own: Gender and land Rights in South Asia.* Cambridge, England: Cambridge University Press.

Batliwala, S. (1994) "The Meaning of Women's Empowerment: New Concepts From Action." In G. Sen, et al (eds.) *Population Policies Reconsidered: Health, Empowerment and Rights,* 17 Cambridge, Mass.: Harvard University Press.

Das, Maitreyi (1992) *The Women's Development Program in Rajasthan: A case study in group formation for women's development.* Policy Research Working Paper. Washington, D.C.: Population and Human Resources Department, World Bank.

Development of Women and Children: A brief on efforts made in Rajasthan (1999) Jaipur: Department of Women, Child Development and Nutrition, Government of Rajasthan.

Dighe, Anita, and JainSharada (1987) *Women's Development Programme: Some insights in participatory evaluation.* Jaipur: Institute of Development Studies (IDS).

Draft Policy for Women in Rajasthan (August 1998) Jaipur: Government of Rajasthan.

Freire, Paulo (1972) *Pedagogy Of the Oppressed.* Translated by Myra Bergman Ramos. London: Penguin.

Jain, Sharda, et al (1986) *Exploring Possibilities* Jaipur, Rajasthan: Institute of Developmental Studies (IDS).

Kabeer, N. (1994) *Reversed Realities: Gendered hierarchies in development thought.* London: Verso.

Ninth Five-Year Plan, section 3.8, "Empowerment of Women and Development of Children" (2000). New Delhi: Planning Commission, Government of India.

Parliamentary Committee on Women and Empowerment: A brief note on Jaipur district September 30, 1997 to October 3, 1997. Jaipur, Rajasthan: Office of the Project Director, District Women's Development Agency(DWDA).

Parpart, Jane L., et al (eds.) (2002) *Rethinking Empowerment: Gender and development in a global/local world.* London: Routledge.

Rajan, Shobhita, and Mathur Kanchan (1994) "Will the Law Dispense its Justice," *The Hindu,* 1 March.

Prashasnik Prativedan avam Pragati Vivaran [The annual reports of the Department of Women, Child Development and Nutrition] (1995–1999) Jaipur: Directorate of Women and Child Development,(WC&N) Government of Rajasthan, Jaipur (Hindi).

"Report on the Training Programme Conducted in Bada Padampura" (1984). Jaipur, Rajasthan: Institute of Development Studies (IDS).

Review of The Women's Development Programme Rajasthan 1984–88 (n.d.) Jaipur: Government of Rajasthan.

The Sathin (1996). New Delhi: National Commission for Women, Government of India.

Sathin Ro Kagad [*Sathin* Monthly Newsletter] (1992) Jaipur: Rajasthan Adult Literacy Society, February.

Sixth Five-Year Plan, chapter 27, "Women And Development" (1981). New Delhi: Planning Commission, Government Of India.

Staudt, Kathleen (2002) "Engaging Politics: Beyond official empowerment discourse." In Jane L. Parpart, Shrin M. Rai, and Kathleen Staudt (eds.) *Rethinking Empowerment: Gender and development in a global/local world.* London: Routledge.

Stein, Jane (1997) *Empowerment and Women's Health: Theory, method, and practice.* London: Zed Books.

Unnithan, Maya, and K. Srivastava (1997) "Gender Politics, Development and Women's Agency in Rajasthan." In R. D. Grillo and R. L Stirrat (eds.) *Discourses of Development: Anthropological perspectives.* Oxford: Berg.

World Bank (2002) *Empowerment and Poverty Reduction: A source book.* Ed. Deepa Narayan. Washington, D.C.: World Bank.www.worldbank.org/poverty/empowerment/sourcebook/index.htm

Women's Development Project Rajasthan: Concept Paper (1984). Jaipur: Department of Rural Development and Panchayati Raj, Government of Rajasthan.

Young, Kate (1993) *Planning Development With Women.* London: Macmillan.

———. (1997) "Planning from a Gender Perspective: Making a world of a difference." In N. Vishvanathan, et al (eds.) *The Women, Gender And Development Reader.* London: Zed Books.

Sumi Madhok *is a visiting lecturer at Centre for the Study of Global Ethics, University of Birmingham. She recently earned a Ph.D. in political studies at the School of Oriental and African Studies, University of London. In addition to published articles, her doctoral thesis, "Autonomy, Subordination, and the 'Social Woman': Examining Rights Narratives of Rural Rajasthani Women," will soon appear in print as a research monograph.*

Negotiating Leadership Roles

Young Women's Experience in Rural Egypt

*Rania Salem, Barbara Ibrahim,
and Martha Brady*

In the midst of an intense debate among academics and those influencing public opinion over whether there is a "deficit of democracy" in the Arab region, it is interesting to note how little attention is given to local arenas, and how young people practice citizenship and "become" citizens. Penetrating even the most isolated locales, community development activities today represent a notable space for civic participation and an emerging agent of political socialization. This article explores the gendered meanings and processes of venturing into public life in four rural communities in Egypt, and how young women in particular forge new roles and relationships beyond their families.

Ideals of youth participation in earlier eras in Egypt focused on young men and typically involved membership in a national party or political movement (Yousef 2000). An Egyptian program of national service existed for female university graduates in the post-revolutionary decades, after 1952, but by the 1990's it was largely defunct. While the ethic of social responsibility remains, what appears to distinguish contemporary forms of youth mobilization is less emphasis on the ideology of nation-building, and more concern for grassroots social development spearheaded by non-governmental actors.

Despite the global proliferation of development activities targeting and enlisting youth,[1] a search of the international literature yields few studies dealing with their introduction to public roles. The mainstream literature has largely concentrated on the transitions to adulthood in the context of work, schooling, marriage, and fertility (Mensch, Bruce, and Greene 1998). Only recently has there been interest in the transition to citizenship roles, and as yet little is published on the Middle East (Neyzi 2000).

Thus, for grounding of this article, we have drawn mainly on the ethnographic literature of community power dynamics in the Arab region. Our contribution may be to extend the insights of that literature to account for the unique position of young women as they enter into public roles. We posit that as young women engage with peers and elders beyond their families, they face a "double bind" of age and gender disparities. In this context, young women both mobilize patriarchal relationships to their advantage and subvert patriarchal formulas to rework their prescribed feminine role. For those who successfully negotiate the hurdles of age and gender discrimination, the rewards may be greater access to public influence in their communities than was available to any previous generation of young women. It is in this sense that we speak of a new dimension of citizenship that deserves fuller exploration.

Review of the Literature

The institutions of patriarchy place women at a remove from direct public participation, but, as many scholars have argued, that does not mean a lack of avenues for public influence. For example, El Kholy (1997) demonstrates with ethnographic data from low-income Cairo that gender politics are governed by a wide range of women's behaviors, falling between passive acquiescence and open revolt. Acts such as disruption, deception, negotiation, avoidance, and accommodation constitute "everyday" forms of contestation and resistance seldom acknowledged in Marxist and other schools of thought concerned with conflict between subordinate and hegemonic groups (El Kholy 1997). Such strategies vis-à-vis men may secure privileges for women in the household and beyond, but importantly, they work within the structural and ideological constraints set by the dominant order, in this case, patriarchy.

Similarly, marital alliances, both of a woman and of her adult children, can be a potent source of women's extended influence; thus the importance of "marriagability" to women as a political strategy (Ibrahim and Singerman 2002). One consequence is the reinforcement of a wide range of behaviors of modesty and reserve in each new generation of girls. This in turn discourages open participation and pushing out of boundaries in women's public roles. The price of transgression, especially for a younger woman, could be lifelong spinsterhood and the attendant economic and social marginality.

Women also effectively mobilize their sons and other male kin to achieve influence beyond the immediate household (Singerman 1997). Indeed, Rola Sharara's work on Lebanon (quoted in Joseph and Slyomovics 2001) suggests that individual interactions with the state are mediated through patriarchy. In particular, women have experienced the state largely through their relationships with men—fathers, sons, brothers, husbands.[2]

Suad Joseph (1996a, 1996b, 2001) and others have made an important contribution by elaborating the ways in which collective identity and the ability to mobilize "primordial" networks are central to the public life of men as well as women in Arab societies. Such "primordial" family and kin groups are regarded as anachronistic to Western conceptions of citizenship, rooted as they are in the notion of the individual as an autonomous social actor. However, this principle of Arab public life finds its formal expression in the constitutions of most Arab countries, which state that the family is the basic unit of society. Clan and other primordial groups can buffer and protect from the state and provide access to public goods for their members (Joseph and Slyomovics 2001).

But scholars may be overstating the case to claim that kin groups form the primary arena for expressions of public life. Rather than establishing a state-versus-clan dichotomy, one can think of those two spheres overlapping in a space occupied by new institutions, such as community development organizations, clubs, and so forth. We argue below that new institutions of civil society are starting to become significant venues for public participation and training grounds for citizenship.

Institutions of civil society are by definition of a voluntary nature—individual citizens participate based on perceived self-interest—which civil society detractors note is problematic in entrenched systems based on patronage, faith, and blood ties (Gellner 1991). Joseph questions whether non-governmental entities can ever be truly autonomous when kin are recruited, power is kept by elders, and patrons are needed in government circles (Joseph 1996a). But the rejoinder from other scholars is to recall that emergent forms of modern association historically began with links to family, clan, and tribe before transforming to more interest-based groups of unrelated individuals (Ibrahim 1994).

Be that as it may, Arab societies are now pervaded by new forms of association that include community development associations, social clubs, political parties, and professional organizations, to name but a few. These institutions have in common the Weberian distinction that individuals participate (in theory) out of perceived interest rather than ascription. However, they interact dynamically with the more long-standing arrangements of kinship, as illustrated above, as well as state institutions. Indeed, the boundaries between state and non-state institutions are often blurred, with many Egyptian non-govermental organizations maintaining a semi-autonomous status vis-à-vis the central government.

Young people who are recruited into these organizations will therefore draw upon their clan and other personal ties, but in their day-to-day social interactions, they will also be connecting with others—officials, teachers, and elected representatives—over work-related matters. We posit that these interactions give rise to a sense of belonging independent of kin affiliation, and an emergent identity as a citizen joined with others for social change, largely independent of the state. We believe that this understanding of citizenship as connection to society and its collective interests is a better characterization of the reality on the ground than thinking of the individual in relation primarily to the state.

The advent of voluntary associations and development projects in even the remotest villages in Egypt has helped to define the spatial community more distinctly as an entity. This challenges older, more rigid definitions of communities in the Middle East, which view community in terms of ethnicity or religion, rather than by spatial, national, or other boundaries (Joseph and Slyomovics, 2001). Identity as a member of a specific place—the *balad,* or village—is not new, of course, but we posit that it may be gaining in importance, as a result not only to official use in documents like identity cards, but also to the nature of civil society organizations in those places. We see in the experiences of young women a new identification with service-oriented values and with new channels for activism focused on the community.

Thesis: Age and Gender: The Double Bind for Young Women

We are particularly interested in the experiences of young women, because their entry into public life in villages would have been unlikely a generation ago. In a system organized hierarchically by gender and age, young women are the least powerful group. In contrast, young men are expected to learn from their elders how to negotiate public positions as a matter of growing up as a male in the community. Senior women also commanded a degree of public influence through male relations. While older women are considered relatively androgynous, young women undergo a post-pubertal phase of "gender intensification" during which conformity with codes of propriety and modesty are critical to ensuring marriageability and maintaining the political standing of male kin.

The hierarchical power balance is shifted when development projects enter a community through local civil society institutions. In theory, such projects benefit all, or the most needy, rather than any particular family or those with traditional access to power. They typically inject both assets and jobs into local economies. Their programs of activity usually require a cadre of local paid workers, and because activities are often targeted to women and girls, there is a need to recruit female staff and volunteers. There may therefore be considerable "'goods'" for distribution community-wide, allocated according to standards and potentially by means other than those that have supported the long-standing local patriarchal alliances. Young girls and women may be offered jobs and training unavailable to their male counterparts. They may be privileged as well in terms of greater access to knowledge and to centers of power outside the community.

For rural young women in Egypt, whose mobility is more restricted than young men's, the local community is acceptable as a place for employment or community service in ways that more distant urban spaces may not be. In order for these realms to be considered appropriate for women or girls, however, several criteria must be met, including the presence of other respected women, and limited or supervised contact with men. Because the objectives of these local organizations are usually defined in terms of social improvement, in areas such as health or education, they often provide a milieu that is considered "natural" or appropriate for female participation.

However, as young women enter these new roles, they risk violating established norms of age and gender. If all youth are somewhat disadvantaged in relation to the adult male world of public power, we argue that young women face a double disadvantage. They must respect the lines of gendered authority in order not to humiliate their families and to remain marriageable. But they must also accede to the authority that comes with age, expressing deference and demonstrating their proper place in that hierarchy. Constantly under the watchful eye of neighbors and kin, young women could risk severe sanctions if they appear too bold or immodest, or if they challenge the sources of community power openly. We therefore expect that the experience of becoming a public actor, of exercising "citizenship," will be one that is accompanied by a degree of conflict and role ambiguity. We illuminate in what follows the dilemmas that community development projects pose to their young participants, and we describe their resourceful responses to those dilemmas.

Data Sources

This paper analyzes the experiences of twenty-four young rural women who were hired to act as "promoters" in an experimental development program, Ishraq, in the Upper Egyptian governorate of Al Minya. The program trains these promoters to offer literacy, life skills, and sports activities to disadvantaged out-of-school girls aged 13thirteen to15 fifteen, the program's intended beneficiaries.[3]

Young women in each of four villages are responsible for a total of

200 beneficiaries divided into smaller learning groups. Promoters are assigned to a group of girls from their own community meeting several times a week. Their main role in the program is to transmit information and skills to adolescent beneficiaries. As mentors and role models, promoters convey messages on health, rights, the environment, civic responsibility, and so forth. They are trained to raise awareness, provide girls with instruction in literacy and numeracy, and help develop other skills, such as negotiation and teamwork. Promoters also gain experience in more public roles by making home visits, organizing and speaking at community meetings, and bringing public services to girls in their communities.[4]

This paper draws upon data collected among the study population prior to the official launch of the program, as well as evidence gathered from promoters after activities were introduced to the villages. The promoters' baseline survey included questions on: education, mobility, time-use, violence, work, marriage, health, gender-role attitudes, self-perceptions, social connectedness, and general knowledge.[5] Focus group discussions were also held with groups of six promoters, each from the same village, at baseline. Once the program was launched, promoters were required to keep personal accounts of noteworthy experiences in notebooks called "diaries." Records also were kept of unstructured discussions and informal interviews conducted throughout the course of the first year and a half of program activities.[6]

A Profile of the Promoters

Work History and Institutional Involvement

Promoters range in age from 18-27, with an average age of 21 years. Before the program began, one out of a total of twenty-four promoters was married, and five others were at some stage of engagement. Most hold vocational diplomas equivalent to secondary school degrees, while four have completed university. The majority (21) had some work experience prior to joining the program. Over half had worked for a wage, but very few were ever self-employed. Many promoters who had worked previously had come from social service jobs or were engaged in what might be stereotypically viewed as "women's work," such as teaching, knitting, or sewing. This reflects both the types of jobs available to young women in these communities as well as notions of acceptable occupations for young women.

In addition to doing the remunerative work discussed above, close to one- half of the young women reported involvement in some form of volunteer work like collecting donations for widows and orphans or giving literacy lessons. More than half reported some prior institutional affiliation, having participated in or frequented a local club, society, or youth center. The majority of promoters had made a visit to a community official (i.e., a community leader, religious figure, or school official) in the past. While we do not have comparable data for non-participating women, we suspect that these relatively high levels of exposure to professional and organizational experience are atypical, and have predisposed this group to continued civic participation.

Promoters' Ideal Public Roles

The ideals and personal goals of this group of young women appear closely linked to their prior experience outside the confines of the family. Most promoters envision some sort of role for themselves in the public life of their communities in the future. For example, a significant number stated that they want to forge links with other people and organizations. Doing well financially did not loom large in promoters' stated ambitions; only one promoter mentioned this.

Promoters expressed a strong belief that the appropriate role for young women in the community entails involvement in the *tatweer* of their villages, that is, the villages' evolution, advancement, or development. For many, participation in *tatweer* meant paid participation in a development project introduced by external agencies or nongovernmental organizations (NGOs). For others, it meant active membership in a Community Development Association (CDA) or in the other clubs and societies present in nearly every community. When asked what they could offer to their communities in their effort to "develop," most promoters cited services that reflect dominant gender patterns of work both inside and outside the home, such as outreach to other women, opening nurseries, teaching literacy, and carrying out environmental "cleanup." One promoter, who holds a law degree, viewed her community role as providing legal services to other villagers.

We note that promoters failed to mention formal political roles as appropriate for young women. Nor did they express any desire to effect change in their communities through political channels, whether by holding political offices themselves, campaigning for others, or voting for candidates. For promoters, *al hukumah* (the government) and its political channels seem remote, inaccessible, and of limited efficacy. Civil society institutions were the preferred medium for their participation to improve conditions in the village.

Promoters' previous work experience and civic involvement were projected onto their ideals regarding public responsibility. In one

village where promoters and many other local women had organized a freestanding Women's Committee, greater emphasis was
placed on young women's formation of and work through local
institutions. Here, promoters stated that young women like themselves should reach out to a range of people in the village, but particularly to youth at large. In another village, where most promoters
had worked or volunteered as teachers or literacy instructors, the
appropriate role for young women was defined as serving disadvantaged groups of women, girls, and children—groups with whom
it is appropriate for young women to interact.

Gender Roles and Public Participation

Contrary to our own expectations, promoters did not perceive any conflict between this ideal role of serving the community and the roles of
wife and mother, which are unanimously held in high regard. When
asked what they would do if a suitor or fiancé demanded that they con-
fine themselves to domestic duties as housewife and mother, almost
every promoter said that she would negotiate with him or leave him
altogether. Whether they will be able to do this in reality remains to be
seen; however, at least two promoters have subsequently dropped out
of the program as a consequence of having married and moved away
from the village.

   This affirmation of personal autonomy is only partially borne out
by attitudes towards marriage and domestic roles expressed in survey
responses. All promoters stated the belief that women should have
some say in the decision-making process about timing of marriage
and groom selection. Only slightly more than half felt that the woman
herself should choose the groom, while others were of the opinion
that the woman and her family should consult on that matter.
Promoters hold fairly traditional notions with regards to spousalage
difference between marriage partners, preferring the husband to be
several years older.

Initial Reservations About Civic Participation

While promoters aspired to greater participation in their communities, further probing during focus group discussions revealed that this
ideal was one that many viewed as beyond their reach. A number of
obstacles to more effective participation in the life of the community
were articulated. One promoter said:

([The men in the village]) hold the projects and they think that women can't fill the role of a man. . . . If it was a woman, she wouldn't be able to move around and do what men do. . . . If she has children. . . . A man can go anywhere far away, like Cairo or Assiut, if his work entrusted him with a task. They think a woman wouldn't be able to go to that place. Of course, I don't think this is right, but we are talking about the village and the people. (Sana')[7]

Underlying this statement is the belief that cultural assumptions regarding women's abilities and their "natural" duties prejudice women's ability to engage in public activities. A perception of local politics as elite and closed in nature emerged repeatedly. Promoters felt excluded from community activities, dominated as they are by a select group of men who leave little opportunity for popular representation, whether by females or others:

In my opinion, people with (vocational) diplomas and higher education should have a role. In the village, you find that those who "hold" the youth center "hold" every activity. In my opinion, everyone should participate in all the activities in the village. Everyone has a different viewpoint, and every time someone new comes in, the viewpoint improves. . . . The men don't leave anything for the women. They don't let in any girls or any women. (Rasha)

While support from leaders and decision -makers is critical, as the promoters also pointed out, that serving disadvantaged groups requires the assistance of males, who have greater control of resources. It is thus difficult for women in the community to address problems independently of men:

I met a man who was collecting donations for the mosque, and I said to him there should be a room for women to pray in. He said go and collect donations from the women. And of course, one will give me 25 piasters, and one will give me nothing at all. How am I supposed to get 400 pounds? If it was a man who went to collect, one man would give him 5 pounds, and the next would give him 10. Because it is a man going to talk to the man of the household. (Mona)

A final constraint to the participation of young women in the community is their own sense of exclusion from institutions that appear opaque to them. The resultant feelings of ignorance and inadequacy may be a consequence of not having the opportunity to engage in some institutions due to gender, age, or elite group hierarchies. At the conclusion of a debate on why women were absent from the membership and board of the local CDA, the promoter Karima said plaintively: "We don't understand a thing about how the Community Development Association works."

Despite these reservations, promoters came to the program with a degree of initial self-confidence and sense of their own efficacy. Even before they had started, they expressed a great deal of confidence in their ability to succeed in program-related duties. Most felt assured that upon completion of pre-service training they would be able to work together to relay information, cultivate skills, maintain discipline, and address the personal problems of girls enrolled in the program. This confidence may be built partially on the prior expectation that females of all ages interact relatively easily and informally within the village.

Confidence is less apparent when promoters anticipated working with older male members of the community. They expressed concern about their responsibilities outside the classroom. Apprehensive at posing as leaders and activists in the community, one promoter said: "Persuading the girl's [male] guardian is a problem. It's difficult because they're older than me. I don't know how to deal with them" (Hind).

Some promoters also explained that they were not personally acquainted with local leaders and therefore were fearful of them. Being equipped with the skills of communication and negotiation imparted during program training was less important for young women than developing a relationship with those community members with whom they would not ordinarily have social exchanges.

Promoters' Personal Strategies in Addressing Challenges

As they introduce activities and values that counter social conventions, and assume roles that challenge the dominant social structure, promoters encounter a variety of obstacles. In what follows, we examine the tactics adopted by young women in their efforts to create a new space in the community both for themselves and for younger girls. We argue that in confronting challenges from individuals and collectivities in their social environment, young women subvert patriarchal values and relationships to work to their advantage. Their tactics pay deference to and evoke patriarchal modes, while drawing on social resources available to them in their capacity as members of communities with strong social cohesion.

Many difficulties promoters must cope with result from the violation of social codes. While some beneficiaries would like to participate in the program but are constrained by poverty and the attendant claims made on their labor by the family. Others are willing to spare time to attend classes but are reluctant to participate in non-traditional elements of the program, such as reproductive health lessons, sports activities, and field trips. While all these activities are considered as compromising the modesty of young girls and therefore somewhat inappropriate, the last two also generate concern for girls' physical safety.

The program also encourages beneficiaries to adopt new behaviors that replace daughters' culturally dictated duty of submissiveness with a new notion: that they have an undeniable *right* to participate in decisions pertaining to them. A girl's choice of spouse and timing of her marriage are a case in point: "An uneducated girl's father would decide and settle everything [with the groom] and afterwards he would tell her your wedding is on such-and-such date and this is who you will take [marry]. . . . They don't give her a chance to state her opinion nor to object to anything" (Amal).

The promoters also encounter regular resistance to their own roles as promoters. Promoters reported that their families had opposed their walking through the streets of the village unescorted to recruit beneficiaries to the program. This breached the custom of confining eligible young women indoors or limiting their physical mobility to protect their reputations. In one village, an early meeting with village notables and leaders was called to correct misconceptions about the content and objectives of the program. When one promoter stood up to contradict a statement made by another participant, the men in attendance protested heatedly, saying that it was indecent for a young woman to address a gathering of men who were not members of her family.

Whether they themselves are contravening norms or are facilitating beneficiaries' contravention of norms, promoters must carefully navigate this site of struggle. By and large, they do so not by directly challenging the status quo but by negotiating and accommodating it. Norms are not transgressed, but rather, boundaries are pushed and stretched, as illustrated by the tactics young women use within this larger strategy.

In confronting many dilemmas, promoters rely on the authority of their male relations for immunity and protection. In the example cited above, the promoter involved was able to violate the rules of gender propriety and speak out publicly on behalf of her colleagues because her father is a leader (*sheikh el balad)* in the village. Though leaders in their own right, all of the other men in attendance were subordinate to *sheikh el balad*. Similarly, in taking on roles that defy those structures, promoters mobilized their personal relations or contacts. Most promoters first heard about the opening for their jobs through networks of friends, relations, or neighbors rather than a public announcement. At least four promoters have fathers, brothers, or husbands active in the local CDA, school, or youth center.

Promoters similarly relied on their own social ties in their recruitment of beneficiaries. They initially recruited young girls who were neighbors, relatives, or acquaintances, thereby investing their efforts in preexisting and therefore more reliable relationships with established trust and rapport.

In their dealings with community leaders and the parents of beneficiaries, young women often invoke their own reputations and standing in the community to persuade, cajole, or embarrass others into agreement. To legitimize the playing of sports, promoters wore training suits and attended sports sessions with beneficiaries and sports trainers. On several occasions, promoters overcame the reservations of community members to girls' participation by stating that if it was shameful to wear a training suit, the promoter herself would not do it. The promoter thereby challenging the individual face to face to declare her indecent, and cornering him or her into assenting. In the same way, when negotiating with a parent, one promoter invoked a sense of community spirit and collective responsibility for the welfare of the daughters of the village:

> There was the situation around the time of the trip to Fayoum . . . there were a lot of people who wouldn't permit their daughters to come. We went to see one man, Neama's father; we sat with him for over an hour. And I spoke with him, and I told him that I was going, and Mariam is going, and Ustaz Talaat the project supervisor, he is like our father, is going, and all the Muslim girls are going. And he said that he is worried for her safety. So I said to him, if you are worried for her, then you should be worried about us too. Are you worried for her and not for us? Aren't we all girls together? If you think that something might happen to us, then why do you consent to our doing something you wouldn't want for your daughter? (Hanem)

Promoters also legitimize their somewhat daring roles in the community by expressing their relationship with the adolescents in their charge in terms of kin relations. Promoters likened themselves to concerned elder sisters or caring mothers. This use of fictive kinship terms underscores that the activities of the young women conform to the ideal feminine roles of wife, mother, and sister rather than alien roles, such as leader or activist.

The language of patriarchy thus emerges as a culturally appropriate medium through which to frame new orientations and behaviors. When negotiating with community members, promoters confirm common adherence to patriarchal norms and values. When a beneficiary objected to thea discussion of circumcision because this was `eib (shameful), one promoter insisted that it was all right since all those present were girls, thereby reinforcing prescribed codes of modesty and sex segregation in discussion of sensitive matters. In this way, the young woman was able to break the taboo on discussion of reproduction and sexuality.

In a discussion with other young women, one promoter contended that, while it is important for girls to learn to stand up for themselves, affirming some of the inequalities of patriarchal relations is a way of building social capital for the future: "[In] a situation where a girl and her brother are sitting at the same table and with them is the mother and the father. . . . If [the brother] is thirsty and the girl gets up to bring him some water . . . when she does that for him one time and another, he will know that he owes her a favor. This is her brother, after all" (Marwa). While acknowledging that a girl should ideally be treated as an equal by a male sibling, this promoter argues that by performing the symbolic act of serving him during a meal a girl ultimately promotes her own interests.

Similarly, promoters avoided creating direct competition between beneficiaries' work duties and the *Ishraq* program by negotiating modified hours with girls' parents and employers on the one hand, and the program's hosting facilities on the other. A collective solution was reached whereby girls could carry out their work during the harvest and still attend classes.

Finally, many young women justified their promotion of activities for young girls to the community by emphasizing the necessity of enhancing the skills and knowledge of the future mothers of the next generation of children. This sort of argument can be considered as appeasing those who wish to maintain the status quo, in which girls are supported only in their quest to become good wives and mothers. It is an argument thought sure to win the approval of those who would question the intentions of young women operating more actively in the community.

Young Women's Advances into Civil Society

As demonstrated above, formidable obstacles stand in the way of young rural women's adoption of active civic roles in their communities. Whether these roles are sustained and will stand the test of marriage and childbearing and the attendant demands they impose on young women remains to be seen. To determine the long-term reverberations of such early exposure to activism on young women as future citizens would require further research beyond the life of this particular program.

However, it appears from the data that these young women believe they are preparing themselves for a life of community service and public participation. This contrasts with the near-universal expectation of young Egyptian factory workers in another recent study that they would *not* continue work after marriage (Amin and al Bassusi 2002). Those women received significantly higher salaries, but worked long hours and did not report a sense of social solidarity or commitment to their jobs. Overall, the first year of experience of promoters suggests that their strategies of negotiation, accommodation, resistance, and manipulation have been fairly effective. Attrition has been minimal, with only those who married outside the village having left the program.

Steps from program participation to other forms of community activism occurred a short way into program implementation. Promoters have on their own initiative intervened in instances where girls are at risk of early marriage or circumcision. Over the course of the first year of the program, at least two promoters joined the local arm of the National Democratic Party and expanded their interactions with locally-elected officials. In one village, young women are now collaborating with several national organizations and grassroots groups to form a Women's Committee, with a promoter as its chairwoman. Another promoter has exploited her new links with the board of the village youth center to secure a room in which she holds seminars for local women on religious topics twice a week. These examples affirm observations from the international literature that early local participation is predictive of later commitment to active citizenship (Flanagan, Jonsson, and Botcheva 1999).

Promoters place great value on their expanded social networks, which now include influential individuals in the village and beyond. Dependence on family members or the connections of family members can now be augmented or replaced by contacts of their own. A new sense of integration was expressed by one young woman: "You'll find that when we walked through the village we took to the houses. . . . To the extent that when we'd be invited in, and we'd drink tea, it would be as if we were one of the family" (Marwa). Perhaps most important in the opinion of promoters is their newly won status in the eyes of the community. Rasha proudly reported that people in the village now append the title *abla* (literally, "elder sister," an honorific similar to "miss") to her first name when addressing her.

Broader Implications and Conclusions

As we saw above, promoters rework the community's dominant gender formula, using traditional images and language to foster new roles. Far from passively accepting the roles recommended by the development agencies overseeing their work, they actively engage in and shape their new roles. But in so doing, do they convolute the messages intended by the development program and therefore alter its outcomes? We posit that promoters are taking largely alien ideas and recasting them in a culturally appropriate way to make success more likely. This also protects them as young women from the ostracism or marginalization that might result if they were to adopt these values unquestioningly. However, this makes the practical task of evaluating program impact both more nuanced and more difficult than often acknowledged. Conventional program monitoring approaches are insufficient for measuring the extent to which promoters internalize and convey faithfully new ideas around, for example, women's individual autonomy and empowerment.

Another pragmatic question this raises is the appropriateness of standard leadership training. The tactics we found young women adopting in their work bear little resemblance to the job skills inculcated during formal training. The ways in which the sociocultural environment serves to foster or impede leadership opportunities and leadership styles of young women must inform program planning and training content.

As grassroots social development led by non-state actors expands, the cadre of young women entering the public arena at the local level will undoubtedly increase. Will these women become development " entrepreneurs," seeking primarily higher salaries and individual career advancement? Or, as they gain practical experience and come to understand the mechanisms of local power, will they begin to lobby for more equal participation in society, greater rights and privileges, and more favorable allocation of resources for their gender? The young women in this study seem to lean in the latter direction, and are beginning to draw on the latent power inherent in the network of promoters themselves to lobby for better treatment within the program. From a policy perspective, both democracy and civil society objectives could be served by creating more opportunities for young development workers like these to engage in broader national or regional initiatives. This group of peers, especially should they join forces with other youth leaders, will be an interesting one to watch over time—as a site of exchange, support, and resources to rally for greater social change.

NOTES

This paper is based on presentations made at the First World Congress for Middle Eastern Studies in Mainz, Germany, held between September 8–13, 2002, and the Middle East Studies Association 2002 Annual Meeting in Washington, D.C., held between November 23–26, 2002. The authors gratefully acknowledge the contributions of Nisha Varia and Michelle Skaer in annotating part of the literature reviewed in this study.

1. *Youth* is a term that conventionally refers to age group, whereas *adolescence* denotes those aged 10–19.

2. Given the various ways in which women lobby for power through male kin relations, the categories "public" and "private" clearly overlap in women's lived experience. Indeed, many feminist scholars have rightly problematized this dichotomy. However, we retain the term "public" as a heuristic one denoting spheres of influence beyond the family, in setting forth the arguments below.

3. The Safe Spaces, or *Ishraq*, program is a nonformal education program tailored for rural adolescent girls. The pilot phase of this intervention has been a collaborative effort among Save the Children, Population Council, Caritas, and CEDPA. Other partners include the Egyptian Ministry of Education, the Ministry of Youth and Sport, and the Ministry of Health and Population.

4. While there is debate in the development community over the virtues of volunteering versus receiving remuneration, this program does provide promoters with a nominal salary equivalent to less than thirty dollars a month.

5. This forms the first round of a longitudinal impact study for the larger program. Promoters are one of several study populations.

6. Promoters may have been motivated to present themselves as successfully carrying out tasks entrusted to them in personal diaries, and a well-known characteristic of focus group data is that it reflects social norms and group consensus. However, the reporting of problems as well as successes was rewarded throughout, and much of the data presented in what follows has been reinforced by direct observation.

7. The names of promoters cited here are pseudonyms.

REFERENCES

Amin, S., al Bassusi, N. (2002). *Wage Work to Prepare for Marriage: Labor Force Entry for Young Women in Egypt.* Cairo, Egypt: Population Council.

El Kholy, H. A. (1997). *"Alam El Bint Kinz":Gender Politics in Low-Income Cairo.* Cairo, Egypt: Population Council.

Flanagan, C., D. Johnsson, D. & and L. Botcheva, L. (1999). Roots of Citizenship in Seven Countries. In Yates, M. & Youniss, J. (eds.), *Roots of Civic Identity: :International Perspectives on Community Service and Activism in Youth.* Cambridge, England: Cambridge University Press.

Gellner, E. (1991). Civil Society in Historical Context. *International Social Science Journal* 43 : 495–510.

Ibrahim, B., & and D. Singerman, D. (2002). Costs of Marriage in Egypt. In *Cairo Papers in Social Science.* Cairo: AUC Press.

Ibrahim, S. E. (1994). Civil Society and the Prospects for Democratization in the Arab World. In Norton, Augustus Richard (ed.).*Civil Society in the Middle East,* edited by Richard Augustus Norton. Leiden, Netherlands: E. J. Brill.

Joseph, S. (1996a). Gender and Citizenship in Middle Eastern states. *MERIP* 126, no. 1: 4-10.

Joseph, S. (1996b). Patriarchy and Development in the Arab World. *Gender and Development* 4, no. 2: 14–19.

Joseph, S. (ed.) (2000). *Gender and Citizenship in the Middle East.*; with a foreword by Deniz Kandiyoti. Syracuse, N.Y.: Syracuse University Press.

Joseph, S. (1996a). Gender and citizenships in Middle Eastern states. *MERIP* 126(1): 4.

Joseph, S. (1996). Patriarchy and development in the Arab world. *Gender and Development* 4(2): 14-19.

Joseph, S., and S. Slyomovics, S. (2001). Introduction. In Joseph, S., & Slyomovics, S. (eds.) *Women and Power in the Middle East,* edited by S. Joseph and S. Slyomovics. Philadelphia: University of Pennsylvania Press.

Mensch, B. S., J. Bruce, J., & and M. E. Greene, M. E. (1998). *The Uncharted Passage: Girls' Adolescence in the Developing World.* New York: Population Council.

Neyzi, L. (2000). Object or Subject: The Paradox of "Youth" in Turkey. MEAwards Regional Papers no. 45. Cairo, Egypt: Population Council *MEAwards Regional Papers* (45).

Singerman, D. (1997). *Avenues of Participation: Family, Politics and Networks in Urban Quarters of Cairo.* Cairo, Egypt: American University Iin Cairo Press.

Yousef, Ahmad. (2000). The Revolutionary Generation. In Meijer, Roel (ed.). *Alienation or Integration of Arab Youth: Between Family, State and Street,* edited by Roel Meijer. Richmond, England: Curzon Press.

Rania Salem *was, at the time of this study, research assistant under the Gender, Family and Development Program of the West Asia and North Africa office of the Population Council. She is currently a graduate student in sociology at the University of Oxford's St. Antony's College.* ***Barbara Ibrahim*** *is regional director for West Asia and North Africa at the Population Council. She is author of many publications on youth, marriage, and the gendered acquistion of adult roles. She was principal investigator of the first nationally representative survey of young Egyptians.* ***Martha Brady*** *is an associate in the Gender Family and*

Develoment Program of the Population Council. She is a public health researcher working on adolescent health and development issues, with special emphasis on program and policy initiatives for girls.

Capacity Building and Change

Women and Development in India

Mangala Subramaniam

Development as a term is being used increasingly to explain a myriad of processes and outcomes, although the emphasis on the economic aspect is continuing (Rai 2002). Recognizing this economic bias, Amartya Sen and other scholars have been calling for incorporating the social dimension of development emphasizing education and health (Sen 1983, 1990, 1997, 1999). Sen asserts that basic education, good health, and human attainments are directly valuable as constituent elements of basic "capabilities" (Dreze and Sen 1997; Sen 1997). While these attempts have initiated a shift in thinking about development, this understanding of the "social" needs to be further expanded to consider everyday dignity, confidence, and courage to demand or seek access to services like education by redefining power relations. Everyday dignity refers to the ability to perform basic day-to-day activities without inhibitions and to have a public voice without being socially excluded (Varshney 2000; Afkhami, Naido, Pitanguy, and Rao 2002). For poor rural women, education or literacy can imply making everyday experiences the basis for understanding and renegotiating the world. Therefore, an essential component of education or literacy for disadvantaged groups like poor women, in the context of development, is to direct efforts at addressing everyday dignity and confidence to demand and access services. Focusing on this aspect of women and development, I draw on the concept of capacity building to explain how training and networking initiatives can serve as a possible route to building courage and confidence among poor women.

Capacity building, development, and/or strengthening refer to actions to create, reform, or support activities that facilitate sharing of experiences, knowledge, and strategies (Edwards and Hulme 1992; Thompson 1995; Chen 1997; Storey 1998; Ferree and Subramaniam 2001). Such sharing of actions demand and create networks. The capacity-building efforts facilitate consciousness raising and serve as sites for interaction among women, thereby connecting women across spatial boundaries of the home and the village. The development of consciousness is an "ongoing process in which groups reevaluate themselves, their subjective experiences, their opportunities, and their shared interests" (Taylor and Whittier 1992, 114). This article adds a new dimension to the understanding of the processes of women's consciousness raising by illustrating how capacity-building initiatives are not merely the means toward bettering individual women's lives in the short term but also involve creating spaces for long-term interaction and building bonds for collectively seeking change in women's status. I seek to show that capacity-building efforts have consequences beyond immediate investment of resources for development and serve as connecting links in the emergence of networks for challenging gender relations.

As women's issues came to the center stage of the development arena in the 1980s, in India a number of empowerment programs for women were formulated. Through protest, lobbying, and critiquing patriarchal structures and institutions, the women's movement created an "alternative space" in the previously forbidden terrain of government programs. Partnerships between women's groups, non governmental organizations and the state, previously seen as impossible, began to be forged. The Mahila Samakhya (MS) program is one such partnership initiative. *Mahila* means "women" and *Samakhya* is a compound of the Sanskrit words *sama*, meaning "equal," and *akhya* meaning "to be valued or weighed" (Mahila Samakhya Karnataka 1996a). Formulated as an Indo-Dutch assistance program, the program is under the direct responsibility of the federal government for its implementation and monitoring, as part of India's Literacy Mission. The program was born out of the emphasis in the government's New Education Policy of 1986 on formulating education programs that play a positive interventionist role for women's equality.

Drawing from field research of the MS program in one southern state, Karnataka, I focus on rural capacity-building initiatives that form a component of this literacy initiative.[1] Mahila Samakhya Karnataka (MSK) serves as an example of a grassroots-based initiative attempting change designed for and with women. The stated objective of the MSK program is education for women's empowerment, where education signifies a process of consciousness raising, organizing, and broadening the awareness and skills of poor rural women to take control over their lives. The aim is to organize poor rural women into village-level collectives, *sanghas*, which are "not merely activity oriented but enable women raise their self-image and confidence" (Mahila Samakhya Karnataka 1996a). At the end of the 1997–98 fiscal year MSK was working with 25,000 poor women, mainly from among the Scheduled Castes, in 1,020 villages in 6 districts of Karnataka.[2]

Focusing on the *sanghas* formed in villages, this article illustrates how capacity-building initiatives, in combination with regular meetings across the organization, facilitate formation of networks, at both the individual level and group levels. I argue that the capacity-building forums serve as spaces for sharing experiences and building bonds among participants. These processes of sharing can facilitate growth of a collective strength that women can draw on to challenge power and inequity. Beginning with an overview of the social dynamics of gender and caste, I explain the concept of capacity building and then provide a brief description of the MSK program before proceeding to an analysis of the program's initiatives.

Theoretical Framework

Economic inequality means differences in economic resources (income or wealth). "Economically conditioned power is not, of course, identical with 'power' as such. Very frequently the striving for power is also conditioned by the social 'honor' it entails" (Weber 1916 [1958], 180). Social honor, the power and advantages organized by and through systems of social deference, finds expression in both caste and gender relations. "Caste is and remains essentially, social rank," and the central position of the Brahmans "rests more upon the fact that social rank is determined with reference to them than upon anything else" (Weber 1916 [1958], 397). The Indian caste system comprises four major castes or *varnas,* and several subcastes are categorized within a single caste (Dumont 1980). The caste system is perceived as a particularly rigid and oppressive form of inequality and its origin is a subject of debate.[3]

"Untouchability," along with rituals and ritual prohibitions are an essential feature of the caste system. The practice of untouchability isolates those in the lowest caste, especially the Scheduled Caste (SC) or *dalits* from those belonging to the upper castes. More than one-sixth of India's population, about 160 million people, is categorized as *dalits* (meaning "downtrodden") (Government of India 1999). Untouchables may not cross the line dividing their part of the village from that occupied by higher castes. They may not use the same wells for drawing water or drink from the cups used by others in tea stalls. As noted by Shah (2001), "though the visible practice of untouchability has declined—certainly in public spheres—incidents of atrocities against dalits have not shown a similar downturn and continue unabated in post-independence India in various forms—murder, grievous hurt, arson, and rape" (20). Shah adds that "conflicts over material interests and political power contribute to a great deal to such incidents" (20). Power and social control find expression in both caste and gender relations (Kannibiran and Kannibiran 1991; Omvedt 1993, 1998). Over the past two decades, the changing status and roles of women combined with the rise of modern feminism have promoted a dramatic increase in concern with the meaning and explanation of gender. Feminist scholarship and women-in-development (WID) research have led to the consensus that gender is a fundamental organizing principle in human societies. Gender is a primary way of signifying relations of power (Scott 1986) and constructing hierarchies. Gender is not "only about women"; it refers to a structural relationship between sex categories that is linked to the state, the economy, and other macro- and micro-processes. Gender is not a homogenous category; it is internally differentiated and elaborated by class, race and ethnicity, age, region, and education. Like caste, gender organizes social prestige and enacts status in rituals of interaction (Ridgeway 1992).

In different ways and for a variety of reasons, all cultures use gender as a primary category of social relations. Sociological analyses of gender emphasize that gender, like race and class, is a social experience of all. Integrating race, class, and gender into feminist thinking requires a process of transformation that involves seeing race, class, and gender in relational ways. In the Indian context, caste also interacts with gender. Social restrictions on the lifestyles of women tend to become more rigid as one moves up in the caste hierarchy. Generally, there is more seclusion of upper-caste women than of lower-caste women (Miller 1981). For instance, within upper-caste communities, women are often denied the right to gainful employment outside their homes. By contrast, lower-caste women have greater freedom to take up gainful employment, not because their people are more liberal or permissive, but because economic conditions do not allow them to remain indoors. In fact, this is freedom based on economic necessity and tied to two predominant forms of power and control. Lower-caste women are often at the mercy of landlords to be hired for wage labor (such as on farms or construction projects). In addition, economic returns for their labor are maintained at the lowest level possible. Thus, the exploitation and control of lower-caste women involve intersecting effects of class, caste, and gender.

Feminist scholars have persuasively argued for analyses of race, class, and gender as intersecting and interlocking systems of oppression (Andersen 1993; Hill-Collins 1990). This model can usefully be applied to gender-class-caste dynamics as well. Focusing on the mechanisms of intersection across caste and gender allows for exploring how individuals negotiate, resist, and struggle against inequalities. In the Indian context, the caste system is an important aspect of the social sphere. The hierarchy and characteristics that govern the caste system constrain life chances gained through acquiring information, skills, and education. Intersections of caste and gender lead to women having less prestige and respect compared with men even within the same caste.

Recognizing the need to address structural inequality, such as that based on gender, the state, international agencies, and nongovernmental organizations (NGOs) are engaged in designing and implementing programs for empowering women.[4] State interventions, especially in developing countries, have been criticized as being "welfare" oriented, that is, ignoring the community and excluding them from design and implementation strategies. Scholars and policy makers have been critical of the "clientalistic" approach of the state and have increasingly called for involving the community (Clark 1992). Recent innovations by the state include programs like the MSK in India. Interventions by agencies outside state institutions, such as NGOs, are usually localized unless the agency is exclusively a conduit for channeling resources. NGOs have advocated self-help models in the form of group-based credit and savings programs to promote income-generating activities.[5] Mixed results are reported for these efforts. While some studies point to the positive social effects for women as a result of income change at the household level, there are others that raise concerns about who controls the credit and income, and particularly question whether there have been positive changes for women.(Amin, Ahmed, and Chowdhury 1994; Goetze and Sen Gupta 1996; Hashmi, Schuler, and Riley 1996.) The case of the MSK *sanghas* can also be viewed as a form of self-help model, although these groups are not initiated as savings groups or for starting an economic activity. An additional angle often raised in the discussions of programs to empower women is the role of men in the community. While it may be meaningful to include men to facilitate change in the community, this can prove counterproductive for women facing the simultaneous effects of class, caste, and gender. Inclusion of men in attempts to alter gender relation might be better assessed based on the context.

Capacity-Building Initiatives

Capacity building allows for sharing, making commonalities recognizable and alternatives imaginable (i.e., raising consciousness). It also increases the possibility of pooling resources and organizing collective resistance (i.e., collective action). Capacity-building initiatives provide community-based groups with information and support that can lead to the creation of formal and informal networks. Debate surrounds the question of appropriate sites for capacity-building initiatives (Cohen and Wheeler 1997; Chen 1997; Myers 1997; Peterson 1997). The scarcity of development resources raises two concerns. The first concern is whether capacity-building initiatives should involve only the government or should also strengthen the capacity of nongovernmental organizations; the second concern is related to where capacity-building initiatives are arranged (e.g., in major cities or rural areas) and what forms of resources are used. Relying on organizational resources for capacity building at the local grassroots level can save valuable resources and make access easier for groups based in remote rural areas.

The capacity-building forums serve as spaces where village women can meet (within and outside their immediate community), be together, and begin the process of reflecting, asking questions, speaking fearlessly, analyzing, and above all feeling confident to articulate their needs. In addition to providing women new learning opportunities and access to information and ideas, the networks permit the narration and sharing of experiences beyond the village collective. Such sharing facilitates consciousness raising. Consciousness raising provides a "framework for criticizing existing reality and for reinterpreting both one's own past and all history. . . . Consciousness-raising as a specific political practice is directed toward challenging dominant ideas (i.e., combating the ideological hegemony of male supremacy)" (Ferree and Hess 1985, 175). The processes associated with learning and sharing within the network(s) can lead to networks themselves becoming actors.

Capacity-building efforts include formal training programs and workshops that explicitly aim to "educate" women. For the women involved, these learning opportunities facilitate making informed choices and taking control over their own lives. Women with similar experiences come together at forums organized across geographical boundaries of the village, the district, and the state. Connections forged in these forums facilitate the formation of networks of groups.

Data and Methods

The data for this article are drawn from fieldwork undertaken between September and December 1998 in four districts of the state of Karnataka where MSK has been working to form *sanghas*. The districts of Bidar, Bijapur, Gulbarga, and Raichur are drought-prone and the most underdeveloped districts of the state of Karnataka. Almost 90 percent of the women covered in this study are *dalit* and are poor.

Multiple forms of data were collected. For this article, I draw from (1) the information I gathered about the program, (2) group meeting discussions, and (3) data on the training programs, seminars, and workshops organized in the four districts. A database of the information about the training programs, workshop, and seminars was constructed from annual reports of Mahila Samakhya Karnataka for the years 1993 through 1998 (Mahila Samakhya Karnataka 1995, 1996b, 1997, 1998, 1999). As the format of reporting of activities organized has varied over the years, I have used the categories for 1997–98 as the basis for classifying the activities in each district for the previous four years. I think these categories reflect the priorities of the organization and most likely form the basis for annual planning.[6]

The MSK Program

The MSK is an autonomous registered society and functions like an independent organization rather than like a government department that adopts a "top-down" approach in administering programs for "beneficiaries" and driven by target dates. In the context of this research, the relatively independent and flexible functioning of MSK is indicative of the intention to involve people at all levels and especially to let women set the pace of change (Subramaniam 2001). Much of the formal structure of the MSK echoes other familiar development and cooperative-based initiatives in India (Rose 1992; Narasimhan 1999). A three-tier structure connects the state-level office, a district-level unit, and the village-level *sangha*. Capacity-building initiatives extend across these levels and beyond the state. Information flows between the state and the village through intermediary structures created by the organization that serve as sites for meetings. The activities of the organization are structured along the three administrative and geographical levels: the state, the district, and the village.

At the state level is a state program office headed by a state program coordinator (SPD). The state office comprises resource persons and accounts and administrative staff. Within MSK, the subunit at the district level is called the district implementation unit (DIU). Headed by a district program coordinator (DPC), the DIU, like the state office, comprises resource persons and accounts and administrative staff. There is no formal subunit at the *taluka* level, although several clusters of *sanghas* exist within a *taluka*. The village-level unit is called the *sangha*. Ten *sanghas* (around the same area, generally neighboring ones) form a cluster and a *sahayogini* (the facilitator) oversees a cluster.

The facilitators, or *sahayoginis,* are a cadre of highly motivated and trained women activists who form the backbone of the MSK program. The *sahayoginis* and other district-level staff as well as visiting state staff encourage and support action by *sangha* women. For instance, during a *sangha* meeting, in a discussion of how to get power reconnected for the *sangha* meeting hall in Mogadal village, Bidar district, *sahayogini* Prema and junior resource person Shyla say, "You have done so much for your *sangha.* Why don't you go to the government office in town to seek reconnection of power? You're at the front, we're at the back. We will teach you and tell you what you can do. You discuss and decide."

Sanghas, like other women's movements, challenge the paternalistic assumption that women are "beneficiaries" by making explicit efforts to specifically empower women who are the least advantaged and most marginalized from the political system (Dugger 1995). MSK trains SC and Scheduled Tribe (ST) women to contest elections to the village *panchayat,* a village-level institution. The 33 percent reservation for women provided through the Seventy-Third Amendment to the Indian Constitution in 1993, which ensures a 'quota' of seats for women in the village panchayats, has opened opportunities for women to contest elections to local institutions. It has provided political power for some women, like Hanumavva of the *sangha* in Dotihal village (Raichur district), who was elected to the village panchayat on the 'quota'. *Sangha* women are trained through organized district-level programs to contest elections. Training in participation in meetings after being elected has been attempted through the *Gramsat* (*Gram* means "village" and *sat* is the abbreviation for "satellite") experiment.[7] The training and guidance on participation are intended to ensure inclusion of women's voices and avoid token representation.

Two to three years after formation, *sanghas* begin to try to find ways to construct their own meeting place. Referred to as the *sangha* "hut," the meeting place is both symbolic of their presence and power in the village and an impetus for women members to make demands on the government. It necessitates seeking allotment and purchasing land through the local administration (at the village, *taluka,* and district levels). "We will go to the government office in town and seek allotment of land for construction of the *sangha mane* [hut]," say women of Gabbur village in Raichur district. *Sangha* women who have almost never entered government offices or have been dissuaded from meeting officials are now emboldened to do so.

Other activities of MSK include the setting up and managing of adult and nonformal education centers and child care centers at the village level. In addition, MSK has set up continuing education centers, residential centers for young girls from villages who have dropped out of school or have had to discontinue school. The continuing education centers are located at the district headquarters (a town, not a village) and are managed by the district implementation unit. Adult and non-formal education centers have been set up in only some of the villages.

Rural Capacity-Building Initiatives for Networking

What does Mahila Samakhya mean to us? In the images which this question brings to life, we are never alone. We are women together, we support and help each other, we embrace each other, we laugh and weep together, we struggle and learn and work together. We are mirrors for each other—we experience ourselves as individuals when our identities are affirmed by our collectives, and recognize our strengths and potentials when we see them reflected in the women who share our lives in Mahila Samakhya (Government of India a, undated, 31).

In the "Green Book," the first project document laying out the ground rules for Mahila Samakhya, training was conceptualized as a critical input into the program (Government of India b, undated). As the nonnegotiable principles of the project mandate, "every intervention and interaction taking place in the project must be a microcosm of the larger processes of change—the environment of learning, the respect and equality, the time and space, the room for individual uniqueness and variation must be experienced in every component of the project" (Bhaiya and Menon-Sen, undated, 14). The term *training,* as used in Mahila Samakhya, refers not to an event or series of events, but to "complex progression of several interconnected and ongoing collective learning processes, which form the warp and weft of the programme and hold together its various elements. The MS training process can therefore be compared to an ongoing, many-stranded and widening spiral of action and reflection" (Bhaiya and Menon-Sen, undated, 15). The document *We Can Change Our World: The Mahila Samakhya Experience,* a compilation of some of the material generated by the process documentation exercises in villages where MS has been operative states, "Our ultimate objective is to build a strong network of women's collectives which can sustain themselves and act independently of the programme" (Government of India a, undated).

The social location of *sangha* women and their customary lack of access to resources are circumstances significant to understanding the linkage between capacity building and networks. In MSK, learning and training through capacity-building initiatives can be seen as occurring in two often interrelated contexts. These include workshops, training programs, and seminars that are often combined with regular meetings and activities of the organization. Both contexts provide opportunities for "in-house" networking.

Activities in the capacity-building initiatives provide impetus for the emergence and/or broadening of both formal and informal networks, which facilitates consciousness raising and leads to networks becoming actors in or agents of change. A major intended consequence of the capacity-building initiatives is to provide women information about such issues as using herbal remedies, treating illnesses, literacy, and personality development. Some of the workshops deal with economic development programs, as was attempted in Shirdona village in Gulbaraga district, where a training program for women for starting an income generating activity was organized by MSK. Basic adult education has been emphasized through the organizing of literacy camps, as occurred in the Gulbarga and Bijapur districts. Women in Kulali village in Bijapur have at their own initiative arranged for literacy classes at night. An unintended consequence of the initiatives' network structure is the availability of space for exchange of information and ideas and reflection for consciousness raising. I discuss these aspects of capacity building below.

MSK has concentrated capacity-building initiatives at the village level and *taluka* or district level. Initial efforts of the organization are targeted at building networks across the immediate boundaries of the village and *taluka* and are later extended to cover larger boundaries of the district and state. These strategies are reflected in the analysis of the data on sites of capacity-building initiatives. A tabulation of the activities listed in the annual reports of MSK for the years 1993-1998 shows that training workshops organized and/or attended by *sangha* women typically exceeded fifty a year. Until the fiscal year 1997–98, over 90 percent of the capacity-building initiatives were organized at the village, *taluka*, and district levels, as Table 1 shows. Further, the deputing of staff for activities at the state level and beyond rose above 1 percent only after 1997. The total number of initiatives in which MSK participated beyond the district level was 16 percent in 1997–98, compared with 4 percent and lower in earlier years. These numbers indicate that linkages beyond state borders increased after 1997. They also indicate an ensuring of exposure for *sangha* women at a pace that may not be overwhelming, since most *sangha* women have limited exposure outside their own villages.

Table 1
Meetings, Workshops, and Conferences Attended by MSK Staff
and *Sangha* Women

Year	Village level	Taluka/District level	State level*	Other*	Total (#)**
1997–98	20 (29%)	39 (56%)	6 (9%)	5 (7%)	70
1996–97	10 (18%)	44 (79%)	2 (4%)	0	56
1995–96	43 (42%)	59 (57%)	1 (1%)	0	103
1994–95	55 (34%)	105 (64%)	4 (2%)	0	164
1993–94	31 (40%)	46 (59%)	1 (1%)	0	78

* Refers to state level within Karnataka or another state.
** Refers to national and international levels.
Note: Because of missing information in the annual reports on the venue of
the activity/program, there is a difference in the total number of activities
organized each year and that available by venue of activity.

In some cases, training and learning do involve differential knowledge and assimilation levels between the trained and the trainers or
between staff at various levels of the organization itself. Recognizing
the strong support structures created by the *sahayoginis*, the MSK program is challenged to create spaces within which these facilitators "can
be affirmed and supported in new roles" (Government of India a
undated, 113). The MSK program provides opportunities for the
sahayogini to connect with other staff as well as other individuals and
organizations. The MSK intervention pays special attention to investment in facilitators through training, workshop participation, and personnel development. In addition, facilitators interact with local
government staff, nongovernmental organizations, and agencies that
provide them access to information. The program thus creates a new
resource in the organization and keeps it active by offering *sahayoginis* the opportunity to rise in the organization's ranks.

While the *sahayoginis* face hardship and challenges, including
threats from village-level power groups, the opportunities they are provided can be empowering. These opportunities create conditions for
facilitators to make demands for bettering their own lives. Although
empowering *sahayoginis* is not explicitly included in the program objectives, it was seen as a necessary and positive means for change. Such
self-empowerment implies greater learning and acquisition of knowledge by *sahayoginis* than by the *sangha* women because the skill level
of the two groups (*sahayoginis* and *sangha* women) varies. This has two

additional unintended consequences, not spelled out in program reports or by the program staff. These are creation of new equations of power between *sanghas* and facilitators in terms of knowledge and information and challenge to the authority of MSK's district- and state-level office. Both outcomes are visible in processes that shape social relations between facilitators and district- and state-level staff, as well as in the interaction of some of the facilitators and *sangha* participants. These outcomes involve evoking existing structures of inequality of caste and class that create new conflicts and challenge formal structures of authority within the organization.

The intersections of the competing forms of inequality, caste, and class result in new dynamics of power relations. The national evaluation report of the Mahila Samakhya program (Government of India 1993) alludes to this issue: "It is important that the staff do some process reflection on how to cope with empowerment, the personal changes it brings, and most importantly working from positions of authority without being drawn into a dehumanization process, which would be anathema to the values of MS" (18).

In spite of these tensions, MSK's capacity-building initiatives have opened avenues for the *sangha* women, the *sahayoginis*, and the district- and state-level staff to access and share resources at both the national and international level. In the analysis that follows, I address the capacity-building efforts of MSK, the forms and sites of the efforts at the level of the *sangha*, and then I focus on the initiatives at the *taluka* and state levels.

At a late-night meeting at Kulali, which I attended with the group facilitator and a staff member from the Bijapur district office, we sat in a dimly lit, partially constructed hall where members laid out a list of three items they planned to discuss. The *sahayogini* or facilitator watched silently and made no move to provide assistance. The *sangha* women discussed what they described as an urgent issue—the need for resources to complete the construction of the meeting hall. One *sangha* member said, "We need to raise money and complete this hall for our meetings. We have some amount from what we raised on the foundation laying day. But we have to quickly decide about visiting the Zilla Panchayat soon." At the end of an hour of discussion the group identified options. The first was to seek the honorarium amount that MSK earmarks for *sanghas*, and the second was to visit the district-level government office (Zilla Panchayat) and seek state funds for the construction work. These deliberations and the consideration of options demonstrate that the *sangha* members were taking on the mantle of leadership and that the *sahayogini* facilitated this. The *sangha* women seemed confident about discussing how and from where to seek resources.

At an early morning meeting I attended in Shirdona village in Gulbarga district, all the *sangha* women spoke at once, yelling at each other, saying, "Why should we give in? . . . Everyone should learn." After unsuccessfully attempting to interrupt, the staff member from MSK's district office watched the heated discussion. The women discussed the criteria they would use to select which of them would attend a three-week training program organized through a state-sponsored initiative. Participation in the program would provide an opportunity to learn a new skill (for starting a small-scale income-generating activity) but could also mean losing daily wage labor in the farms as substitutes would be put in the women's places. The training program offers a stipend to women to make up for the wages lost. However, two of the women who work in the village crèche and receive a monthly salary were also interested in the training program, considering that they were *sangha* members too. *Sangha* women were concerned that the two crèche employees would receive their salary and a portion of the stipend, too. The *sangha* women discussed and debated the basis for selection of women for the training and did not allow any intervention by the staff member of the district office. Following acrimonious discussion, they decided that all the *sangha* participants would attend the training program. Their experiences in the decision-making process were critical to their realization of their own abilities.

Similar processes can be noted in issues related to violence against women. At a weekly *sangha* meeting in Gabbur village, as we waited for tea from the nearby tea stall, some women explained how the daughter of a *sangha* member had to deal with violence by her husband, the tea stall owner:

> [The *sangha* member's] daughter lives here, in this village. Her husband abuses her. He owns a tea stall, works and earns money. And at night he goes to the liquor shop with other men, gets drunk, and comes home and abuses her. We, in the *sangha*, had to find a way to deal with this. First, we thought we would get him to come during one of our *sangha* meetings—like by ordering tea from his tea stall. Then, we felt that it might be difficult to speak to him with all of us here. We, then, decided that [a] few of us, older women, would speak to him one day, and warn him about abusing his wife. We warned him that the *sangha* will take this matter very seriously if he does not mend his ways. And, now we have been keeping track and following up. He has still not completely given up on drinking.

The space created through the *sangha* meetings enabled the *sangha* member to bring this issue before the group. The *sangha* members recognized that they needed to confront this issue and consider possibilities for dealing with the case of violence in a home in the village. The processes experienced by women in discussing ways and means to seek control over their lives and bodies further builds courage and confidence to challenge power and control. The above instances of in-house capacity-building initiatives at the level of the *sanghas* indicate that women connect with each other to seek change collectively. This form of in-house networking extends beyond the village *sangha* to the *taluka*, district, and state levels. The Mahila Samakhya Karnataka annual reports emphasize this point: "Networking is an important agenda in the Mahila Samakhya activities. It provides the needed exposure and experience to our women and the samakhya family" (1995) and "in the past year, the *Ghataka* [cluster] and *Taluk* [administrative units of a district] level meetings have been good forums to plan new inputs with the sangha women" (1998).

The cluster-level meetings organized once in two months by the *sahayogini* link women from across ten *sanghas*. *Taluka*-level meetings are held once in a quarter and are referred to as the *taluka mahasabhas*. These meetings have selective participation. Two participants from each *sangha* within the *taluka* attend the *mahasabhas* by rotation. Thus, members from across *sanghas* have an opportunity to meet other *sangha* women. As I observed in the *mahasabhas* of Gulbarga taluka (Gulbarga district) and Muddibehal taluka (Bijapur district) *sangha* women often carry their food and share it with MSK staff. The *sangha* women play games, raise questions, and share concerns. In addition, *sangha* women engage in activities like role plays and songs that focuse on social issues, such as child marriage and violence. The *taluka mahasabha* extends for a day. The *mahasabhas* of Gulbarga taluka and Muddebhial taluka provide *sangha* women the opportunity and time to build allies outside their own village. Such cluster-level and *taluka*-level meetings facilitate formation of a network of *sanghas*.

Networks of *sanghas* also emerge across the boundaries of the *taluka* to the district level through the regular district-level meetings. In addition, MSK has been organizing an "MSK Day" once a year to bring together the *sangha* women and the MSK staff. In addition to facilitating formation of networks among village-level participant women as well across *sanghas*, MSK provides opportunities for staff to network and interact with other employees at the district and state levels. These opportunities include monthly *sahayogini* meetings at the district level and training programs and workshops at the district and state levels.

Conclusions

The analysis in this article is specific to poor *dalit* women in rural
North Karnataka. It is important to recognize that these women may
already be negotiating power relations within their homes and their
communities. Acknowledging such agency is critical to dispelling
notions of *dalit* women as being only victims, as the example of the
women in Kulali village who are organizing literacy classes for themselves illustrates. The capacity-building initiatives discussed in this article provide an additional or alternative route to acting for change.

I have argued for recognizing capacity-building initiatives as key to
creating sites for consciousness raising among women. The networks
created through the capacity-building initiatives across various levels
of the organization are a resource that *sangha* women can draw upon.
Thus, capacity-building initiatives should be viewed not only as facilitating the transfer or development of tangible skills but also as a most
likely route to addressing oppression and thereby changing gender
relations. It is important to note that this analysis is not intended to
stereotype all poor women as victims of oppression. It calls for recognizing these women as key agents of change in communities.

Capacity-building initiatives are directly linked to construction of
networks allowing for information flow between and across local grassroots groups, as in the case of *sanghas*. MSK concentrated its initiatives
at the village, *taluka*, and district levels during the initial years and later
extended efforts at capacity building beyond the level of the state to
other states and to the national and international levels. The capacity-
building initiatives have intended and unintended consequences. The
intended consequences are reflected in the specific training and workshop programs organized by MSK or by other organizations, while the
unintended consequences are the creation of spaces for interaction
and the transformation of the network structures as actors. The initiatives provide women the space to interact with each other at the
grassroots village level, as in the excerpts of discussions from the meetings in Kulali village (Bijapur district), Shirdona village (Gulbarga district), and Gabbur village (Raichur district). These instances are
indicative of the ability of *sangha* women to relate to each other, share
experiences, and engage in discussing options available for seeking
resources or addressing violence. The local, village-level connections
for women extend to the *taluka* and district level, through the *taluka*-
and district-level meetings. *Taluka mahasabhas*, such as those in
Gulbarga taluka and Muddebihal taluka, are illustrations of efforts to
connect women across villages in the state and share information on

activities and efforts made for change. The connections that women build serve as intangible resources that the *sangha* can draw upon for collective resistance.

MSK is therefore engaged in raising the self-confidence of women who can then begin to seek access to resources that were previously denied to them. The program has been progressively emphasizing involvement in capacity building across organization and geographical levels as well as facilitating the transformation of consciousness among women. Arguing for conditions to make education possible for women is implicitly admitting that women's educational needs are different. This is the first step to facilitating access and creating conditions so that women themselves will question gender stereotypes seriously. Such a process will open the world of education for women.

NOTES

I wish to thank the four anonymous reviewers for their comments and suggestions on an earlier version of this article.

1. In India, every state is divided into districts, and several *talukas* make up a district. A *taluka*, in turn, comprises villages.

2. Under articles 341 and 342 of the Indian Constitution, certain castes, specified by public notification, have been deemed to be Scheduled Castes. Castes in this category were and are still among the poorest sections of Indian society. Considered unclean, hence untouchable, and outside the pale of the caste system, the Scheduled Castes are subject to various types of discrimination ranging from physical avoidance to exclusion from Hindu temples. Hindered in their development by socioeconomic and cultural factors, these categories receive protection under provisions of the constitution, and special laws safeguard their civil rights and representation in various spheres, such as education, employment, and elected bodies. The Scheduled Castes are from among the lowest in the caste hierarchy. Other descriptive terms used to refer to them are "untouchables," *harijan* (a term coined by Mahatma Gandhi and meaning "children of God"), and *dalits*. In this article I use these terms interchangeably.

3. See Joshi (1986) for details of the debate.

4. *Empowerment* as a term has been used in a variety of ways, but there is little consensus on the definition. Feminist discourses of empowerment are constructed around a cluster of recurring concepts of social power: rights, respect, integrity, autonomy, interests, choices, and control (e.g., Bookman and Morgen 1988; Batliwala 1993, 1996; Karl 1995; Molyneux 1985). This recent body of literature emphasizes the significance of intangible social "resources"—voices, public presence, internal strength and confidence, collective organization, reflection and analytical skills, information, political participation, and knowledge. Such resources matter socially at different levels (from the level of the individual to the macrosocial structure)

and in different domains (within the intimate domain of the family as well as in the public arena). Feminist literature also stresses the role of male violence in disempowering women (e.g., Bookman and Morgen 1988; Jejeebhoy 1998; Omvedt 1993; Rao 1999).

5. The growing trend is visible in the Indian state of Tamil Nadu, where the DHAN Foundation has been working on this idea.

6. Missing information regarding the affiliation of the resource persons as well as the venue (i.e., whether the site was the village, *taluka,* district, state, capital, or another state) of the capacity-building activity was noted.

7. A project using a satellite-based interactive communication system for training of development functionaries in Karnataka state was jointly organized by several government agencies and departments, including the Indian Space Research Organization (ISRO), the State Institute for Rural Development (SIRD), and SIRD's Administrative Training Institute (ATI).

REFERENCES

Afkhami, Mahnaz, Kumi Naido, Jacqueline Pitanguy, and Aruna Rao. 2002. "Human Security: A Conversation." *Social Research* 69 (fall 2002): 657–73.

Amin, Ruhul, A.U. Ahmed, and J. Chowdhury. 1994. "Poor Women's Participation in Income-Generating Projects and their Fertility Regulation in Rural Bangladesh: Evidence from a Recent Survey." *World Development* 22, no. 4: 555–65.

Andersen, Margaret L. 1993. *Thinking About Women: Sociological Perspectives on Sex and Gender.* New York: Macmillan

Batliwala, Srilata. 1993. *Empowerment of Women in South Asia: Concepts and Practices.* New Delhi: (FAO-FFHC/AD).

———. 1996. "The Meaning of Women's Empowerment: New Concepts from Action." In *Population Policies Reconsidered: Health, Empowerment, and Rights,* edited by G. Sen, A. Germain, and L. C. Chen., 127–138. Cambridge, Mass.: Harvard University Press.

Bhaiya, Abha, and Kalyani Menon-Sen. Undated. *Feminist Training: Precepts and Practice. Experiences in the Mahila Samakhya Programme.* Report written for Mahila Samakhya

Bookman, Ann, and Sandra Morgen. 1988. *Women and the Politics of Empowerment.* Philadelphia: Temple University Press.

Chen, Martha A. 1997. "Building Research Capacity in the Nongovernmental Organization Sector." In *Getting Good Government: Capacity Building in the Public Sectors of Developing Countries,* edited by Merilee S. Grindle, 229–53. Harvard, Mass.: Institute for International Development, Harvard University

Clark, John. 1992. *Democratizing Development. The Role of Voluntary Organizations.* West Hartford, CT: Kumarian

Cohen, John M., and John R. Wheeler. 1997. "Training and Retention in African Public Sectors: Capacity Building Lessons from Kenya." In *Getting Good Government: Capacity Building in the Public Sectors of Developing Ccountries,* edited by Merilee S. Grindle, 125–53. Harvard, Mass.: Institute for International Development, Harvard University

Dreze, Jean, and Amartya Sen (eds.). 1997. *Indian Development: Selected Regional Perspectives*. Delhi: Oxford University Press.

Dugger, Celia W. 1995. "Lower-Caste Women Turn Village Rule Upside Down." *New York Times*, May 3.

Dumont, Louis. 1980. *Homo Hierarchicus: The Caste System and Its Implications*. Translated by Mark Sainsbury, Louis Dumont, and Basia Gulati. Chicago: University of Chicago Press.

Edwards, Michael, and David Hulme. 1992. "Scaling-up the Developmental Impact of NGOs: Concepts and Experiences." In *Making a Difference: NGOs and Development in a Changing World*, edited by Michael Edwards and David Hulme, 13–27. London: Earthscan.

Ferree, Myra Marx, and Beth Hess. 1985. *Controversy and Coalition: The New Feminist Movement*. Boston, Mass.: Twayne.

Ferree, Myra Marx, and Mangala Subramaniam. 2001. "The International Women's Movement at Century's End." In *Gender Mosaics: Social Perspectives*, edited by Dana Vannoy, 496–506. Los Angeles: Roxbury.

Goetze, Anne Marie, and Rina Sen Gupta. 1996. "Who Takes the Credit? Gender, Power, and Control Over Loan Use in Rural Credit Programs in Bangladesh." *World Development* 24, no. 1: 45–63.

Government of India. 1993. *Mahila Samakhya National Evaluation Report*. New Delhi: Ministry of Human Resource Development.

———. 1997. *Mahila Samakhya. (Education for Women's Equality) Ninth Plan Document 1997–2002*. New Delhi: Ministry of Human Resource Development, Department of Education.

———. 1999. *India's Ninth Five-Year Plan*. New Delhi: Planning Commission.

———. Undated a. *We Can Change Our World: The Mahila Samakhya Karnataka Experience*. New Delhi: Ministry of Human Resource Development, Department of Education.

———. Undated b. *Mahila Samakhya*. New Delhi: Ministry of Human Resource Development, Department of Education.

Hashmi, Syed M., Sidney Ruth Schuler, and Ann P. Riley. 1996. "Rural Credit Programs and Women's Empowerment in Bangladesh." *World Development* 24, no. 4: 635–53

Hill-Collins, Patricia. 1990. *Black Feminist Theory: Knowledge, Consciousness and the Politics of Empowerment*. Cambridge, Mass.: Unwin Hyman

Jejeebhoy, Shireen J. 1998. "Wife-Beating in Rural India: A Husband's Right? Evidence from Survey Data." *Economic and Political Weekly*, 33, NO. 15: 855-862

Joshi, Barbara R. 1986. "Introduction" In *Untouchable! Voices of the Dalit Liberation Movement*, edited by Barbara Joshi, 1–14. London: Zed.

Kannabiran, Vasanth, and Kalpana Kannabiran. 1991. "Caste and Gender: Understanding Dynamics of Power and Violence." *Economic and Political Weekly* 26, no. 37: 2130–33

Karl, Marilee. 1995. *Women and Empowerment: Participation and Decision-Making*. London: Zed.

Mahila Samakhya Karnataka. 1995. *Annual Report 1993–94*. Bangalore: Mahila Samakhya Karnataka.

————. 1996a. *Beacons in the Dark: A Profile of Mahila Samakhya Karnataka.* Bangalore: Mahila Samakhya Karnataka

————. 1996b. *Annual Report 1994–95.* Bangalore: Mahila Samakhya Karnataka.

————. 1997. *Annual Report 1995–96.* Bangalore: Mahila Samakhya Karnataka.

————. 1998. *Annual Report 1996–97.* Bangalore: Mahila Samakhya Karnataka.

————. 1999. *Annual Report 1997–98.* Bangalore: Mahila Samakhya Karnataka.

Miller, Barbara D. 1981. *The Endangered Sex: Neglect of Female Children in Rural North India.* Ithaca, N.Y.: Cornell University Press

Molyneux, Maxine. 1985. "Mobilization Without Emancipation? Women's Interests, the State and Revolution in Nicaragua." *Feminist Studies* 11 (summer 1985): 227–54.

Myers, Charles N. 1997. "Policy Research Institutes in Developing Countries." In *Getting Good Government:Capacity Building in the Public Sectors of Developing Countries,* edited by Merilee S. Grindle, 177–98. Harvard, Mass.: Institute for International Development, Harvard University.

Narasimhan, Sakuntala. 1999. *Empowering Women. An Alternative Strategy from Rural India.* New Delhi: Sage.

Omvedt, Gail. 1993. *Reinventing Revolution: New Social Movements and the Socialist Tradition in India.* London: East Gate.

————. 1998. "The Anti-Caste Movement and the Discourse of Power." In *Region, Religion, Caste, Gender, and Culture in Contemporary India* , edited by T. V. Sathyamurthy, 334–354. Vol. 2, *Social Change and Political Discourse in India: Structures of Power, Movements of Resistance.* Delhi: Oxford University Press.

Peterson, Stephen B. 1997. "Hierarchy versus Networks: Alternative Strategies for Building Organizational Capacity in Public Bureaucracies in Africa." In *Getting Good Government: Capacity Building in the Public Sectors of Developing Countries,* edited by Merilee S. Grindle, 157–75. Harvard, Mass.: Institute for International Development, Harvard University.

Rai, Shirin. 2002. *Gender and the Political Economy of Development.* Malden, Mass.: Blackwell.

Rao, Anupama. 1999. "Understanding Sirasgaon: Notes towards Conceptualizing the Role of Law, Caste, and Gender in a Case of Atrocity." In *Signposts: Gender Issues in Post-Independence India,* edited by Rajeswari Sunder Rajan, 204–247. New Delhi: Kali for Women.

Ridgeway, Cecilia (ed.). 1992. *Gender, Interaction, and Inequality.* New York: Springer-Verlag.

Rose, Kalima. 1992. *Where Women are Leaders. The SEWA Movement in India.* London: Zed.

Scott, Joan. 1986. "Gender: A Useful Category of Historical Analysis." *American Historical Review* 91(5): 1053–75.

Sen, Amartya. 1983. "Development: Which Way Now." *Economic Journal* 93 (December): 745-62.

————. 1990. "Capability and Well-Being." In *The Quality of Life,* edited by Martha Nussbaum and Amartya Sen, 30–53. Oxford, England: Oxford University Press.

————. 1997. "Editorial: Human Capital and Human Capability." *World*

Development 25 (December): 1959–61.

———. 1999. *Development as Freedom.* New York: Knopf.

Shah, Ghanshyam. 2001. *Dalit Identity and Politics.* New Delhi: Sage.

Storey, Donavan. 1998. "Towards an Alternative Society? The Role of Intermediary Non-Governmental Organizations (INGOs) in Urban Poor Communities, the Philippines." *Urban Anthropology and Studies of Cultural Systems and World Economic Development* 27 (fall–winter): 345–92.

Subramaniam, Mangala. 2001. "Translating Participation in Informal Organizations into Empowerment: Women in Rural India." Ph.D. Diss., University of Connecticut, Storrs.

Taylor, Verta, and Nancy E. Whittier. 1992. "Collective Identity in Social Movement Communities: Lesbian Feminist Mobilization." Aldon D. Morris and Carol McClurg Mueller (eds.) In *Frontiers in Social Movement Theory,* edited by Aldon D. Morris and Carol McClurg Mueller, 104–129. New Haven: Yale University Press.

Thompson, John. 1995. "Participatory Approaches in Government Bureaucracies: Facilitating the Process of Institutional Change." *World Development* 23 (September): 1521–54.

Varshney, Ashutosh. 2000. "Is India Becoming More Democratic?" *Journal for Asian Studies* 59, no. 1: 3–25.

Weber, Max. [1916] 1958. *From Max Weber: Essays in Sociology.* Translated and edited by H. H. Gerth and C. Wright Mills. Reprint, New York: Oxford University Press.

Mangala Subramaniam is assistant professor of sociology and women's studies at Purdue University. Her areas of interest include gender and change, social movements, and quantitative methods. Her current research focuses on the dalit women's movement in India. She is coediting a book with Bandana Purkayastha titled "The Power of Women's Informal Networks: Lessons in Social Change from South Asia and West Africa" (forthcoming, Lexington Books).

Beyond Gender

Towards a Feminist Analysis of Humanitarianism and Development in Sri Lanka

Jennifer Hyndman and Malathi de Alwis

Gender has become something of a household word among development practitioners. Gender is also a buzzword in agencies and staff providing humanitarian assistance to people affected by conflict, but its integration into everyday operations is less apparent. In Sri Lanka, humanitarian agencies and development organizations work side by side in a country affected by war since 1981. Most people working in these organizations at senior levels know well that gender does not simply refer to women. They have come to understand that gender is a relational concept that juxtaposes femininity and masculinity, women's work and men's work, and that the concept varies across cultures. In efforts to integrate a gender analysis into humanitarian assistance, however, the ways in which gender relations and identities change in conjunction with the war economy and with competing Sinhalese and Tamil nationalisms are rarely mentioned. The centres of prostitution that are generated around new army bases at the frontlines of the war and the mothers' movements that emerge as soldiers' lives are endangered by the war do not fit inside the "gender box"; hence they are often ignored. Gender is treated as a portable tool of analysis and empowerment that can be carried around in the back pockets of both international humanitarian and development staff. It has become part of the development and humanitarian lexicon to be employed when preparing proposals and evaluating programs. Our objective in this paper is to move beyond gender in this context and reintroduce an analytical approach that engages disparate power relations inherent in both humanitarian and development work.

We are not interested in highlighting the shortcomings of specific policies or staff in the fields of development and humanitarianism. Rather we contend that the root of the problem lies in the way in which gender has been conceived and disseminated within these fields. Accordingly, we outline a more comprehensive, and still portable, feminist analytic that provides a more sophisticated approach to understanding the *production* of gender identities and relations. The idea that gender identities and relations are generated differently across space and time, and have no essential pre-established qualities, is critical to changing them. This feminist analytic, then, is at once a tool for understanding social, economic, and political relations and a tool for changing them. We define *feminist* for the purpose of this article as reflecting analyses and political interventions that address the unequal and often violent relationships among people based on real or perceived social, economic, political, cultural, and sexual differences. The analysis and elimination of patriarchal relations of power within each of these fields is a primary focus. We recognize that there is more than one kind of feminism, and we do not wish to fix the category "feminist" in any singular manner nor to create a typology of feminisms. We contend that gender analysis has fallen prey to such rigidities, and has thus limited its analytical strength.

Gender remains a central concern of feminist politics and thought. However, its primacy over other social, economic, cultural, and political locations is not fixed across time and place. Daiva Stasiulis (1999) elaborates on the importance of relationality, positionality, and "relational positionality" to feminist politics: "They refer to the multiple relations of power that intersect in complex ways to position individuals and collectivities in shifting and often contradictory locations within geopolitical spaces, historical narratives, and movement politics" (194). Stasiulus continues, "Central to my interpretation of relational positionality is also a rejection of poststructuralist deconstructions that deny the material bases for power relations, however complicated their discursive representations" (196). We agree with Stasiulus to an extent, although we argue that poststructuralist analyses do not categorically deny the material bases of power relations. A poststructuralist analysis can, in fact, reveal the very processes by which particular constellations of power are effaced or naturalized (Butler 1992).

Gender versus Woman: WID, WAD, GAD . . . FAD?

Gender policies in humanitarian organizations provide a "grid of intelligibility" for field officers and other staff working with displaced populations. They furnish concepts and checklists to assist in the organization and functioning of camps, but they do not generally allow dimensions of gender or culture to change the assumptions of the overall planning framework in which field staff work. Historical context, regional geopolitics, cultural dynamics, and gender relations are left for field workers to "fill in" once in the field. Such policies are flawed because they do not take these "variables"—historical arrangements, proximate politics, and so forth—as integral to all operations (Hyndman 1998).

The institutionalization of women in development (WID) in the early 1970s was largely a result of liberal feminist agitations globally. Since then, several permutations of this formulation have been proposed, reformed, and challenged. These can be most clearly traced through the conceptual shifts delineated by now-familiar acronyms, from WID to WAD (women and development) to GAD (gender and development). As Eva Rathgeber (1990) notes, the WID approach is linked closely with modernization theory and "is understood to mean the integration of women into global processes of economic, political, and social growth and change" (489). This approach became the dominant paradigm for understanding women's roles in development in the early 1970s. But by the end of the decade, another approach had emerged, namely women and development (Moser 1993; Lind 1995). This approach focused on the "relationship between women and development processes" rather than purely on strategies to integrate women into development (Rathgeber 1990, 492). WAD proponents considered the integration of women into a masculinist project of development as insufficient, and advocated separate projects for women designed by them. Gender and development, or GAD, emerging in the 1980s as an alternative to WID and WAD, were influenced by socialist feminist critiques of the modernization paradigm. Instead of focusing on women per se, GAD approaches were primarily concerned with the "social construction of gender and the assignment of specific roles, responsibilities, and expectations to women and to men" (Rathgeber 1990, 494). GAD not only goes further in questioning the underlying assumptions of social, economic, and political relations but in fact "demands a degree of commitment to structural change and power shifts that is unlikely to be found either in national or international agencies" (Rathgeber 1990, 495). This commitment to structural and relational change is lost when agencies simply invoke the categories of "women" or "gender" in an effort to include gender programming in their projects. GAD attempts to probe the implications of male and female identities, and examines the power relations between men and women

The transformative potential of the GAD paradigm is often diluted by organizations that maintain that it is not practically applicable, especially in emergency situations where logistical challenges are acute and survival is deemed the goal. Feminists working in conflict areas characterized by crisis talk of the "emergency excuse," whereby gender is considered a luxury, not integral to people's survival.[1] Many NGOs, humanitarian NGOs in particular, have sought instead to compromise by following strategies of "gender sensitizing" and "gender mainstreaming." Such strategies may take into account the social construction of gender and its iterative intersections with other bases of identity, but most often they reduce gender to an exercise in "adding on" women beneficiaries or women's perspectives to their larger frameworks of intervention, which remain unchanged and unproblematized (de Alwis and Hyndman 2002; Parpart 2000).

What we wish to stress here is that every humanitarian project, in its design, method, evaluation, and impact, is gendered. In Sri Lanka, the fact that most income-generation projects for women enable them to work from or near home (i.e., in poultry rearing and home gardening) carries with it an implicit assumption that women are inextricably linked to the private and gendered sphere of the home. Similarly, stereotyped roles in society are perpetuated through the training of women in particular kinds of skills and professions. Women are more often taught sewing and weaving—"feminine" skills—than masonry or carpentry. (In Sri Lanka, one Canadian nongovernmental organization, World University Services of Canada, does attempt to change the existing gender regime by providing training in nontraditional sectors, such as carpentry, masonry, welding, and bicycle and tractor repair.) To include "gender balance" or a "gender analysis" in the evaluation of a project, as some international NGOs operating in Sri Lanka do, without integrating gender into the very conception of a project, is to the miss the point.

Situating Sri Lanka

War between the Liberation Tigers of Tamil Eelam (LTTE) and the armed forces of the Government of Sri Lanka has been raging for twenty years. The conflict has spawned large-scale displacement within the country and well beyond its borders, where a significant Tamil diaspora has emerged. Statistics suggest that there are more than 800,000 internally displaced persons in Sri Lanka (Refugee Council 2002). The death toll now exceeds 60,000. Mass displacement, multiple displacements, long-term displacement, and attacks on communities of displaced persons amid intense militarization across the country present massive challenges to both national and international organizations positioned to address the human needs these crises generate. Displaced persons exist on both sides of the lines, and are from Tamil, Sinhala, and Muslim groups, though the vast majority of displaced persons in Sri Lanka are Tamil. The government-controlled "cleared"/ "unliberated" areas (depending on whom you ask) stand in contrast to the LTTE-controlled "uncleared"/"liberated" areas—spaces that continually shift and frontlines that are ever-evolving in these "border areas." A ceasefire agreement between the government and the LTTE was drawn up in February 2002 and at the time of this writing was still holding. This has meant that a number of military checkpoints have been dismantled and that major transportation routes to the north and east have been reopened. No comprehensive peace agreement or plan for the demobilization of the warring factions has been initiated, although preliminary peace talks between the LTTE and the Sri Lankan government were held in September 2002.

Numerous Sri Lankan and Sri Lankanist scholars whose work spans several decades have provided incisive analyses about developments within the country. Sri Lanka's present is an expression of a long history of conflict and struggle that cannot be covered in depth in this article (see Abeysekera and Gunasinghe 1987; Committee for Rational Development 1984; Jayawardena 1985a; Jeganathan and Ismail 1995; Spencer 1990). Discriminatory measures in education, employment, and use of language were introduced after Sri Lanka's independence from Britain in 1948 and these measures denied equal rights to the Tamil minority. In addition, "the failure of successive Sinhalese-dominated Sri Lankan governments to implement agreements with Tamil leaders saw the deterioration of relations between the two communities" (Refugee Council 2002, 4).

A brief note on the methods employed in conducting the recent research discussed here is appropriate. The research was carried out by both authors over a period of two years, from January 1999 to December 2000. Our choice of field sites within Sri Lanka was based on a desire to capture the variety and complexity of different conflict areas. As a result, we concentrated on the districts of Trincomalee, Batticaloa, and Ampara in the Eastern Province, and the Wanni region in the north. We had originally hoped to include the city of Jaffna as well, but the challenges of transportation, security clearances, and other logistics in the region soon convinced us that this would not be a viable venture. In each of the regions, we met with aid beneficiaries, non–aid beneficiaries, community leaders, members of community-based organizations (CBOs), and senior and junior staff in the branch offices of both international and national (or local) nongovernmental organizations (NGOs) working in development and humanitarian assistance. We jointly visited each region at least twice over the research period. In Colombo, we conducted more formal interviews with country representatives and programme officers in the head offices of international and national NGOs, while also engaging in extensive library and archival research at these offices where possible. Because of the instability of the political situation and the sensitivity of issues addressed, we decided not to use a tape recorder or a formal questionnaire in our meetings. We nevertheless took detailed written notes, including specific information and quotations gleaned during our conversations and meetings, in order to preserve the accuracy of our information.

Feminist Analysis of the Sri Lankan Conflict

Men and women are affected differently by war, just as they are affected differently by the antidotes, services, and interventions that are made in the name of humanitarian assistance. Women and other minority groups can be disadvantaged or even harmed by such activities if assistance is gender-blind, that is, based on the assumption that assistance will affect all displaced persons equally. We found that displaced women in the north and east of Sri Lanka are frequently disadvantaged in terms of access to employment or services by humanitarian agencies because they are less likely to speak up, or to speak English, than their male counterparts. While it may be true that women are systematically worse off than men (economically, politically, socially), women from the majority nation in a region or from the middle and upper classes would certainly enjoy less vulnerability and more privilege, on average, than men from a minority national group. Hence, extant hierarchies of power that include control over land, official language, and religion—as in the case of Sri Lanka—produce specific gender relations depending on one's location within the hierarchy. The links between gender and nation in this context provide a case in point, and one that we will return to later in the article.

In Sri Lanka, the impact of war has been both disabling and enabling for women and men. The conflict has, for example, destabilized the sexual division of labor, resulting in the redefinition of women's roles in society (Rajasingham-Senanayake 1998). We found that the training of young women in unconventional trades and skill sets by NGOs was more viable during such periods of change. The training of women as mechanics, for example, something unheard of before the war in Sri Lanka, was reported both in areas controlled by the militant LTTE and in those controlled by the government (de Alwis and Hyndman 2002). Just as the fictional Rosie the Riveter represented new possibilities for women during the World War II, new roles and spaces have emerged for Sri Lankan women amid ongoing conflict and war. Change precipitated by war, however, does not necessarily benefit women. Our research shows that women increasingly lead lone-parent families, often becoming the sole income earner when menfolk are absent, and are also more prone to sexual harassment, societal censure, and surveillance. The consequences of war, especially displacement, are profoundly gendered, as de Alwis (2004) demonstrates in her analysis of Sri Lankan Muslims living in refugee camps[2] in northwestern Sri Lanka:

> Shifts in property ownership and the inversion of patterns of income-generation within the refugee camps, where many women go out to work while their husbands stay home, has made women's positioning within pre-existing patriarchal power structures a fraught one. Not only has the incidence of domestic violence increased [probably exacerbated by the increasing emasculation of refugee men] within the camps but the women's mobility has been drastically curtailed. Their every movement is now open to scrutiny and questioning under the guise that it is they who have to uphold the honour and cultural traditions of their family and community. (182)

Thus, both men and women are adversely affected in distinctive ways. The positions of men and women within nationalist discourse tend to be distinct, especially along gender lines. Women are often constructed as reproducers of the nation, while men are its warriors and protectors.

Programs that target women as the sole "beneficiaries" represent an inadequate approach to addressing issues of gender inequality within the context of displacement. The term *beneficiary* is unproblematically mobilized in humanitarian and development discourse, but highlights the asymmetrical relationships within which "assistance" is bestowed. Such forms of "gifting" among unequals symbolically disempowers the recipients, who become "clients of those upon whom they are dependent for the means of survival and security" (Harrell-Bond 2000, 2). In Sri Lanka, gender concerns are frequently reduced to a concern with women's welfare. Accordingly, credit schemes for "war widows" are numerous. To qualify as beneficiaries, women are often pushed to take on such an identity, when their status might be much more ambiguous (for example, their spouse might be missing or "disappeared"). The stigma associated with widowhood is, however, rarely addressed in this context.[3]

The reduction of gender to women's welfare appears also to have led most international NGOs to appoint women as gender coordinators. The particular gendering of this job title produces several unfortunate consequences. First, most gender coordinators end up working exclusively with women's groups and/or on women's projects, thus rarely interacting with male beneficiaries or being provided with opportunities to make men rethink and change unequal gender hierarchies that they might be perpetuating within Sri Lankan society. Second, in a context where no trained gender coordinator is available within an NGO, responsibility for gender often devolves to a junior female program officer. Her womanhood, it is assumed, automatically makes her sensitive to issues of gender. Such practices serve only to marginalize gender analysis and politics within organizations. Third, the appointment of only women as gender coordinators absolves other field and program officers from taking responsibility or being accountable for promoting gender equality in the programs that they implement. This becomes the separate responsibility of the gender coordinator. Finally, gender is increasingly considered a "soft" issue, one that will not warrant the apportioning of significant resources if it does not produce "hard" results based on monitoring and evaluation outcomes.

The final point is further solidified through an argument commonly made by many international and national NGOs that things are better for women in Sri Lanka than elsewhere in South Asia, and therefore gender politics need not be an issue of concern. While it is true that Sri Lankan society is relatively free of such practices as female infanticide, honour killings, dowry deaths, and *sati*—the usual bugbears of its neighbours—this does not mean that gender inequalities do not exist in the country or that sexual harassment, rape, incest, and domestic violence are not part of the lived reality. No society, in any part of the world, is free of such unsafe and unfair conditions for women. When deployed, such rationale for gender inaction only serves to reinforce the "us/them" distinction, instantiating different standards for women in different societies.

What we are calling for here, then, is a feminist approach to understanding gender in the context of development or humanitarian crises, one that analyzes and integrates considerations of history, location, and politics. This more feminist approach allows greater flexibility in assessment of need and program development. Gender cannot be prioritized ahead of religion, nationality, caste, or class in all places nor at all times. Gender is one part of an adaptable, practical, analytical package that international development and humanitarian agencies use in collaborating with local and national partners, and that all NGOs employ in conducting programs in areas affected by displacement. In Sri Lanka, efforts to assist women in the Wanni, Batticaloa, and Puttalam will each be distinct because of the geopolitics, national groups, and governing authorities in place. What it means to be a woman in each of these places is different. This is compounded by differences in class, caste, and nation. In a town such as Batticaloa or Akkaraipattu, mobility and opportunities for Tamil women are markedly different than they are for Muslim women. Hence, there is no single approach to working with women in the Eastern Province. In the following section, we move to a discussion of gender and nation in conjunction, arguing that gender cannot be separated out from historical and geographical contingencies of nation and the related conflict in Sri Lanka.

Feminist Perspectives on Nationalism and Gender

In Sri Lanka and elsewhere, membership in a particular nation shapes one's political, economic, and social locations at least as much as one's gender identity, and in ways specifically articulated through gender differences. Over the past few decades, feminists in many countries have produced an extensive literature that examines and analyses the links between gender and nation, often contextualizing such relations within postcolonial societies. Research on nationalism has focused on the role of gender in the construction and reproduction of ethnonationalist ideologies (Enloe 1989; Jayawardena 1986; Moghadam 1994; Yuval-Davis 1998). The mutually constitutive identities of gender and nation position women and men in particular ways, for example, rendering women the bearers of "tradition" and national culture, on the one hand, and men the protectors of the faith-nation and its property, women (Moghadam 1994), on the other. As Partha Chatterjee (1996) notes, nationalism is a project of asserting difference through internal unity, but one within which hierarchies of gender, race, class, and caste are hardly unifying. Kumari Jayawardena and Malathi de Alwis (1996) further note that "ultra-nationalist movements have used women as cultural representatives and constructed them in relation to western domination. Women are the carriers of 'authenticity'; this puts them in a difficult position vis-à-vis their gender and religious identities" (xiii). The subaltern school of historians in India (and those they have inspired) as well as feminist scholars in various parts of South Asia have played a central role in this endeavour of writing back, of producing their own knowledge of place and history and decolonizing (neo)colonial epistemologies of knowledge production (Chatterjee 1986).

While nationalism may seek to homogenize differences through the unifying discourse of the nation, it nonetheless generates contradictory positions for women as symbols of cultural purity, agents of resistance against western domination, and "role models for the new nationalist patriarchal family" (Moghadam 1994, 4). Nationalism is not a fixed notion, nor can it claim a unitary subject that bears nationality separate from gender, caste, class, and religious identities (Giles and Hyndman 2003). The construction of national identity and gendered nationalism in Sri Lanka has been traced and debated by a number of scholars (de Alwis 1994, 1996; Hellman-Rajanayagam 1990; Ismail 1995; Jayawardena 1986, 1993, 1995; Maunaguru 1995). These analyses highlight the intersection of gender with nationalism and their connections to state building in Sri Lanka. Sri Lankan women, be they Sinhala, Tamil, or Muslim, continue to be constructed as the reproducers, nurturers, and disseminators of tradition, culture, community, and nation. Such perceptions have not only legitimized the surveillance and disciplining of women's bodies and minds in the name of communal and national "morality" and "honour" but have also re-inscribed the expectation that whatever women may do, they are primarily mothers and wives; they have to marry and have children, and the domestic burdens are solely theirs.

The 1980s and 1990s have also witnessed the political mobilization of "motherhood" as a counter to violence, both in the context of the civil war in the north and east as well as the second youth Janatha Vimukthi Peramuna (JVP) (People's Liberation Front) uprising in the south. The seemingly unquestionable authenticity of these women's grief and espousal of traditional family values has provided the Mothers' Fronts, movements made up of soldiers' mothers, with an important space for protest at a time when feminist and human rights activists who were critical of either state or JVP violence were being killed with impunity. While women have been the victims and survivors of violence, they have also been its perpetrators. Though some women participated in the JVP youth insurrection of 1987–89, the issue of women militants has come to the fore in the 1990s with the increased participation of Tamil women militants in combat. In fact, the women's wing of the LTTE, Suthanthirap Paravaikal (Birds of Freedom), has acquired almost as much notoriety as their male counterparts since a female suicide bomber killed Rajiv Gandhi, the prime minister of India, in 1991. The increased visibility of these women in recent LTTE campaigns against the Sri Lankan forces has also generated much discussion among feminists in Sri Lanka on the role of female militants in antistate movements, a familiar question to those who have studied the positioning of female fighters in guerrilla groups. Much of this feminist debate is framed in binary terms of whether the women in the LTTE are liberated or subjugated (de Silva 1994; Coomaraswamy

1997), agents or victims (de Mel 1998). Such exclusivist categories of either/or, and us and them, tend to obscure the fraught and multiple locations of women in the context of war.

The anti-Tamil pogroms of 1983 and the start of a civil war in the north and east also led the feminist movement in Sri Lanka to expend a great deal of energy towards promoting a peaceful and politically negotiated settlement to the violent nationalisms underlying the conflict. Various feminist groups have spoken out against the increased militarization of Sri Lankan society; published articles and books on the ideological underpinnings of conflict; documented and protested human rights violations by the state as well as militant groups; set up peace education programmes in schools; and organized peace demonstrations, pickets, and vigils. The committed efforts of several feminist groups not only call for an end to the war but also highlight the shared suffering of both Tamil and Sinhala women as a result of this war. These activists have emphasized, through articles, songs, and videos, the shared histories and cultures of the Sinhalese and Tamils and have fostered greater understanding between the two groups by offering free Tamil classes, organizing goodwill missions to the north and east, and setting up various trauma-counseling and income-generating projects in the conflict zones.

Colombo-based feminist groups have demonstrated active concern for women refugees of all ethnic and national groups, including Tamil women prisoners and detainees, as well as Tamil women civilians in the north and east who were raped and abused by the Sri Lankan military. Such efforts have frequently antagonised the Sinhala press. These groups' critique of patriarchal structures of power within Sri Lankan society has also drawn a great deal of criticism in the media (see de Alwis 1998; Jayawardena 1985b) and has led to group members being harassed and beaten by the police on many occasions (see de Rosairo 1992). In the mid-1980s, for example, the extremely nationalist, mainstream Sinhala newspaper, the *Divaina*, was at the forefront of a campaign to "expose" Sinhala feminists, who were supposedly funded by foreigners and controlled by religious (meaning Christian) organizations (*Divaina*, May 25, 1986). These groups were said to be publicizing the plight of the Tamil people all over the world, and thus not only discrediting their own country, but their race and religion as well. More recently, feminists' demands for peace and the resumption of talks between the government and the LTTE, with third-party facilitation, has led to the renewal of attacks against feminist peace activists both by the media as well as sections of the Sinhala populace (*The Island*, July 26, 1999).

Concluding Notes

We contend that a thoroughly feminist analysis incorporates *multiple* bases of identity and power relations, not exclusively gender. In the case of Sri Lanka, gender identity cannot be neatly separated from national identity; they are mutually constitutive. Gender relations are part and parcel of nationalist discourses, be they Sinhalese, Tamil, or Muslim. A feminist approach—one that combines multiple analytical axes contingent on time and place—provides a more powerful lens with which to examine the place of both women and men in society and a more compelling position from which to transform relations that provoke or perpetuate violence, hate, and inequality. A brief inventory of humanitarian and development practices pertaining to gender in the Sri Lankan context points to the professionalization of gender among development and humanitarian organizations in Sri Lanka. Thus, remarkably, gender has ceased to have much analytical or political valence in a context of war; gender has been so thoroughly incorporated into proposal development, monitoring, and evaluation that it has little substantive content or transformative potential.

We seek, then, to reintroduce a feminist analytic to both humanitarian and development work in an effort to understand and engage the displacement, insecurity, and trauma that shape people's lives. Crosscutting relations of gender, nation, geography, class, even birthplace, produces distinct patterns of dislocation and instability. A feminist analysis resists typologies, eschews modules, and allows for examination of multiple bases of identity that shape, and are shaped by, the geographically and historically specific dynamics of conflict. The feminist analysis promulgated here resists any singular production or understanding of gender; instead, we highlight the ways in which gender identities and relations are produced differently through and by nationalist and humanitarian discourses. Conflict destabilizes gender norms, and while this may generate openings for women to take on new responsibilities, it heightens uncertainty and insecurity for those displaced by war.

NOTES

1. We thank Kerry Demusz, former Oxfam project coordinator for the Northern Province of Sri Lanka, for this insight. Her work highlights feminist methods for conducting community-based research in conflict-affected areas. See Demusz 2000.
2. Although these camps are for the internally displaced, they are referred to as refugee camps in common parlance, in Sri Lanka.

3. Some NGOs prefer to give loans to women because they are considered better repayers. When asked about their gender policies, the NGOs tried to spin this as an example of their gender sensitivity and balance.

REFERENCES

Abeysekera, Charles, and Newton Gunasinghe (eds.) (1987). *Facets of Ethnicity in Sri Lanka.* Colombo: Social Scientists' Association.

Butler, Judith. (1992). "Contingent Foundations: Feminism and the Question of 'Postmodernism.'" In *Feminists Theorize the Political,* edited by Judith Butler and Joan W. Scott, 3–21. New York: Routledge.

Chatterjee, Partha. (1986). *Nationalist Thought and the Colonial World.* London: Zed.

———. (1996). "Whose imagined community?" In *Mapping the Nation,* edited by G. Balakrishnan, 214–25. London: Verso.

Coomaraswamy, R. (2003). "A Question of Honour: Women, Ethnicity, and Armed Conflict." In *Feminist Under Fire: Exchanges Across War Zones,* W. Giles, M. de Alwis, E. Klein, and N. Silva (eds), 91–102. Toronto: Between the Lines.

Committee for Rational Development. (1984). *Sri Lanka The Ethnic Conflict: Myths, Realities and Perspectives.* New Delhi: Navrang.

de Alwis, Malathi. (1994). "Towards a Feminist Historiography: Reading Gender in the Text of the Nation." In *Introduction to Social Theory,* edited by R. Coomaraswamy and N. Wickremasinghe, 86–107. New Delhi: Konark.

———. (1996). "Sexuality in the Field of Vision: The Discursive Clothing of the Sigiriya Frescoes." In *Embodied Violence: Communalising Women's Sexuality in South Asia,* edited by Kumari Jayawardena and Malathi de Alwis, 89–112. London: Zed.

———. (1998). "Maternalist Politics in Sri Lanka: A Historical Anthropology of Its Conditions of Possibility." Ph.D. diss., University of Chicago. Ann Arbor, Mich.: UMI Dissertation Services.

———. (2003). "The 'Purity' of Displacement and the Re-territorialization of Longing: Muslim Women Refugees in North-Western Sri Lanka." In *Sites of Violence: Feminist Politics in Conflict Zones,* edited by Wenona Giles and Jennifer Hyndman. Berkeley: University of California Press (forthcoming).

de Alwis, Malathi, and Jennifer Hyndman. (2004). *Capacity-Building in Conflict Zones: A Feminist Analysis of Humanitarian Assistance in Sri Lanka.* Report. Colombo: International Centre for Ethnic Studies.

De Mel, N. (2003). "Agent or Victim? The Sri Lankan Woman Militant in the Interregnum." In *Feminists Under Fire: Exchanges Across War Zones,* 55–74. Toronto: Between the Lines.

Demusz, Kerry. (2000). *Listening to the Displaced: Action Research in the Conflict Zones of Sri Lanka.* Oxfam Working Papers.

de Rosairo, Khema (pseud.). (1992). "Gender Agenda: State Co-option of International Women's Day," *Pravada* 1, no. 4: 10–11.

Enloe, Cynthia. (1989). *Bananas, Beaches and Bases: Making Feminist Sense of International Politics.* Berkeley: University of California Press.

Giles, Wenona, and Jennifer Hyndman (eds). (2003). *Sites of Violence:*

Feminist Politics in Conflict Zones. Berkeley: University of California Press (forthcoming).

Harrell-Bond, Barbara. (2000). "Can Humanitarian Work with Refugees Be Humane?" Paper presented at the on Recovery and Development after Conflict and Disaster Conference, Norwegian University of Science and Technology, April 5–6, 2000.

Hellman-Rajanayagam, Dagmar. (1990). "The Politics of the Tamil Past." In *Sri Lanka: History and the Roots of Conflict,* edited by Jonathan Spencer, 107–22. New York: Routledge: 107–22.

Hyndman, Jennifer. (1998). "Managing Difference: Gender and Culture in Humanitarian Emergencies," *Gender, Place, and Culture* 5, no. 3: 241–60.

Ismail, Qadri. (1995). "Unmooring Identity: The Antimonies of Elite Muslim Self-Representation in Modern Sri Lanka." In *Unmaking the Nation: The Politics of Identity and History in Modern Sri Lanka,* edited by Pradeep Jeganathan and Qadri Ismail, 55–105. Colombo: Social Scientists' Association.

Jayawardena, Kumari. (1985a). *Ethnic and Class Conflicts in Sri Lanka.* Colombo: Sanjiva Books.

———. (1985b). "Some Aspects of Feminist Consciousness in the Decade 1975–1985." In *UN Decade for Women: Progress and Achievements of Women in Sri Lanka,* 171–80. Colombo: Centre for Women's Research in Colombo(CENWOR).

———. (1986). *Feminism and Nationalism in the Third World.* London: Zed.

———. (1993). "Some Aspects of Religious and Cultural Identity and the Construction of Sinhala Buddhist Womanhood." In *Religion and Political Conflict in South Asia,* edited by Douglas Allen, 161–80. Delhi: Oxford University Press.

———. (1995). *The White Woman's Other Burden: Western Women and South Asia During British Colonial Rule.* New York: Routledge.

Jayawardena, Kumari, and Malathi de Alwis. (1996). Introduction to *Embodied Violence: Comunalising Women's Sexuality in South Asia,* edited by Kumari Jayawardena and Malathi de Alwis, ix–xxiv. London: Zed.

Jeganathan, Pradeep, and Qadri Ismail (eds). (1995). *Unmaking the Nation: The Politics of Identity and History in Modern Sri Lanka.* Colombo: Social Scientists' Association.

Lind, Amy. (1995). "Gender, Development and Women's Political Practices in Ecuador." Ph.D. Diss., Cornell University. UMI Dissertation Services.

Maunaguru, Sitralega. (1995). "Gendering Tamil Nationalism: The Construction of 'Woman' in Projects of Protest and Control." In *Unmaking the Nation: The Politics of Identity and History in Modern Sri Lanka,* edited by Pradeep Jeganthan and Qadri Ismail, 158–75. Colombo: Social Scientists' Association.

Moghadam, Val. (1994). Introduction and overview to *Gender and National Identity,* edited by Val Moghadam, 1–17. London: Zed.

Moser, Caroline. 1993. *Gender Planning and Development.* London: Routledge.

Parpart, Jane. (2000). "Rethinking Participation, Empowerment, and

Development from a Gender Perspective." In *Transforming Development: Foreign Aid for a Changing World*, edited by Jim Freeman, 222–34. Toronto: University of Toronto Press.

Pateman, Carole. (1989). *The Disorder of Women: Democracy, Feminism and Political Theory.* Stanford: Stanford University Press.

Rajasingham-Senanayake, Darini. (1998). "After Victimhood: Cultural Transformation and Women's Empowerment in War and Displacement." Paper presented at Women in Conflict Zones Network Conference, Hendela, Sri Lanka, December 7–10.

Rathgeber, Eva. (1990). "WID, WAD, GAD: Trends in Research and Practice," *Journal of Developing Areas* 24, no. 4: 489–502.

Refugee Council. (2002) "Sri Lanka: Return to Uncertainty." Sri Lanka Project. London, July; http://www.refugeecouncil.org.uk/downloads/rc_reports/srilanka_uncertainty.pdf. Accessed October 3, 2002.

Spencer, Jonathan (ed). (1990) *Sri Lanka: History and the Roots of Conflict.* New York: Routledge.

Stasiulis, Daiva. (1999). "Relational Positionalities of Nationalisms, Racisms, and Feminisms." In *Between Woman and Nation: Nationalisms, Transnational Feminisms, and the State*, edited by C. Kaplan, N. Alarcón, and M. Moallem, 182–218. Durham, N.C.: Duke University Press.

Yuval-Davis, Nira. (1998). *Gender and Nation.* London: Thousand Oaks. New Delhi: Sage.

Jennifer Hyndman *is associate professor of geography at Simon Fraser University in Vancouver and author of* Managing Displacement: Refugees and the Politics of Humanitarianism *(University of Minnesota Press).* ***Malathi de Alwis*** *is visiting associate professor of anthropology at New School University in New York and senior research associate with the International Centre for Ethnic Studies in Colombo.* Both authors appear in Sites of Violence: Gender in Conflict Zones, *a feminist volume forthcoming with the University of California Press.*

Feminist Post-Development Thought

"Women in Development" and the Gendered Paradoxes of Survival in Bolivia

Amy Lind

Let Me Speak!

—Title of the English translation of Domitila Barrios de Chungara's published testimony, 1978

More than 20 years have gone by since [the inaugural conference of the United Nations Decade for the Advancement of Women, 1975–1985, in Mexico City]. There have been so many workshops, so many conferences. Nonetheless, the situation of women has not improved. It has remained the same. Nothing has changed.

—Domitila Barrios de Chungara, personal interview, 1999

Typically, in development studies, women's lives and political struggles in so-called Third World[1] countries have been understood from within the ethnographic imagination of the West, through a Western lens (Mohanty 1991). Feminist scholars, teachers, and policy makers from around the world have analyzed and supported the struggles of poor women in impoverished nations, although with mixed results. Feminists from Third World countries are perhaps more aware of how local communities must negotiate male-based power embedded in local social relations and cultural practices, on one hand, and the "Western gaze," which involves a universal agenda influenced by Western ideas promoted particularly by international development and human rights organizations, on the other (Coomaraswamey 2002). Nonetheless, Third World feminists[2] continue to grapple with how to address gender discrimination and interrelated issues of racial, economic, and religious oppression from an autonomous standpoint.[3] In the industrialized "West,"[4] the location from which I write this article, scholars are faced with the educational task of explaining "Third World difference" (Mohanty 1991) during a period of much confusion and fear about what these differences really are (or are not) and whether they constitute the need for military intervention, humanitarian aid, or "help" of any kind. In this article I address the dilemmas of researching about women's lives in global perspective and examine feminist post-development thought and its potential contributions to women's studies curriculum and scholarship. On one hand, feminist post-development scholars have called for further attention to Western feminism's role in reproducing global inequalities faced by many women in poor countries (Marchand and Parpart 1995). Yet despite the need for this project we know, from a variety of media and studies, that there is still a need for "an anthropology of place" (see Starn 1999), including an examination of regional histories prior to, during, and following colonization; a study of geography, including a critical examination of the role of maps in constructing a global reality (e.g., most maps purchased in the United States divide India into two); further research on women's lives in poor countries, including issues surrounding poverty, but also women's contributions to art, media, literature, politics, and policy making, to name only a few arenas; and an examination of how gender and women's bodies themselves have become "battlefields" for broader movements against modernization, Westernization, or U.S. imperialism (Williams 1996; Enloe 1989, 2000).

To address these issues, I draw from my 1999 research on women's movements in Bolivia, in which I analyzed how community-based women's organizations negotiate the terms of international development agency agendas in their local struggles for survival. My research methods included discourse analysis; policy analysis; participant observation in organizational meetings and events; and semi-structured interviews and in-depth, open-ended interviews with key female political leaders, including Domitila Barrios de Chungara, a leader of Bolivia's tin-mining wives' associations and former vice-presidential candidate, whose testimony has been published and used in women's studies classrooms throughout the United States (Barrios de Chungara 1977, 1978). Utilizing insight from feminist post-development studies, I address the dilemmas of researching these issues. In conclusion, I suggest ways in which we can best integrate this area of research into women's studies curricula and the gender and development field. More generally, I address how we can understand and locate women's lives in a global context, rather than merely through a Western lens.

Feminist Visions of Post-Development

Since the 1975 inaugural conference of the United Nations Decade for the Advancement of Women (1975–1985) in Mexico City, scholarly understandings of "women's roles in development," based on Ester Boserup's (1970) original research, have significantly changed. Following more than three decades of scholarship on women's lives in poor countries and globally, including the women in development (WID), women and development (WAD), and gender and development (GAD) approaches (see Rathgeber 1990; Tinker 1990; Moser 1993; Chua et al. 2003) scholars now speak of a "post-development" era (Escobar 1995, 2000; Sachs 1992; Rahnema and Bawtree 1997). This envisioned era of post-development is commonly characterized by the perceived inevitability of globalization, combined with the rise of local cultural and ethnic struggles attempting to survive in the new "McWorld" (see Bergeron 2001), a market-based world in which corporations like McDonald's prevail and set standards not only for business but also for how we perceive, for example, national and international governance, citizenship laws, and subjective identities (Phillip 1998). Post-development scholars address how the international development field, including global financial institutions (e.g., the World Bank, the International Monetary Fund, the World Trade Organization), governments (e.g., the United States, Canada, European nations), and philanthropic institutions and charity organizations (e.g., Oxfam, the Ford Foundation, the American Friends Service Committee, to name only a few), has been framed through a Western lens, creating a number of biases in thought and practice (Escobar 1995) and contributing to the reinforcement of global patterns of domination.[5] Some scholars envision life "after development," an era in which the world might redistribute resources differently, organizing itself according to an altogether different vision of what constitutes "progress," "the market," "standard of living," or "wealth" (see Sachs 1992). This vision involves a major shift in power relations between rich and poor countries and a rethinking of development theories that rely upon Western forms of knowledge about countries within and outside the "West."

Feminist post-development thought involves a critique of the liberal foundations of the WID field, the area of scholarship that "remains hegemonic at the level of feminist developmental practices" (Saunders 2002a, 1; see also Marchand and Parpart 1995; Saunders 2002b). It attempts to provide a new gendered vision of development, or alternative to development, including a proposed alternative to the current economic arrangements of globalization, a term that scholars challenge and contest (Harcourt 2000; *Signs* 2001; Bergeron 2001). Feminist post-development scholars address the cultural contradictions of feminist approaches to "integrating women into development," including the tension among culturally specific, gendered forms of societal organization and global forms of change and domination. At this stage, post-development "is not a distinct spatial region constituted through a self-conscious post-developmental mode of life"; rather, as Kriemild Saunders explains (2002a), "post-development is . . . currently limited to a form of criticism or deconstructive practice that is just beginning to emerge" (24).

At the heart of the academic, policy, and activist field of gender and development studies, whether the approach be liberal, Marxian, or postmodern, lies a commitment by many to address the needs, identities, and roles of women from poor communities in impoverished nations. Yet what continues to be lacking is a more complex understanding of how "we"—feminist scholars and teachers of global studies, along with our students—are trained to "see" (Mohanty 1991) and understand the lives and struggles of women in contexts of poverty in postcolonial societies.[6] This includes how we understand women's daily-life situations as well as how they are seen and represented in scholarly publications and classroom discussions. As a women's studies professor, I think about how students can best locate and understand the struggles of prominent Third World activists, such as Domitila Barrios de Chungara of Bolivia,[7] Rigoberta Menchú of Guatemala,[8] and the millions of unnamed women who struggle within their communities for survival and social change. One question I have is, How have their struggles contributed to feminist post-development thought?

The Gendered Paradoxes of Development

Paradoxically, Third World women's movements have emerged, become institutionalized (Alvarez 2000), and strengthened since 1980. This has occurred despite the fact that the global economic situation for poor women and men has deteriorated, leading to some of the highest inequalities we have seen in the past century. In some countries, the gap between rich and poor has increased, partly as a result of the governments' foreign debt burdens (George 1997). In this section I discuss the paradoxes of women's community organizing in the context of the WID field, global feminism, and globalization.

Undoubtedly, the professional women in development (WID) field has contributed to enormous global and local change for many sectors of women in various national and cultural contexts. Universal notions of "human rights" and "equality," for example, have been integrated into government legislation around the world, and civic organizations have participated actively in reformulating democratization agendas.

The 1980s phrase "sisterhood is global" (Morgan 1984) was in many ways a precursor to today's phrase "global feminism" (Alvarez 2000), which refers to an international movement that includes United Nations (UN) agencies as well as thousands of nongovernmental organizations (NGOs) around the world that have developed international networks, including their own conferences, which parallel the UN meetings. Since 1980, in cities as diverse as New Delhi, Lima, and Johannesburg, urban and rural sectors of poor women have organized at the community level to combat economic crisis, foreign debt (especially in Latin America, although increasingly in Africa and elsewhere), racism and ethnic genocide, and associated political corruption or instability. Through this process, many of these women have acquired political visibility—for example, through their participation in global conferences and regional networks and through their recognition by development professionals and feminists as crucial contributors to the national and international political economy.

Yet despite the political advances that have taken place in international institutions and national governments, many politicians and development practitioners continue to assume that poor families can survive on their own, in two ways: explicitly, through market-based policies that support the defunding of state welfare and, implicitly, through policy frameworks that assume that the "private sphere," including families, households, and women's work, are "outside" the economy and therefore do not need to be examined (Kabeer 1994; Elson 1995; Bakker 1994). Since the 1980s, development policies that emphasize the market (e.g., neoliberal policies),[9] including the integration of nations into the global economy, the loosening of trade and tariff barriers, the privatization of state-owned enterprises, and massive layoffs and the defunding of state welfare programs, have done so largely under the pretext that families, and especially women, will "absorb" the costs of economic restructuring (Benería and Feldman 1992; Bakker 1994). In addition, some scholars—particularly those outside women's studies—have viewed women's community-based struggles as apolitical and/or easily conforming to the interests of the state or international development organizations. This scenario depicts women as passive recipients, conservative, and/or reinforcers of the dominant social order, rather than as agents of change (see Lind 2003; Marchand and Parpart 1995).

Although most poor countries have never had strong welfare states, their recent cuts in social spending have had dramatic effects in poor and marginalized communities. Some neoliberal development policies explicitly target poor women to participate in their projects, for example, in food distribution programs or micro-entrepreneur collectives. In these cases, it is assumed that women want to participate and, perhaps more importantly, that they will participate on a volunteer basis or for substandard wages (i.e., as "secondary" breadwinners) (see Lind 2002). Although, clearly, feminist policy makers and scholars from First World countries are interested in the welfare of women from poor communities and countries, development policies that frame women in these ways, on the basis of conventional notions of gender and family, can hurt the beneficiaries of these policies more than they help. At the very least, these policies, and the projects that stem from them, could be more sensitive to the tensions at play in attempting to "empower" women through a universal notion of empowerment rather than one grounded in the local reality. After all, this type of understanding affects the success or failure of development policies and programs. In relation to this, it is important to acknowledge the role of international development agencies in funding and supporting women's antipoverty struggles. How women organize, including how they define their "survival" and form of politics, cannot be understood without addressing how international institutions such as the World Bank and the International Monetary Fund (IMF), along with Western governments (especially the United States), shape poor countries' development agendas. The way in which sectors of poor women are framed in development policies, and the very notion of poverty itself, strongly influences the outcomes of these policies. Today, while many urban poor women in Third World cities have developed innovative strategies to deal with economic and political restructuring, they are faced with a paradox. On one hand, some groups have gained significant political power and visibility in local and sometimes in international arenas. From the mid-1980s to the present, Lima's soup kitchen movement, in which over 40,000 women collectively prepare and serve food in 2,000 kitchens throughout the city's poor neighborhoods, reaching over 200,000 people on a daily basis (Barrig 1989; Delpino 1991; Lind and Farmelo 1996), is one example of a local "success story" that has made international headlines and has been emulated by development and philanthropic institutions in other countries. Yet despite this movement's perceived success, many participants did not anticipate working there permanently, and many complain about being exhausted, underpaid, and living in continual poverty. What is considered a "success" by some in the development field may be a bigger burden for the women involved. Another example involves the few women leaders who have gained international attention for their leadership in local struggles, including Domitila Barrios de Chungara, whose story has been published in Spanish (1977) and English (1978). Although she has been embraced by Western feminists and discussed in women's studies textbooks and classrooms (e.g., DeLamotte et al. 1997), Barrios de Chungara, like many other women activists, continues to live in deep economic poverty.

Indeed, despite these perceived grassroots successes, studies have shown that most organized poor women are living in deeper poverty and facing greater structural inequalities in their societies than prior to the 1980s, when the so-called foreign debt crisis first began (Kuczynski 1988).[10] Because of this, feminist post-development scholars have addressed the fact that some feminists and development practitioners have romanticized women's antipoverty struggles, including in studies of women's "anti-development" movements, such as the Chipko movement in India and the IMF riots in Latin America (see Walton and Seddon 1994). It is true that women have been among the first to protest against foreign banks (e.g., against Citibank in Quito, Ecuador [see Lind 1992]), McDonald's (e.g., in Brazil and Bolivia [see *Arizona Republic* 2001]), the World Bank and the IMF (Daines and Seddon 1994), and foreign oil companies, as in the case of the recent women's mobilization against Chevron Oil Company in Nigeria (see Environmental Rights Action 2002). Yet these protests are not typical of the majority of women's forms of participation in community development initiatives. As Sonia Alvarez states, "[W]e vest great hopes in the 'resistance' everywhere in evidence in women's daily lives, household survival strategies, and collective struggles. Yet we too often ignore the less glorious, more contradictory, more paradoxical dimensions and sometimes ephemeral qualities of those struggles" (1996, 139). Thus, an important issue concerns how researchers can best define and assess women's perceived "power," as there is not a causal relationship between women's increased political participation and their economic empowerment. Rather, what we see is a mix of empowerment and exploitation, survival and transformation, triumphs and losses.

Neither of these visions of women's roles in development—as passive and conservative or as committed to "anti-development" struggle—adequately grasps the complexity of the challenges women face for survival in postcolonial cities. Rather, in addressing development, women's organizations, including "self-help" movements for housing or infrastructure, soup kitchens, "mothers' movements" for human rights, movements against fundamentalism and communal violence, antiracist movements, and IMF protests, often must negotiate among men in their communities and Western development policy makers and practitioners who view them as part of a cohesive and/or homogenous urban neighborhood without gender conflict.

'Let Me Speak!': Community Women's Organizing in Bolivia

In Bolivia, a poor country by many standards, there is a radical history of peasant and indigenous women's organizing. Many women who participated originally in peasant, indigenous, labor, and leftist struggles have become self-defined feminists or women activists who contribute in important ways to national politics and decision making. Indigenous and peasant women began organizing primarily in the 1960s and 1970s, during a period of military dictatorship that was followed by processes of democratization. The state has also played a role in organizing women, primarily through inviting them to participate, often on a volunteer basis, in community development initiatives ranging from mothers' clubs (*clubes de madres*) and communal kitchens (*ollas comunes*) in the 1980s (Salinas Mulder 1994) to food-for-work programs in the 1990s (Ochsendorf 1998). The mothers' clubs, although they were organized initially by the state, became important spaces of political expression and resistance for some groups of women (Salinas Mulder 1994; Jiménez and Soruco 1989).

Between 1978 and 1982, Bolivian politics were marked by political change; a sequence of ten presidents and a military junta led the country during that period. During this time women of various social sectors became involved in the anti-authoritarian mobilizations (especially in 1978) and in reconstructing leftist political parties. Some also began to establish their own organizations.

The Bolivian state has undergone an intense process of restructuring since 1985. Beginning with decree 21060, initiated in 1985 by then-president Paz Estenssoro, Bolivia underwent a series of measures, including privatization of state-owned enterprises, economic liberalization, and later, decentralization. The privatization of Bolivia's tin-mining industry had drastic effects on workers; over 26,000 were laid off within a year. Thousands of women displaced by the layoffs became politicized during this period (McFarren 1992), including Domitila Barrios de Chungara, the daughter of a tin miner. In addition, some Bolivian women's organizations were among the first to directly protest international banks and lenders for their roles in the debt crisis. The film *Hell to Pay* (directed by Alexandra Anderson and Anne Cottringer, 1988), documents the efforts of indigenous groups of women in Cochabamba that resisted the Bolivian government's economic policies and the associated political corruption among wealthy industrialists. It was women such as these—women primarily of poor, working-class, peasant, and/or indigenous backgrounds—who first took to the streets to protest the rising cost of living resulting from the inflationary costs of structural adjustment measures (Benería and Feldman 1992). Their efforts have included protests against the closing of Bolivia's tin mines in the mid-1980s and the recent mobilizations of female coca producers against the U.S.–inspired, Bolivian government–backed campaign to eradicate coca in Bolivia's Chapare region (the "War on Drugs") (see Agreda et al. 1996).

One of the best-known Bolivian activists is Domitila Barrios de Chungara, whom I interviewed in April 1999 in her current hometown of Cochabamba, Bolivia. In many ways, Barrios de Chungara's political trajectory, from local activist to global feminist and back to local activist, reflects power relations embedded in the globalization process and in the Western production of knowledge about "women's roles in development" in Bolivia. Despite her active presence in antipoverty struggles and subsequently in global feminist networks, her own situation, made difficult by poverty and exploitation, has changed very little. Below I describe my interview with Barrios de Chungara to highlight the paradoxes of women's lives, and to focus especially on women's actual conditions of poverty, the role of WID scholarship in framing women's struggles, and the ways in which Third World female leaders are understood in the Western classroom.[11]

Barrios de Chungara's political career began when she became a leader of a tin-miners' housewives committee (*comité de amas de casa*), one of hundreds of housewives committees organized in the early 1970s to address the exploitative working and living conditions of families in Bolivia's mining communities. Barrios de Chungara is from one of Bolivia's largest mining communities, Siglo XX, a town built and managed entirely by the mining company. Siglo XX was particularly hard-hit by Bolivia's harsh economic measures in 1985, including the privatization of the mining industry. At its peak in 1971, the Siglo XX housewives committee had over one hundred members and was organized to address the immediate survival of mining families displaced by economic restructuring

Domitila appears tired, much older, and perhaps less idealistic than the person I remember from reading her published testimony, *Let Me Speak!*, when I was an undergraduate in women's studies and Latin

American studies in the 1980s. We are sitting in her office in a self-built, small house in a working-class neighborhood in southern Cochabamba. It is hot outside and children are playing in the yard. Her office is adorned with awards and honorary degrees she has received from European governments and at United Nations conferences and international meetings. Having been an invited guest of many countries in the 1970s and 1980s (as Rigoberta Menchú was after the publication of her autobiography), Barrios de Chungara has collected an array of diplomas and honors. Despite these impressive honors, the office is small and modest; an old wooden desk and a few rows of chairs make it look more like an aged schoolroom. One of Barrios de Chungara's current projects is education and literacy, and so her office is also a classroom. I am struck by her extremely modest standard of living, given her status as a leader among feminists around the world. In many ways, she has returned to her political roots; she now focuses primarily on change within the local arena, rather than on national or international politics. Although this may be due in part to her age (she was born in 1937), it also appears that she has been forgotten by the Western press and feminists. This is so, despite the fact that conditions for miners, and for the majority of Bolivians, have hardly improved, if at all, since her years of political glory in the 1970s. Domitila herself pointed this out: "Why in Bolivia, a country so rich, do people live so poorly?" It is ironic to think about the ease with which one person's life and struggle can be made invisible, or forgotten, by those who read and consume her story.[12] In many ways, her experience reveals the contradictions of the international development agenda, an agenda first proposed by industrialized countries (especially the United States) as a way to frame foreign policy, international aid, and cooperation, and humanitarian intervention in Third World countries (Escobar 1995).

During our interview, it is clear that Domitila has spoken these words perhaps hundreds of times before. I am no different than any other interviewer; someone whom she cannot trust intimately but with whom she instead uses her diplomatic tongue to tell about peasant and indigenous women's lives in Bolivia. Our only connection is that we share two friends in common—two people whom she clearly likes and trusts very much. I am happy that, probably because we have mutual friends, she has chosen to answer my questions.

Born to a tin miner's family, a tin miner's wife, and the mother of seven children, Domitila has witnessed dramatic political and economic changes in Siglo XX and throughout Bolivia. Much of the history she shared in her interview is told in *Let Me Speak!*. She spoke of the feudalistic living conditions of miners, who were reliant not only upon company wages but also company stores for their daily sustenance and survival. Conditions worsened in the 1980s with President Estenssoro's introduction of decree 21060. Privatizations resulting from this decree led to the massive migration of miners from mining communities such as Siglo XX to El Alto, Cochabamba, Santa Cruz, and Bolivia's Amazon region. In Barrios de Chungara's case, her family migrated to Cochabamba, a nearby, midsized city. Cochabamba continues to be a city in motion and has an increasing rate of homelessness due to economic and violence-related displacement. As Domitila commented, "We had to look for other places to survive."

Barrios de Chungara's fundamental message to me was that "classism is what . . . Bolivians most need to fight," perhaps more than gender or ethnic or racial oppression, although she acknowledges that they are related. Greatly influenced by Marxism, as most people in Bolivia's labor movement have been, she once ran for vice president on the Communist Party ballot. Although she lost, her campaign symbolized hope for peasant women and men who until then had not seen a woman from her background run for a national office. Her struggle has not come without costs; she has received many threats and has had to live underground at times, for fear of political persecution and to protect the immediate safety of her family. This is true even now. "Before, we were communists or terrorists; now we are drug dealers," she says to me, in reference to Bolivia's new, harsh drug laws, which criminalize small-scale (e.g., family-based) producers and sellers of coca in local markets and demonize (particularly, indigenous) individuals as "drug addicts" rather than viewing coca as part of long-standing historical, cultural practice in many Bolivian communities.[13] The political context and discourse have changed; the fear of persecution and global power imbalances has not.

In a sense, the struggle of Barrios de Chungara and other women in tin-mining communities in the 1970s was a prelude to women's struggles "in and against" development in the 1980s and 1990s. Women like Barrios de Chungara continue to strive in Bolivia, from various geographical locations, for a number of reasons, often related to development and survival. An irony of these women's efforts is that the women are fighting for access to resources, and thus access to development, as well as against it, in the sense that they are opposed to development policies that do not lead to equitable distributions of wealth and resources in Bolivian society. In Barrios de Chungara's case, she was embraced by Western WID feminists, yet the underlying causes of her community's and country's situation remain unexamined. This is a great paradox of women's struggles for survival—one that plagues the WID field and the development field in general and lies at the heart of feminist post-development perspectives on the hypocrisy of foreign aid.

Re-Imagining Gender and Development

Constructing an alternative to development is nearly impossible, despite the best intentions of post-development scholars. Yet envisioning a different kind of society is not, nor is critiquing the economic, political, and cultural arrangements within which we currently live. Deconstructing the philosophical and material foundations of the development field is one important starting point for re-imagining gender and development and envisioning a "feminist future" (Bhavnani, Foran, and Kurian 2003).

Below are suggestions for teachers, policy makers, and scholars of gender, development, and Third World women's movements. They are meant to contribute to an ongoing discussion about how we can best reconceptualize women's studies based on insight from post-development and postcolonial studies.

Imagining a Post-Development Era: In a world increasingly characterized by large institutions, corporations, and global communication, is it possible to envision an alternative social order? When Wal-Mart and McDonald's are examples of global prosperity in the corporate world, how can we envision a form of social justice that adequately addresses the inequalities stemming from the new global economic relationships, particularly as they affect sectors of women? These are just two questions that might inform the way scholars and teachers imagine a post-development era. Although some scholars have pointed out that the economy is too often viewed as unchangeable (see Bergeron 2001), an important item in a post-development agenda is to rethink "the economy" itself (Gibson-Graham 1996) and address the cultural effects of policies, including the very ways in which policies themselves are sites of struggle and resistance (Shore and Wright 1997; Alvarez 2000; Lind 2003).

Rethinking Poverty: GAD scholars have attempted to rethink poverty from a gender perspective, including from the perspective of the so-called global feminization of poverty (Heyzer 1995). In addition, some scholars have addressed how violence against women, sexuality (Harcourt 1993-94; Lind and Share 2003), and sexual rights (Hartmann 1995) are themselves "survival issues" for women.

Particularly in poor countries the assumption has been made about poor women that sexuality and sexual rights are secondary to their daily struggle to survive. For women demonized for perceivably being single, unmarried, lesbian, or otherwise not fitting into conventionally prescribed gender roles, this is far from the truth. Standard international measurements of poverty rarely take these less-quantifiable factors into consideration, thus creating an overly simplistic view of why women organize collectively and how they define their survival. Researchers could focus more attention on how, for example, domestic violence and institutionalized heterosexuality limit women's ability to earn an income, manage the household, maintain social ties, and survive economic hardship.

Turning the Lens Back on the West: More studies could be done to address development and modernization in Western industrialized countries. In the United States, for example, similar processes of state welfare defunding and privatization have been taking place, although more often than not scholars and policy makers do not locate these processes within a global context. In addition, the role of internal colonization and global migration patterns in shaping federal and state government development agendas and private sector strategies of employment and industrial restructuring are rarely addressed. Policy fields and liberal arts disciplines in the United States could benefit greatly from examining the scholarship on development and postcolonial studies with an eye toward rethinking women's lives and political struggles within the country. This would include an examination of the contradictions involved in economic development and antipoverty policies in a wealthy country that has significant power in the global political and economic arena.

Mapping Women's Lives: There is a great need to educate people about world geography, including historical and contemporary relations among countries and regions. Some high school students still do not know where to place the United States on a global map (Weiss et al. 2002), and many people are uninformed about U.S. foreign policy and were surprised by what they learned following the events of September 11, 2001. In Phoenix, Arizona, where I reside, many students (white, latino/a, and other) have visited Chicago, San Francisco, or New York but have never made the two-and-a-half-hour trip to Nogales, Mexico. As teachers and scholars, we must ask ourselves why, and how people's inattention to Mexico, a neighboring country, stems from our socialized understandings of being "American," "white," and/or members of a "developed" nation. Geographic maps and national borders greatly limit our way of seeing the world, and it is important to continue researching the anthropology of societies throughout the world, albeit with the insight of postcolonial studies, including Edward Said's work on "orientalism" (1978).

Internationalizing Women's Studies: To date, women's studies programs in the United States are Eurocentric to the extent that they are framed in Western terms and based largely on the experiences and theories of women of European descent. This is so, despite the fact that Third World feminists (e.g., "women of color" and feminists from poor countries) have contributed massively to the formation of women's studies scholarship from the start (Moraga and Anzaldúa 1981; Sandoval 2000). Beginning an introductory course from the perspective of, for example, Sojourner Truth as opposed to that of Elizabeth Cady Stanton radically transforms the context in which we all understand colonization, whiteness, the global economy, and categories of "race" as they relate to our gendered experiences.

These suggestions are meant to stimulate dialogue about what, I recognize, is a vast and diverse field of scholarship, policy, and activism. At the very least, they are meant to encourage debate about how all feminists can make connections among their personal struggles and the distinct perspectives and experiences of women in contexts other than their own, be they within their own cities or across national boundaries. At the root of these issues lies an overarching need to envision a world different from what exists today, a world without massive inequalities between rich and poor, both within and among countries around the world. Feminist post-development thought is one contribution to this ongoing debate, although it will require women and men acting locally, in the interest of broader communities or publics (Fraser 1997), to enact true global change.

NOTES

The research for this article was funded by a Fulbright Senior Scholar Grant (1999). Additional funding was provided by the Arizona State University Women's Studies Program. I thank Stephanie Brzuzy for her comments on earlier drafts of this article. Most importantly, I thank Domitila Barrios de Chungara and the many other Bolivian women who shared their experiences with me.

1. I recognize the controversies surrounding the usage of the terms *Third World, First World,* and so forth. Although in original modernization theory these terms were used in a pejorative sense (see Escobar 1995), I prefer their usage over the terms *underdeveloped, developing,* or *in development* for one important reason: the term *Third World* has been reclaimed by feminists and other activists and reappropriated as a way to invoke a positive sense of identity, both within poor regions, such as Africa, Latin America,

and parts of Asia, and in industrialized countries, such as the United States. Likewise, I use the terms *Western* and *nonwestern* with caution, understanding that they too reinforce rich countries and the West as the source of power. For lack of better terminology, I use these terms in this article.

2. By *Third World feminists* I am referring to feminists from and working in Third World countries. I recognize, however, that this term is also used to describe the activism and scholarship of feminists of color and/or feminists of Third World origin in the United States, and was first coined in the influential publication, *This Bridge Called My Back: Writings By Radical Women of Color* (Moraga and Anzaldúa 1981). Chela Sandoval (2000) develops a useful framework for understanding Third World feminism globally, in rich and poor countries.

3. Add to this the fact that many Third World feminists themselves are educated in the same, or similar, Westernized systems of knowledge production and professional formation, something they carry with them in their own political movements and places of employment.

4. I place the term "West" in quotations to highlight the fact that this term itself is socially constructed and was created in what we now call Western societies. Edward Said was perhaps the first person to conduct a study of how Asian countries were labeled, through Western colonization processes, as "the Orient" (1978) and the "Middle East" (1979).

5. This global pattern of domination includes, for example, the concentration of wealth in the hands of a few, and biases regarding (1) which groups of people or countries receive foreign aid and for what purpose; (2) whether wars and associated humanitarian interventions are needed or not in a given context; and (3) what the overall goal of development is, including who benefits from it and who loses out (George 1997).

6. In this regard I am referring to countries throughout the world that have been former colonies or territories, including Latin American and Caribbean, Asian, and African countries, as well as industrialized countries, such as Australia and the United States. With regard to the United States, I am referring primarily to native communities colonized by European settlers, including today's so-called reservations, in addition to states such as Hawaii. Also relevant to this discussion are current U.S. territories, including Guam and the U.S. Virgin Islands, as well as Puerto Rico. Highlighting the parallel historical processes among "internal colonies" and former colonies that are now independent nations is one way to bridge our own locations, as part of the national community of the United States, with those of marginalized groups of women in some of the world's poorest countries. This also demonstrates how, for example, the social construction of whiteness (Frankenburg 1993) and the history of colonialism are current aspects of our lives, regardless of where we live.

7. I discuss the example of Domitila Barrios de Chungara's life and activism in a later section of this article.

8. Rigoberta Menchú, an important social justice activist for Guatemalan indigenous groups, has struggled for years against ethnic genocide and associated forms of domination in Guatemala and throughout the region. In 1984 her autobiography was published in English, and in 1992 she won the Nobel Peace Prize.

9. Scholars define *neoliberal* in a variety of ways, too many to mention here. In general, neoliberal development policies include an emphasis on the market and a de-emphasis on the state's role in guiding the economy. For further information see Phillips 1998; Lind 2002.

10. Mexico was the first country to default on a loan payment to foreign lenders. When the Mexican government first announced the default in 1982, the lending community, including private banks, such as Citibank and Bank of America, as well as the World Bank and the IMF (the two institutions that drafted the framework for poor countries' debt allevia-tion plans that we now see throughout the world) panicked and imme-diately designed plans for governments to refinance their debts over a longer-term period. Today, most Latin American countries, along with Caribbean, African, and Asian countries, as well as Eastern European and former–Soviet Union countries, have adopted some version of World Bank- and IMF-inspired policies. The foreign debt crisis that swept Latin America in the 1980s led some analysts to call this period Latin America's "lost decade" (see Kucsynski 1988).

11. All quotations in this section by Domitila Barrios de Chungara are from an interview I conducted with her on April 15, 1999.

12. This point has been taken up in studies of women's testimonial writing. See, for example, Carey-Webb and Benz 1996.

13. The Bolivian government has followed several recommendations made by the United States government to eradicate coca production in the country, despite massive critiques by Bolivians and others of the state's complicity in the U.S. "War on Drugs" in the Andes. A new set of laws was introduced in the 1990S to address drug-related offences. Generally speaking, these laws have disproportionately affected small-scale coca pro-ducers who depend upon selling coca for their livelihoods and are not necessarily involved in cocaine production or trafficking; many of them have been imprisoned for two or more years and are still awaiting their initial hearings. See Agreda et al. 1996; Léons and Sanabria 1997.

REFERENCES

Agreda R., Evelin, Norma Rodríguez O., and Alex Contreras B. 1996. *Mujeres cocaleras marchando por una vida sin violencia.* Cochabamba, Bolivia: Comité Coordinador de las Cinco Federaciones del Trópico de Cochabamba.

Alvarez, Sonia. 1996. "Concluding Reflections: Redrawing the Parameters of Gender Struggle." In *Emergences: Women's Struggles for Livelihood in Latin*

America, edited by J. Friedmann, R. Abers, and L. Autler, 153–84. Los Angeles: Latin American Center, University of California.

———. 2000. "Translating the Global: Effects of Transnational Organizing on Local Feminist Discourses and Practices in Latin America." *Meridians* 1, no. 1: 29–67.

Arizona Republic. 2001. "Women Protest Against McDonald's," March 9.

Bakker, Isabella (ed.). 1994. *The Strategic Silence: Gender and Economic Policy.* London: Zed.

Barrig, Maruja. 1989. "The Difficult Equilibrium Between Bread and Roses: Women's Organizations and the Transition from Dictatorship to Democracy in Peru." In *The Women's Movement in Latin America: Feminism and the Transition to Democracy*, edited by Jane Jaquette, 114–48. Boston: Unwin Hyman.

———. 1996 "Women, Collective Kitchens and the Crisis of the State in Peru." In *Emergences: Women's Struggles for Livelihood in Latin America*, edited by John Friedmann, Rebecca Abers, and Lilian Autler, 59–77. Los Angeles: Latin American Center, University of California.

Barrios de Chungara, Domitila. 1977. *Si me permiten hablar,* edited by Moema Viezzer. Mexico City: Siglo XXI Editores.

Barrios de Chungara, Domitila, with Moema Viezzer. 1978. *Let Me speak!: Testimony of Domitila, a Woman of the Bolivian Mines.* New York: Monthly Review Press.

———. 1999. Interview with the author, April 15.

Benería, Lourdes. 1992. "The Mexican Debt Crisis: Restructuring the Economy and the Household." In *Unequal Burden: Economic Crisis, Persistent Poverty and Women's Work*, edited by L. Benería and S. Feldman, 83–104. Boulder: Westview.

Benería, Lourdes, and Shelley Feldman (eds.). 1992. *Unequal Burden: Economic Crisis, Persistent Poverty and Women's Work.* Boulder: Westview.

Bergeron, Suzanne. 2001. "Political Economy Discourses of Globalization and Gender." *Signs.* Special issue on gender and globlization. 26, no. 4: 983–1006.

Bhavnani, Kum-Kum, John Foran, and Priya Kurian (eds.). 2003. *Feminist Futures: Re-Imagining Women, Culture and Development.* London: Zed.

Boserup, Ester. 1970. *Woman's Role in Economic Development.* New York: St. Martin's.

Burgos-Debray, Elisabeth. 1994. *I, Rigoberta Menchú: An Indian Woman in Guatemala.* New York: Verso.

Carey-Webb, Allen, and Stephen Benz (eds.). 1996. *Teaching and Testimony: Rigoberta Menchú and the North American Classroom.* Albany, N.Y.: State University of New York Press.

Chua, Peter, Kum-Kum Bhavani, and John Foran. 2000. "Women, Culture, Development: A New Paradigm for Development Studies?" *Ethnic and Racial Studies* 23, no. 5: 820–41.

Coomaraswamy, Radhika. 2003. "Are Women's Rights Universal? Re-Engaging the Local," *Meridians: Feminism, Race, Transnationalism* 3, no. 1: 1-18.

Daines, Victoria, and David Seddon. 1994. "Fighting for Survival: Women's Responses to Austerity Progams." In *Free Markets and Food Riots: The Politics* of *Global Adjustment*, edited by John Walton and David Seddon, 57–96. Cambridge, Massachusetts: Blackwell.

Delamotte, Eugenia C., Natania Meeker, and Jean F. O'Barr. 1997. *Women Imagine Change: A Global Anthology of Women's Resistance*, New York: Routledge.

Delpino, Nena. 1991. "Las organizaciones femeninas por la alimentación: un menú sazonado." In *La otra cara de la luna: nuevos actores sociales en el Perú*, edited by Luís Pásara et al., 29–72. Buenos Aires: Centro de Estudios de Democracia y Sociedad (CEDYS).

Elson, Diane, ed. 1995. *Male Bias in the Development Process*. Manchester, England: Manchester University Press.

Enloe, Cynthia. 1989. *Bananas, Beaches and Bases: Making Feminist Sense of International Politics*. Berkeley: University of California Press.

———. 2000. *Maneuvers: The International Politics of Militarizing Women's Lives*. Berkeley: University of California Press.

Environmental Rights Action. 2002. "Chevron Ignores Demand of Women for Employment and Clean Environment." Nigeria Environmental Rights Action, http://www.waado.org/Environment/OilCompanies/Women/Women2002Rebellion/.

Escobar, Arturo. 1995. *Encountering Development*. Princeton: Princeton University Press.

———. 2000. "Beyond the Search for a Paradigm? Post-Development and Beyond." *Development* 43, no. 4: 11–14.

Frankenberg, Ruth. 1993. *White Women, Race Matters: The Social Construction of Whiteness*. Minneapolis: University of Minnesota Press.

George, Susan. 1997. "How the Poor Develop the Rich." In *The Post-Development Reader*, edited by Majid Rahnema and Victoria Bawtree, 207–13. London: Zed Books.

Gibson-Graham, J. K. 1996. *The End of Capitalism (As We Knew It): A Feminist Critique of Political Economy* Cambridge, Massachusetts: Blackwell.

Harcourt, Wendy. 1993–94. "Women, Sexuality and the Family." *Development* 36, no. 4: 25–27.

Harcourt, Wendy (ed.). 2000. *Development*. Special issue on post-development. 43, no. 4.

Hartmann, Betsy. 1995. *Reproductive Rights and Wrongs: The Global Politics of Population Control*, Boston: South End Press.

Heyzer, Noeleen (ed.). 1995. *A Commitment to the World's Women: Perspectives on Development for Beijing and Beyond*. New York: UNIFEM.

Jiménez, Maritza, and Teresa Soruco. 1989. "Movimientos de mujeres y participación política y social en Bolivia." In *Mujer y Participación Social y Política*. La Paz, Bolivia: Fundación San Gabriel and UNICEF.

Kabeer, N. 1994. *Reversed Realities: Gender Hierarchies in Development Thought*, London: Verso.

Kuczynski, Pedro Pablo. 1988. *Latin American Debt*. Baltimore, Md.: Johns Hopkins University Press.

Léons, Madeline Barbara, and Harry Sanabria (eds.). 1997. *Coca, Cocaine, and the Bolivian Reality*. Albany, N.Y.: State University of New York Press.

Lind, Amy. 1992. "Power, Gender and Development: Popular Women's Organizations and the Politics of Needs in Ecuador." In *The Making of Social Movements in Latin America*, edited by A. Escobar and S. Alvarez, 132–49. Boulder: Westview.

————. 2002. "Making Feminist Sense of Neoliberalism: The Institutionalization of Women's Struggles for Survival in Ecuador and Bolivia," *Journal of Development Societies* 18, nos. 2–3): 228–58.

————. Forthcoming. *The Paradoxes of Survival and Struggle: Women's Organizations and the Cultural Politics of Neoliberalism in Ecuador.* Penn State University Press.

Lind, Amy, and Martha Farmelo. 1996. "Gender and Urban Social Movements: Women's Community Responses to Restructuring and Urban Poverty." United Nations Research Institute for Social Development (UNRISD) Occasional Paper no. 76. Geneva, Switzerland: UNRISD.

Lind, Amy, and Jessica Share. 2003. "Queering Development: Institutionalized Heterosexuality in Development Theory, Practice and Politics in Latin America." In *Feminist Futures: Re-Imagining Women, Culture and Development*, edited by K. Bhavnani, J. Foran, and P. Kurian, 55–73. London: Zed.

Marchand, Marianne, and Jane Parpart (eds.) 1995. *Feminism/Postmodernism/ Development*, London: Routledge.

McFarren, Wendy. 1992. The Politics of Bolivia's Economic Crisis: Survival Strategies of Displaced Tin-Mining Households. In *Unequal Burden*, edited by L. Benería and S. Feldman, 131–58. Boulder: Westview.

Mohanty, Chandra Talpade. 1991. "Under Western Eyes: Feminist Scholarship and Colonial Discourses." In *Third World Women and the Politics of Feminism*, edited by Chandra Talpade Mohanty, Ann Russo, and Lourdes Torres, 1–50. Bloomington: Indiana University Press.

Moraga, Cherríe, and Gloria Anzaldúa (eds.). 1981. *This Bridge Called My Back: Writings by Radical Women of Color*. Watertown, Mass.: Persephone.

Morgan, Robin. 1984. *Sisterhood is Global.* New York: Anchor Press/Doubleday.

Moser, Caroline. 1993. *Gender Planning and Development.* New York: Routledge.

Ochsendorf, Ann. 1998. *Constructing Power Through Food-for-Work Projects in El Alto, Bolivia.* Undergraduate honors thesis, Wellesley College.

Phillips, Lynne (ed.). 1998. *The Third Wave of Modernization in Latin America: Cultural Perspectives on Neoliberalism.* Wilmington, Del.: Scholarly Resources Books.

Rahnema, Majid, and Victoria Bawtree (eds.). 1997. *The Post-Development Reader.* London: Zed.

Rathgeber, Eva. 1990. "WID, WAD, GAD: Trends in Research and Practice." *Journal of Developing Areas* 24 (July): 489–502.

Sachs, Wolfgang (ed.). 1992. *The Development Dictionary: A Guide to Knowledge As Power.* London: Zed.

Said, Edward. 1978. *Orientalism.* New York: Vintage.

————. 1979. *The Question of Palestine.* New York: Vintage.

Salinas Mulder, S., et al. 1994. *Una protesta sin propuesta: situación de la mujer en Bolivia: 1976–1994*, La Paz, Bolivia:

Sandoval, Chela. 1995. "U.S. Third World Feminism." In *Oxford Companion to*

Women's Writing in the United States, edited by Cathy Davidson, 880–82. New York: Oxford University Press.

———. 2000. *Methodology of the Oppressed.* Minneapolis: University of Minnesota Press.

Saunders, Kriemild. 2002a. "Introduction: Towards a Deconstructive Post-Development Criticism." In *Feminist Post-Development Thought: Rethinking Modernity, Post-Colonialism and Representation,* edited by Kriemild Saunders, 1–38. London: Zed.

Saunders, Kriemild (ed.). 2002b. *Feminist Post-Development Thought: Rethinking Modernity, Post-Colonialism and Representation.* London: Zed.

Shore, Cris, and Susan Wright (eds.). 1997. *Anthropology of Policy: Critical Perspectives on Governance and Power.* New York: Routledge.

Signs. 2001. Special issue on globalization and gender. 26 (summer).

Starn, Orin. 1999. *Nightwatch: The Politics of Protest in the Andes.* Durham, N.C.: Duke University Press.

Tinker, Irene. 1990. "The Making of a Field: Advocates, Practitioners, and Scholars." In *Persistent Inequalities: Women and World Development,* edited by Irene Tinker, 27–53. New York: Oxford University Press.

Walton, Joh, and David Seddon. 1994. *Free Markets and Food Riots: The Politics of Global Adjustment.* Cambridge, Massachusetts: Blackwell.

Weiss, Andrew R., A.D. Lutkus, B.S. Hildebrandt, and M.S. Johnson. 2002. *The Nation's Report Card: Geography 2001.* Washington, D.C.: U.S. Department of Education, National Assessment of Educational Progress (NAEP).

Williams, Brackette (ed.).1996. *Women Out of Place: The Gender of Agency and the Race of Nationality.* New York: Routledge.

Zabala, María Lourdes. 1995. *Nos/otras en democracia: mineras, cholas, y feministas (1976–1994).* La Paz, Bolivia: Instituto Latinoamericano de Investigaciones Sociales (ILDIS).

Amy Lind is an independent scholar based in Phoenix, Arizona. She has taught women's studies and Latin American studies at Arizona State University, Brown University, and the University of Massachusetts-Amherst. Her book, The Paradoxes of Survival and Struggle: Women's Organizations and the Cultural Politics of Neoliberalism in Ecuador, *is forthcoming from Penn State University Press.*

Reflections on Working in Post-Conflict Afghanistan

Local Versus International Perspectives on Gender Relations

Rebecca Winthrop

Afghanistan is currently recovering from two decades of war, including ten years of Soviet occupation and ensuing civil strife. The process will not be easy, and the post-Taliban government is facing problems of drought, insecurity, and decimated infrastructure and social services. I recently spent a month working with Afghan women and men on rebuilding Afghanistan's shattered education system. I was an education specialist for the International Rescue Committee (IRC), a humanitarian agency working in conflict and post-conflict countries. Our education work with the Afghan community includes working with girls' education programs for Afghan refugees in Pakistan and for Afghans inside Afghanistan in areas of high repatriation. While I have worked for the past eight years on education issues related to refugees, migrants, and war-affected populations in Latin America, Africa, and the Balkans, my experience in Afghanistan served to remind me anew of the importance of recognizing the lived realities of the people for whom development is intended. In the face of the newly arrived throngs of international actors working on the reconstruction of Afghanistan, it becomes all the more important to listen to the voices of Afghan men, women, and children because, to be successful, development must involve local perspectives.

Kabul in the beginning of 2003 was a city in flux. It was teeming with international experts and specialists working for the United Nations, nongovernmental organizations (NGOs), and the U.S. government, with a new batch arriving every day. The airport had been significantly spiffed up during the preceding months with the installation of new glass windows, although there still was no heat and no one had removed the heap of destroyed airplanes at the end of the runway. The Chinese restaurant in Kabul had just opened a bar, and there were rumors of Thai and Mexican restaurants opening soon, which would practically double the dining options catering to "internationals" flying into Kabul. A few women (non-Afghans, of course) were seen in public with form-fitting clothing and no headscarf. Many "internationals" recognized each other from working in past "hot spots." Indeed, there was a running joke among the internationals that, touching on the culture of professional development practitioners, everyone now working in Kabul had served either in Kosovo or East Timor.

For anyone who has worked in analogous crisis, post-conflict, or development settings, this scene is familiar. The logistics of development work, especially in post-conflict areas receiving international attention, usually entail a massive influx of international actors where previously only a few were present. This surge of international people, money, and action only exacerbates the already existing tension between international and local perspectives. While many organizations are committed to development strategies that attend to local knowledge and operate from the ground up—indeed, much writing has been done on this subject—there is inevitably an encounter between different frameworks. This encounter can occur on many levels and can be as basic as international organizations having staff-hiring procedures based on merit whereas local mechanisms are based on family networks. The cultural relativism debate is becoming increasingly sophisticated, and few would argue that, categorically, international organizations must always defer to local knowledge or vice versa. This is especially true when local practices prevent women from participating in development work. But in the hubbub of throngs of international actors descending into a post-conflict country, it is imperative to ensure that local voices have a sustained place at the table, or else development efforts, however well planned or thought out, will be stymied. This is certainly the case with Afghanistan.

The organization with which I am affiliated, the IRC, has been working with and for Afghans for over twenty years, since long before the Taliban was covered in the international press. Very few workers in our organization are from outside Afghanistan; the IRC relies on the input and skills of a large Afghan staff, providing training where needed. As an international aid and development worker, I try to be cognizant of the many assumptions I take into any given situation and act with the knowledge that there are many more assumptions I cannot conceive of until they confront me. Despite this level of awareness and reflexivity, I was reminded anew when I arrived in Kabul of the need to attend to Afghan lived realities. This realization came about because the contrast between local and international frameworks is so stark, and nowhere is this more the case than with gender relations.

There is great need in Afghanistan now for professional women; there is a dearth of female teachers, social workers, medical personnel, policy makers, business persons, office managers, and assistants.

Gender segregation is a strict norm, and the country needs female professionals to meet the needs of its girls and women. For example, in most places girls must have female teachers, or else, with the exception of those in the early primary grades, they cannot be taught at all. One of the assets that IRC has as an organization in the region is a wealth of highly trained female staff in our Pakistan education program, which works with Afghan refugees and has a focus on girls' education, female teacher training, and female professional development. As refugees are increasingly returning from Pakistan to their homes in Afghanistan, I helped IRC design a reintegration strategy, which seeks, among other things, to hire wherever possible our returnee staff from Pakistan to be senior managers in our Afghanistan education program.

While in theory this sounds like an excellent idea, numerous tensions arise when professional refugee women are brought into a majority male staff, many of whom have lived under the Taliban for several years and remain resistant to working alongside women who have higher or equal positions. By and large, the Afghan refugees living in Pakistan received through nongovernmental refugee education programs and private training schools a far superior education to that received by anyone living in Afghanistan under the Taliban, especially girls and women, but boys and men as well. Many of the female staff from Pakistan that we seek to transfer to Afghanistan have had educational opportunities that the staff in Afghanistan—male and female—have never had, especially regarding desirable professional skills such as typing, computer usage, English language, and professional writing. This tension between returning refugees and those who never left home or left only briefly can combine with the hierarchical Afghan gender norms to create an inhospitable and unwelcoming work environment for female returnees.

Several of our senior male staff, veterans of NGO education programming in their own right, had difficulties accepting the young, highly skilled, professional women returning from life in exile in Pakistan. These women in many ways had outstripped our male veteran education staff; they were Microsoft ready, could meet a deadline, and knew how to devise a strategic plan. In short, they were NGO-equipped in a world of equipped NGOs. The male "veterans" had given their best years to NGO work in a time when NGO operations in Afghanistan were clandestine, rough, tough, poorly supplied, and virtually without e-mail. In the bustling center of today's Kabul, the veterans are relics of their time, overtaken by the digitally trained younger generation of women and men. And, in general, they are not happy about it. For many years, they have lived on the top, given that women have had limited access to public life. The pace of social change has outstripped the ability of many veterans to become accustomed to the idea of women professionals. Some are insulted, affronted, and angry, especially if the women receive higher salaries or positions. Some find the challenge to be too much, and they may harass or lash out at the women. Others have younger minds and are more agile in adaptation; they learn to live with it and may even come to support the women with whom they now work.

When planning development projects, this potential friction between male and female staff is an important encounter to consider in order to successfully mainstream women back into professional life in Afghanistan. For the IRC, this particular situation is one in which the local framework is unacceptable; not only does it go against one of our core organizational principles—gender equity in hiring—but it is programmatically detrimental, as women are needed as staff to serve the needs of 50 percent of the population. We chose to opt for recognition of the local gender framework coupled with intense training in the required professional behavior while in the office.

While social change is visible on a daily basis in Kabul, change in the rural areas is not moving at such a rapid pace. Communities recognize the political changes in their country, but do not immediately translate this into changes in social norms. While girls and women can now go back to school, in many parts of the country gender relations remain much the same. On my trip, I was working with IRC's home-based schools, which were created to give Afghan girls and boys access to education under the Taliban. The Taliban had prohibited girls from attending school after the third grade, and so many courageous Afghan women and men opened up their homes to conduct clandestine classes for the girls in their communities. The IRC supported their efforts through provision of school materials and training. Today girls are allowed to go to school, but education is still inaccessible to many girls who live in rural areas because of a lack of government or home-based schools in close proximity, or because parents feel it is inappropriate for their girls to go to school or believe there is a better use of their girls' time (e.g., rug weaving or working in the home). In areas where the IRC works, we support local government schools, but we also continue to support home-based schools for those communities that do not have functioning government schools yet, out of a commitment to the right of all children to education. Our support takes the form of training government teachers and training community members to be teachers, providing materials, and working with parents and communities to build their interest in and capacity to support the schools.

On a visit to one home-based school we support in a rural village with no government school, I met two sisters who were attending the school on a regular basis. Neither of the girls had been in school the year before because their father did not think it was a worthwhile activity for them. The head of the school had spoken with the father repeatedly, and eventually he acquiesced in sending his youngest daughter to school. Over time, the father began to notice that his young daughter was learning useful skills in school and grew impressed with her reading and writing abilities. He was so happy with her new skills that he sent his older daughter to school the next year. Needless to say, the school head was most proud, and rightfully so.

This story brought home to me the importance of operating within the framework of the lived realities of the people with whom one is working. Gender issues have received much attention from international organizations and are not directed just at women and girls, but at men and boys, too. Certainly in the context of rural Afghanistan, it is crucial to involve men, as they are the key decision makers. Granted, many men do not support girls' education and, as they are the primary power holders in the country, it can be difficult to work with men on gender issues. But, as evidenced by the father who sent his two girls to school, it can be quite fruitful when we are able to involve men in meaningful ways in the promotion of gender equity.

Overall, my trip to Afghanistan left me with a lasting impression of the difficulties of working in a context of rapid political change and slower social change, a context where international expert voices have the potential to drown out local ones. The past twenty years have slowly stamped out many of the socially cosmopolitan elements in Afghanistan. A Ministry of Education official bemoans Afghanistan's destroyed education system and tells me how well respected it once was. A refugee woman puts on her burka as she shows me a picture of herself twenty years ago as a teenager in Kabul wearing a miniskirt and leather boots. She tells me that she was a chemistry teacher before she fled her country. The past twenty years have not done much to help rural communities, either. A villager describes the fear of Taliban officials and their rampant abuse of power that he and his family lived with. Another man describes the lack of resources available to his community as the government—past and present—was, and remains, unable to help significantly with the loss of crops and water from drought. Now, there are new political changes and the country has new plans. Plans to rebuild, rehabilitate, and renew. But this process will take time, and many social adjustments will have to be made. As international experts work to assist the government and civil society in this process, it is becoming even more important for them to attend to the people of Afghanistan and the expressed needs and desires of both women and men in rural and urban areas. It is important to remember that social change takes longer than political change. To be successful, development efforts must work *with* instead of *for* the people for whom they are intended.

Rebecca Winthrop currently works as an education specialist for the International Rescue Committee where she supports education programs in countries throughout Africa, East Asia, the Caucasus, and the Balkans. She leads IRC's "Healing Classrooms" initiative, and her present area of focus is on teacher education and transformative learning in conflict and post-conflict contexts. Publications include "Emergency education and psychosocial adjustment: Displaced Chechen youth in Ingushetia" (Forced Migration Review, *October 2002), "Opportunities in Crisis: A Case Study of Afghan refugee Teacher Education" (forthcoming in companion volume to "Transformative Learning in Action: Building Bridges across Contexts and Disciplines," an upcoming conference at Teachers College, Columbia University).*

Limited Choices

A Look at Women's Access to Health Care in Kiboga, Uganda

Lara Knudsen

Nabaloga had been in labor for two days with a traditional birth attendant (TBA) out in a village before the TBA referred her to Kiboga Hospital. But she didn't have the money for transport, so she remained in obstructed labor for two more days before finally making it to Kiboga somehow. Her uterus had ruptured and the baby was dead. When the doctor did the C-section he had to do a hysterectomy as well. She only had two children at home and, despite her state of illness, she seemed most preoccupied by what her husband would think of her, no longer able to bear children.

—Author's fieldnotes, October 24, 2001

Nabaloga's story was one of many I heard during my stay in Kiboga, Uganda. I had traveled to this rural area to live with a family in Butemba, a village about five miles from Kiboga town, and to do an internship in the maternity wing of a government hospital—all research for my undergraduate thesis at Marlboro College in the United States.[1] As time went on, as I heard more and more stories like Nabaloga's, common themes began to emerge: lack of financial independence, lack of power, and a sense of self-worth closely tied to fertility. While numerous barriers impede access to health care for every Ugandan, women face an additional set of obstacles as a direct result of their gender. Though the health status of the general population in this East African nation is low, women suffer the most from ill health. Yet they have the least access to health services.

Located just seventy-five miles northwest of Kampala, Uganda's capital city, Kiboga town serves as the political and medical center for the district's population of 171,000 people (Republic of Uganda 1991). Referred to by many as the "forgotten corner" of Uganda, Kiboga is surprisingly remote, given its proximity to the capital city. Throughout the district, only 1.3 percent of households have electricity[2] and 0.7 percent have access to safe drinking water[3] (Republic of Uganda 1991). There are no phone lines district-wide, and even cellular phones have no reception. Education levels are low (only 16.9 percent

253

of fifteen-year-olds have completed primary school) and life expectancy at birth is nearly five years less in Kiboga than in Kampala (44.7 versus 49.5 years). Not surprisingly, Kiboga's fertility rate of 7.4 children per woman exceeds the national average of 6.9 and far surpasses Kampala's average of 5.2 (Republic of Uganda 1991). During my stay in Butemba, I lived with a married couple that had nine children, ranging in age from four days to fifteen years.

Perhaps the most visible and devastating obstacle to accessing health care in Uganda is the general lack of transportation and communication infrastructure across the country, as shown in Nabaloga's story. Kiboga is primarily an agricultural area and its population is scattered throughout the countryside. Small villages are connected to each other and to the main town by bumpy dirt roads that are barely wide enough to accommodate a car. Automobiles are rare, though; the preferred mode of transportation for privileged inhabitants is the *bodaboda* (moped) and, for the majority of the population, bicycles or walking. In rural areas, the most common mode of transportation to a health clinic is a bicycle—clearly not the ideal for someone who is already in a physically compromised state, not to mention someone who needs emergency care. During Uganda's rainy seasons (September to November and April to June), these roads become difficult to traverse and are occasionally even impassable. The 1995 Safe Motherhood Needs Assessment, conducted by the Ministry of Health with support from the World Health Organization, revealed that, in most areas, the local "ambulance" was a bicycle pulling a trolley, or a stretcher that could be carried to the nearest health center (Republic of Uganda 2000, 22–23). With no way to contact the nearest health center when an emergency arises, the patient often arrives at the hospital only to find staff that are not ideally prepared for the event. Valuable minutes are lost while the doctor is summoned, the operating room prepared.

Communication lines are important not only in emergency situations but also in transmitting to the community crucial health-related messages and information about the value and use of available health services. Rural women are the most disadvantaged in this regard, as they often have no access to newspapers, radio, or television, and they are more likely than men to be illiterate. (Fifty-five percent of Ugandan women cannot read or write compared to thirty-five percent of men [Neema 1999, 100]). Further compounding the communication dilemma is the fact that health promotional materials are often written in English, which few people in rural areas can read or understand (Neema 1999, 100).

The disproportionate number of government health centers located in urban areas exacerbates the transportation and communication difficulties that many patients face. The Ministry of Planning and Economic Development estimates that less than half of Ugandans (49.0 percent) have access to static health units (Republic of Uganda 1991). Over 50 percent of hospitals are located in urban areas, where 11 percent of the population resides, and in 1992 urban areas housed 76 percent of all doctors, 80 percent of midwives, and 70 percent of nurses in Uganda (Republic of Uganda 2001, 7). When one considers the dearth of medical professionals to begin with—the doctor-to-population ratio in Uganda is 1:28,000—this unequal distribution is even more alarming (Republic of Uganda 2001, 7). Attracting health professionals to rural areas has proved to be a daunting task for the Ugandan government. The majority of physicians I came to know at Kiboga Hospital were stationed there involuntarily, fulfilling a mandatory term set by the government to work in a rural area. Specialist physicians on one-month rotations fill the sole position for an obstetrician-gynecologist at Kiboga Hospital. Health professionals' reluctance to live in rural areas is easy to understand when one compares health facilities available in Kampala and other urban areas to what is found in rural areas like Kiboga.

Often called "the pride of the district," Kiboga Hospital appears at first glance to be not much more than a dilapidated building; a road sign concealed by rust and dirt announces its presence. Yet this hospital is the most impressive health center in the area; it serves about 15,000 people per year, though its patients are disproportionately from subcounties closest to the hospital (Kiboga Hospital 1999). Even though Lyantonde subcounty (where I lived) is only six to seven miles from Kiboga town, residents of the area often spoke of the hospital as an impossibly distant last resort, inaccessible to most of the local population.

If a patient is able to overcome the numerous barriers to reaching a government health unit, she or he finds upon arrival a limited range of services offered. Ministry of Health statistics from 1998 show that only two-thirds of health units provide ante-natal care, less than half offer maternity services, and only 39 percent have the capacity for inpatient care (Mugaju 1999, 128). As the district's largest health center and the one responsible for tertiary care, Kiboga Hospital is expected to offer a broad range of services, such as X rays, laboratory tests, immunizations, and microscopy for tuberculosis diagnosis. Yet the reality is that many of these services are not always available. Grossly underfunded, like all public hospitals in Uganda, Kiboga

Hospital often runs out of such basic supplies as latex gloves and essential drugs. It is not uncommon for women who have had Cesarean sections on Thursday, or later in the week, to go without the antibiotics necessary to prevent sepsis; the hospital often runs out of such drugs by Wednesday, and most women do not have the financial resources necessary to buy the drugs from private pharmacies. More often than not, the hospital has no blood supplies, and patients who need emergency transfusions are referred to Hoima Hospital, fifty miles away. Kiboga Hospital is unable to provide transportation to patients referred to Hoima; those patients who have already faced difficulty scraping together sufficient funds to travel five miles from their village to Kiboga town may very well not make it to Hoima.

Several sociocultural factors place women at greater risk than men, both for becoming ill in the first place and for delaying (or never receiving) health care. Uganda's female morbidity rate is staggering; Stella Neema, at the Makerere Institute of Social Research, reports that over 70 percent of the country's women are sick at any one time (Neema 1999, 96). Though morbidity rates are notoriously difficult to estimate accurately, there is no doubt that a large portion of Ugandan women are suffering suboptimal health. Yet these women have little opportunity to improve their health status. Since cultural preferences dictate that men eat the best food, women already living in malnourished communities have the worst nutrition of all. This inequality persists despite the fact that pregnant and lactating women are most in need of balanced diets to prevent anemia—an especially dangerous condition for pregnant women. Repeated, frequent childbearing compounds the problem (Republic of Uganda 2000, 51). In the household where I lived, on the infrequent occasions when we ate meat, the father enjoyed first claim, followed by the children and the mother (even though the mother was breastfeeding her infant twins at the time).

Once women do fall ill, restoring their health can be a low priority in the family's budget. Often women seek health care solely in relation to their reproductive health, partly because their societal value is closely linked with their fertility, and partly because these are the services offered to them, frequently at the expense of other services. Since most women have little or no independent income, the decision of whether or not they will seek health services rests largely with a woman's husband. Women account for 70 to 80 percent of Uganda's agricultural workforce, yet only 7 percent of them own land and only 30 percent have access to or control over the proceeds of their work (Republic of Uganda 2001, 7). Nationally, only 15 percent of women are self-employed or employed in the formal sector, and nearly all of these women live in urban areas (Republic of Uganda 2001, 7). Women work an average of fifteen to eighteen hours each day, compared to the eight to ten hours that men work (Neema 1999, 102). They often cannot afford to leave their domestic duties for a day to seek health care. Even where public health care is free, transportation to the health unit and sometimes the need for additional drugs can cost women money they do not have, requiring the notification and consent of the husband. This lack of financial autonomy becomes especially crucial in relation to family planning services.

The consequences of this lack of access to services are partially evident in high mortality rates; the infant mortality rate in Uganda is 97 deaths per 1,000 live births, compared to a rate of 6.9 deaths per 1,000 live births in the United States (and mortality rates in the United States are among the highest of all developed countries). The maternal mortality rate is equally staggering, at 506 deaths per 100,000 live births, compared to 7.5 deaths per 100,000 live births in the United States (Republic of Uganda 1991; Centers for Disease Control 2002a, 2002b).[4] The Ministry of Health estimates that, nationally, only 38 percent of women are attended by a trained health person during childbirth; it is safe to assume that in Kiboga this number is even lower (Republic of Uganda 2000, 3). Indeed, among the many pregnant women I met in Butemba, not one intended to have a hospital birth. The majority of women deliver at home, with the assistance of female relatives, older children, and sometimes a traditional birth attendant.

A striking 22 percent of all maternal deaths are caused by unsafe, illegal abortions, according to the Ministry of Health (Republic of Uganda 2001, 9). Although this societal problem could partly be addressed on the policy level by legalizing abortion, the number of deaths from clandestine abortions could be significantly reduced if proper post-abortion care were available; today, only 30 percent of health units offer such care, which is needed for both induced abortion and spontaneous abortion (miscarriage) (Republic of Uganda 2000, 20).

Available family planning services often fall short of the ideal. Anthony Mbonye, commenting on Uganda's low contraceptive prevalence rate of 15 percent, estimates that over three-quarters of Ugandan women lack access to family planning services (quoted in nSalasatta 2001, 30). Those who do enjoy access to family planning may not receive adequate counseling, follow-up care, or access to the full range of contraceptives they deserve. Hardon et al. call for minimal requirements in the range of contraceptives offered that include methods for both men and women; temporary and permanent, hormonal and nonhormonal, user-controlled methods (i.e., the Pill and barrier methods); and methods that are safe for breastfeeding women. They also call for postcoital methods, such as emergency contraception and abortion (the latter, as mentioned, is illegal in Uganda and the former is practically nonexistent) (Hardon et al. 1997, 32). Yet these ideals, though often embraced in theory, are rarely delivered in practice. In Kiboga Hospital, I observed that, by far, the most common contraceptive given to women is Depo Provera, a hormonal injection that provides protection from pregnancy for three months. A survey of the clinic revealed that the only other options available are the Pill and condoms.

In the face of such dire health conditions, what have international donor agencies and the national government done to try and improve the situation? Development efforts in the field of women's reproductive health have largely been misdirected and ineffective. Undue emphasis has been placed on curbing fertility levels via aggressive family planning campaigns, rather than on addressing the forms of structural inequities that lead to women's disempowerment. When the United States Agency for International Development(USAID) first came to Uganda, they were not willing to put resources into any non–family-planning programs. Now, with domestic and international pressure, the agency is slowly widening its focus to related issues, like safe motherhood.[5] Still, despite gains made after the 1994 International Conference on Population and Development (ICPD), donors place disproportionate emphasis on promoting family planning as the chief strategy for fertility reduction. Donors are less willing to fund basic supplies and equipment other than contraceptives (gloves and drugs, for example) at health centers, even though such support would dramatically increase the quality of services offered and decrease mortality rates.[6]

If the newly adopted language of "improving women's reproductive health" from the ICPD is to be taken seriously, then the government and donors alike need to address barriers to health care access both within the health care system and external to it. Women have a right to comprehensive health services and not merely services aimed at reducing their fertility. In order to achieve this, health centers need to be adequately equipped with essential supplies like gloves and drugs (particularly antibiotics), in addition to basic amenities like running water and electricity. Health centers should be committed to providing a wide range of health services and not only those related to controlling women's fertility. Within family planning services, women have a right to truly "informed choice" from a full range of contraceptives, including user-controlled, nonhormonal methods. Beyond the health care system, improvements in infrastructural elements, like roads and communication lines, would directly benefit women's health. Likewise, increasing women's access to financial resources would ease their dependence on men when it comes to making health-related decisions.

Returning to Nabaloga, whose story opens this essay, we can see that the health care system's failure to help her is by no means a random occurrence. A multitude of factors combined to impede her access to health services and her ability to give birth to a healthy child. Without adequate means of transportation, financial resources, and the power to make decisions regarding her body, this woman had few opportunities to avoid the tragedy that unfolded. Faced with the loss of her child, she has to cope with the additional stress of questioning her status in society now that she cannot bear any more children. This woman, like so many others, is more likely to fall ill than the men in her family, and she is less likely to receive adequate medical care. Efforts to "empower" these women solely through increased access to contraceptives drastically fall short of what is needed. Women in Kiboga, like women in many developing countries, will have difficulty claiming power over their bodies and health care decisions until fundamental changes, both inside and outside the health care system, take place.

NOTES

1. The name of the village and subcounty in Kiboga District has been changed.
2. Compared to an average of 2.6 percent in the rest of Uganda, excluding Kampala, and 5.6 percent nationally.
3. Compared to an average of 23.6 percent in the rest of Uganda, excluding Kampala, and 25.7 percent nationally.
4. The risk of death from pregnancy in developing countries is 1 in 16, compared to 1 in 1,800 in developed countries (Republic of Uganda 1999, 2).
5. Assistant commissioner of Reproductive Health, personal communication, March 18, 2002.
6. Project manager, Reproductive Health Division, personal communication, April 2, 2002.

REFERENCES

Centers for Disease Control. (2002a). "Infant Mortality." http://www.cdc.gov/nchs/fastats/infmort.htm. Accessed November 14, 2002.

———.(2002b). "Maternal Mortality—United States, 1982-1996" http://www.cdc.gov/\epo/mmwr/preview/mmwrhtml/00054602.htm. Accessed November 14, 2002.

Hardon, Anita, Ann Mutua, Sandra Kabir, and Elly Engelkes. (1997). *Monitoring family planning and reproductive rights: A manual for empowerment.* London: Zed.

Kiboga Hospital. (1999). Kiboga hospital attendance by sub-county, 1999. Unpublished data.

Mugaju, Justus. (1999). District rural health systems: Case studies of Bushenyi, Kisoro, and Sembabule. In *Rural health providers in south-west Uganda*, edited by Mhammad Kisubi and Justus Mugaju, 119–40. Kampala, Uganda: Fountain Publishers.

Neema, Stella. (1999). Women and rural health: The gender perspective. In *Rural health providers in south-west Uganda*, edited by Mohammad Kisubi and Justus Mugaju, 96–118. Kampala, Uganda: Fountain Publishers.

nSalasatta, Dan. (2001). Bear children by choice, not chance. *The New Vision*. October 10. 30.

Republic of Uganda. (1991). Some salient population and development indicators for Uganda. Kampala, Uganda: Population Secretariat and Ministry of Planning and Economic Development.

———. (1999). Sexual and reproductive health minimum package for Uganda. Kampala, Uganda: Ministry of Health, Earnest Publishers.

———. (2000). Reproductive health division 5-year strategic framework 2000–2004. Kampala, Uganda: Ministry of Health.

———. (2001). National adolescent health policy. Entebbe, Uganda: Ministry of Health.

Lara Knudsen graduated from Marlboro College in Vermont in May 2003. She plans to pursue a career in medicine and public health. She is currently working on a book about women's reproductive rights in seven countries.

Women of the Tent

Nancy Nye Knipe

Izmit, Turkey

October, 1999

Tents are everywhere. Tents of canvas and plastic, tents blue, white, green, and transparent. I can see inside some of them, where a bed sits, a table, two chairs, a striped cloth draped for a bit of privacy. The tents are set up in parking lots, in city parks, and on sidewalks. Whole villages of tents have sprung up beside buildings that have collapsed, buildings ready to collapse, rubble, twisted rebar, a stairway leading to air, a mosque with a cracked wall.

Around this destruction, children chase each other, men sit drinking tea, women hurry in the streets carrying babies and plastic bags of groceries. Vendors sell vegetables and fruit from wooden carts, clothes and cooking pots from the backs of vans. In the air I smell freshly baked bread. From minarets, muezzin call the faithful to pray. The sound is mournful and hopeful at once.

On one hand, the city looks as if a bomb has fallen. On the other, people carry on with their lives, adapting to the destruction around them. This dichotomy is the result of a major earthquake with a magnitude of 7.4 that shook central Turkey on August 17, 1999, causing from 15,000 to 35,000 deaths, depending on whether the estimates are governmental or unofficial.

It is October now, and the dead are buried. The living have found alternatives to their ruined apartment buildings. I have come to Turkey and to Izmit, the epicenter of the earthquake, along with my husband, a psychologist who will train Turkish therapists in a method to treat trauma and post-traumatic stress. I will visit a women's center in Izmit sponsored by the Kadin Emegini Degerlendirme Vakfi (Foundation for the Support of Women's Work), with headquarters in Istanbul, dedicated to programs that provide training and educational and economic opportunities for women throughout Turkey.

Izmit is an industrial city two hours southeast of Istanbul on the Sea of Marmara. High-rise apartments, still intact, cluster on hills above the sea. Below them in the city center, windowless buildings lean at odd angles next to buildings that suffered no damage. Failure to comply with building codes, hasty and poor construction, greed

261

and disregard for soil conditions all contributed to a range of problems that resulted in varying degrees of damage.

A Turkish friend drives us to the edge of town, where one of the organized tent villages is situated on the grounds of a former navy munitions depot. Cephanelik Çadirkent, funded by an organization of Turkish textile manufacturers, provides shelter, food, a community center, and medical facilities to 1,600 people living in 178 green tents supplied by U.S. Marines. The tents are set up in a wooded area along a main road and in rows angling off from the road like streets in a small village. Boys play soccer, women hang laundry, a family gathers outside their tent on a variety of stools and chairs with their two-tiered Turkish teapot.

I walk around the camp one morning to get a sense of it and to take photographs if people are willing. I speak little Turkish, and few are able to speak English, but my camera held in the air seems to convey the question. I am aware of the inherent problem in photographing people, as opposed to tents and collapsed buildings. How to document and not objectify or exoticize? I always ask permission and, when possible, bring copies to the people I photograph. On this day, I take photographs of women washing clothes at an outdoor faucet, women visiting the canteen to pick up bread and hot meals prepared in huge stainless steel pans three feet in diameter, a woman peeling potatoes in front of her tent, young mothers holding babies lined up outside the infirmary. The tent village seems to be a woman's world. This impression is reinforced in the afternoon when I am introduced to the women's tent, a Quonset-shaped structure made out of white parachute cloth. The space is bright, its curved walls shadowed with patterns of leaves from trees outside. About fifteen women smile and stare at me from where they sit around a long white table covered with pieces of fabric and yarn.

"*Merhaba,*" I say in greeting.

They laugh, surprised and pleased as they answer, "*Hosgeldinez,*" a welcome given.

"*Hosbulduk,*" I reply, a welcome taken.

The women offer me a chair at the head of the table and set plates of sweets and glasses of tea amidst the fabric and strands of yarn used in making dolls and puppets, a small-income project that is part of the Foundation's program in the tent village. Each day the women gather at the tent while their children attend an adjacent day care center and kindergarten. Throughout the afternoon, children come and go, standing shyly beside their mothers or sitting on their laps.

A couple of women sit cross-legged on mats along the walls of the tent. All of them are dressed in layers of clothes, striped sweaters over

tunic tops, with long and loose flowered skirts. On their heads, they
wear flowered scarves, tied in a variety of ways. I am fascinated by their
scarves, a typical Western preoccupation with Islamic head covering.
The scarves, referred to as covers in Turkish culture, are beautiful—
brightly colored, edged in intricate chains of tiny crocheted flowers.
The women either tie them at the back of the neck with some hair visible at the forehead and nape, or below the chin, pulled forward over
the forehead to cover all wisps of hair. I'm curious about the different
styles and whether it matters if their hair shows.

Nuriye, the Foundation's coordinator at the women's tent, explains
that the scarves reflect Islamic religious practice. "A few years ago," she
says, "the scarves were worn loose, allowing some hair to show. Now,
very often they are tied tightly, with sometimes two scarves layered one
on top of the other, so that no hair shows."

In contrast, Nuriye wears her dark hair short and uncovered. She is
a retired chemical engineer, recruited for the Izmit tent village by a
friend in Istanbul who directs the Foundation. Before the earthquake,
Nuriye had never been involved in volunteer work. I hear many such
stories of professional people who began to participate in relief efforts
following the earthquake, and their involvement has an ongoing
impact on the social structure of the earthquake areas. Nuriye and I
talk in simple English; she does most of the work. Over several visits I
will make to the women's tent and, later, a center in the new prefab
housing, Nuriye and I become friends. Much of what I learn about the
women and their lives comes from my conversations with her.

In subsequent visits, the covers and how the women wear them, or
don't wear them, become a barometer of changes the women are
undergoing as a result of the earthquake. Covering of the head is a
complex and politicized issue in Turkey. As a secular, democratic
republic, Turkey is unusual in the Islamic Middle East. Women were
granted certain social, legal, and political rights in 1923 as part of
Kemal Ataturk's modernization process. Women's right to vote was
granted for local elections in 1930, and for national elections in 1934,
and is therefore comparable with U.S. women's suffrage, granted in
1920. However, rather than changing underlying traditional values
regarding women's relations with men and within the family, many of
the new legal rights affected only the highest socioeconomic elite.
Turkish feminists point out that these reforms came paradoxically
from the governing male class, rather than from within the women's
community, and were an effort to convince Europeans that Turkey
was a modern nation (Müftüler-Bac 1999, 303–4). As a result, adoption of western codes of conduct and modern dress actually inhibited

evolution of feminist consciousness and a women's movement because the rights granted to women gave the impression that there were no issues for women to coalesce around. In recent years, young university women have reclaimed "the veil" to distinguish themselves both from Western women and from traditional women who wear the cover to obscure their sexuality. These students say covering is a statement of their "personality rather than their sexuality." Turkish feminists contend that political debate over dress impedes broader discourse on issues common to all women (Kadıoglu 1994, 645).

As we talk in the women's tent, the women glance at me and smile. I am as different in their midst as they are to me, and we want to look at each other to compare. Their faces represent the diversity of the Turkish population, people from Central Asia, the Balkans and Caucasus, and Mediterranean countries, such as Italy and Spain. I am the only American they have seen, aside from those they have seen on television, and the first American they have met. To them, I am the exotic one.

We eat the sweets and drink our tea, and the women begin to ask questions. Nuriye translates. They want to know when I will be back, if I will be back, to visit them. It seems a test of seriousness and whether I am worth their interest, and not just their curiosity. When I tell them that I will be back, I ask a question in return, "Will you still be here?" One woman answers, "*Insallah,*" God willing.

Before the earthquake, the women lived in scattered apartments in Izmit or the surrounding area. Often a mother-in-law lived with them, and they were fairly isolated in these family groups. In the close quarters of the tent village, their lives are more communal. Before the earthquake, one of their main activities was shopping for and preparing food. Since food is now distributed from a central canteen, the women have time to gather at the women's tent or with other women in neighboring tents. During the day, men leave the tent city, either for jobs in Izmit, if their employment wasn't affected by the earthquake, or to sit in cafés with other men drinking tea and playing backgammon.

As a result of these changes, women have a much larger role in the social structure of the tent city than they did in their former communities. One social worker told me, "Women are in charge of life at the camp." They serve on camp councils and participate in collective activities organized by groups such as the Foundation or government social services. Provided with day care, in some instances for the first time, women are able to take part in programs outside of their tents, including earning income from handicrafts they make in the women's tent.

As a result, this activity is given value and the women are still near their children and homes in the tent village. Among the programs Nuriye has organized are classes in reading and writing. Some of the women never went to school, others attended through eighth grade, but very few finished high school. Most who have finished high school went to a vocational high school. I ask them to sign my notebook as I write out my name so they can see it. Naming gives each of us a place in this afternoon of glances, smiles, and laughter. For the ones who can't write, Nuriye enters their names into the list: Aynur, Sevim, Zeliha, Döne, Narin, Asumaa, Meryem, Nigar, Ayten, Gülizar, who knows a little English and writes, "U.S.A. Nensi [the Turkish pronunciation of Nancy], Tankyou very muc." I thank them, too, and say that I am glad to have met them, *"Tesekkür ederim; memnun oldum,"* which makes them laugh again.

Nuriye and I exchange e-mail addresses before I leave with a doll and a puppet, gifts from the women, who worry that the crafts are not good enough to give away since the women are still learning to make them. Nuriye and Gülizar give me the traditional Turkish good-bye kisses on each cheek, with a firm hug, and I tell them I will be back again in winter.

Cephanelik Çadirkent

January, 2000

It is a snowy day when I return to Izmit. Fewer people live at Cephanelik Çadirkent than in October—705 in single-family tents heated with catalytic stoves. Ninety-one tents are vacant, reflecting movement from the tent village to prefabricated houses outside of Izmit. A new communal dining hall has replaced the central canteen, which operated during the warmer months. New laundry facilities and indoor showers have been added. Snow covers the ground in patches and dusts the tops of the tents. The ground is muddy. The air is cold.

The women have baked cookies and baklava for me in their tents. We sit around the table, warmed by the stove and the presence of twenty women who are busy sewing. Bare light bulbs hang from the ceiling. Layers of plastic have been added to the parachute cloth, and the feeling inside is enclosed and intimate. The women have left their shoes at the entrance, just inside a heavy flap that allows an occasional brisk burst of cold air to sweep across the floor. The shoes are caked with gray mud. We drink tea and pass around the photographs I took in the fall and they point at themselves and each other and laugh. Some of the women are new, some of the women of the fall are gone. Other changes become obvious as I eat and drink. The scarves are worn loose now, and some heads are bare, the hair cut short, dark, and spiky. I ask Nuriye about the change, and she tells me, "One day a woman removed her cover, and I told her she had beautiful hair. She began to leave off her cover, and then other women began to do the same. I asked another woman about it, and she said, 'When I came here [to the tent village], my head was dark and covered. Now I am open.'" I imagine a domestic revolution among these traditional Islamic families and ask Nuriye if uncovering causes problems at home. "Mostly they do it only in the tent, where we are all women," she explains.

When we finish our tea, we share bits of language, speaking Turkish and English in turn. My pronunciation is funny to them. One woman wants to know how to say, "Where are you coming from?" I tell them, "I come from Colorado, U.S.A.," and "Today, I come from Istanbul," which makes them laugh again. How can I, an American, "come from" Istanbul, in the sense of belonging to a place where I was not born, did not grow up, have never lived? Yes, I'd like to tell them, I wonder this too. But when I first came to Turkey in 1992, I stood on Galata Tower in Istanbul and looked out over the red-tiled roofs toward the Bosphorus, domed mosques and pointed minarets in every direction, and I had an unerring sense that I had come home.

We go around the tent, and each woman says where she is from, what city, what village, what part of Turkey. One of the women says, "I come from Japan," and we all laugh at her joke.

We are warm and laughing together in the winter women's tent. We have little in common except this afternoon, and another afternoon in October. We speak different languages, wear different clothes, have different histories and opportunities. Just as there are earthquakes, there are also cultural fault lines that divide us. But something seems to happen in this tent, both to the Turkish women and to me. Our differences don't seem to have much significance. The women's enthusiasm and playfulness convey a level of trust and comfort for all of us. As I leave, they line up to kiss my cheeks, and then I walk out into the deep dusk through mud and snow, the air purple with winter's waning light.

Izmit Government Housing

February, 2001

This is my second visit to the prefabricated housing built by the government. I first came last summer, on a sweltering June day when the women chose a representative to the housing's central council. Two candidates stood for the election amidst a great deal of joking and teasing. Having a choice was radical, and they enjoyed it immensely. The women are now self-governing and no longer have a coordinator, such as Nuriye. They publish a newsletter; photographs of their activities and visitors line the walls.

The prefabricated housing area consists of rows of identical houses crowded within a fenced enclosure. The women's center and day care facility occupy a separate building at the top of a hill overlooking the prefab houses, Izmit, and the Sea of Marmara. Higher still are towering new apartment buildings under construction. Most of the women will live in the prefab houses for years, since they do not qualify for the new housing. In order to qualify, a family has to have owned an apartment lost in the earthquake, and of the twenty-five women present at the center this February, only one formerly owned an apartment. Most of the women were too poor before the earthquake to own a home, and since the earthquake there have been few opportunities to earn money.

Once again, the changes in the women are pronounced. Their conversation is animated as we eat the lunch they have prepared for me— börek, a pastry with many varieties; *tavuk gögsü,* a wonderful pudding; salads; baklava. They want me to know how the center and visitors like me have affected their perceptions of themselves. As they talk, I realize that this conversation would not have happened a year ago when I visited, either in content or delivery. The women speak fervently, urging my Turkish friend, who drives me to Izmit from Istanbul and who helps with translation, saying, "Tell her, explain it to her, what we say."

Döne says, "Nuriye has shown us that women can do anything. Before we thought that women can't or must not do certain things like drive cars or work. We've learned it is okay to work in the fields in the countryside, but not in factories in the city. We don't drive, but we *can!*"

Another woman adds, "Women can be productive in the city too; we can contribute to income with our work at the women's center; we can learn and improve our capabilities."

Sevgi talks about wanting to further her education. "When I finished vocational high school, I wanted to go on." Her eyes are fierce as she says this and waits for the translation. "My father said no, but when I insisted then on working, he allowed this. After I married, my husband wouldn't let me work."

One of the other women says, "What did you expect?" When Nuriye and I discuss this conversation later, she explains that if women work outside the home, men feel it reflects badly on them.

All the women want their children to have higher education, which they view as the only way to break the "shell" they are in. Through the women's center, they have met teachers, their coordinators Nuriye and Oya, and visitors like me; without the center they say it would be impossible for them to meet different kinds of people. More than half of the women are uncovered when my friend drops me off at the center. When he joins us later for lunch, they put on their scarves, observing the traditional code. But they talk freely with him. He says that they accept him as a brother and feel that it is safe to be honest with him since they know him from the tent village.

When it is time to leave, they ask, as they always do, "When will you be back?" They line up to give the traditional kisses—on both cheeks, or bad luck will come from the side not kissed. They gather outside the center with their children as I take one last photo. Then they wave after me, pouring water on the road to make my journey flow as the water flows, smoothly and surely.

I see them one more time in late summer, just before the terrorist attacks on the World Trade Center. On September 11, Nuriye calls from Izmit. "We are all with you," she says. The women want you to know our friendship goes beyond religion and country. We know terrorism. We think of you, and we send our sadness for your country."

REFERENCES

Kadıoglu, Ayse. "Women's Subordination in Turkey: Is Islam Really the Villain?" *Middle East Journal* 48 (1994): 645–60.

Müftüler-Bac, Meltem. "Turkish Women's Predicament." *Women's Studies International Forum* 22 (1999): 303–15.

Nancy Nye Knipe writes fiction and essays. She was a women's studies liaison and part-time reference librarian at Colorado College. Her work has appeared or is forthcoming in Inkwell, bananafish, Writer's Forum, Glimmer Train, *and an anthology,* Higher Elevations: Stories from the West. *She lives in Green Mountain Falls, Colorado, and most recently visited the women in Izmit, Turkey, in spring 2003.*

Seminar on Women and Development, Lahore, 2003

Fawzia Afzal-Khan

In the grand auditorium
next to Shirkat Gah
off Ferozepur Road near
Kalma Chowk in the
city of my birth, Lahore

I tore my hair out
whirling whirling
playing the mad dervish
poor dancing girl caught
between the sufi saints and
military dictators with
religion on their minds

Dictators, fundamentalists, call them
what you will, men all
snatched my character
dancing at her sufi's shrine
beat her
cursed her
raped her
threw her in prison for her sinfulness

dancing
prancing
free as a bird
on an empty stomach
how dare she be so in an Islamic state
where only mullahs and military mustachioes
may drink and dance at private parties
the public mustn't find out about

And so;
twenty years later
here I am
at a seminar on

Women and Development
in the city of my birth
playing
the same old whore I did then

Lahore hasn't changed much
I see
the same familiar faces in the
audience
older
grayer
still clamoring for Human Rights
for themselves and their daughters
for the poor
for the minorities

Pakistan is still in debt
to the IMF and the World Bank
another military dictator in thrall
to the mullahs
has replaced the one
from twenty years ago
both blessed
by the Greatest Secular Democracy
in the world

So you see
we still need these seminars
on Women and Development
on my trips back home
to the developing world
I can count
on playing
the madwoman role of my youth

what a comforting thought
for an aging actress

Fawzia Afzal-Khan is professor of English at Montclair State University. She is author of books, essays, poems, original music, and poetry. Her current book projects include "Shattering the Stereotypes: Muslim Women Speak Out (Interlink, forthcoming 2004) and "Women and Alternative Theater in Contemporary Pakistan" (Seagull Press, India, and Oxford University Press, Pakistan, forthcoming 2004). She is winner of several research grants, among them the Dubois Fellowship at Harvard University, Fulbright Fellowship, Rotary International Fellowship, and the American Institute of Pakistan Studies Fellowship.

Four Hundred Tons or Twenty-Five Thousand Dollars a Day

Paola Corso

My sister is the one who told me
about the woods behind our childhood home,

the peach trees, lilac bushes and wild rhubarb
the old barn foundation where we played hopscotch,

the willow tree bullrope we used to swing on just so
I could feel my menstrual pad rub against the knot,

the treehouse to smoke cigarettes and play strip poker,
the place where I wasn't anybody's daughter or virgin.

I wasn't surprised by what she said
having grown up in an industrial river town

where more members of my family worked themselves black
in the steel mill or glass plant or salt works than didn't

so the smokestack was our church steeple,
the haze rising in the sky our ascending angel.

She told me since they bulldozed the woods I'd be able to see
clear to the river if I could look out our old kitchen window,

a naked river now once clothed in emerald green.
I shiver for it and I shiver for myself, for all the times

I was exposed in those woods, for the first time I was
wed in nakedness. With each chill I wish I could keep

thinking it was pure and so was I as long as my secret
remained hidden in the thicket's immaculateness.

But how can I come home and walk behind the house
when my secret is bare and dirty, born from a bigger one.

How can I tell the new owners it was different
when they think of it as a toxic waste dump the company

stalled to clean up until ordered to pay fines
and what's it matter to them that I smell rotting fruit

when they can look out the window to tender saplings,
to a wide river that sees beyond.

Paola Corso *is a 2003 New York Foundation for the Arts poetry fellow. Her forthcoming book of poems,* Death by Renaissance, *is set in her native Pittsburgh and draws from her working-class, Italian American background. She currently teaches writing at Fordham University and the City University of New York.*

Peace Time

Kylie Thomas

Dedicated to those people with HIV/AIDS who are dying because they are denied access to treatment by the South African government. Their suffering and deaths go on regardless of whether or not war is being waged.

600 people dead every day.
600 strangers.
600 dead strangers.
The dead bodies of 600 strangers.
I can't see them.
Can you see them?

600 people dead every day.
Nobody knows their names.

600 people dead every day.
Nobody imagines their faces.

600 people dead every day.
They can't be forgotten since they never were remembered.

600 people dead every day
1,200 eyes that are shut
6,000 fingers that won't move again

600 people dead every day
600 people dead

If you hear nothing else that I say
Hear this:

600 people dead every day

There is really nothing else to say.
600 people dead every day
600 people dead

let me add it all up for you now
600 people dead every day

4,200 dead every week
16,800 dead every month
200,000 people dead every year

this is called peace-time

600 people dead every day

Kylie Thomas *was born in Zimbabwe in 1976 and grew up in South Africa,
where she has spent the last two years working with people living with
HIV/AIDS. She is a doctoral student at the University of Cape Town and is
currently writing her dissertation, "Writing HIV/AIDS: Towards A Living
History in Post-Apartheid South Africa."*

Teaching Gender, Development, and Cultural Change from an Interdisciplinary Perspective

Problems and Prospects

Barbara Burnell

The College of Wooster adopted a new curriculum, A Wooster Education, that went into effect in the fall of 2001. An important feature of the new curriculum is to make interdisciplinarity a central focus through support of the Program in Interdisciplinary Study (PIDS). Faculty members were asked to propose courses that would be team-taught (with full course credit for each faculty member) and to design courses that had no prerequisites. The lack of prerequisites was intended to attract as many students as possible to the course, with the hope that a large fraction of the student body would come to appreciate and critically evaluate the role that interdisciplinary study plays in a liberal arts education.

In this article, I first describe the process by which my co-teacher Pamela Frese and I designed the course, and then I discuss the course itself. I will also suggest some of the ways in which we might change the course when it is offered again.

Course Design

All faculty interested in teaching in the PIDS program were asked to submit a course proposal to the administration, including a course description, a list of possible resources that would be used, and an explanation of how the course would meet the objectives of the program. Once our proposal for the course was approved, we began to do research on the structure and content of the course, first independently and then together. One of the first things we did when we began working together was to exchange articles from our own disciplinary perspectives, to see where we each thought we were "coming from" in our ideas for the course. Each of our courses—Barbara Burnell's course on the Economics of Gender and Pamela Frese's course on Gender in World Cultures—has provided disciplinary perspectives on feminist issues, but we were interested in expanding beyond the boundaries of our disciplines. We then each wrote preliminary course descriptions and compared them; although the final description was somewhat different from our starting versions, we discovered that we had fairly similar ideas about the objectives of the course and its structure and content. As our syllabus explains, the course

> explores the relationship between gender, the development process, and cultural change from anthropological and economic perspectives. The approaches used by anthropologists and economists to understand the process of development and change will be explored and critiqued from a feminist perspective, with the goal of providing a more complete understanding of the link between gender and culture in the developing world.

Our ideas for the course differed most radically on issues of methodology. These differences arose not primarily because of "who we were" as individuals, but because of our disciplinary training and also because of the different impacts feminist critique has had on anthropology and economics. As an economist exploring anthropological literature, Professor Burnell discovered that anthropologists have been studying issues of gender, development, and cultural change for a long time. While such analysis has certainly not always been feminist, it has always proceeded "from the bottom up." Anthropologists have explored the relationships between cultural context and the resulting cultural change resulting from development in many societies around the world, initially as a way to document and preserve "disappearing" traditions different from Western social and cultural traditions. One of the key dimensions to anthropology is the manner in which scholars embrace a holistic view of society, tracing the important connections between social institutions, such as politics, kinship, economics, and religion, and cultural beliefs and practices. Most anthropologists attempt to explain the world from an "insider's" point of view, rather than imposing the researcher's own way of viewing the world on the data. Moreover, feminist criticism in anthropology has a longer history than in economics, and feminist theory has had a relatively greater impact on the discipline.

In contrast, Professor Frese discovered through her reading of the economics literature that, while economists also have a long tradition of studying development issues, their approach is almost always a "top-down" one. This approach relies on formal, abstract mathematical models of the economy as a whole, and the factors of interest are income, wealth, and material well-being. The terms *development* and *growth* are often used interchangeably in the economics literature.

Because of this approach, traditional economic development analysis has only recently paid attention to gender, and it has had virtually no focus on the relationship between development and cultural change. Moreover, because of the "top-down" methodological approach, gender is often not incorporated in a meaningful way.[1] Because of this, feminism has had a more limited impact on economic development analysis, and the use of formal, abstract models makes it difficult to reconcile this analysis with the anthropological approaches.

In addition, we found that we had different definitions and understandings of the same terms, and we came to perceive these differences as disciplinarily specific, but certainly potentially confusing for students. Most significantly, we took the meanings attached to the concepts of development and gender for granted until well into the planning process, when we realized that we needed to deal with our own disciplinary assumptions embedded in these key dimensions to our course. Professor Frese tended to understand development as primarily a "bad thing" that brought about unwelcome change to a society, frequently destroying tradition for a group of people and providing totally different and unsatisfying models in its place. Many anthropologists who work in applied fields serve as mediators for directed cultural change in situations where change is inevitable, but in most cases these professionals actively serve to provide the disadvantaged indigenous peoples with a voice in their future. In addition, gender studies in anthropology require us to look beyond the Western construction of only two genders in the world. There did not appear to be literature that allowed for this perspective on development and gender.

Professor Burnell was well aware of the feminist critiques of mainstream neoclassical economic models.[2] She also knew, however, that neoclassical development models are predicated on the assumption that growth is a "good thing," and that in most cases, economists do not make a distinction between economic growth and development. Since most analyses of economic growth/development are based on the macro, or aggregate level, the impact of growth on individuals or groups is typically ignored. Gender, if it is considered at all in traditional analysis, is considered as a variable, or as a means to an end— that is, "we will consider gender if it helps to facilitate the growth process." Clearly, this perspective on gender is extremely difficult to reconcile with the multidimensional anthropological conception. These stark contrasts made us strongly aware of the scope and complexity of the job of course design.

As we continued our reading and research, we were amazed at the sheer volume of material on gender and development. Both of us have done reading, research, and advising of student research in this area, but we were unaware of how much new research there is in this area. It was clear from the beginning that this was not going to be a course in which we could simply assign a textbook or two. While textbooks on gender and development provided excellent discussions of the impact of development on women in many different cultures, they were primarily rooted in feminist perspectives in political science, policy analysis, and work done under the auspices of nonprofit organizations and the United Nations. It also became quickly apparent that readers on gender, development, and cultural change would not adequately address the issues of interdisciplinarity between anthropology and economics that were central to our course.

As we determined criteria for the resources we would use in the course, we decided that, with rare exceptions, we wanted to work with materials that had been published since the mid-1990s and we wanted to include a balance of anthropological and economic sources. We also hoped to find resources that would integrate the two disciplinary perspectives. In addition, the material had to be accessible to an undergraduate audience whose backgrounds in anthropology, economics, and/or women's studies were unknown to us at the time.

We also hoped to develop assignments for the course and a pedagogical approach that would draw students into productive thinking about and discussion of the importance of the subject, as well as what could be gained by considering alternative disciplinary frameworks and attempting to integrate them. We wanted to provide a way for students to understand our own disciplinary ways of thinking before moving into the more challenging interdisciplinary perspective we hoped to develop. Initially we identified the crucial areas that we believed should be represented in our course from our survey of the existing literature. These topical areas included agricultural development, tourism and cultural change, globalization and sexual trafficking, multinational corporations and gendered development, and the process of empowering women through grassroots organizations. We clearly had our work cut out for us.

The Course

As our syllabus shows, we assigned two books that the students were required to purchase—an ethnography on the women of Belize and a more theoretical book on economic perspectives on gender and development and critiques of these perspectives. These two books were complemented with many other articles from journals, edited volumes, and government agency publications. All of these readings were placed on electronic reserve so that students would have relatively easy access to them via the Internet. We also made extensive use of film and Internet sources in class.

The variety of our assignments was intended to reflect, first, the fact that we were likely to have students with varied backgrounds and different learning styles and, second, our desire to get the students involved in the course as much as possible. We provided a class listserv on which students were responsible for posting their comments on the reading and class discussion at least once a week throughout the semester. Through an in-class examination we attempted to gauge students' knowledge of basic terms and concepts in the fields of anthropology and economics. Through a take-home essay exam we sought to generate more interdisciplinary thinking and to analyze ways in which media such as film helped to facilitate it. Around Halloween, we asked students to come to class wearing a costume. We discussed the Anglo-American categories that were represented in these costumes and asked students to reflect critically on the countries in which these costumes were made. While we did not know precisely which countries would emerge as costume producers in this class exercise, it became apparent that the three countries that were most frequently represented (China, Mexico, and the Philippines) were ones we had been discussing in terms of development and cultural change. Students were offered the opportunity to write extra credit papers on this exercise. About half of the students chose to complete this assignment, and many expressed surprise—and some dismay—that the impact of U.S. culture, economics, and beliefs was so pronounced in these nations.

Students also wrote research papers on a particular culture and/or development issue; these were presented orally in class and critiqued by other class members. Each student then provided us with a question that had resulted from these in-class critiques and we selected several of the best to appear on the final exam. The in-class final exam was cumulative; in one question we asked students to reflect on what they had learned since they wrote the first-day essay (which had posed three questions about their expectations for the course) and the roles of their countries and themselves in the development process. Several of the responses to the question are quoted below:

> *The Question:* Reread what you wrote for us on the first day of class. Have your perspectives on these questions changed after taking this course so that you might provide different answers to these questions today? Explain.

Student One: I no longer think that if women in developing countries just "tried" harder, they could escape their circumstances. . . . The most important concept I learned was feminist standpoint theory. It has caused me to think about my world in a different way. . . . This is the class I spoke most about this semester because I found it simultaneously frustrating, overwhelming, and intellectually stimulating. My views have changed and I now have a working knowledge of anthropological jargon. My initial understanding at the beginning of the course was not as great as other students, but I feel I have made great growth. I'm still confused and puzzled by some areas, but feminism is no longer the dirty word it once was for me. My definition of feminism now may not be straight out of *Cosmo* and is neither anthro- or econ-based, but it is evolving and growing as my understanding increases.

Student Two: This class has allowed me to better understand some complex issues as well as helped me determine what my role in society is given my social and academic background. . . . Throughout the course it has been remarkable to me how patterns of patriarchy tend to replicate themselves in different areas of the world. It does not seem to be based on cultural differences, but on the simple, basic fact that powerless individuals can be subordinated through economic power. I had a much more positive outlook on development when I first started and therefore viewed the course as one that redefined gender roles over time. It is interesting to note that though there is some redefinition of these roles in some parts of the world, it is the stagnation and perpetuation of traditional roles that tend[s] to be the problem. "Redefining" a role is a complex one because it entails going against societal norms.

In terms of the role that [I] personally play in this world when it comes to gender and development, I have found that having knowledge of both anthropology and economics has served to better understand my role. I find that the two disciplines go together so well and have allowed me, as an economics major, to think "out of the box." This is something that is important to do and needs to be done more often in economics. Breaking out of the "chalk and talk" mode through interdisciplinary classes is a good way to go about doing this! (and I'm not just saying that—I really mean it!) Thanks!

Student Three: When I first enrolled in this course, I did not have a firm grasp of the concept of development and the ways in which that term is used in anthropology and economics. I also lacked a substantial knowledge base of economics, which might have given me a better understanding of the ways in which the Western dominance in terms of the structure of the economic framework contributes to the exploitation of societies that are supposedly being developed "for their own good." On the first day of class, I understood that as a member of the most overpowering culture and society in the world, I play a fundamental role in either the reproduction of the American mindset and values elsewhere, or in the culturally relativistic exhibition of respect for the individual cultures. Looking back, I now realize that I had little knowledge of the impact of my society on the rest of the world. Multinational corporations, the majority of which are American, ruthlessly exploit less-developed countries, viewing people as objects rather than subjects, in order to help the economy be productive in the neoclassical sense and to improve and impose the Western values of lifestyle domestically and abroad. Before I took this class I had a firm grasp of how gender often serves as a variable, as a part of culture not to be taken into account . . . . I see now that gender is not only a factor that cannot be ignored, but is also one that should be examined within . . . cultur[al] contexts in an attempt to fully understand societal roles.

Nineteen students were enrolled in the class—seventeen women and two men. Most of the students were upper-level students, and they ranged widely with respect to major, from economics, anthropology, and women's studies to a host of other fields. Needless to say, their backgrounds in these three areas were extremely diverse; there were, in fact, some students who had not taken courses in any of these three areas. This diversity made it somewhat difficult to teach the course so that all students could assimilate and integrate different disciplinary perspectives.

We did try to structure the class in pedagogically diverse ways. Each of us did some lecturing, particularly in the first part of the course, when we were attempting to introduce students to discipline-specific concepts and terminology. In lectures, we tried to incorporate as many of the student listserv comments as possible. We had some fairly open-ended discussions of the readings, as well as more structured discussions in which we asked students to think for the next class about specific questions raised in readings or issues presented in the films. And, in the interest of allowing students to present the knowledge they had gained in the course, the last part of the semester was devoted to the student presentations.

The Experience

Our experiences in the course and the student performance and reactions to it were as about as diverse as the composition of the class, the material presented, and the nature of the assignments. Some students enjoyed the course and believed that they learned a great deal from it while others felt overwhelmed at the volume and variety of material covered. Indeed, it was our sense that a few students never engaged in the material at all. There was also diversity of opinion regarding how much class time was devoted to different activities, such as lecture and student presentations.

Similarly, the two of us had somewhat different notions of what went well in the course and what modifications would be useful in subsequent teaching of the course. Perhaps as a result of our previous disciplinary training and teaching experience, Professor Frese tended to favor the free-flowing, open-ended discussions, while Professor Burnell felt comfortable in a more structured class environment in which discussion was more closely tied to interpretations of the texts.

There were also several areas of agreement. The use of a class listserv, which Professor Burnell had assigned in previous courses but Professor Frese had not, generally went well, and perhaps the use of this could be expanded and more fully integrated into class discussions in the future. Assigning readings in government documents from the World Bank and on Web sites on particular countries were successful ways to relate our theoretical constructs to real-world experiences. Many of our students chose to include Web sites among the sources for their final papers. Our use of the electronic reserves for student readings was fairly successful and allowed us to assign wide-ranging sources without asking students to buy several books. The use of film to illustrate various gendered aspects of the processes of development and cultural change was perhaps the most successful aspect of the course. It seems that the films spoke to all students—regardless of their disciplinary training or background—about the importance and complexity of the issues we were considering in the course. We did not necessarily like all of the films we used, but they all generated useful discussions about the important issues. In the future, the role of film will be expanded and reading and discussion will be more closely tied to it.

Prospects for Change

This course provided us with a wonderful opportunity to enhance our thinking about and teaching of issues related to gender, development, and culture. There are times when colleagues think you're getting off easily in team-teaching; after all, you're only teaching half a course. Of course, the reality is much different. We both spent the majority of a summer reading, researching, and collaborating for this course. We found team-teaching to be far more challenging and demanding than teaching a course alone on, say, gender and world culture or gender and economic development might be. It is true, though, that neither of us could teach these discipline-centered courses now without incorporating some of the interdisciplinary insights that we have gained from this recent course, and we hope that students who take further courses in these areas will likewise find their interdisciplinary experience informing their learning.

Overall, the course successfully provided us with an important learning experience that will affect our teaching and research. For example, in her research with retired military wives Professor Frese had neglected to address the significant role that the American military plays in the development of prostitution in countries in which the military is stationed. Her research has benefited immensely from the discussions and readings in this class.

For Professor Burnell, it is probably her advising of student research on gender and development that will be most profoundly affected by this course. Research in economics usually adheres to a fairly standard and narrow procedure, and it usually has to be mathematical and quantitative to be considered "good" research. Although Professor Burnell has never subscribed to this view, this course has made her more aware of the importance of multiple methods, descriptive analysis, and case studies in understanding the complex intersections between gender, cultural change, and development.

As noted previously, the course was favorably received by many students. Thus, for both of us, probably the biggest puzzle is why several students in the course didn't seem to "get it." These students simply didn't seem to be able to grasp the overall goals of the course and how the integration of various objectives might help us to achieve them. Certainly, some of this may be attributed to different backgrounds and learning styles, but we attempted to accommodate these with varied assignments, review sheets, classroom activities, and the opportunity to revise work. Pedagogically, all of these approaches seemed to anticipate any problems that different backgrounds would cause, and we attempted to provide the basic concepts in detail at the beginning. As teachers we cannot predict students' success in a class. It is obvious, however, that some students in our class were never able to assimilate both disciplinary perspectives and this was indeed a challenge for us. The weaker students in our class struggled to understand the abstract nature of some of the materials we used. In the future, we may want to clarify what we hope students will learn and how that learning will be assessed. It may also help to attempt some convergence in our teaching styles. Finally, we need to develop pedagogical devices that allow students to better internalize basic concepts.

We will certainly continue to use and enhance the assignments and pedagogical tools that were successful. But we need to evaluate how much time we should spend on core concepts and the differences between disciplines. It seems impossible to us to teach interdisciplinary knowledge without understanding the roots of particular disciplines. However, the readings were overwhelming for several of our students, so we should perhaps reduce the number of things we try to do with readings and allow time for more explicit discussion of the reading assignments in class. We may also want to consider expanding the roles of the students in actual classroom presentation throughout the semester, either through expanded use of the listserv, or by having groups of students present various topics to the class. Perhaps this would give them a greater sense of ownership over and command of the material, particularly if we were to relate these presentations to areas of student expertise identified at the beginning of the semester. This would also foster a greater collaborative learning environment throughout the semester, a quality that we believe is essential to the course. We should probably require meetings with both professors together for all students, especially to discuss the final research projects. We began our grading of exams with each of us reading and grading the questions we put into the exam. But we concluded that every exam question should be graded by both professors and averaged for the final student grade. It would also be possible, but for many reasons undesirable, to institute prerequisites for the course; doing so would in many ways be antithetical to a program in interdisciplinary learning.

It will be a challenge and an opportunity to offer this course again. Both of us learned a great deal, not only about the subject but also about pedagogy and the dynamics of team teaching. From the perspective of an economist, the significant investment made in this course will hopefully have a future payoff. On a more serious note, we both firmly believe that the continuation of courses such as ours plays an important role in our students' liberal education, and has the not insignificant effect of allowing us to learn from one another, and from our students, as teachers and scholars.

NOTES

An earlier version of this article was presented at the Great Lakes College Association (GLCA) Women's Studies Conference at the College of Wooster in spring 2002. I would like to thank the participants in this conference for their helpful comments, the anonymous referees for their insights, and, of course, Pamela Frese for her willingness to undertake this adventure in teaching.

1. See, for example, the World Bank report (2001) and critiques of this approach by Elson (1991, 1994) and Kabeer (2000), all cited in the readings sections of the syllabus.

2. See the critiques in Elson (1991, 1994) and Kabeer (2000), as well as the more general discussion in Ferber and Nelson (1993), all cited in the readings sections of the syllabus.

GENDER, DEVELOPMENT, AND CULTURAL CHANGE

Description of the Course

This course explores the relationship between gender, the development process, and cultural change from anthropological and economic perspectives. The approaches used by anthropologists and economists to understand the process of development and change will be explored and critiqued from a feminist perspective, with the goal of providing a more complete understanding of the link between gender and culture in the developing world.

Course Requirements

One in-class midterm examination (15%); one take-home midterm examination (20%); one research paper (12–15 pages) (20%); class presentation of research (10 minutes) (5%); class participation (on class listserv and questions submitted during class presentations (15%); a cumulative final exam (25%). An extra credit option will be made available during the course of the semester (a potential of 15 points to be added to the second midterm grade).

Listserv

A listserv has been established for the class in order to help facilitate class discussion. The class will be divided into three groups, and each group will be responsible for participating in the listserv once a week. On the days you are assigned to participate, you are expected to submit a post no later than 10 P.M. the prior evening (i.e., Sunday, Tuesday, or Thursday) that raises questions or presents a critical evaluation of the reading/topic for the next class. If the listserv is to serve its purpose, you need to think seriously about your contributions. They should be detailed and clearly written, so that we and other students can determine what issues you find particularly thought-provoking or problematic and worth discussing. Please refer to the handout for directions on how to subscribe to the listserv.

Required Readings to Purchase

Kabeer, Naila 2000[1994] *Reversed Realities: Gender Hierarchies in Development Thought.* London: Verso.

McClaurin, Irma 1996 *Women of Belize: Gender and Change in Central America.* New Brunswick, N.J.: Rutgers University Press.

Required Readings on Reserve (in library and on electronic reserve)

Acosta-Belén, Edna, and Christine E. Bose 1995 "Colonialism, Structural Subordination, and Empowerment: Women in the Development Process in Latin America and the Caribbean" in Christine E. Bose and Edna Acosta-Belén (eds.) *Women in the Latin American Development Process.* Philadelphia: Temple University Press, 15–36.

Benería, Lourdes, and Amy Lind 1995 "Engendering International Trade" in Noeleen Heyzer (ed.) *A Commitment to the World's Women.* New York: United Nations, 69–86.

Bienefeld, Manfred 1995 "Global Markets: Threats to Sustainable Human Development" in Noeleen Heyzer (ed.) *A Commitment to the World's Women.* New York: United Nations, 87–100.

Case, Karl, and Ray Fair 2002 "Economic Growth in Developing and Transitional Economies" in *Principles of Economics.* Upper Saddle River, N.J.: Prentice Hall. 6th edition, 719–43.

Ekejiuba, Felicia I. 1995 "Down to Fundamentals: Women-centred Hearth-holds in Rural West Africa" in Deborah Fahy Brycesan (ed.) *Women Wielding the Hoe: Lessons from Rural Africa for Feminist Theory and Development Practice.* Oxford: Berg, 47–61.

Elliott, Lorraine 1996 "Women, Gender, Feminism, and Environment" in Jennifer Turpin and Lois Ann Lorentzen (eds.) *The Gendered New World Order: Militarism, Development and the Environment.* New York: Routledge, 13–24.

Elson, Diane 1991 "Male Bias in the Development Process: An Overview" in Diane Elson (ed.) *Male Bias in the Development Process.* Manchester, England: Manchester University Press, 1–28.

———. 1994 "Micro, Meso, Macro: Gender and Economic Analysis in the Context of Policy Reform" in Isabella Bakker (ed.) *Strategic Silence: Gender and Economic Policy.* London: Zed, 33–45.

Enloe, Cynthia 1993 "Bananas, Beaches, and Bases" in Linda S. Kauffman (ed.) *American Feminist Thought at Century's End: A Reader.* Cambridge, Mass.: Blackwell, 441–64.

Fernandez Kelly, M. Patricia, and Saskia Sassen 1995 "Recasting Women in the Global Economy: Internationalization and Changing Definitions of Gender" in Christine E. Bose and Edna Acosta-Belén (eds.) *Women in the Latin American Development Process.* Philadelphia: Temple University Press, 99–124.

Hanochi, Seiko 2001 "Japan and the Global Sex Industry" in Rita Mae Kelly, Jane H. Bayes, Mary E. Hawkesworth, and Brigitte Young (eds.) *Gender, Globalization, and Democratization.* New York: Rowman & Littlefield, 137–48.

Kapadia, Karin 1999 "Every Blade of Green: Landless Women Labourers, Production and Reproduction in South India" in Naila Kabeer (ed.) *Institutions, Relations and Outcomes: A Framework and Case Studies for Gender-Aware Planning.* London: Zed, 80–101.

McKay, Lesley 1993 "Women's Contribution to Tourism in Negril, Jamaica" in Jane Momsem (ed.) *Women and Change in the Caribbean: A Pan-Caribbean Perspective.* Bloomington: Indiana University Press, 278–86.

Moore, Henrietta 1998 "Feminist Anthropology: What Difference Does It Make?" in *Feminist Anthropology.* Minneapolis: University of Minnesota Press, 186–98.

———. 1994 "Social Identities and the Politics of Reproduction" in *A Passion for Difference: Essays in Anthropology and Gender.* Bloomington: Indiana University Press, 86–106.

Rocheleau, Dianne, Mohamud Jama, and Betty Wamalwa-Muragori 1995 "Gender, Ecology, and Agroforestry: Science and Survival in Kathama [Kenya]" in Barbara Thomas-Slayter and Dianne Rocheleau (eds.) *Gender, Environment, and Development in Kenya: A Grassroots Perspective.* Boulder: Lynne Rienner, 47–73.

Warren, Kay B., and Susan C. Bourque 1991 "Women, Technology, and International Development Ideologies: Analyzing Feminist Voices" in Micaela di Leonardo (ed.) *Gender at the Crossroads of Knowledge: Feminist Anthropology in the Postmodern Era.* Berkeley: University of California Press, 278–311.

World Bank 2001 "Introduction" and "Chapter Three" in *Engendering Development: Through Gender Equality in Rights, Resources, and Voice.* New York: Oxford University Press. http://www/worldbank.org.

Related Texts (for your information)

Appadurai, Arjun 1996 *Modernity at Large: Cultural Dimensions of Globalization.* Minneapolis: University of Minnesota Press.

Aubrey, Lisa Marie 1997 *The Politics of Development Cooperation: NGOs, Gender and Partnership in Kenya*. London: Routledge.

Blumberg, Rae Lesser 1995 *EnGENDERing Wealth and Well-being: Empowerment for Global Change*. Boulder, Colo.: Westview.

Chao, Shiyan (ed.) 1999 *Ghana: Gender Analysis and Policymaking for Development*. World Bank Discussion Paper no. 403. Washington, D.C.: World Bank.

Dube, Leela, Eleanor Leacock, Shirley Ardener (eds.) 1986 *Visibility and Power: Essays on Women in Society and Development*. Delhi: Oxford University Press.

Edwards, Louise, and Mina Roces 2000 *Women in Asia: Tradition, Modernity and Globalisation*. Ann Arbor: University of Michigan Press.

Ehlers, Tracy Bachrach 2000 [1990] *Silent Looms: Women and Production in a Guatemalan Town*. Austin: University of Texas Press.

Ferber, Marianne, and Julie Nelson 1993 *Beyond Economic Man: Feminist Theory and Economic Analysis*. Chicago: University of Chicago Press.

Henderson, Helen Kreider, and Ellen Hansen 1995 *Gender and Agricultural Development: Surveying the Field*. Tucson: University of Arizona Press.

Hodgson, Dorothy L., and Sheryl A. McCurdy (eds.) 2001 *"Wicked" Women and the Reconfiguration of Gender in Africa*. Westport, Conn.: Greenwood Press.

Jain, Shobhita, and Rhoda Reddock (eds.) 1998 *Women Plantation Workers: International Experiences*. New York: Berg.

Lazreg, Marnia 1994 *The Eloquence of Silence: Algerian Women in Question*. New York: Routledge.

Lockwood, Victoria S. 1993 *Tahitian Transformation: Gender and Capitalist Development in a Rural Society*. Boulder, Colo.: Lynne Rienner.

Momsen, Janet (ed.) 1993 *Women and Change in the Caribbean: A Pan-Caribbean Perspective*. Bloomington: Indiana University Press.

Pankhurst, Helen 1992 *Gender, Development and Identity: An Ethiopian Study*. London: Zed.

Peña, Devon G. 1997 *The Terror of the Machine: Technology, Work, Gender, and Ecology on the U.S.-Mexico Border*. Austin: University of Texas Press.

Ryan, Chris 2001 *Sex Tourism: Marginal People and Liminalities*. London: Routledge.

Snyder, Margaret C., and Mary Tadesse 1995 *African Women and Development: A History*. London: Zed.

Sweetman, Caroline 1998 *Gender and Technology*. Oxford: Oxfam.

Sylvester, Christine 2000 *Producing Women and Progress in Zimbabwe: Narratives of Identity and Work from the 1980s*. Westport, Conn.: Greenwood Press.

Venkateswaran, Sandhya 1995 *Environment, Development and the Gender Gap*. New Delhi: Sage.

Movies

Between Light and Shadow: Maya Women in Transition (27 min.; $50.00;
  #38398; University of California Extension)
Eternal Seed (43 min.; $90.00; #01566; Women Make Movies)
The Ladies of the Lake: A Matriarchal Society (20 min.; $55.00; Filmmakers
  Library)
Love, Women, and Flowers (58 min.; COW)
Not The Numbers Game: Indonesian Factories (10 min.)
Performing the Border (42 min.; $60.00 rental; #01644; Women Make
  Movies)
Sisters and Daughters Betrayed (28 min.; $50.00; #38352; University of
  California Extension)
Tokyo Girls (57 min.; $75.00; #38510; University of California Extension)
The Toured: The Other Side of Tourism in Barbados (38 min.; $60.00; #38226;
  University of California Extension)
Who's Counting? (60 min.; COW)

Course Schedule

Section I. Introduction

Class 1: Disciplinary perspectives used during course; semester overview
Class 2: Read: "Intro" in the U.N. report, http://www/worldbank.org.
  Movie: "Who's Counting?"
Class 3: What is anthropology? Read: Henrietta Moore's "Feminist
  Anthropology: What Difference Does It Make?"
Class 4: Read: Kay Warren and Susan Bourque's "Women, Technology, and
  International Development Ideologies: Analyzing Feminist Voices"
Class 5: Lecture on anthropological approaches to the study of gender
Class 6: What is economics? Read: Karl Case and Ray Fair's "Economic
  Growth in Developing and Transitional Economies"; class lecture on
  economic approaches to gender and development
Class 7: Read: Diane Elson's "Male Bias in the Development Process: An
  Overview" and "Micro, Meso, Macro: Gender and Economic Analysis
  in the Context of Policy Reform"
Class 8: Read: Naila Kabeer's "The Emergence of Women as a
  Constituency in Development" in *Reversed Realities* (pp. 1–10) and
  "Introduction: Feminism and International Development" by Martha
  Nussbaum (1–33).
Class 9: Read: Naila Kabeer's "Connecting, Extending, Reversing:
  Development from a Gender Perspective" in *Reversed Realities* (pp.
  69–95). Class discussion; review for Midterm Examination I
Class 10: Midterm Examination I

Section II. Agricultural Development: Women's Production and the Environment

Class 11: Read: Henrietta Moore's "Social Identities and the Politics of Reproduction." Movie: "Love, Women, and Flowers"

Class 12: Read: Naila Kabeer's "Benevolent Dictators, Maternal Altruists and Patriarchal Contracts: Gender and Household Economics" in *Reversed Realities* (pp. 95–135)

Class 13: Read: World Bank, "Chapter Three"

Class 14: Read: Felicia Ekejiuba's "Down to Fundamentals: Women-centered Hearth-holds in Rural West Africa." Movie: "Eternal Seed"

Class 15: Read: Karin Kapadia's "Every Blade of Green: Landless Women Labourers, Production and Reproduction in South India"

Class 16: Read: Dianne Rocheleau, Mohamud Jama, and Betty Wamalwa-Muragori's "Gender, Ecology, and Agroforestry: Science and Survival in Kathama [Kenya]"

Section III. Tourism and Cultural Change

Class 17: Read: "Women's Contribution to Tourism in Negril, Jamaica" by Lesley McKay. Movie: "The Ladies of the Lake"

Class 18: Movie: "The Toured: The Other Side of Tourism in Barbados"

Section IV. Globalization and Sexual Trafficking

Class 19: Read: Seiko Hanochi's "Japan and the Global Sex Industry." Movie: "Tokyo Girls"

Class 20: Movie: "Sisters and Daughters Betrayed"

Class 21: Review for Midterm Examination II

Section V. Multinational Corporations and Gendered Development in Latin America

Class 22: Read: M. Patricia Fernandez Kelly and Saskia Sassen's "Recasting Women in the Global Economy: Internationalization and Changing Definitions of Gender" (pp. 99–124)

Class 23: Read: Edna Acosta-Belén and Christine E. Bose's "Colonialism, Structural Subordination, and Empowerment: Women in the Development Process in Latin America and the Caribbean" (pp. 15–36)

Class 24: Midterm Examination II due in class. Movie: "Performing the Border"

Class 25: Read: lecture on Mayan culture and Meso-American civilizations; begin *Women of Belize*

Class 26: Turn in research topic; class discussions of research methods and

Mayan women

Class 27: Halloween Lecture. Wear Costumes! (Extra credit paper on origin of costume designs available in local stores and implications for constructions of gender)

Class 28: Read: *Women of Belize.* Movie: "Between Light and Shadow: Maya Women in Transition"

Class 29: Read: Naila Kabeer's "Empowerment from Below: Learning from the Grassroots" in *Reversed Realities* (pp. 223–63); class discussions on guidelines for student presentations on research paper (3 per day, with discussion)

Classes 30 through 32: *Women of Belize*

Classes 33 through 36: Student presentations

Class 37: Extra credit paper due in class. Read: Cynthia Enloe's "Bananas and Beaches." Presentation of Professor Frese's 2001 American Anthropological Association paper: "Guardians of the Golden Age: Custodians of U.S. Military Culture"

Classes 38 through 40: Student presentations

Class 41: Read: Naila Kabeer's "Beyond the Poverty Line: Measuring Poverty and Impoverishing Measures" in *Reversed Realities* (pp. 136–62) and Manfred Bienefeld's "Global Markets: Threats to Sustainable Human Development" in *Gender at the Crossroads: Feminist Anthropology in the Post Modern Era* (240–56).

Class 42: Last day of class; review for final examination

Barbara Burnell *is professor of economics at the College of Wooster. She has taught many courses in women's studies and has been published in several edited volumes on feminism and economics. She is interested in feminist philosophy as it applies to methods in economics and the sciences.*

Topics in Development
Gender and Development

Sara Curran

Course Description

This course examines men and women's lives in less developed countries and the impact upon them as a result of development and incorporation into global, economic, and political systems. The course begins with theoretical approaches to gender and development, development theory, and feminist critiques. We then turn to how social change (positive or negative development) happens. We will examine in detail issues of production (formal and informal work), reproduction (health, child survival, and fertility), and the family/household nexus (where production and reproduction meet). Woven throughout the course will be themes about (1) micro and macro processes, perspectives, and levels of analysis and (2) research methods and policy applications, given a practitioner's structural position. The course will offer two applied projects for students to work on. The first is the development of material for a Web page and two Internet network discussions to take place on the Gender and Development Policy Network (*http://www.wws.princeton.edu/~gender/*). The second project is to assist the new Gender Division of the World Bank in assessing the gender content of bank projects. This will involve summarizing the gender content of forty to fifty projects at the bank, selecting and analyzing five case studies among the projects, and writing an evaluative report for limited circulation within the Bank.

Requirements

1. Reading and class participation: This is one of the most important requirements. To facilitate your participation each week two people will be required to provide a one-paragraph summary of each reading and questions for discussion. Every person is expected to participate each week.
2. Participation in two projects:
The Gender and Development Policy Network (GDPN, http://www.wws. princeton.edu/~gender/)—you may choose to work on the planning and evaluation discussion group or the gender and globalization discussion group. You should participate in the two, two-week Internet discussions

organized by the liaisons and members of the GDPN Advisory Council. A gender critique for the Gender Division of the World Bank—provision of project summaries and a report to the Bank.

3. Attendance at the Center for Migration and Development Lec-ture Series.

4. Books and articles: Books and articles are all on reserve in the Woodrow Wilson School library.

5. Extra credit: Guidelines for how to do a gender country profile (this can be a group effort).

Part 1. Gender, Development, and Theoretical Perspectives

Week 1. Introductions and Planning for the Semester— Leveling the Field: Understanding Social Change and Development

Readings

Boserup, Ester. 1970. *Woman's Role in Economic Development.* London: Allen & Unwin.

Fernandez Kelly, Patricia M. 1994. "Broadening the Scope: Gender and the Study of International Development." In Douglas Kincaid and Alejandro Portes (editors) *Comparative National Development: Society and Economy in the New Global Order.* Chapel Hill, N.C.: University of North Carolina Press. Pp. 143–68.

Portes, Alejandro. 1997. "Neoliberalism and the Sociology of Develop-ment." *Population and Development Review* 23(2): 229–60

Recommended

Jaffee, David. 1990. *Levels of Socioeconomic Development Theory.* New York: Praeger.

Kincaid, Douglas, and Alejandro Portes (editors). 1994. *Comparative National Development: Society and Economy in the New Global Order.* Chapel Hill, N.C.: University of North Carolina Press.

Class Schedule

1st hour: Personal introductions, overview of course and requirements.

2nd hour: Lecture on theories of social change (economic, political and social) and the gender perspective.

3rd hour: Assignment of liaisons for the World Bank and for the Gender and Development Policy Network, brainstorming of projects and plan-ning, establishing tentative schedule for production of reports and dis-cussion sessions.

Week 2. From Women to Gender: The Development of the Field— What is Efficient, Equitable, and Equal?

Readings

Elson, Diane. 1991. "Male Bias in the Development Process: An Overview"
   In *Male Bias in the Development Process.* Edited by Diane Elson
   Manchester, England: Manchester University Press. Pp. 1–15 (just the
   first half of the chapter).
Fernandez Kelly, Patricia. 1993. "Political Economy and Gender in Latin
   America: The Emerging Dilemmas." Latin American Program Working
   Papers. Washington, D.C.: Woodrow Wilson Center.
Moser, Caroline O. 1993. *Gender Planning and Development.* Chapter 1. New
   York: Routledge.
Razavi, Shahrashoub, and Carol Miller. 1995. *From WID to GAD: Conceptual
   Shifts in the Women and Development Discourse.* Geneva: United Nations
   Research Institute for Social Development.

Recommended

Fyree, Myra Marx. 1990. "Beyond Separate Spheres: Feminism and Family
   Research." *Journal of Marriage and the Family* 52 (November): 866–84.
Sen, Gita, and Caren Grown. 1987. *Development, Crises and Alternative
   Visions.* New York: Monthly Review Press.
Tinker, Irene. 1990. *Persistent Inequalities.* Chapters 1 and 3. New York:
   Oxford University Press.

Class Schedule

1st hour: Lecture on efficiency, equity and equality, multilevel and multisectoral issues.
2nd hour: Discussion of reading (Estela and Tyler).
3rd hour: Brainstorming and project planning—Heather Graham from
Gender and Development Policy Network. Finalize schedule and planning
horizon for both projects.
   Trip to Washington, D.C., with liaisons, Curran, and other class members to the World Bank to meet Bamberger, Fort, and other representatives and to pick up materials.

**Week 3. Contending Perspectives, Differing Voices—
Globalization of Feminism and Human Rights?
Who Is to Say What Is Right?**

Readings

Goetz, Anne Marie. 1991. "Feminism and the Claim to Know:
   Contradictions in Feminist Approaches to Women in Development."
   Gender and International Relations. Bloomington: Indiana University
   Press. Pp. 133–55.
Mohanty, Chandra Talpade. 1991. "Under Western Eyes: Feminist

Scholarship and Colonial Discourses." In Chandra Talpade Mohanty, Ann Russo and Lourdes Torres, eds. *Third World Women and the Politics of Feminism.* Bloomington: Indiana University Press. Pp. 51–80.

Parpart, Jane. 1993. "Who is the *Other?* A Post Modern Critique of Women and Development Theory and Practice." *Development and Change* 24(3): 439–64.

Tinker, Irene. *Persistent Inequalities.* Chapter 5.

Whelan, Daniel. 1998. "Recasting WID: A Human Rights Approach." International Center for Research on Women, Working Paper no. 6. September.

Recommended

Dixon-Mueller, Ruth. 1993. *Population Policy and Women's Reproductive Rights.* New York: Praeger. Chapter 1.

Class Schedule

1st hour: Lecture on globalization of feminism/human rights.
2nd hour: Discussion of readings.
3rd hour: Discussion of projects.

Part 2a. Development and Social Change Viewed with a Gender Lens— Production

Week 4. Work and Gender Relations (Inside/Outside the House)— Intrahousehold Resource Allocation and Income Sources

Readings

Katz, Elizabeth. 1995. "Gender and Trade Within the Household: Observations from Rural Guatemala." *World Development.* 23(2): 327–42.

Moser, Caroline. *Gender Planning and Development.* Chapter 2.

Summerfield, Gale. 1997. "Economic Transition in China and Vietnam: Crossing the Poverty Line Is Just the First for Women and Their Families." *Review of Social Economy* 55(2): 201–23.

Tinker, Irene. *Persistent Inequalities.* Chapters 8, 9, and 10.

Tinker, Irene. 1997. "Family Survival in an Urbanizing World." *Review of Social Economy* 55(2): 251–60.

Recommended

Dwyer, Daisy and Judith Bruce. 1988. *A Home Divided: Women and Income in the Third World.* Stanford, CA: Stanford University Press. Pp. 1–19, 143–54, 248–64.

Class Schedule

1st hour: Lecture on families, households, and resource allocation (causes and consequences—who earns, who spends, and who gets).

2nd hour: Discussion of readings.

3rd hour: Discussion of gender summaries for the World Bank—what to look for, how to write one, and planning for the report.

Week 5. Work and Gender Relations (Formal/Informal)

Readings

Collins, Jane. 1993. "Gender, Contracts and Wage Work: Agricultural Restructuring in Brazil's São Francisco Valley." *Development and Change* 24(1): 53–82.

Malhotra, Anju, and Deborah DeGraff. 1997. "Entry Versus Success in the Labor Force: Young Women's Employment in Sri Lanka." *World Development* 25(3): 370–94.

Ward, Kathryn (editor). 1990. *Women Workers and Global Restructuring.* Ithaca, N.Y.: ILR Press, Cornell University. Chapters 1, 2 3, 4, and 5.

Scott, Alison MacEwen. 1991. "Informal Sector or Female Sector? Gender Bias in Urban Labor Market Models." In Diane Elson, ed. *Male Bias in the Development Process.* Manchester, England: Manchester University Press.

Recommended

Benaría, Lourdes, and Shelley Feldman. 1992. *Unequal Burden: Economic Crises, Persistent Poverty, and Women's Work.* Boulder, CO: Westview Press.

Tinker, Irene. *Persistent Inequalities.* Chapter 7.

Cagatay, N., and S. Ozler. 1995. "Feminization of the Labor Force: The Effects of Long-Term Development and Structural Adjustment." *World Development* 23(11): 1883–94.

Haddad, Lawrence, Lynn R. Brown, Andrea Richter, and Lisa Smith. 1995. "The Gender Dimensions of Economic Adjustment Policies: Potential Interactions and Evidence to Date." *World Development* 23(6): 881–96.

Pyle, Jean. 1997. "Women, the Family and Economic Restructuring: The Singapore Model." *Review of Social Economy* 55(2): 215–23.

Tanski, Janet. 1994. "The Impact of Crisis, Stabilization, and Structural Adjustment on Women in Lima, Peru." *World Development* 22(11): 1627–42.

Howes, C., and A. Singh. 1995. "Long-Term Trends in the World Economy: The Gender Dimension." *World Development* 23(11): 1895–1912.

Dwyer, Daisy and Judith Bruce. 1988. *A Home Divided.* Pp. 120–42, 173–94, 229–47. Stanford, CA: Stanford University Press.

Class Schedule

1st half-hour: Remeasuring work—guest lecture, Debra Donahoe, Office of Population Research.

2nd half-hour: Discussion of readings.

2nd and 3rd hours: Computing and Information Technology (CIT) training on Website construction at CIT.

Week 6. Work and Gender Relations (Globalization)

Readings

Elson, Diane. 1995. "Household Responses to Stabilisation and Structural Adjustment: Male Bias at the Micro Level." In Diane Elson, Ed. *Male Bias in the Development Process.* Manchester, England: Manchester University Press.

Fernandez Kelly, Patricia M., and Saskia Sassen. 1995. "Recasting Women in the Global Economy: Internationalization and Changing Definitions of Gender." In Christine E. Bose and Edna Acosta-Belén (editors) *Women in the Latin American Development Process.* Philadelphia: Temple University Press. Pp. 99–124.

Ghorayshi, Parvin, and Clarie Belanger. 1996. *Women, Work, and Gender Relations in Developing Countries: A Global Perspective.* Westport, Conn.: Greenwood Press. Pp. 40–147.

Joekes, Susan, and Ann Weston. 1994. *Women and the New Trade Agenda.* New York: United Nations Development Fund for Women.

Raijman, Rebeca, and Moshe Semyonov. 1997. "Gender, Ethnicity and Immigration: Double Disadvantage and Triple Disadvantage among Recent Immigrant Women in the Israeli Labor Market." *Gender and Society* 11(1): 108–25.

Recommended

Bilsborrow, Richard. 1993. "Internal Migration of Women in Developing Countries: An Overview." In *Internal Migration of Women in Developing Countries: Proceedings of the United Nations Expert Meeting on the Feminization of Internal Migration, October 1991.* New York: United Nations. Pp. 1–17.

Constable, Nicole. 1997. *Maid to Order in Hong Kong: Stories of Filipina Workers.* Ithaca, N.Y.: Cornell University Press.

Special Issue of *World Development* 23 (11).

Class Schedule

1st hour: New Economic Order.

2nd hour: Discussion of readings.

3rd hour: Discussion of program planning and evaluation (both World Bank and Gender Network)—two-week online discussion on gender and globalization begins.

Part 2b. Development and Social Change Viewed with a Gender Lens—

Reproduction

Week 7. Population and Health Policy with a Gender Lens

Readings

Greenhalgh, Susan, and Jiali Li. 1995. "Engendering Reproductive Policy and Practice in Peasant China: For a Feminist Demography of Reproduction." *SIGNS* 20(3): 601–39.

Harpending, H. C., and R. Pennington. 1991. "Age Structure and Sex-Biased Mortality among Herero Pastoralists." *Human Biology* 63(3): 329–53.

Heise, Lori, Kirsten Moore, and Nahid Toubia. 1995. *Sexual Coercion and Reproductive Health: A Focus on Research.* New York: Population Council.

Petchesky, Rosalind. 1998. *Negotiating Reproductive Rights.* New York: International Reproductive Rights Research Action Group. Selections.

Santow, Gigi. 1995. "Social Roles and Physical Health: The Case of Female Disadvantage in Poor Countries." *Social Science Medicine* 40(2): 147–61.

Recommended

Dixon-Mueller, Ruth. 1993. *Population Policy and Women's Reproductive Rights.* New York: Praeger.

Class Schedule

1st hour: Generalizations, gender, and reproductive health—guest lecture, Denise Roth, Office of Population Research.
2nd hour: Discussion of readings.
3rd hour: Presentation of summaries and sector chapter (either multi-sectoral or infrastructure).

Week 8. Health Sector Reform: HIV/AIDS and Gender

Readings

Cassels, A. 1995. "Health Sector Reform: Key Issues in Less Developed Countries." *Journal of International Development* 7(3): 329–47.

Frenk, J. 1994. Dimensions of Health System Reform. *Health Policy* 27: 19–34.

Long, Lynellyn D., and E. Maxine Ankrah. 1996. *Women's Experiences with HIV/AIDS: An International Perspective.* New York: Columbia University Press. Pp. 297–396.

UNAIDS/WHO. 1998 *Report on the Global HIV/AIDS Epidemic.* New York: United Nations.

Class Schedule

1st hour: Lecture by guest speaker—Melissa Huang, "Integration of Disease Control to Health Sector Reform: The Case of HIV/AIDS."
2nd hour: Discussion of lecture and readings.
3rd hour: Case study presentation. Beginning of online program planning and evaluation discussion.
    Discussion: Health sector summaries and initial draft of chapter for World Bank.

Social Reproduction: Education and Its Consequences

Readings

Knodel, John, and Gavin W. Jones. 1996. "Post-Cairo Population Policy: Does Promoting Girls' Schooling Miss the Mark?" *Population and Development Review* 22(4): 683–702.

Bledsoe, Carolyn, John Casterline, Jennifer A. Johnson-Kuhn, and John Haaga (editors). 1999. *Critical Perspectives on Schooling and Fertility in the Developing World.* Washington, D.C.: The National Research Council. Selections.

Class Schedule

1st hour: Lecture on the globalization of education— the politics and consequences of empowerment.
2nd hour: Discussion of readings.
3rd hour: Presentation of education summaries and first draft of chapter. Presentation of summary of online discussion of gender and globalization.

Part 3. Gender, the "Doing" of Development, and the "State"

Week 10. Doing Development Examples

Readings

Cohen, Monique. 1997. "A Road Map for Measuring Development Impact: A Woman's and Family Perspective." *Review of Social Economy* 55(2): 243–49.

Leonard, Ann. 1995. *SEEDS 2: Supporting Women's Work Around the World.* New York: Feminist Press.

Khandker, Shahidur, Baqui Khalily, and Zahed Khan. 1995. "Grameen Bank: Performance and Sustainability." World Bank Discussion Papers #306. Washington, D.C.: World Bank.

Class Schedule

1st hour: Lecture.
2nd hour: Discussion.

3rd hour: Presentation of multisectoral or infrastructure summaries and chapter.

Week 11. Agriculture, Environment, and Gender

Readings

Argawal, Bina. 1994. "Gender and Command Over Property: A Critical Gap in Economic Analysis and Policy in South Asia." *World Development* 22(10): 1455–78.

Jackson, Cecile. 1993. "Environmentalisms and Gender Interests in the Third World." *Development and Change* 24: 649–77.

Rocheleau, Dianne, and David Edmunds. 1997. "Women, Men and Trees: Gender, Power and Property in Forest and Agrarian Landscapes." *World Development* 25(8): 1351–71.

Thomas-Slayter, Barbara, and Dianne E. Rocheleau. 1995. "Research Frontiers at the Nexus of Gender, Environment, and Development: Linking Household, Community, and Ecosystem." In Rita S. Gallin, Anne Ferguson, and Janice Harper (editors) *The Women and International Development Annual, Volume 4*. Boulder Colo.: Westview. 80–116.

Recommended

Argawal, Bina. 1992. "Gender Relations and Food Security: Coping with Seasonality, Drought, and Famine in South Asia." In Lourdes Beneria and Shelley Feldman, eds. *Unequal Burden: Economic Crises, Persistent Poverty, and Women's Work*. Boulder, CO: Westview Press. Pp. 181–218.

Carney, Judith A. 1996. "Converting the Wetlands, Engendering the Environment: The Intersection of Gender with Agrarian Change in Gambia." In Richard Peet and Michael Watts (editors) *Liberation Ecologies*. New York: Routledge. Pp. 165–87.

Hecht, Susanna. 1985. "Women and the Latin American Livestock Sector." In Jamie Monson and Marion Kalb (editors) *Women as Food Producers in Developing Countries* . Los Angeles, CA: UCLA African Studies Center. Pp. 51–69.

Leach, Melissa. 1992. "Women's Crops in Women's Spaces: Gender Relations in Mende Rice Farming." In Elisabeth Croll and David Parkin (editors) *Bush Base: Forest Farm*. New York: Routledge. Pp. 76–96.

Zwarteveen, Margreet Z. 1997. "Water: From Basic Need to Commodity: A Discussion on Gender and Water Rights in the Context of Irrigation." *World Development* 25(8): 1335–49.

Class Schedule

1st hour: Guest lecture—Agnes Quisumbing, International Food Policy Research Institute.

2nd hour: Discussion of readings.

3rd hour: Presentation of World Bank Agriculture Group's initial findings
and suggestions.

Week 12. Social Change: Politics, Social Movements, and the State

Readings

Kardum, Nuket. 1991. *Bringing Women In: Women's Issues in International
Development Programs.* Boulder, CO: L. Rienner Publishers.

Cooper, Barbara. 1995. "The Politics of Difference and Women's
Associations in Niger: of 'Prostitutes,' the Public, and Politics." *SIGNS*
20(4):851–82.

Lind, Amy. 1997. "Gender, Development and Urban Social Change:
Women's Community Action in Global Cities." *World Development* 25(8):
1205–23.

MacLeod, Arlene Elowe. 1992. "Hegemonic Relations and Gender
Resistance: The New Veiling as Accomodating Protest in Cairo." *SIGNS*
17(3): 533–57.

Recommended

Moser, Caroline. *Gender Planning and Development.* Chapters 3, 4, and 9.

Tinker, Irene. *Persistent Inequalities.* Chapters 11 through 15.

Class Schedule

1st hour: Lecture and discussion.

2nd hour: Discussion and presentation of program planning and evaluation chapter.

Week 13. Course Review, Finalization of Report

Class Schedule

Draft presentation of report—attendance of Gender and Development
Policy Network Advisory Council.

Week 14. Trip to the World Bank to Present Report

*Sara Curran is assistant professor of sociology and director of undergraduate
studies in sociology at Princeton University. Curran researches internal migration in developing countries, family demography, environment and population,
and gender. She is currently writing a book, "Shifting Boundaries, Transforming
Lives: Globalization, Gender and Family Dynamics in Thailand."*

Child Care and Inequality: Rethinking Carework for Children and Youth, edited by F. M. Cancian, D. Kurz, A. London, R. Reviere, and M. Tuominen (New York: Routledge, 2002)

Beth Blue Swadener and Karen Ortiz

Child Care and Inequality offers sociological framings of an array of critical issues in the fields of child care, health care, and other "carework" for children and youth, primarily in the United States. The editors have been involved in research addressing a wide range of carework, including family care, center-based and community-based care, neighborhood and youth work, and a variety of advocacy approaches in care-related fields. In describing their use of the term *carework*, the editors convey their struggle to name and frame complex and embedded issues related to the gendered and economically stratified "caring" fields. An example of this is found in the first chapter, by Emily Abel, which provides a history of women in the U.S. caring for children who are sick and disabled – often other people's children. Most chapters are based on papers given at the first Carework Network conference in 2000.

The chapters in this volume underscore sociologists' analytic focus on inequalities, perspectives that have been developing for some time in the early childhood care and education literature—particularly in the reconceptualizing early childhood "movement" of the past decade. Previous sociological work in the United States addressing child care and early education has included the work of Wrigley (1991). Among the obvious ironies of carework are issues of low status and pay in these gender-ghettoized professions, in which careworkers typically do not earn a living wage or have benefits. These conditions perpetuate a field of allied professions that form a "permanent underclass" in Western patriarchal societies, particularly those in post-welfare or post-socialist states (Fraser 1997; Mink 1998; Schram 2000).

The process of untangling the web of early care and education is difficult and complex. Many in the caring fields and beyond still tread softly when speaking of motherhood; but until we deconstruct discourses such as those of early experiences (e.g., of mother, child, and "the poor") and begin to frame these topics in ways that reflect multiple power relationships within historical, social, and political contexts, we will not succeed in elevating the profession of caring.

Several contributors also appear at times to struggle with how explicitly to name and deconstruct power, patriarchy, and oppression. While many contributors confront these issues with data, stories, and narrative analysis, others use primarily historical analysis and sociological theory. As child advocates, we found this book to be refreshing, in part because it was not framed from dominant child development and early education perspectives. We also found the historical analysis in some chapters compelling, and noted ways in which such work complements the growing body of early childhood historical literature, as well as emerging literature on "governing children and families" (e.g., Bloch and Popkewitz 2003; Hultqvist and Dahlberg 2001; Rose 1989).

When many white, middle-class researchers talk as advocates, there is a tendency to frame issues in middle–class–dominant culture assumptions, and this has contributed to a child-saving mentality that is usually rooted in a deficit model of families in poverty or families of color. Several chapters in *Child Care and Inequality* reinforce this point, including discussions of foster care "reform" and policies designed on the basis of middle-class assumptions (e.g., Barbara Bennett Woodhouse's chapter on the privatization of foster care) and definitions of "good" child care (e.g., Francesca Cancian's chapter on hegemonic and democratic standards).

While we were completing this review, the U.S. Congress was in the midst of welfare reform reauthorization, proposing even more punitive requirements. We found ourselves wishing that policy makers or their aides had read the chapters concerning impacts of the 1996 Personal Responsibility and Work Opportunity Reconciliation Act of 1996—particularly the chapter by Andrew London, Ellen Scott, and Vicki Hunter, "Children and Chronic Health Conditions: Welfare Reform and Health-Related Carework," which draws from longitudinal ethnographic case studies of single mothers in the welfare system who have significant dependent-care issues.

In "Care, Inequality, and Policy," Paula England and Nancy Folbre explore reasons for the link between care and inequality, including problems in access to care, negative effects of caregiving on income, and caregivers' vulnerability to discrimination in the labor market. The authors assert that none of these aspects of inequality is directly related to market-driven criteria, but rather, is directly related to societal and cultural processes. In describing the limitations of access to care, the authors tend to stray toward the premise that individuals with higher income can purchase more and higher-quality care services in the marketplace, just as they can with other commodities.

While there is a pervasive scarcity of affordable, quality child care affecting all social classes in the United States, many poor and working-class families are forced to choose child care based on non-quality criteria, and most use informal care. Underlying the persistent stratification of child care is the predominant discourse that child care is a family responsibility. Thus, middle-class families also have difficulty accessing quality child care, not just because of inaffordability, but also because of the lack of available quality care.

In "Child Care Across Sectors," Heather Fitz Gibbon discusses viewpoints of family child-care providers; for-profit, center-based providers; and nonprofit, center-based providers. She argues that child-care providers "adopt one of two models of caring—one based on caring as teaching, and the other emphasizing the relations and nurturing aspect of caring" (145–146). Gibbon places these models of caring under the umbrella of a societal environment that devalues the importance of the emotional aspects of carework and accepts the needless limitations of this field. The permeating theme in Gibbon's analysis of child-care choices points to defective societal branding. Many in the public and in policymaking are guilty of placing little value or importance on the teaching and nurturing of children younger than age five.

Though most of the chapters address carework inequities in the United States, three chapters provide critical cross-national analyses. In "Las Madres en el Barrio," JoAnn DeFiore describes her study of a "community of caregiving" in a small rural pueblo in Paraguay. Her ethnographic work documents ways in which women create a network of godmothers and "othermothers" that supports their role as mother within a high-poverty and oppressive context. In "Caregiving, Welfare States and Mothers' Poverty," Karen Christopher contributes to the growing body of literature on rapidly changing policies and gendered experiences of mothers in nine Western socialist and post-socialist states. In "Support Organizations for Parents of Children with Cancer: Local, National, and International Problems and Prospects," Mark Chesler addresses support organizations for parents of children with cancer. He examines the roles of parents and professionals and contrasts the services and supports available in wealthy and less wealthy national contexts.

While most chapters focus on carework related to younger children, Eric Wright and Robert Connoley , in "Empowering Forces," focus on the roles played by careworkers in support networks for gay, lesbian, and bisexual (G/L/B) youth. Drawing from a mixed-method exploratory study of a national network for G/L/B youth, the authors foreground the voices of participants and highlight the specialized roles played by careworkers in this critical area of carework.

We recommend this book for multiple audiences, including those who are teaching social policy, family sociology, early childhood education, child development, and allied health professions. We feel that the book will also appeal to readers outside the academy, including those who labor without pay in various carework capacities. As in most edited volumes, the chapters are a bit uneven in their theoretical framing and the amount of new knowledge they contribute to related fields. Yet, this book takes on, in insightful ways, critical contemporary issues, such as, impacts of welfare reform on families, particularly with medically fragile children and those who are victims of family violence; standards debates and related class/culture bias; G/L/B/T youth work issues; and the continuing struggle for living wages in predominantly female care fields. Child care and inequality is relevant to a number of fields, including sociology, women's studies, early childhood education, child development, and policy studies, and we strongly recommend it.

REFERENCES

Bloch, M. N., and T. Popkewitz (eds.) (2003). *Restructuring the Governing Patterns of the Child, Education and the Welfare State.* New York: Palgrave Macmillan.

Fraser, N. (1997). *Justice Interruptus: Critical Reflections on the "Postsocialist" Condition.* New York: Routledge.

Hultqvist, K., and G. Dahlberg (eds.) (2001). *Governing the Child in the New Millennium.* London: Routledge/Falmer.

Mink, G. (1998). *Welfare's End.* Ithaca, N.Y.: Cornell University Press.

Rose, N. (1989). *Governing the Soul: The Shaping of the Private Self.* 2nd ed. London: Free Association Books.

Schram, S. F. (2000). *After Welfare: The Culture of Postindustrial Social Policy.* New York: New York University Press.

Swadener, B. B. (1995). "Stratification in Early Childhood Policy and Programs in the United States: Historical and Contemporary Manifestations." *Education Policy* 9, no. 4: 404–25.

Wigley, J. (1991). "Two-Tiered Systems of Child Care in the U.S." In L. Weis, P. G. Altbach, G. P. Kelly, and H. G. Petrie (eds.) *Critical Perspectives on Early Childhood Education.* Albany: State University of New York Press.

Beth Blue Swadener *is professor of early childhood education and policy studies at Arizona State University. She conducts research on social policy, anti-bias curriculum, and early education in Kenya. Her books include* Reconceptualizing the Early Childhood Curriculum, Children and Families "At Promise": Deconstructing the Discourse of Risk, Semiotics of Dis/ability, Does the Village Still Raise the Child?: A Collaborative Study in Changing Childrearing and Early Education in Kenya, *and*

Decolonizing Research in Cross-Cultural Contexts. *She is also active in a number of peace, social justice, and child advocacy groups.* **Karen Ortiz** *has worked in the field of child care advocacy since 1985 and is currently the senior program analyst for early care and education with the Arizona State Board on School Readiness. Prior to that, she served for three years as early care and education senior program associate for Children's Action Alliance, an advocacy organization. She is also one of the founders and the former Executive Vice President for Dependent Care Network, a company offering dependent care benefits, a network of child care providers, and sick care programs to employees of contracted corporations nationwide.*

Engendering International Health: The Challenge of Equity, edited by Gita Sen, Asha George, and Piroska Ostlin (Cambridge, MA: The MIT Press, 2002)

Sheryl McCurdy

This edited volume begins to fill a gap in the international public health literature by demonstrating the importance of conducting gendered analyses when examining health and illness experiences. Some authors examine gendered experiences of illness in particular social contexts. Other authors discuss gendered experiences of particular diseases across social settings. The editors' introduction underlines the need to tie health-related and gendered behavior to structural inequities in access to resources (7).

The editors discuss the unequal relations of power in society and various ways the powerful dominate and shape public debates, programs, and policies. The authors point out that gendered notions of ways of being will influence not only what is thought about health, but what men and women, as individuals, families, communities, and nations, do about health (10).

The first seven contributors to the book focus on key health areas, while the last five focus on research and policy. Pamela Harrigan, Janet Price, and Rachel Tolhurst explore the ways in which infectious disease is related to gender and poverty. Piroska Ostlin discusses occupational health and women's participation in the world economy. Jane Cottingham and Cynthia Myntti create a conceptual map through which to examine reproductive health. Claudia Garcia-Moreno examines violence against women, and Jill Astbury investigates mental health. Rachel Snow brings the discussion around to chronic disease with a discussion of hip fractures, primarily in high-income-earning countries. Jacqueline Sims and Maureen Butter complete the health issues section of the book with their insistence on the need for a broader approach to environmental health, and they link health to poverty, development, and equity issues.

Garcia-Moreno and Astbury's chapters examine women's global experiences of violence and subsequent physical and mental health problems. Garcia-Moreno provides data from around the globe that demonstrate women's universal experiences of domestic and sexual violence and relates these to women's experiences of ill health. Astbury's chapter aptly follows on Garcia-Moreno's, noting the links between the experiences of violence and subsequent depression. Astbury's analysis includes a note on the ways that ethnographic studies "identify the role [of] social and cultural mores, including those around gender relations, in the acceptance and promotion of violence against women" (128).

The policy section of the book begins with Nancy Breen's study of social discrimination and health in the United States, followed by Maggie Banser's study of macroeconomics, programming, and participation. Banser argues that gender equity can be addressed if we develop policies and interventions that take into consideration women's agency, include the poor in planning strategies, and promote public accountability(258). She suggests that analysts examine the strategies poor families use to manage their scarce resources as they begin to develop intersectoral approaches to improving health status (270).

Gita Sen, Aditi Iyer, and Asha George provide readers with an examination of the relationship between class, gender, and health equity in India. They note the ways that treatment-seeking behaviors and morbidity experiences of rural and urban men and women of different classes altered in relation to the deterioration of health services and privatization of medical services. Kara Hanson discusses gender and equity in the context of disease burden and critiques the use of terms like global burdens of disease (GBDs) and disability-adjusted life-years (DALYs). Hilary Standing discusses the complexities involved in conducting gendered analyses of health-sector reform. Women's roles as producers and consumers of health care must be considered. She insists that analysts must also account for women's differential access to income and their unpaid domestic and reproductive labor.

The volume is a good introduction to the study of health and gender for public health, nursing, and medical students interested in international health work. It provides basic and important information about gender, gender inequity, and gender analysis. Authors give examples of gendered behavior and demonstrate the ways that gendered actions are constrained by generation, class, and ethnicity. Basic information about the ways that specific chronic and infectious diseases differentially affect men's and women's health is presented.

Some articles detail the ways that programs and policies, like the structural adjustment programs initiated by the International Monetary Fund in Africa, reduce the capacity of countries to provide adequate health and other social services to their citizens. Each chapter concludes with suggestions for new approaches and interventions that will expand our understanding of gendered differences in health and will improve the ways that we attempt to address inequities. Each of the chapters offers readers with limited international experience concrete examples of the ways that policy and programs play out on the ground. For students and researchers familiar with feminist research in the social sciences and humanities literature, the discussion of gender analysis presented here is not new. Conducting gender analysis to promote more equitable health programs and policies, is, however, new, important, and useful. As the contributors note, simply disaggregating the data by sex does not reveal the ways that gender-coded behavior influences health and illness experiences. In their suggestions for future research some contributors note that qualitative research or the combination of qualitative and quantitative research is key to the process of understanding the relationship between gendered practices and health equity.

A number of authors suggest that multisectoral approaches at the community level are necessary for there to be improvements in women's health. They advocate policy changes and grassroots initiatives. In a typical public health and international health style, the authors suggest broad-based policy and programmatic solutions. The need for more nuanced gendered analyses of what is occurring on the ground and the ways that local actors are influencing macro and micro health factors are considered and promoted in the introduction and suggested in several chapters.

This book provides basic concepts about international health from a gendered perspective not often found in international public health literature. The concepts, definitions, and examples the authors use are accessible to students unfamiliar with the idea that gender is about learned role behaviors and that gendered experiences affect women and men's health. More importantly, the contributors offer important insights into the complexities of conducting gender analyses. They also offer specific proposals for ways that policy makers, development workers, and researchers can communicate with one another and work with local communities to make multi-sectoral changes that will enhance people's health. I expect to use this volume in my public health courses.

Sheryl McCurdy *is an assistant professor at the University of Texas-Houston Health Sciences, School of Public Health. She is coeditor of and contributor to* "Wicked" Women and the Reconfiguration of Africa. *She has published work on women's health and women's associations in East and Central Africa and has articles forthcoming about HIV/AIDS, drug use, and sex workers in Tanzania.*

Gender, Race, and Nation: A Global Perspective, edited by Vanaja Dhruvarajan and Jill Vickers (Toronto: University of Toronto Press, 2002)

Carolyn Kissane

As Vanaja Dhruvarajan, Jill Vickers, and three contributing authors make clear in *Gender, Race and Nation: A Global Perspective,* the field of gender studies has changed dramatically over the last two decades. The authors contributing to this edited volume devote substantial time to targeting Western feminist studies for fostering narrow, homogeneous conceptions of gender. Gender as studied in the past centered on a perspective assuming common interests and feminist goals while ignoring the multiplicity of voices and experiences of women around the world. Today, as the authors emphasize, it is vital not only to understand the differences that exist among women but also to acknowledge the types of hierarchies that are built into institutional structures and perpetuate and legitimate inequalities for women in their various contexts and locations. The authors seek to use the study of difference as a source of learning and understanding and as a point of challenge from which to unlock assumptions concerning women's experiences and histories in order to move progressively forward toward a more diverse and inclusive view of women and their lives.

The chapters expand and confront the way gender is studied by offering a one-world theoretical perspective from which to study gender. Although this might sound like a paradoxical approach for the study of diversity, the one-world framework used throughout the text challenges former generalizations surrounding women and seeks to make the diverse lives of women the focus, while integrating the connections between race and nation and gender. The book draws attention to Amrita Basu's work (1995) highlighting how "women's identities within and across nations are shaped by a complex amalgam of national, racial, religious, ethnic, class and sexual identities" (4). The one-world approach, therefore, represents a much-needed paradigm shift, challenging past scholarly tendencies to singularize women's movements and activities. The authors in this volume contribute to Chandra Mohanty's (1991) critique of mainstream feminist scholarship by calling upon scholars and practitioners conducting empirical research on gender to break down the universal and show the heterogeneity of women, to move beyond categories predicated as natural, and to understand the categories of difference as relational. The book is structured in two parts. The first part addresses theoretical and methodological approaches to the study of gender. This section serves as an excellent overview of the transition from a mainstream approach to the study of gender to a more expanded and inclusive framework acknowledging differences and similarities of women globally. The second part presents studies of women and work, women of color, body and culture, men and feminism, feminists and nationalism, religion, spirituality and feminism, and reproduction and violence. Carla Rice, in her chapter on body and culture, presents individual stories of women's struggles to assert their own body ideals rather than accept the constricted and often manipulated version of what it is to be normal and female in a mainstream-defined world.

The title of this volume suggests an in-depth look at the intersection of race and nation with gender, but the text does not provide as cohesive a treatment of this intersection as it might because of the wide range of issues presented. This is the one shortcoming of the text. It is important to acknowledge the limitations of Western studies of women, but it is also necessary to examine how developing nationalisms and the rise of symbolic and social boundaries around the world block women's rights and usurp spaces for resistance and transformation. The book as a whole is successful in moving research on gender away from stand-alone feminism to a wider and richer understanding of the challenges and possibilities for women. In brief, the authors provide a readable, wide-ranging, and informative look at the changing nature of gender studies. The volume is therefore an important contribution to the field of gender studies and will be useful to scholars, students, and practitioners.

REFERENCES

Basu, Amrita, ed. (1995). *The Challenge of Local Feminisms: Women's Movements in Global Perspective.* Boulder, CO: Westview.

Mohanty, Chandra T. (1991). *Third World Women and the Politics of Feminism.* Bloomington: Indiana University Press.

Carolyn Kissane *is an adjunct professor at Columbia Teachers College and New York University.*

Feminist Post-Development Thought: Rethinking Modernity, Post-Colonialism, and Representation, edited by Kriemild Saunders (London: Zed, 2002)

Ravinder Kaur

The key words "feminist thought" and "post-development" in the title to this book at once open the overwhelming debates in which development is seen as the excruciating test of the entire body of feminist thought in practise. The highly contested meanings of development (in terms of whose, why, and how) and feminist thought (structured by race, class, and ideological and global hierarchies) point to the obvious pitfalls that such a project is likely to encounter. Such contradictions are often problematised and convened in the collective body of "Third World women," who are seen not only as incapacitated in terms of gender, like their counterparts in rest of the world, but also as suffering additional deprivations on account of regional underdevelopment. Therefore, the symbolic Third World woman presents the ultimate challenge of development to the visionaries and practitioners. An advanced form of Pierre Bourdieu's "field" of contesting social forces is embodied in this woman as the development experts are now joined by "First World" feminists who campaign for and draw attention to the plight of this ubiquitous woman. This brings together the non-representational character of "the women in 'other' non-European/North American places" in the world and the frequently voiced project of letting the "other" women speak for themselves. The challenges and visions of development then become a source of critique of prevalent feminist thought that unwittingly tends to focus on the Third World and the female bodies therein as laboratories for experiments in "development".

This collection of seventeen lucidly written essays attempts a bold step further in reviewing feminist thought vis-à-vis visions of post-development. The task is simultaneously to present a critique of current development ideologies as well as to recognise and theorise the inherent schisms in feminist thought. The introductory chapter by Kriemild Saunders makes a systematic overview of the various debates opened by the feminist discourses on development. The historical moorings of the various debates are collectively described as the "opening of a sub-field" within the larger field of development (3). But the subsequent writings show that the auxiliary nature of the sub-field has over a period trans-muted into a full field complete with its own little codes and phrases that are used and understood by others in the field. The point here is that the entire discourse is presented in terms of a number of acronyms that carry certain obvious and immediate meanings to the "insiders"' in the field. The examples include "women in development" (WID), "society for international development" (SID), "women and development" (WAD), "gender and development" (GAD), "development alternatives with women for a new era" (DAWN), and "participatory rural appraisal" (PRA). These acronyms are not shortened titles but rather boiled-down versions of full-fledged concepts with specific theoretical histories that are central to our understanding of feminist development debates. In a way, the wide acceptance and usage of these coded concepts stand in contrast to the frequently voiced wish to bring development debates out of the "expert" discourses. The feminist (post) development discourse also operates in its self-instituted discourses that make it accessible only to the specialist. The distance between objects of development and spe-cialists who practise their knowledge on these objects has been widened, even though the feminist project was always to bring development closer to women.

Marnia Lazreg in her essay "Development: Feminist Theory's Cul-de-Sac" partly challenges this tendency by posing basic questions about the approaches to "women/gender in/and development," which com-prise the very nature of the concept of development, and which fem-inist theories try to grapple with. She puts it rather succinctly: "Accounting for these women's forms of life and liberating them (from themselves, their men, their cultures, their former colonisers) to be more or less like 'us' has always been the dream of feminists in their symbolic conquest of the world of Otherness" (123). Piya Chatterjee, in her essay "Ethnographic Acts: Writing Women and Other Political Fields," continues this interrogation in her discussion of the Third World and native-women–turned-development-practitioners, many of whom come from the "field" and "themselves embody the absent, but still powerfully resonant, space of nativism" (244).

Once the reader is familiar with the prevalent debates and concepts in the field, this volume offers a ready confluence of ethnographic, empirical, and theoretical issues pertinent to the current feminist development thought. The wide range of regions, disciplines, and themes treated in the essays makes it an excellent reference book not only for readers well inculcated in the field but also for students and beginners.

Ravinder Kaur *is a Ph.D. researcher at Institute for International Studies, Copenhagen, and affiliated with the department of international development studies, Roskilde University, Denmark.*

Gender and Imperialism, edited by Clare Midgley (New York: St. Martin's, 1998)

Tanfer Emin-Tunc

Within the past thirty years, the field of women's studies has revolutionized the study of history by serving as a catalyst in the shift away from the white male narrative towards the narrative of the historically marginalized (i.e., women, peoples of color, gays, lesbians, etc.). While this new gynocentric epistemology has affected nearly every area of historical inquiry, arguably it has had the most profound impact on the field of postcolonial studies. In the 1950s, Octave Mannoni, Frantz Fanon, and Albert Memmi set the stage for this transformation by challenging colonial paternalism and the binary of the benevolent "colonizer" and the savage "colonized." Through their rejection of racial essentialism, these theorists helped establish a new field of scholarly inquiry: postcolonialism. Women's studies, with its explicit deconstruction of patriarchal discourses and its focus on gender as a category of analysis, has incited yet another epistemological shift in the field. While these early theorists and their intellectual heirs (i.e., Stuart Hall and Paul Gilroy) maintain that women also participated in colonialism, they do not, by any means, adequately focus on women in their analyses. Moreover, any references they do make to female contributions to the colonial project are given mostly in passing, and in an almost apologetic tone. In 1998, Clare Midgley, a British feminist historian who works in the area of postcolonial studies, called for a revision of such patriarchal analyses and a reexamination of women within the context of the colonial experience. Her groundbreaking anthology, *Gender and Imperialism*, offers an escape from patriarchal academic rhetoric by providing scholars with a remarkable glimpse of how feminist theory can revolutionize the study of history and the sub-specialty of postcolonial studies.

As Midgley posits in the introduction to her anthology, Joan Scott's *Gender and the Politics of History* (1988) was instrumental in changing the face of postcolonial academia. Scott's claim that "gender is a method of signifying relationships of power" almost instantaneously invalidated the scholarly rationale for separating the study of gender from the study of imperialism (Midgley 1998, 2). Whereas gender and imperialism have been perceived by historians, particularly those studying Great Britain and its empire-building tactics, as separate categories of analysis, feminist postcolonial theory has effectively deconstructed imperial history as a powerful form of colonial discourse in and of itself, and has allowed gender to enter serious scholarship on imperialism and empire. More importantly, such epistemological shifts have invalidated the statement that *"gender* is a *special interest* area which can be safely left to feminist or female historians" (2).

Midgley argues that feminist theory has also allowed historians to reconceptualize imperialism as a highly gendered process and has prompted a reexamination of culturally loaded concepts such as masculinity, femininity, and the conqueror/conquered dichotomy. As feminist historians of the 1960s and 1970s discovered, "words like 'manly' and 'effeminate,' each of them normatively loaded, were seldom far from the lips of imperial rulers and others involved in the colonial complex" (vii). Processes of conquest and domination, including the alleged capacity to penetrate and mold the environment to the will of the "manly" conqueror, made these gender divisions and socially constructed binaries more strongly evident. However, a dilemma arose in the unveiling of such dominant masculinities: how could one even begin to deconstruct patriarchal institutions when, as Luce Irigaray has argued, phallic symbolism is so deeply ingrained in the English language? In "traditional" historical writing, not only were European and indigenous women being portrayed as either victims of, or accomplices in, the imperial program, but also their experiences were being universalized as men's experiences through gendered words like "he" (vii). As Midgley aptly points out, recent feminist postcolonial examinations, such as Antoinette Burton's *Burdens of History* (1994), have begun the slow process of eliminating such crude dichotomies and identities by providing alternatives to relativism and absolutism, which have in common the objectification of women and the production of racialized and gendered propaganda. As a result of this epistemological shift, gender relations, interactive and intertwining, responsive and mutually transformative, have become much clearer in both imperial and indigenous societies.

One of the strengths of Midgley's collection is that it illustrates how historians have responded to the challenges posed by feminist theory and postcolonial perspectives by producing new, and nuanced, areas of scholarship. Such categories of study include sexuality and empire, masculinity and empire, the impact of empire on colonizing nations (i.e., metropole studies), empire and the indigenous experience, relationships between feminism and nationalism, female authority in the imperial context, and gender and Foucauldian discourse analysis. This feminist approach marks an effort to remedy the shortcomings of traditional social history, which, while it explores the interaction between gender and class, completely ignores racial and ethnic categories. By including contributions by feminist historians who study India, such as Himani

Bannerji and Jane Haggis, Midgley offers new perspectives on the nature of British imperial power by exploring the implications of race, class, ethnicity, *and* gender on British control. Bannerji's "Age of Consent and Hegemonic Social Reform" contributes to the growing body of scholarship contesting indigenous and colonial patriarchies in India. Haggis's "White Women and Colonialism: Towards a Non-Recuperative History" draws on poststructuralist, anthropological, and postcolonial theory to describe British female missionaries in India, without condemning them as racists or portraying them as benevolent victims of the imperialist patriarchy. Moreover, by questioning concepts like complicity, resistance, and agency, Haggis presents a critical analysis of British women's relationships with indigenous women and also explores the extent to which women, in general, impacted the colonial project.

In this volume, feminist historians also critique postcolonial theory for its tendency to deny social significance to colonized women. In her essay "Indian Christian Women and Indigenous Feminism, c. 1850–c. 1920," Padma Anagol focuses on the Maharashtrian women of India who converted from Hinduism to Christianity and highlights their woman-centered approach to religion and the challenges they posed to the cultural hegemony of the Indian patriarchy (79–103). Similarly, Margaret Ward focuses on female authority and counter-hegemonic actions, this time in Ireland, in her essay "National Liberation Movements and the Question of Women's Liberation: The Irish Experience" (104–22). Ward explores the gendered nature of Irish nationalism and stresses the need to reexamine Irish nationalism, which, until recently, has been portrayed as a masculine tradition in which women did not participate. Through their reassessment of historical events, these feminist historians have begun the important and difficult task of rethinking "patriarchal" knowledge in light of the new perspectives made available when women's experiences are taken as a valid starting point. This new methodological approach is truly revolutionary, for it does not simply attempt to "insert" women into the broad context of the human condition, but instead seeks to restructure our understanding of the world by emphasizing a gynocentric epistemology that prioritizes female participation, and more significantly, the female condition.

What distinguishes Midgley and these feminist historians from other historians examining gender and imperialism is the nature of the questions they pose regarding women and historical configurations of "knowledge-power," or the ways women used their minds and bodies to engage in the colonial project. As Ann Laura Stoler demonstrates in *Race and the Education of Desire*, feminist interpretations of Foucault's work have been extremely influential in postcolonial studies, particularly in the study of gender, colonial discourses, and knowledge-power (1995, 1). Drawing on Robert Young's *Colonial Desire* and Edward Said's *Orientalism*, Stoler illustrates how nineteenth-century discourses regarding race and sexuality constructed the "exotic" female colonial body as a dense transfer-point for desire and knowledge-power (Midgley 1998, 11). Through her emphasis on the Foucauldian notion of normalization, Stoler also provides a more nuanced interpretation of the vague "Other." Like Stoler, Bannerji and Anagol use the Foucauldian concepts of discipline and the panopticon to illuminate how Indian women became the sources of sexual, cultural, and religious knowledge-power, and how these women used the same technologies of power to challenge and subvert male hegemony.

Rather than relying on antiquated discourses of the colonial experience, Clare Midgley and the authors included in her anthology have used the field of women's studies to respond to the dilemmas posed by postcolonialism . They have challenged the historical hegemony by creating new approaches to race, class, gender, culture, ethnicity, and sexuality, and have used the discipline of women's studies to formulate woman-centered postcolonial theories that have questioned, reshaped, and reinvigorated the ways in which historians investigate problems. Although the socially constructed category of "woman" is one that also requires criticism, by taking a gynocentric position, these scholars have begun to reconfigure historical phenomena, such as counter-hegemonic resistance and knowledge-power, through a feminist lens. Historians such as these have proven to the rest of the profession that women's studies can always provide alternative, and empowering, analytic tools to illuminate the mysteries of the past.

REFERENCES

Burton, Antoinette. 1994. *Burdens of History.* Chapel Hill: U of North Carolina.
Scott, Joan. 1988. *Gender and the Politics of History.* New York: Columbia U.
Stoler, Ann Laura. 1995. *Race and the Education of Desire: Foucault's History of Sexuality and the Colonial Order of Things.* Durham, N.C.: Duke U.

Tanfer Emin-Tunc received her B.A. and M.A. in history, and a graduate certificate in women's studies, from Stony Brook University in New York. Her latest article, "Freaks and Geeks: Coney Island Sideshow Performers and Long Island Eugenicists, 1910–1935," can be found in The Long Island Historical Journal, *Volume 14, Numbers 1/2 (Fall 2001/Spring 2002). She is in the process of completing her Ph.D. dissertation, which deals with the history of abortion technology in the United States between 1850 and 1980.*

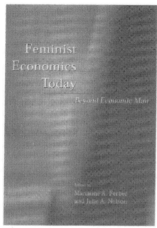